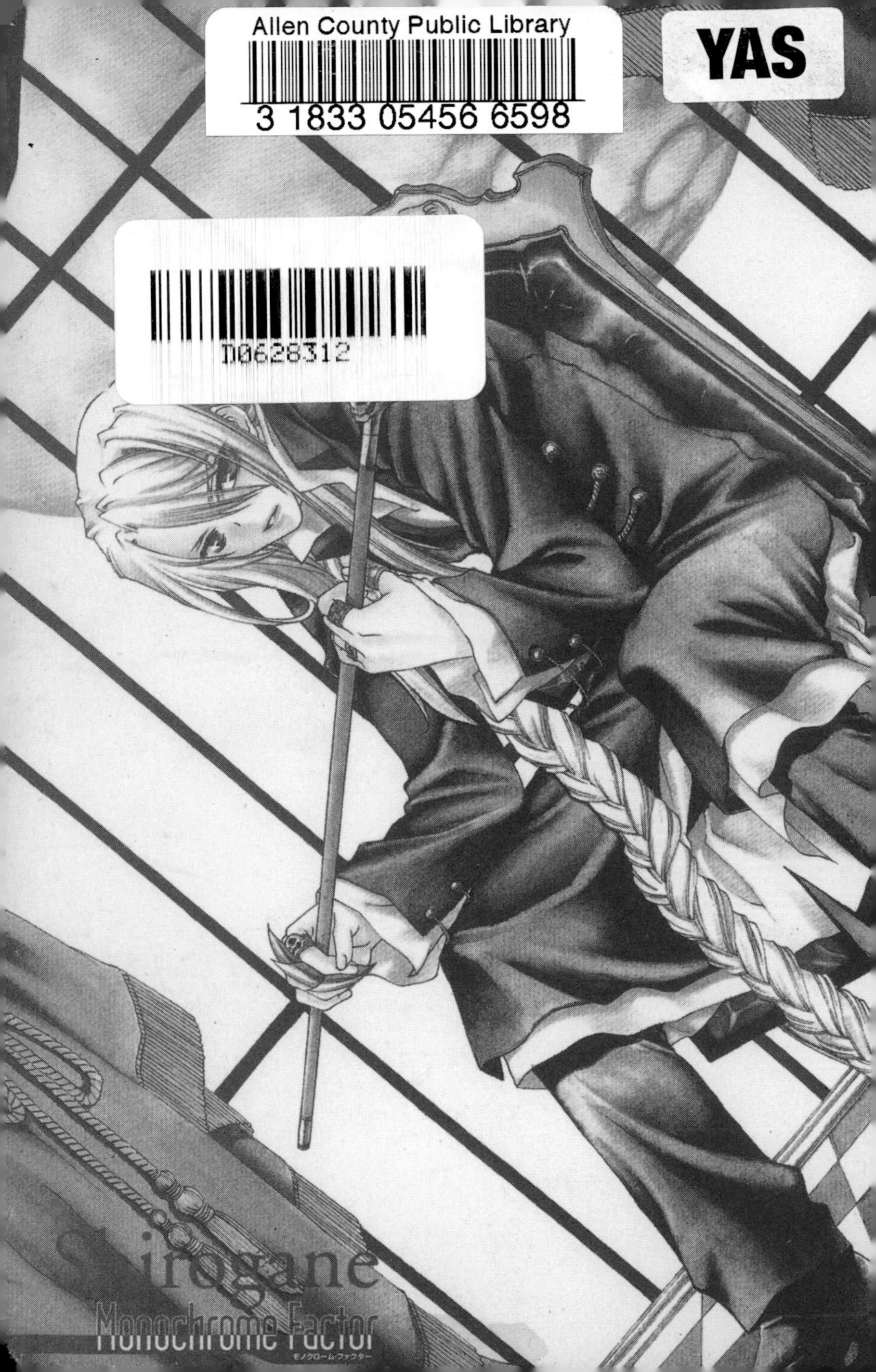
irogane
Monochrome Factor
モノクローム・ファクター

Monochrome Factor Volume 2
Created By KAILI SORANO

Translation - Takae Brewer
English Adaptation - Laura Wyrick
Retouch and Lettering - Star Print Brokers
Production Artist - Keila N. Ramos
Graphic Designer - Colin Graham

Editor - Peter Ahlstrom
Digital Imaging Manager - Chris Buford
Pre-Production Supervisor - Lucas Rivera
Production Manager - Elisabeth Brizzi
Managing Editor - Vy Nguyen
Creative Director - Anne Marie Horne
Editor-in-Chief - Rob Tokar
Publisher - Mike Kiley
President and C.O.O. - John Parker
C.E.O. and Chief Creative Officer - Stu Levy

A TOKYOPOP Manga

TOKYOPOP and are trademarks or registered trademarks of TOKYOPOP Inc.

TOKYOPOP Inc.
5900 Wilshire Blvd. Suite 2000
Los Angeles, CA 90036

E-mail: info@TOKYOPOP.com
Come visit us online at www.TOKYOPOP.com

ISBN: 978-1-4278-0070-1

First TOKYOPOP printing: May 2008
10 9 8 7 6 5 4 3 2 1
Printed in the USA

Monochrome Factor

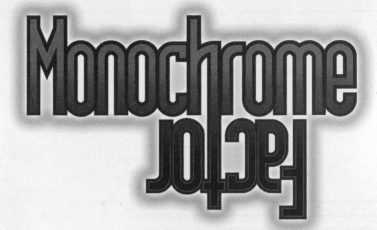

Vol. 2

by Kaili Sorano

TOKYOPOP®

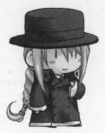

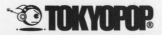

HAMBURG // LONDON // LOS ANGELES // TOKYO

Shirogane

A shin from the shadow world. It seems he's been looking for Akira for some time, but his motivations are unclear. He acts as Akira's shadow when necessary.

Akira (Shin form)

In shin form, Akira's hair turns from brown to black, and his outfit changes as well. When he transforms, two short blades appear in his hands.

Akira Nikaido

Akira was a typical slacker high school student until he lost his shadow and was forced to become a shin. Since he currently has nothing better to do, he's going along with it.

Master

The man who is so far known only as "Master" runs a bar named Aging. Though he's blind, he's an adept with the ability to sense shin. He can heal with his hands.

Aya Suzuno

At school, Aya is on the discipline committee and in the kendo club. Everyone except Akira seems to fear her tongue and her practice sword.

Kengo Asamura

Kengo is Akira's best friend from school, though Akira's definition of "friend" seems a bit...off. His sister Mayu keeps getting possessed.

Previously in

Akira Nikaido thought he had a normal life until he met Shirogane, who told him that the balance between the human world and the shadow world has been distorted. In order to help restore the balance and fight kokuchi shadow monsters, Akira has become a shin—a creature of the shadow world. Not that Akira had much choice—since his doppelganger (his shadow) accidentally got destroyed, his shin form is all he has left. Being shadows themselves, shin can't be seen by normal human eyes, but Akira can appear human again if Shirogane acts as his shadow.

It seems that the balance distortion is having an effect on normal humans as well, however. Normally only an adept can see shin and other shadow creatures, but Akira's friend Kengo's sister Mayu, who has become particularly susceptible to possession by kokuchi, was able to see Shirogane. And during Akira's successful fight with the kokuchi that possessed Mayu, Kengo gained the ability to see Shirogane as well. Now the scene shifts to the shadow realm...

CONTENTS

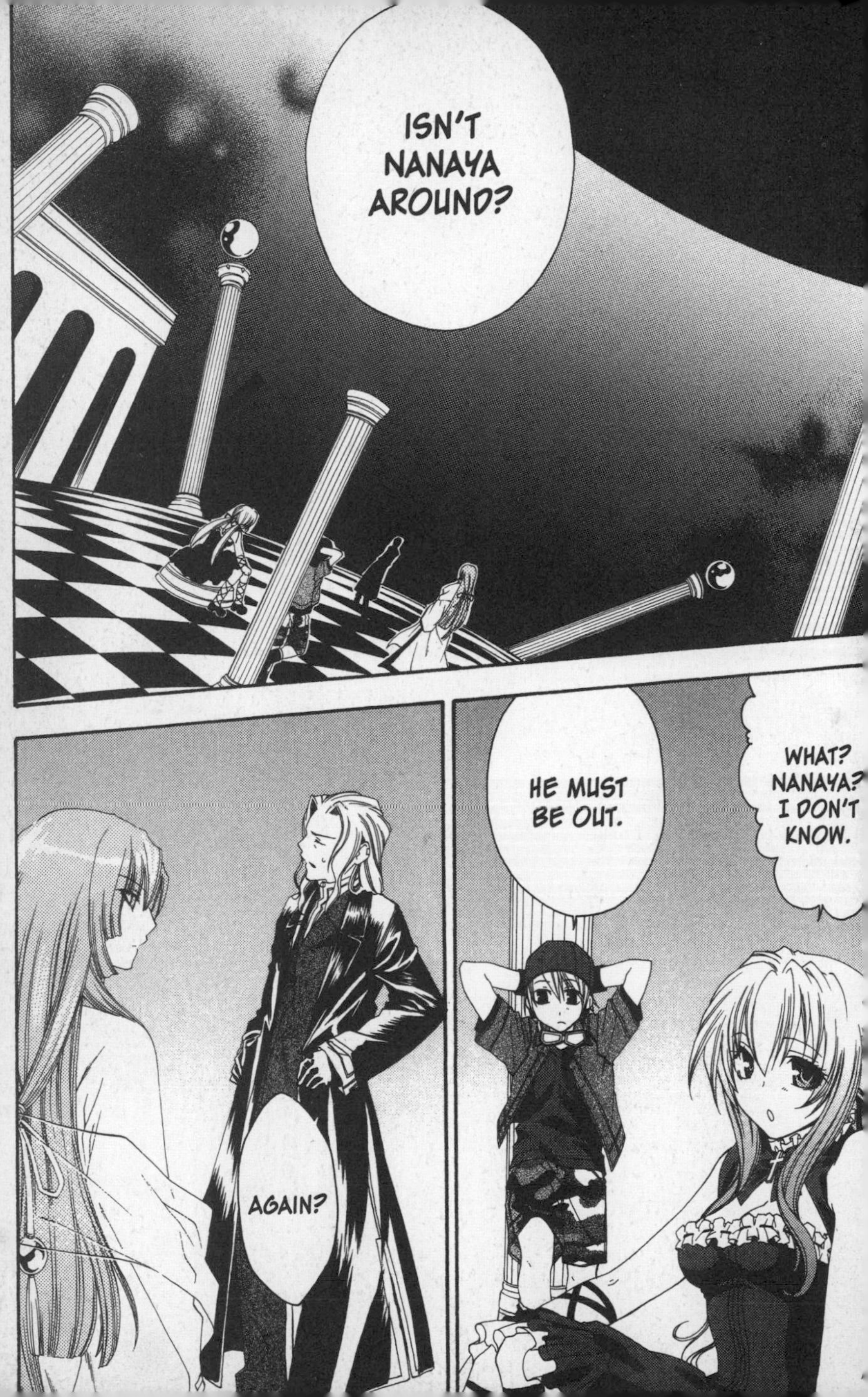
ISN'T NANAYA AROUND?
WHAT? NANAYA? I DON'T KNOW.
HE MUST BE OUT.
AGAIN?

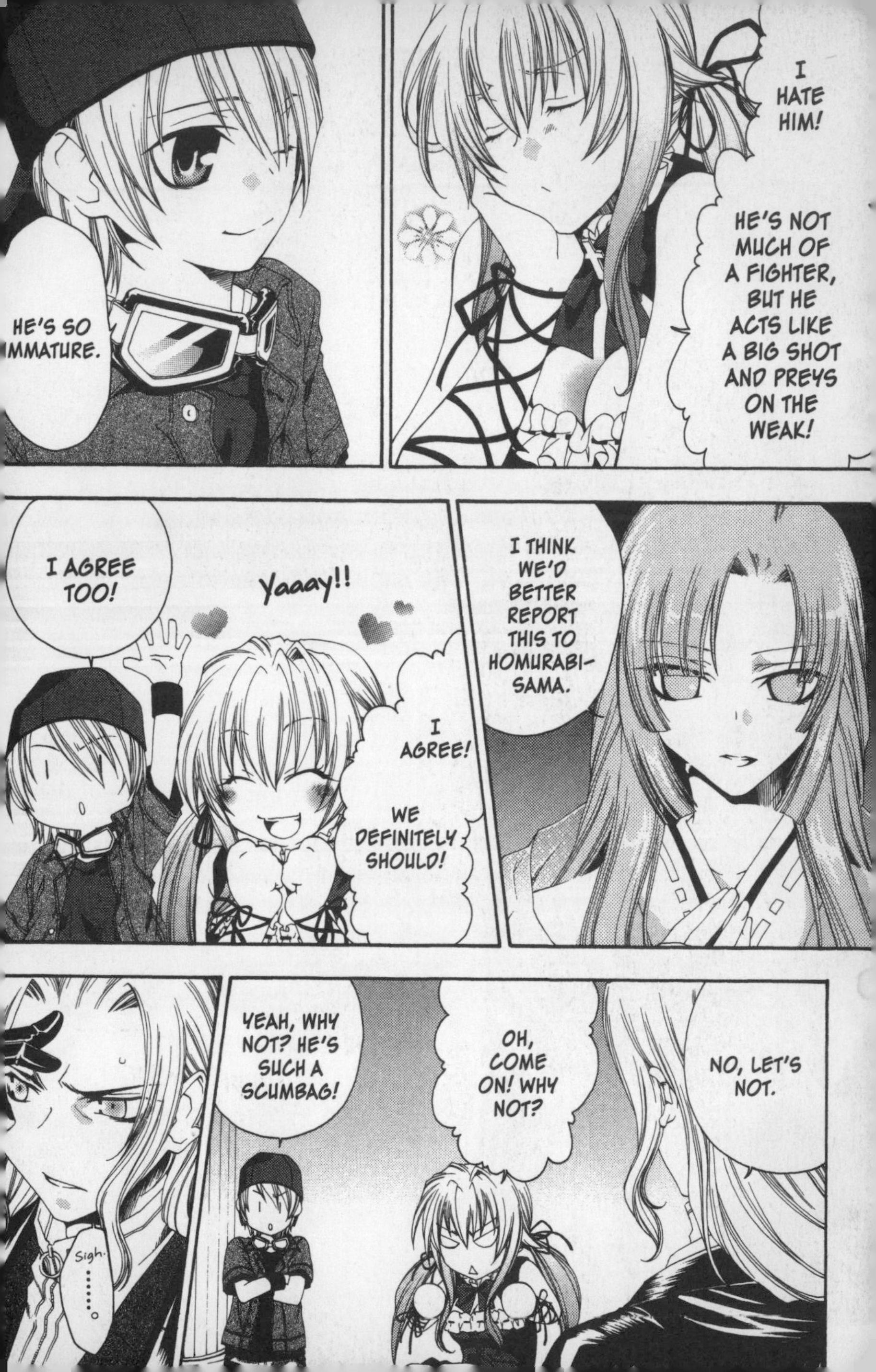
I HATE HIM!
HE'S NOT MUCH OF A FIGHTER, BUT HE ACTS LIKE A BIG SHOT AND PREYS ON THE WEAK!
HE'S SO IMMATURE.
I THINK WE'D BETTER REPORT THIS TO HOMURABI-SAMA.
I AGREE!
WE DEFINITELY SHOULD!
Yaaay!!
I AGREE TOO!
NO, LET'S NOT.
OH, COME ON! WHY NOT?
YEAH, WHY NOT? HE'S SUCH A SCUMBAG!
Sigh.
......

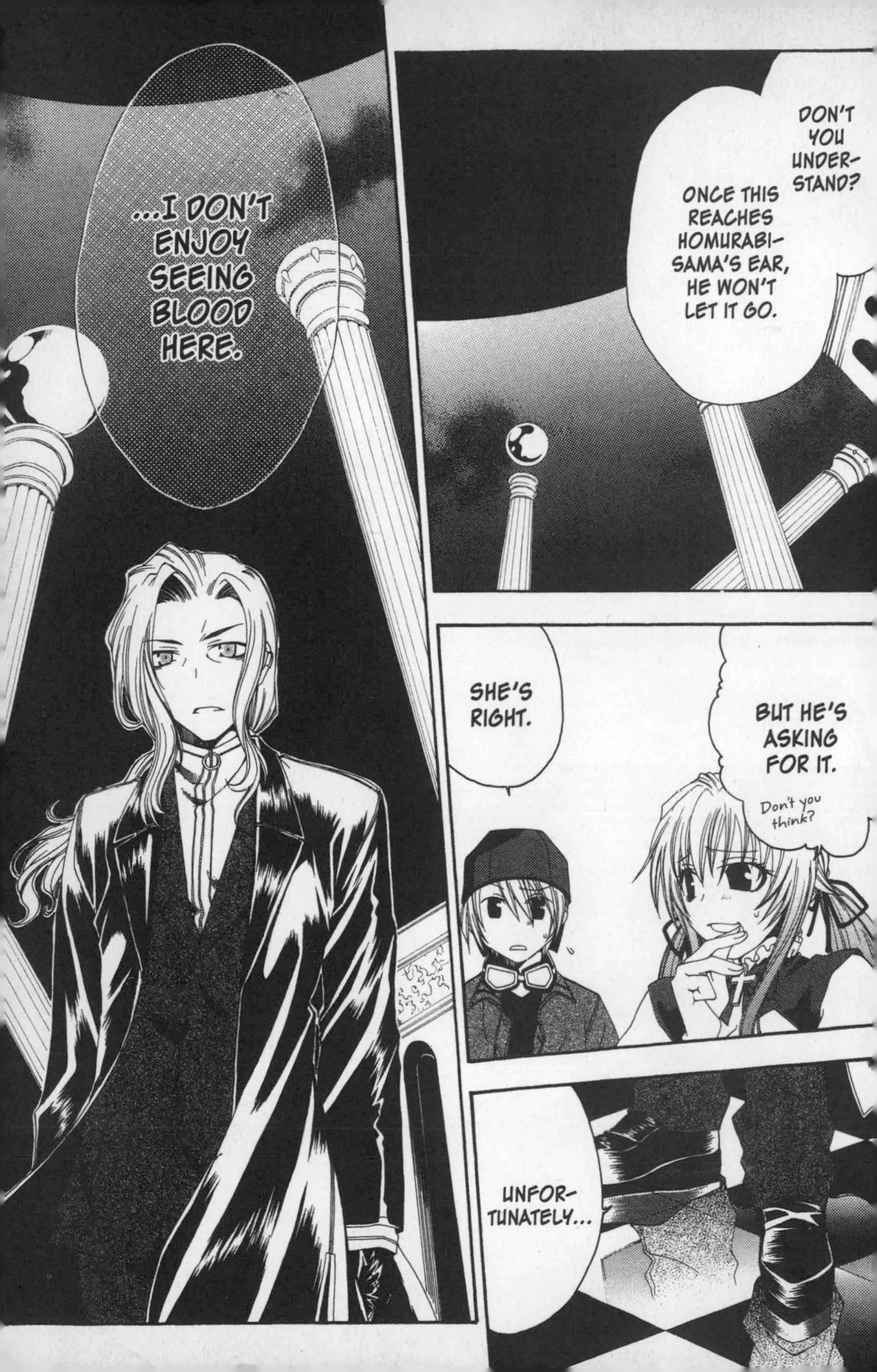

DON'T YOU UNDER-STAND?
ONCE THIS REACHES HOMURABI-SAMA'S EAR, HE WON'T LET IT GO.
BUT HE'S ASKING FOR IT.
Don't you think?
SHE'S RIGHT.
UNFOR-TUNATELY...
...I DON'T ENJOY SEEING BLOOD HERE.

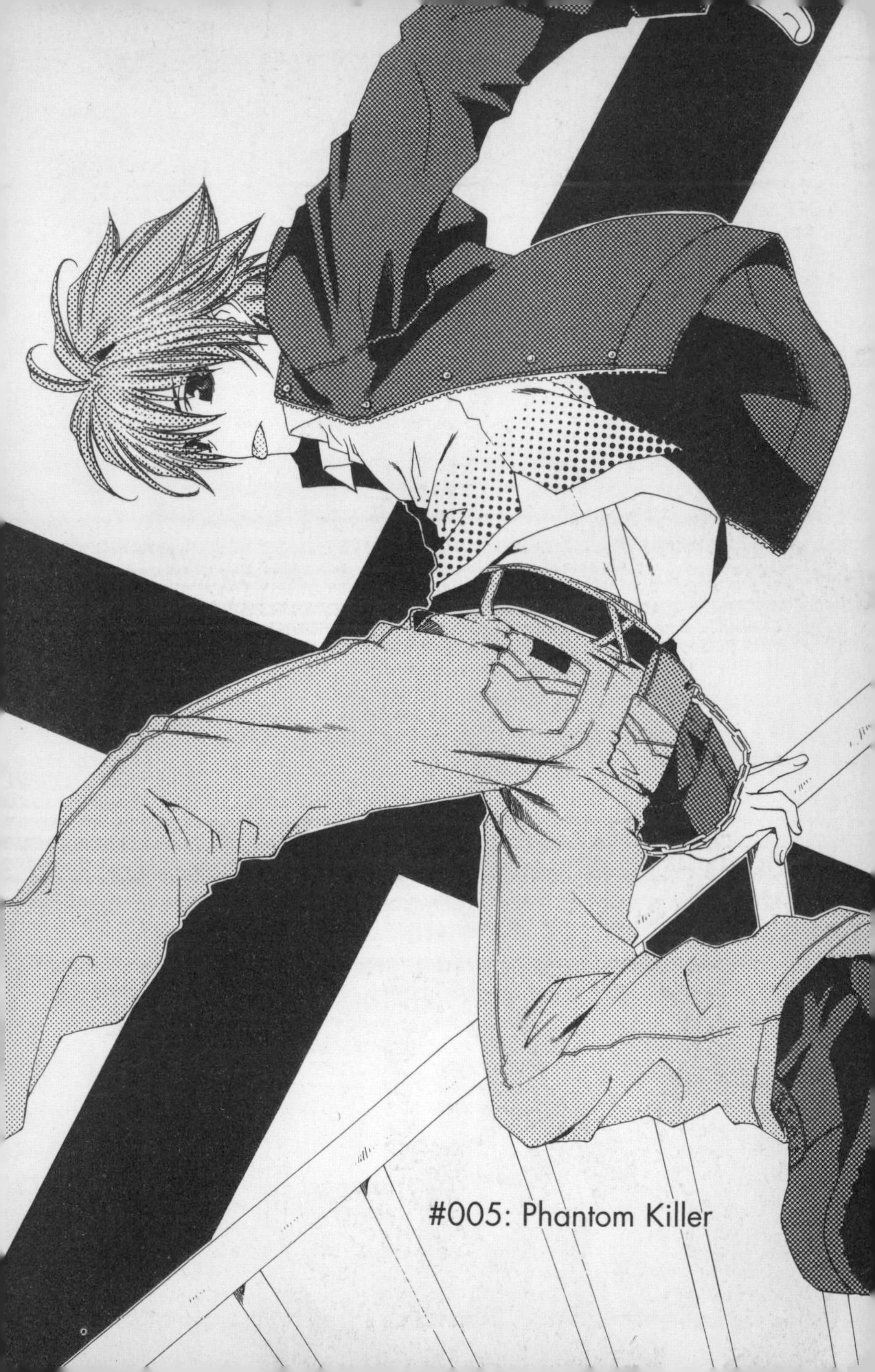

#005: Phantom Killer

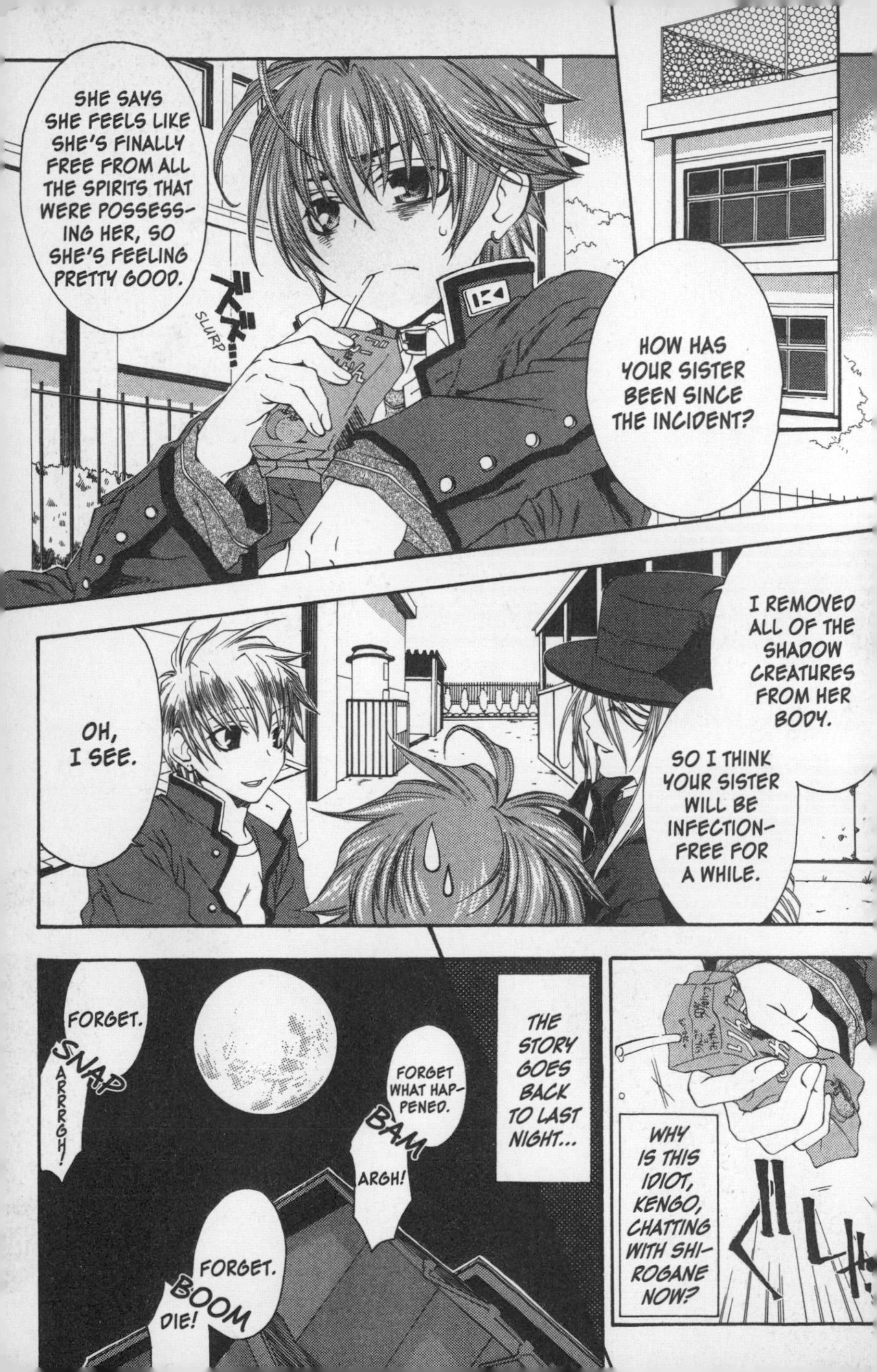
HOW HAS YOUR SISTER BEEN SINCE THE INCIDENT?
SHE SAYS SHE FEELS LIKE SHE'S FINALLY FREE FROM ALL THE SPIRITS THAT WERE POSSESS-ING HER, SO SHE'S FEELING PRETTY GOOD.
SLURP
I REMOVED ALL OF THE SHADOW CREATURES FROM HER BODY.
SO I THINK YOUR SISTER WILL BE INFECTION-FREE FOR A WHILE.
OH, I SEE.
WHY IS THIS IDIOT, KENGO, CHATTING WITH SHI-ROGANE NOW?
THE STORY GOES BACK TO LAST NIGHT...
FORGET WHAT HAP-PENED.
BAM
FORGET.
SNAP
ARRRGH!
ARGH!
FORGET.
BOOM
DIE!

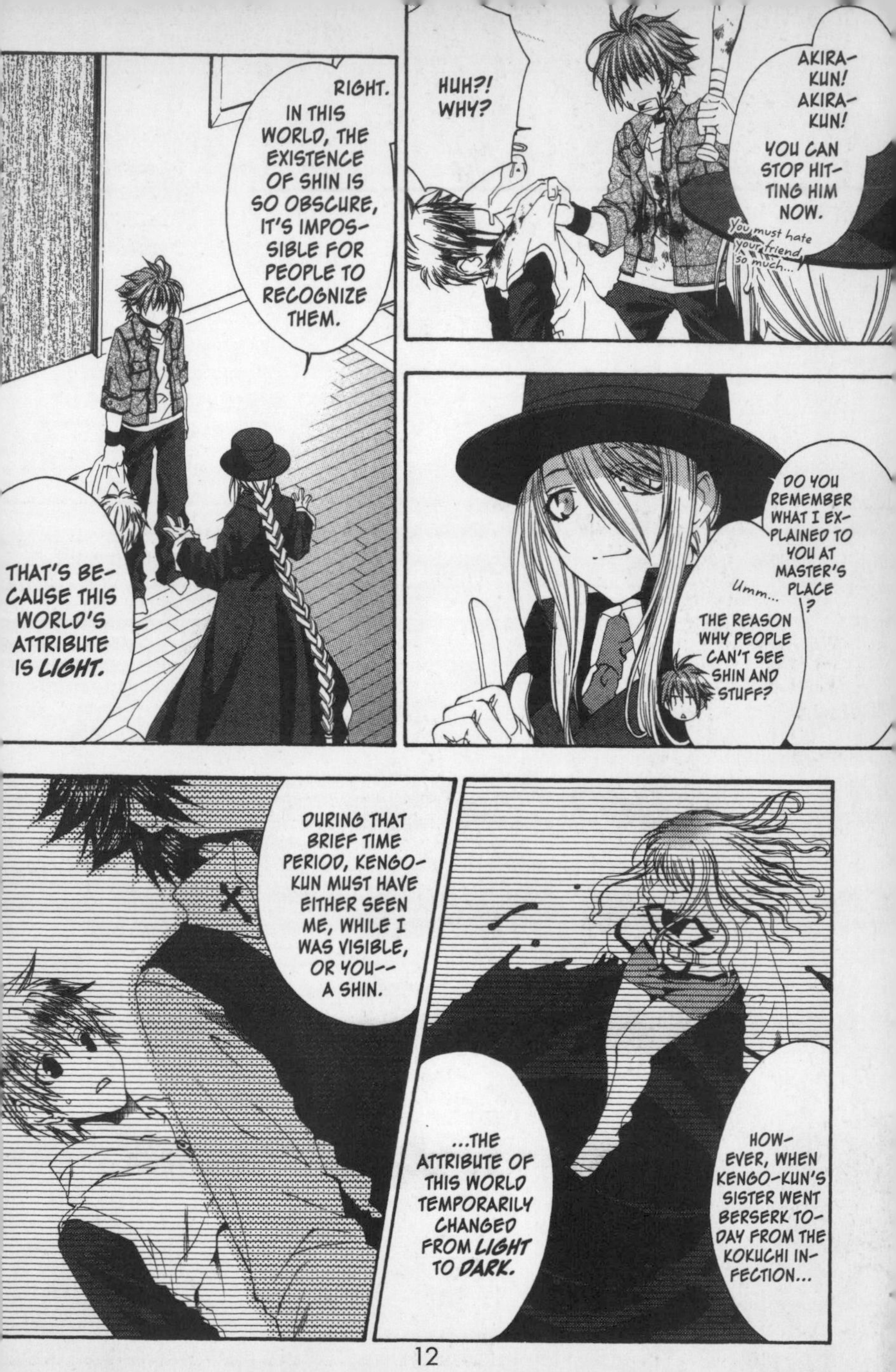
AKIRA-KUN! AKIRA-KUN! YOU CAN STOP HITTING HIM NOW.
You must hate your friend so much...
HUH?! WHY?
RIGHT. IN THIS WORLD, THE EXISTENCE OF SHIN IS SO OBSCURE, IT'S IMPOSSIBLE FOR PEOPLE TO RECOGNIZE THEM.
THAT'S BECAUSE THIS WORLD'S ATTRIBUTE IS *LIGHT*.
DO YOU REMEMBER WHAT I EXPLAINED TO YOU AT MASTER'S PLACE?
Umm...
THE REASON WHY PEOPLE CAN'T SEE SHIN AND STUFF?
HOWEVER, WHEN KENGO-KUN'S SISTER WENT BERSERK TODAY FROM THE KOKUCHI INFECTION...
...THE ATTRIBUTE OF THIS WORLD TEMPORARILY CHANGED FROM *LIGHT* TO *DARK*.
DURING THAT BRIEF TIME PERIOD, KENGO-KUN MUST HAVE EITHER SEEN ME, WHILE I WAS VISIBLE, OR YOU--A SHIN.

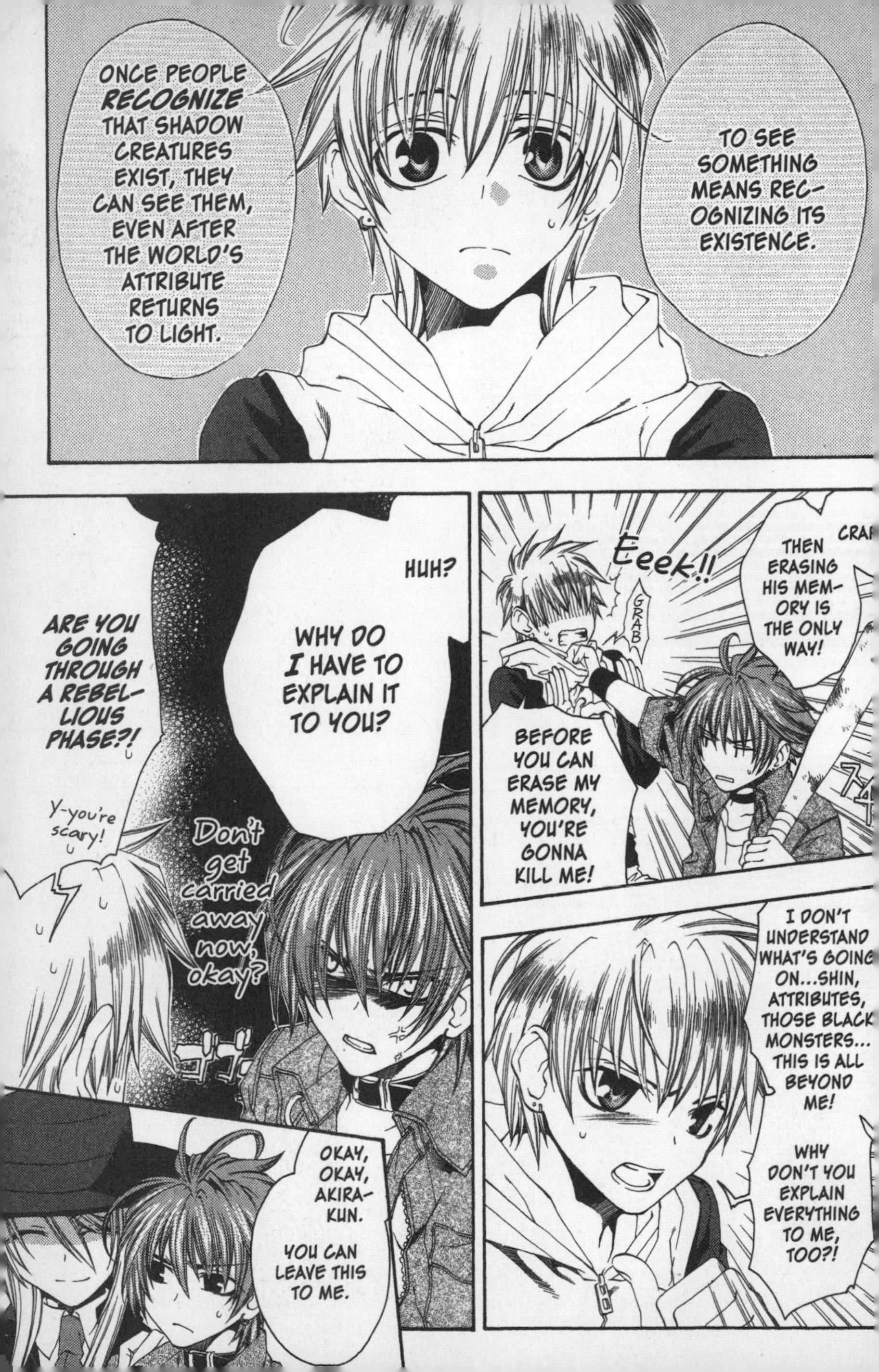
TO SEE SOMETHING MEANS REC-OGNIZING ITS EXISTENCE.
ONCE PEOPLE *RECOGNIZE* THAT SHADOW CREATURES EXIST, THEY CAN SEE THEM, EVEN AFTER THE WORLD'S ATTRIBUTE RETURNS TO LIGHT.
CRA
THEN ERASING HIS MEM-ORY IS THE ONLY WAY!
Eeek!!
GRAB
BEFORE YOU CAN ERASE MY MEMORY, YOU'RE GONNA KILL ME!
HUH?
WHY DO *I* HAVE TO EXPLAIN IT TO YOU?
ARE YOU GOING THROUGH A REBEL-LIOUS PHASE?!
Don't get carried away now, okay?
Y-you're scary!
I DON'T UNDERSTAND WHAT'S GOING ON...SHIN, ATTRIBUTES, THOSE BLACK MONSTERS... THIS IS ALL BEYOND ME!
WHY DON'T YOU EXPLAIN EVERYTHING TO ME, TOO?!
OKAY, OKAY, AKIRA-KUN.
YOU CAN LEAVE THIS TO ME.

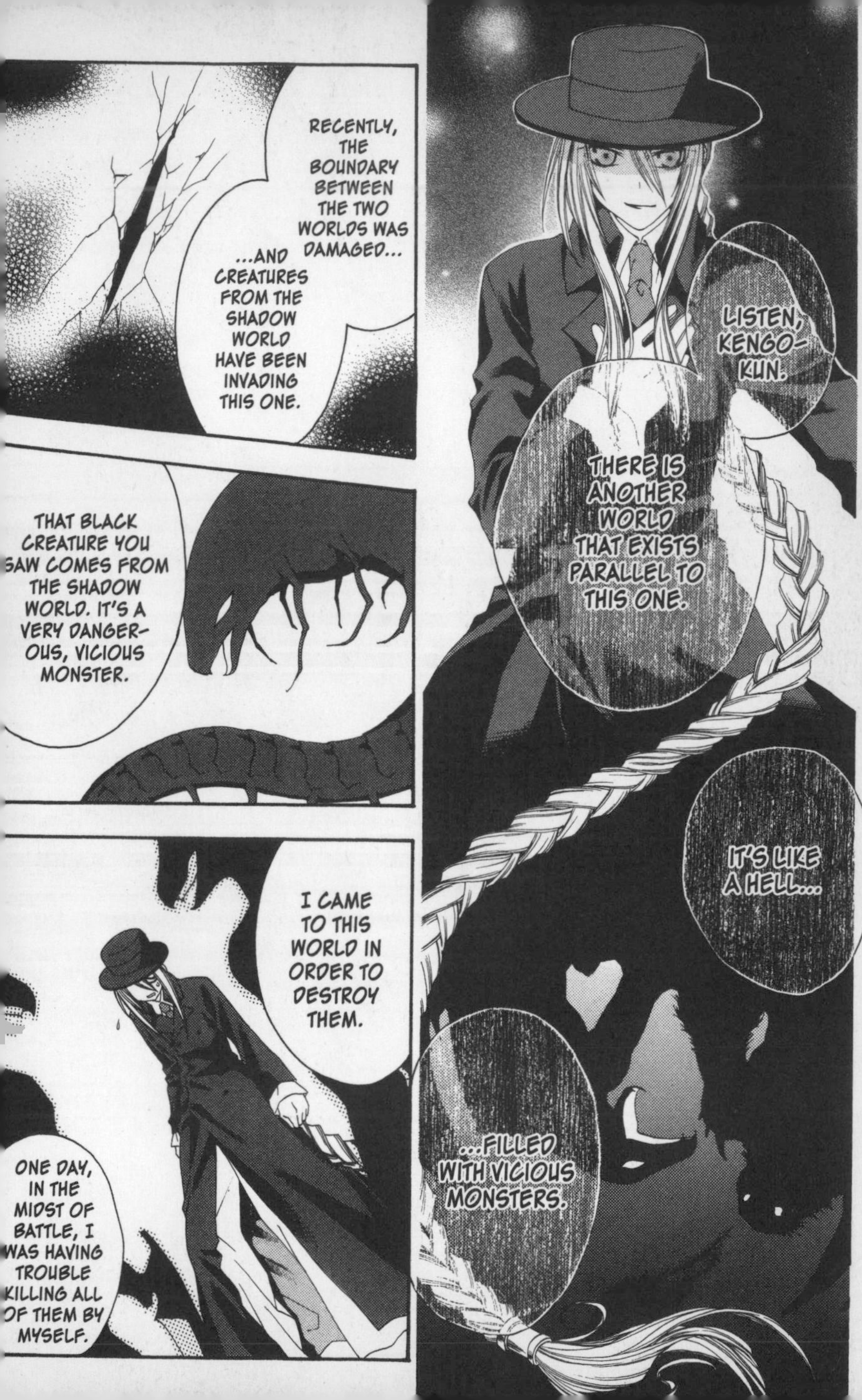
LISTEN, KENGO-KUN.
THERE IS ANOTHER WORLD THAT EXISTS PARALLEL TO THIS ONE.
IT'S LIKE A HELL...
...FILLED WITH VICIOUS MONSTERS.
RECENTLY, THE BOUNDARY BETWEEN THE TWO WORLDS WAS DAMAGED...
...AND CREATURES FROM THE SHADOW WORLD HAVE BEEN INVADING THIS ONE.
THAT BLACK CREATURE YOU SAW COMES FROM THE SHADOW WORLD. IT'S A VERY DANGER-OUS, VICIOUS MONSTER.
I CAME TO THIS WORLD IN ORDER TO DESTROY THEM.
ONE DAY, IN THE MIDST OF BATTLE, I WAS HAVING TROUBLE KILLING ALL OF THEM BY MYSELF.

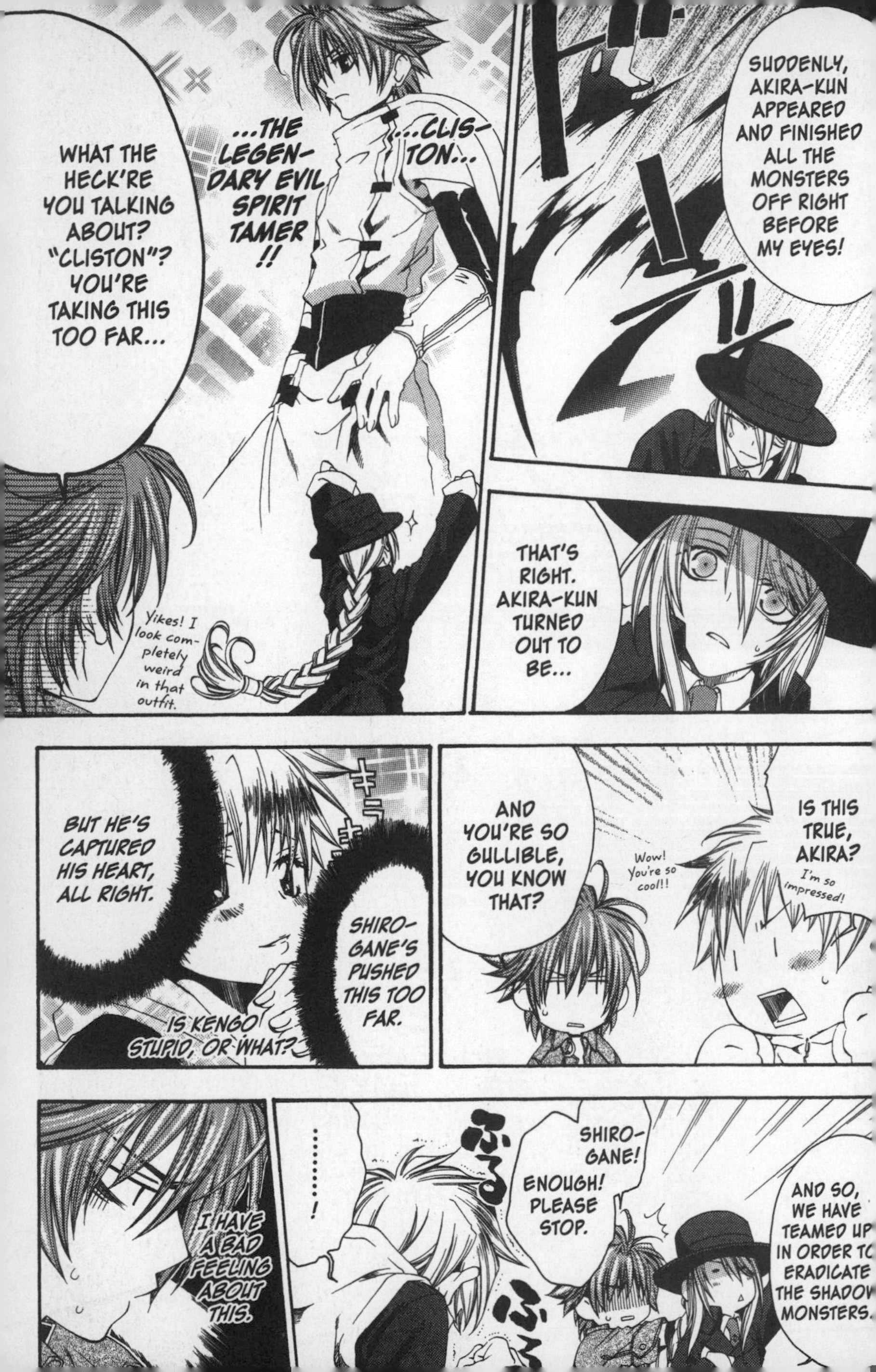
SUDDENLY, AKIRA-KUN APPEARED AND FINISHED ALL THE MONSTERS OFF RIGHT BEFORE MY EYES!
THAT'S RIGHT. AKIRA-KUN TURNED OUT TO BE...
...THE LEGEN-DARY EVIL SPIRIT TAMER !!
...CLIS-TON...
WHAT THE HECK'RE YOU TALKING ABOUT? "CLISTON"? YOU'RE TAKING THIS TOO FAR...
Yikes! I look com-pletely weird in that outfit.
IS THIS TRUE, AKIRA?
I'm so impressed!
Wow! You're so cool!!
AND YOU'RE SO GULLIBLE, YOU KNOW THAT?
SHIRO-GANE'S PUSHED THIS TOO FAR.
BUT HE'S CAPTURED HIS HEART, ALL RIGHT.
IS KENGO STUPID, OR WHAT?
AND SO, WE HAVE TEAMED UP IN ORDER TO ERADICATE THE SHADOW MONSTERS.
SHIRO-GANE! ENOUGH! PLEASE STOP.
.......!
I HAVE A BAD FEELING ABOUT THIS.

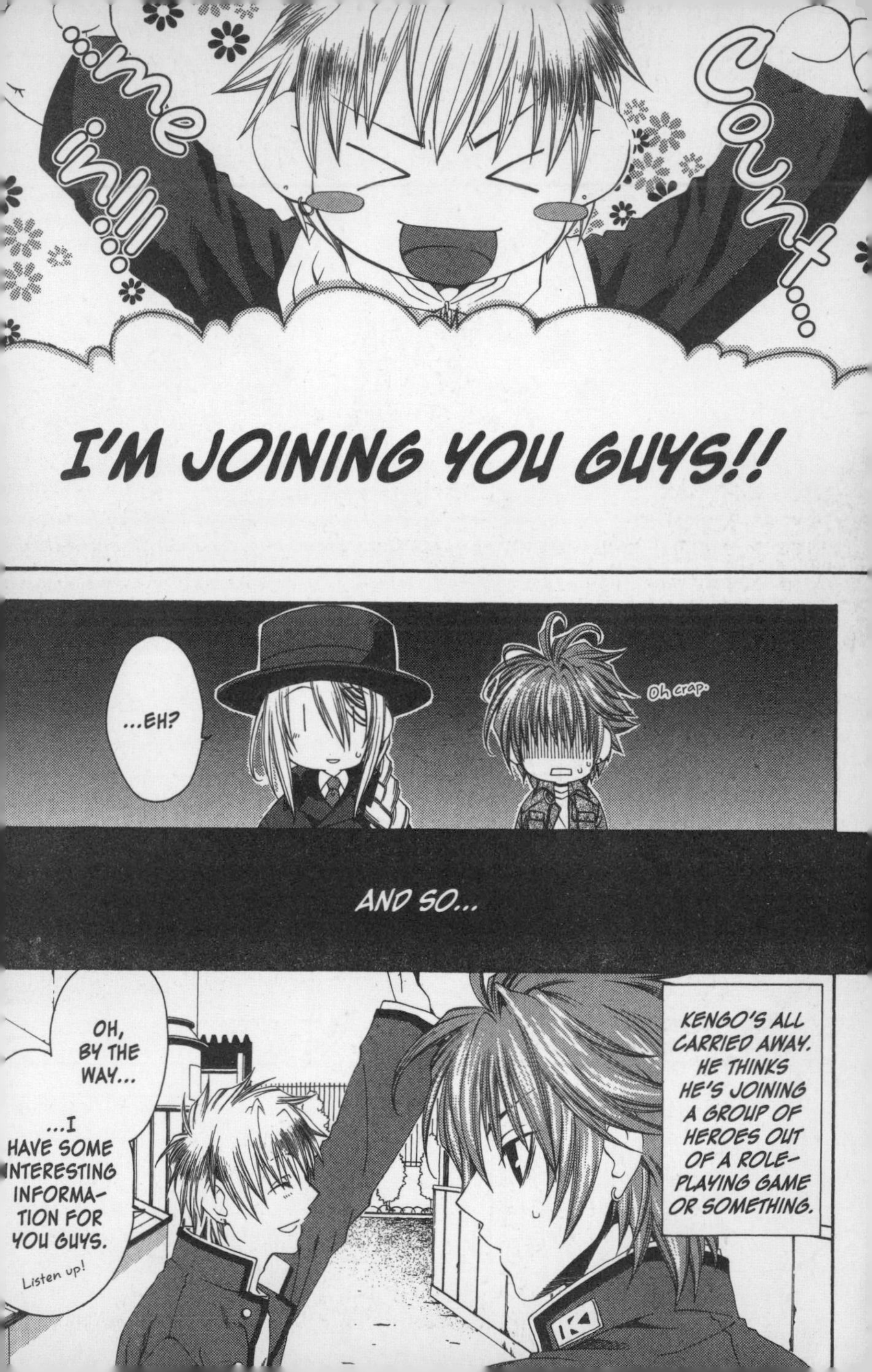
Count...
...me in!!!...
I'M JOINING YOU GUYS!!
Oh crap.
...EH?
AND SO...
KENGO'S ALL CARRIED AWAY. HE THINKS HE'S JOINING A GROUP OF HEROES OUT OF A ROLE-PLAYING GAME OR SOMETHING.
OH, BY THE WAY...
...I HAVE SOME INTERESTING INFORMATION FOR YOU GUYS.
Listen up!

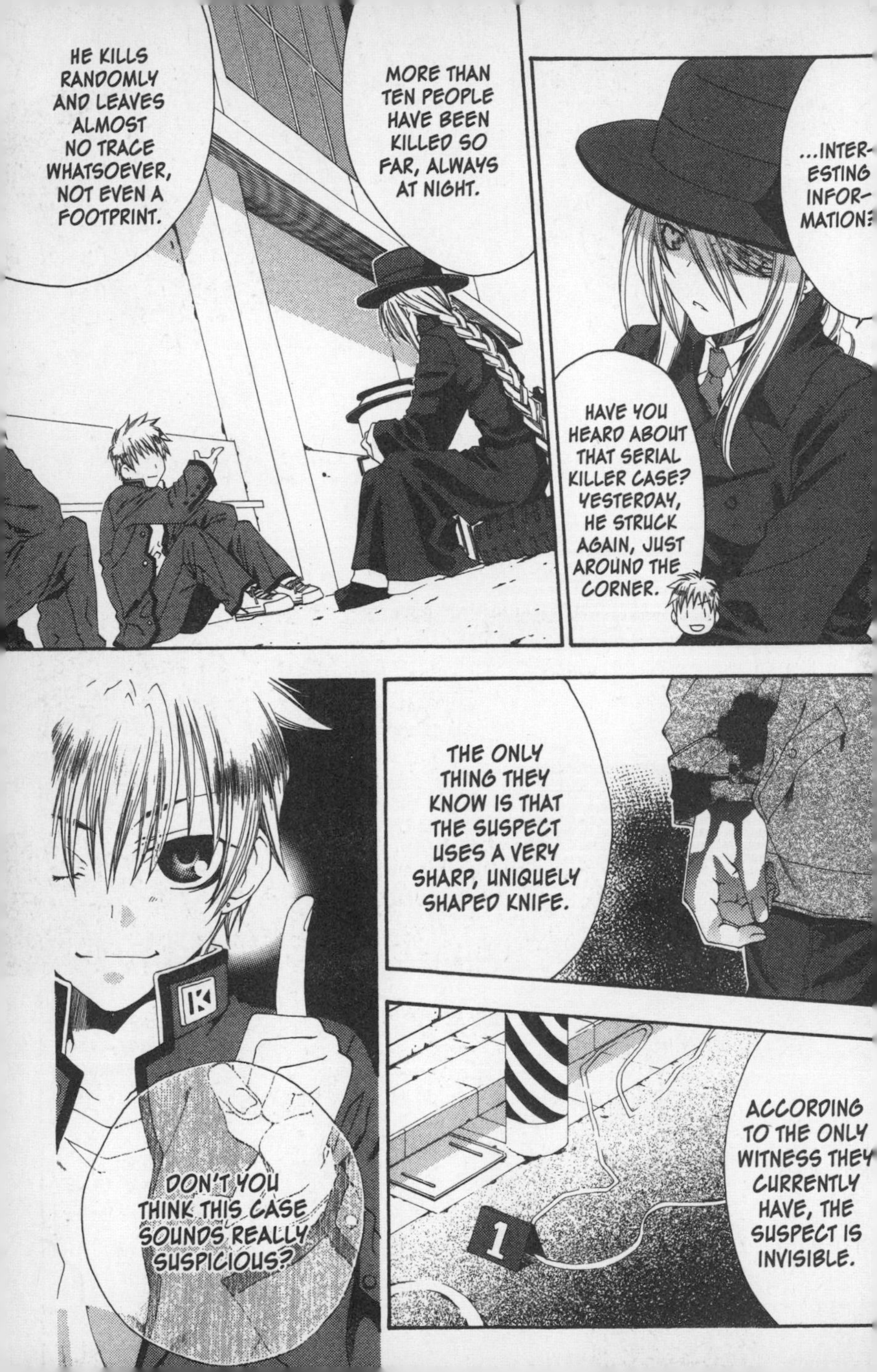
...INTERESTING INFORMATION?
HAVE YOU HEARD ABOUT THAT SERIAL KILLER CASE? YESTERDAY, HE STRUCK AGAIN, JUST AROUND THE CORNER.
MORE THAN TEN PEOPLE HAVE BEEN KILLED SO FAR, ALWAYS AT NIGHT.
HE KILLS RANDOMLY AND LEAVES ALMOST NO TRACE WHATSOEVER, NOT EVEN A FOOTPRINT.
THE ONLY THING THEY KNOW IS THAT THE SUSPECT USES A VERY SHARP, UNIQUELY SHAPED KNIFE.
ACCORDING TO THE ONLY WITNESS THEY CURRENTLY HAVE, THE SUSPECT IS INVISIBLE.
DON'T YOU THINK THIS CASE SOUNDS REALLY SUSPICIOUS?

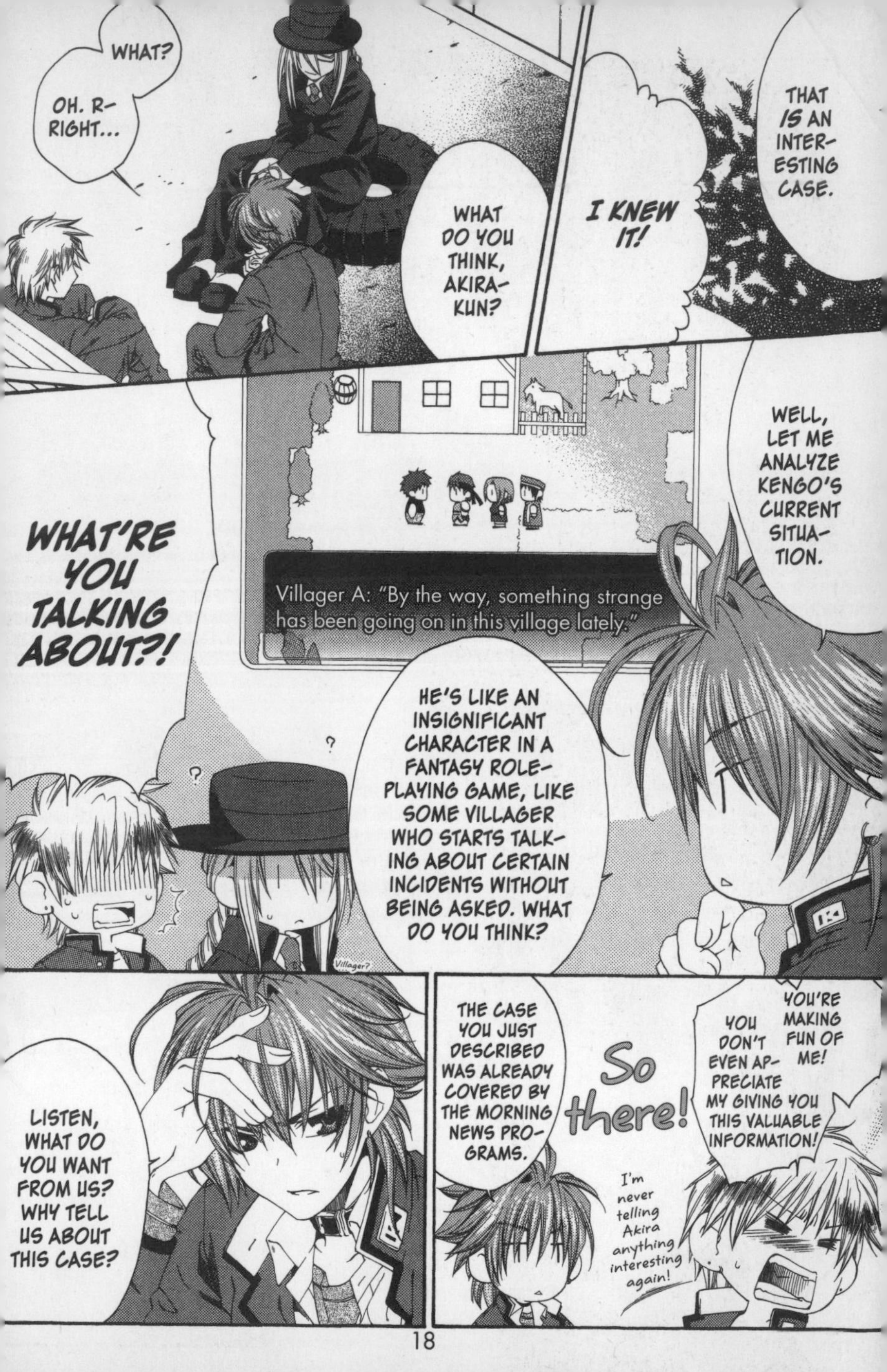
THAT IS AN INTERESTING CASE.
I KNEW IT!
WHAT DO YOU THINK, AKIRA-KUN?
WHAT?
OH. R-RIGHT...
WELL, LET ME ANALYZE KENGO'S CURRENT SITUATION.
Villager A: "By the way, something strange has been going on in this village lately."
WHAT'RE YOU TALKING ABOUT?!
HE'S LIKE AN INSIGNIFICANT CHARACTER IN A FANTASY ROLE-PLAYING GAME, LIKE SOME VILLAGER WHO STARTS TALKING ABOUT CERTAIN INCIDENTS WITHOUT BEING ASKED. WHAT DO YOU THINK?
?
?
Villager?
YOU'RE MAKING FUN OF ME!
YOU DON'T EVEN APPRECIATE MY GIVING YOU THIS VALUABLE INFORMATION!
So there!
I'm never telling Akira anything interesting again!
THE CASE YOU JUST DESCRIBED WAS ALREADY COVERED BY THE MORNING NEWS PROGRAMS.
LISTEN, WHAT DO YOU WANT FROM US? WHY TELL US ABOUT THIS CASE?

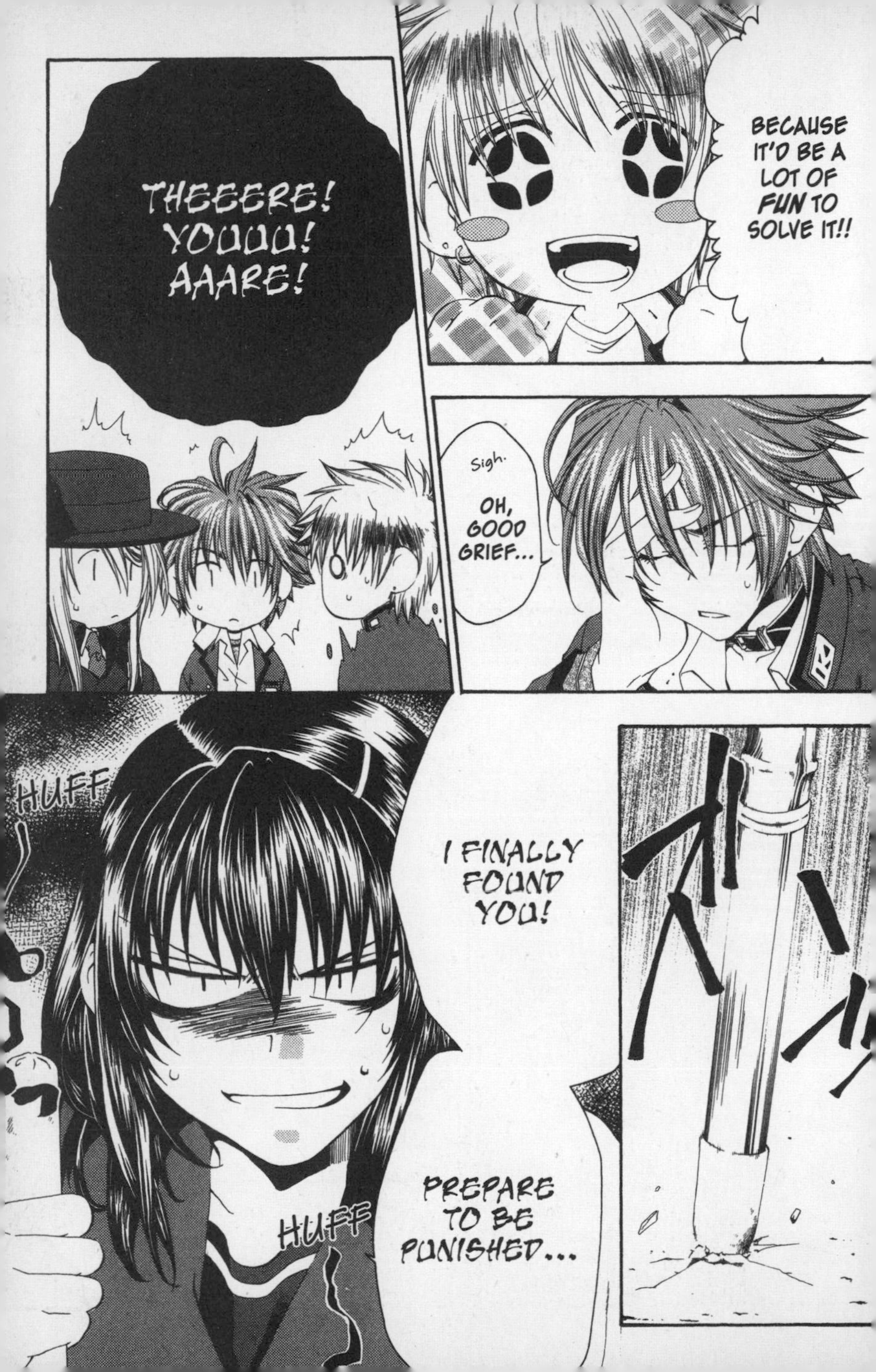
BECAUSE IT'D BE A LOT OF FUN TO SOLVE IT!!
THEEERE! YOUUU! AAARE!
Sigh.
OH, GOOD GRIEF...
HUFF
I FINALLY FOUND YOU!
PREPARE TO BE PUNISHED...
HUFF

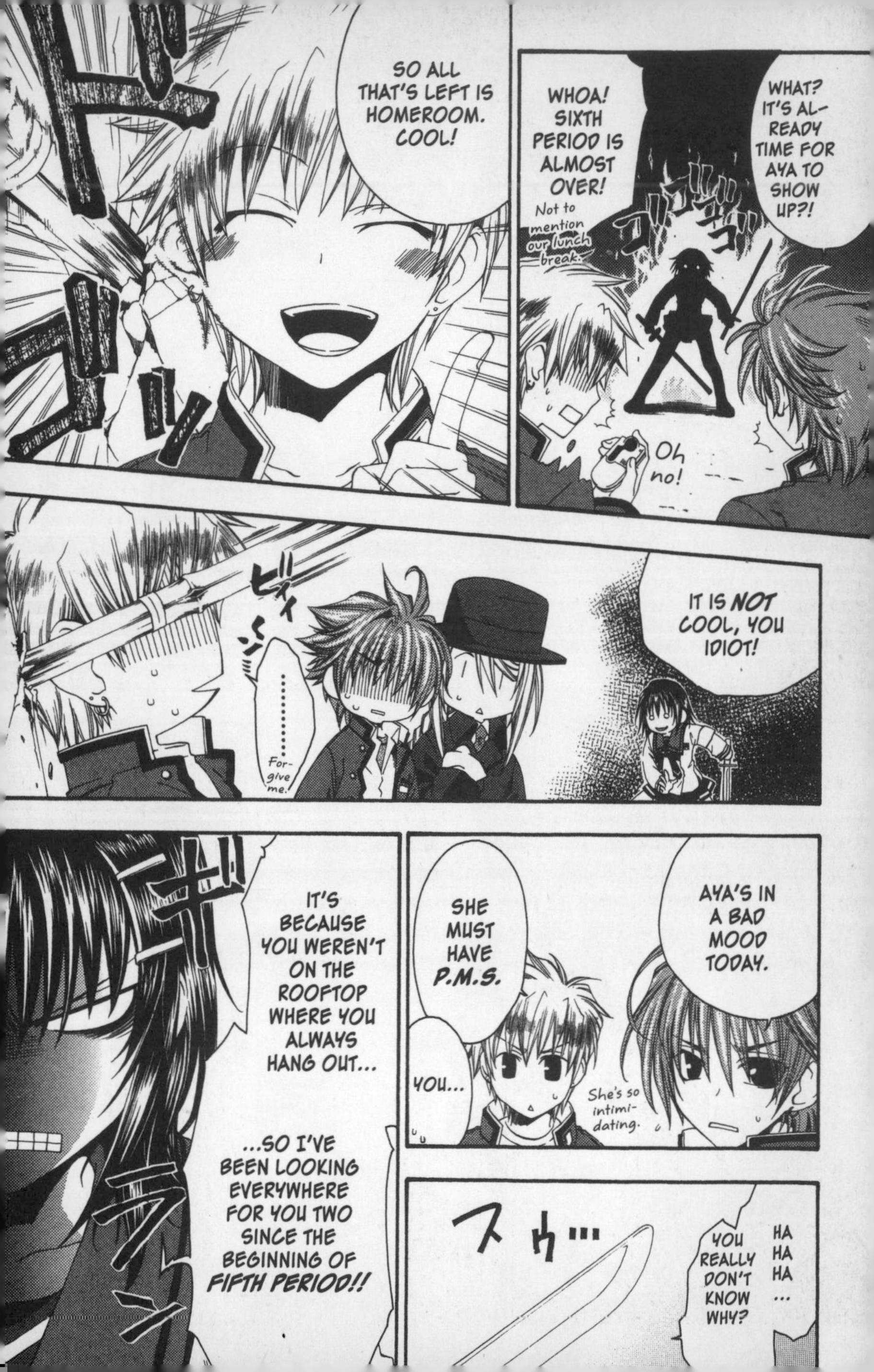
WHAT? IT'S AL-READY TIME FOR AYA TO SHOW UP?!
WHOA! SIXTH PERIOD IS ALMOST OVER!
Not to mention our lunch break.
Oh no!
SO ALL THAT'S LEFT IS HOMEROOM. COOL!
IT IS NOT COOL, YOU IDIOT!
……
Forgive me.
AYA'S IN A BAD MOOD TODAY.
SHE MUST HAVE P.M.S.
She's so intimidating.
YOU...
HA HA HA...
YOU REALLY DON'T KNOW WHY?
IT'S BECAUSE YOU WEREN'T ON THE ROOFTOP WHERE YOU ALWAYS HANG OUT...
...SO I'VE BEEN LOOKING EVERYWHERE FOR YOU TWO SINCE THE BEGINNING OF FIFTH PERIOD!!

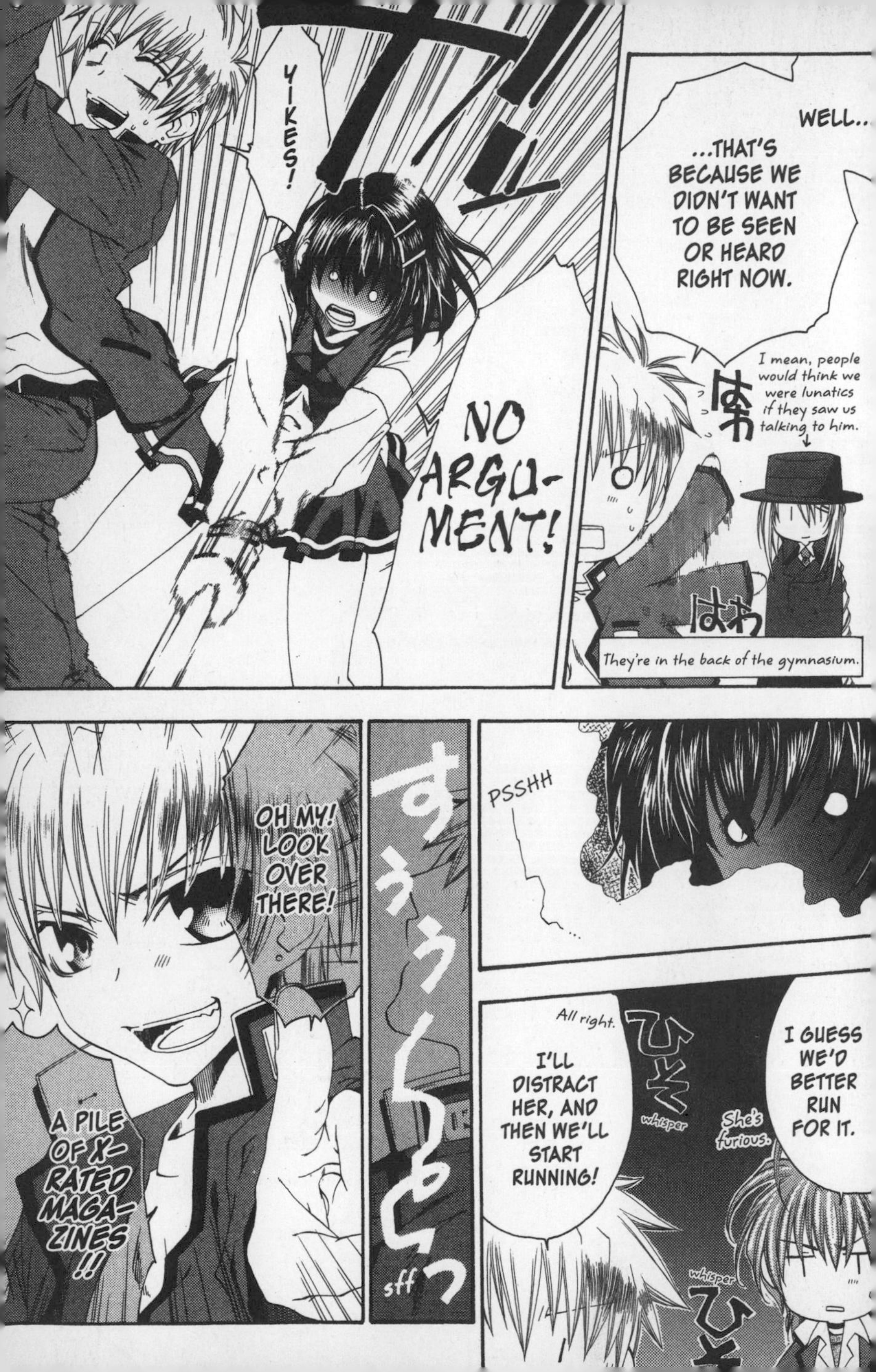

WELL...
...THAT'S BECAUSE WE DIDN'T WANT TO BE SEEN OR HEARD RIGHT NOW.
I mean, people would think we were lunatics if they saw us talking to him.
はわ
はわ
They're in the back of the gymnasium.
NO ARGUMENT!
YIKES!
PSSHH
I GUESS WE'D BETTER RUN FOR IT.
She's furious.
whisper
ひそ
All right.
I'LL DISTRACT HER, AND THEN WE'LL START RUNNING!
whisper
ひそ
sff
OH MY! LOOK OVER THERE!
A PILE OF X-RATED MAGAZINES!!

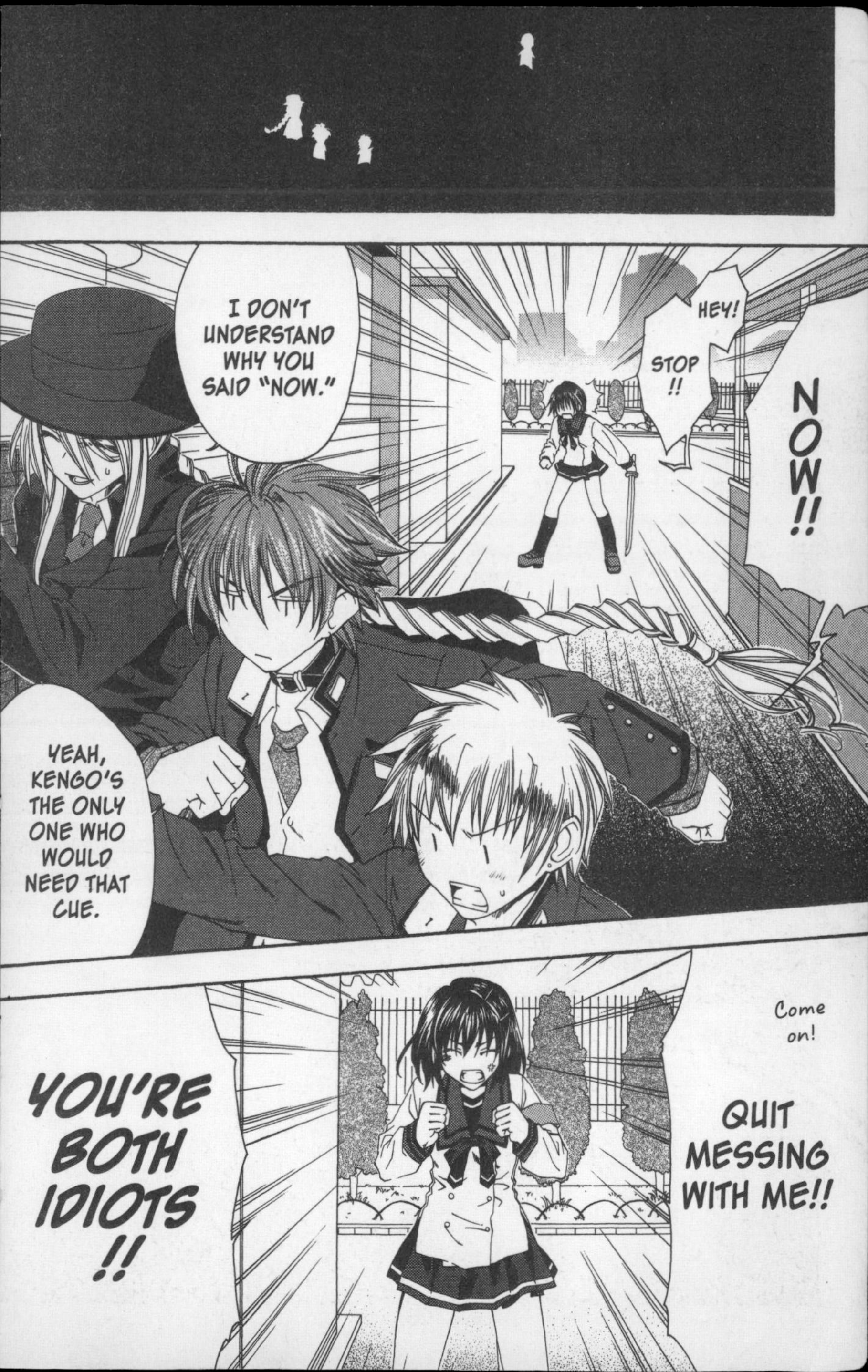
NOW!!
HEY! STOP!!
I DON'T UNDERSTAND WHY YOU SAID "NOW."
YEAH, KENGO'S THE ONLY ONE WHO WOULD NEED THAT CUE.
Come on!
QUIT MESSING WITH ME!!
YOU'RE BOTH IDIOTS!!

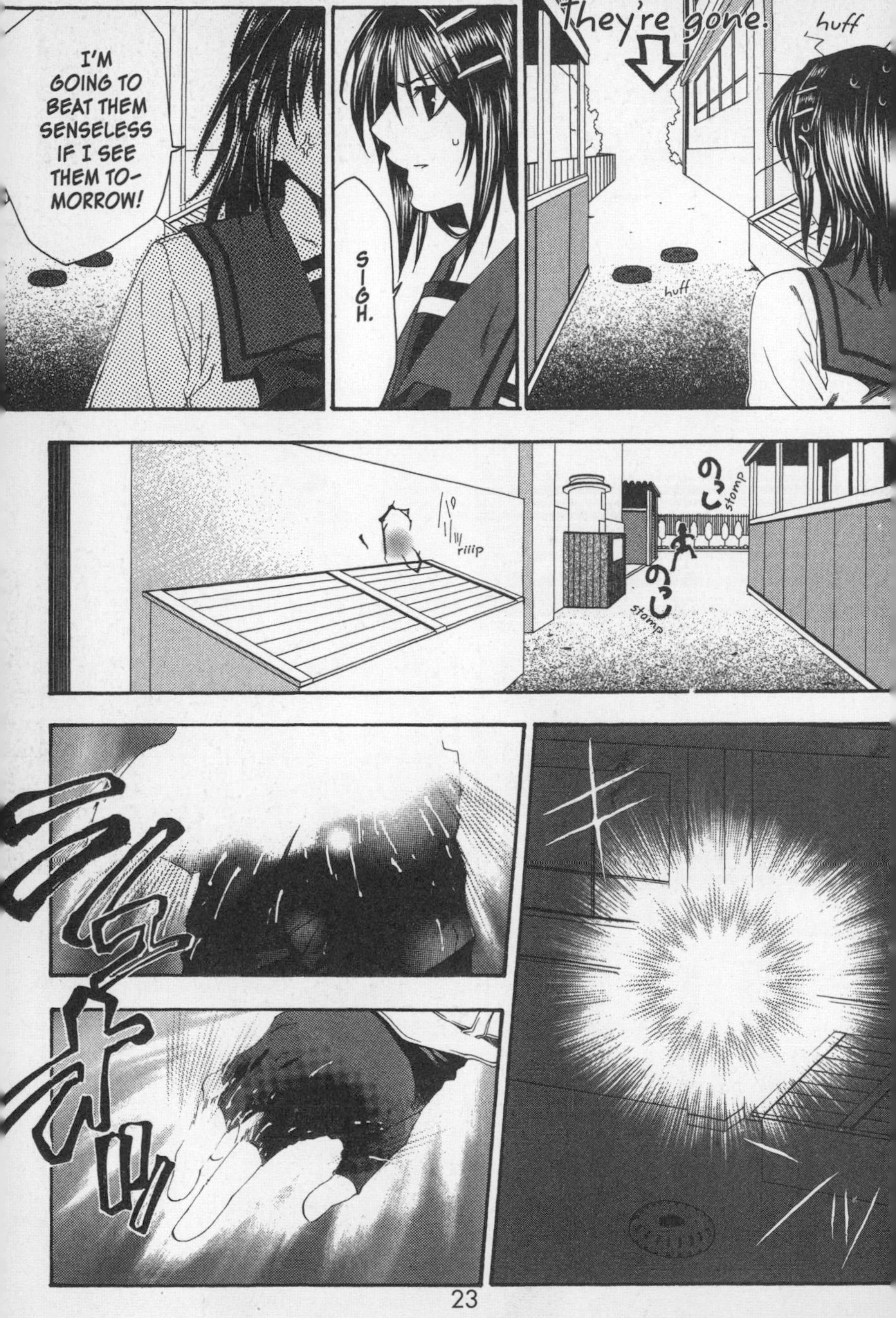
They're gone.
huff
huff
SIGH.
I'M GOING TO BEAT THEM SENSELESS IF I SEE THEM TO-MORROW!
stomp
stomp
riiip

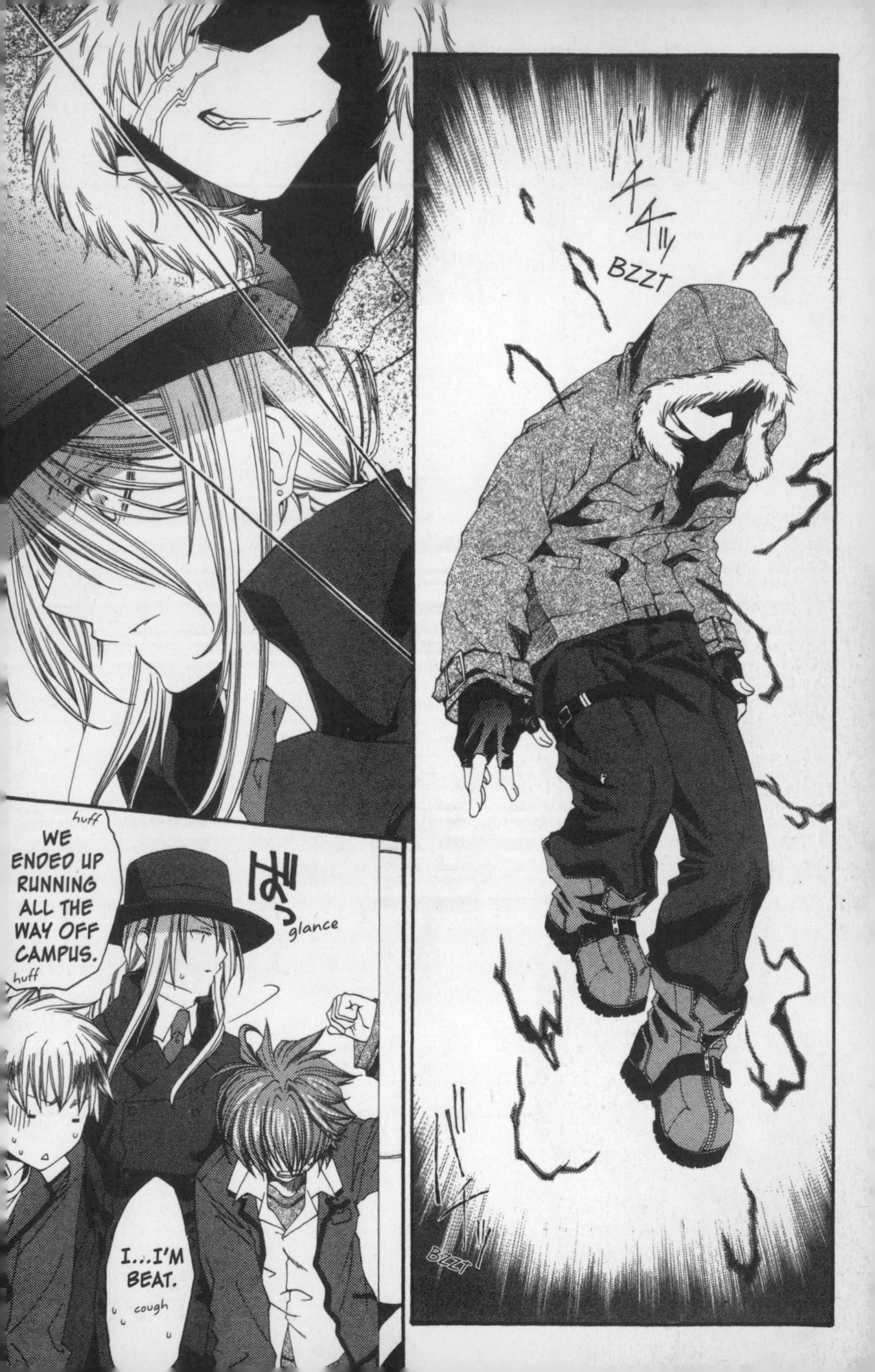
BZZT
BZZT
huff
WE ENDED UP RUNNING ALL THE WAY OFF CAMPUS.
huff
glance
I...I'M BEAT.
cough

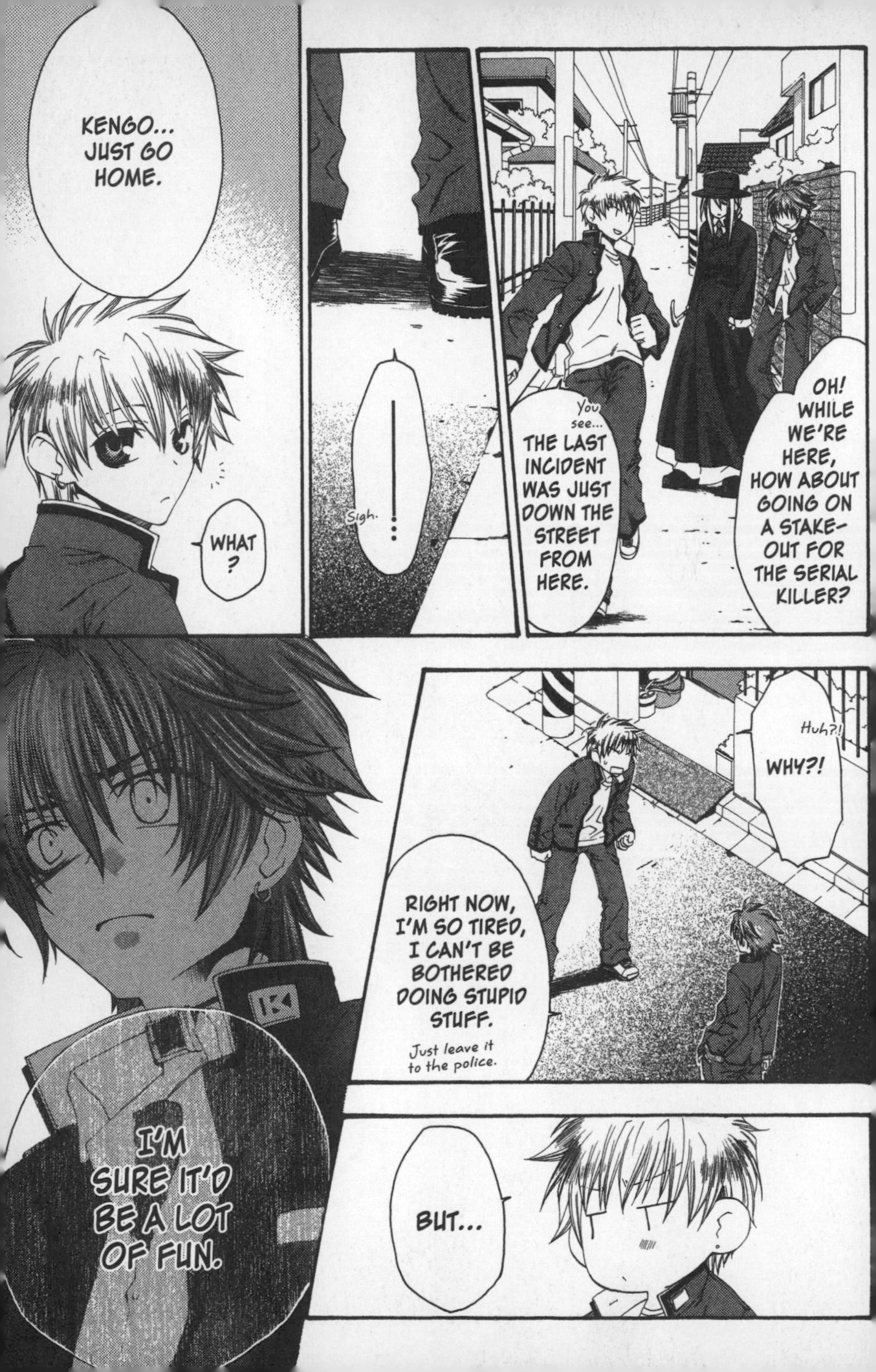
OH! WHILE WE'RE HERE, HOW ABOUT GOING ON A STAKE-OUT FOR THE SERIAL KILLER?
You see... THE LAST INCIDENT WAS JUST DOWN THE STREET FROM HERE.
Sigh.
......
KENGO... JUST GO HOME.
WHAT?
Huh?! WHY?!
RIGHT NOW, I'M SO TIRED, I CAN'T BE BOTHERED DOING STUPID STUFF.
Just leave it to the police.
BUT...
I'M SURE IT'D BE A LOT OF FUN.

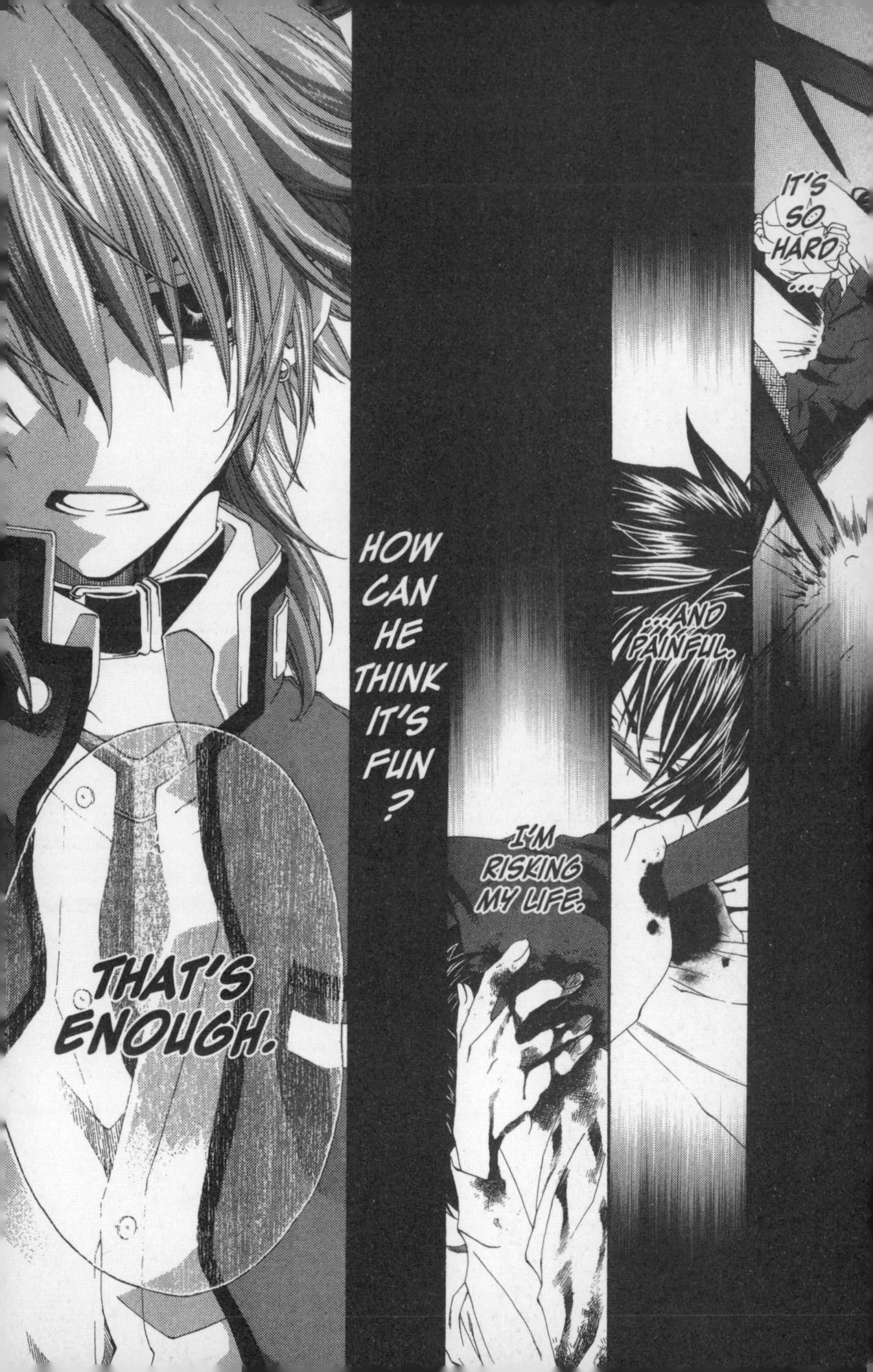
IT'S SO HARD...
...AND PAINFUL.
I'M RISKING MY LIFE.
HOW CAN HE THINK IT'S FUN?
THAT'S ENOUGH.

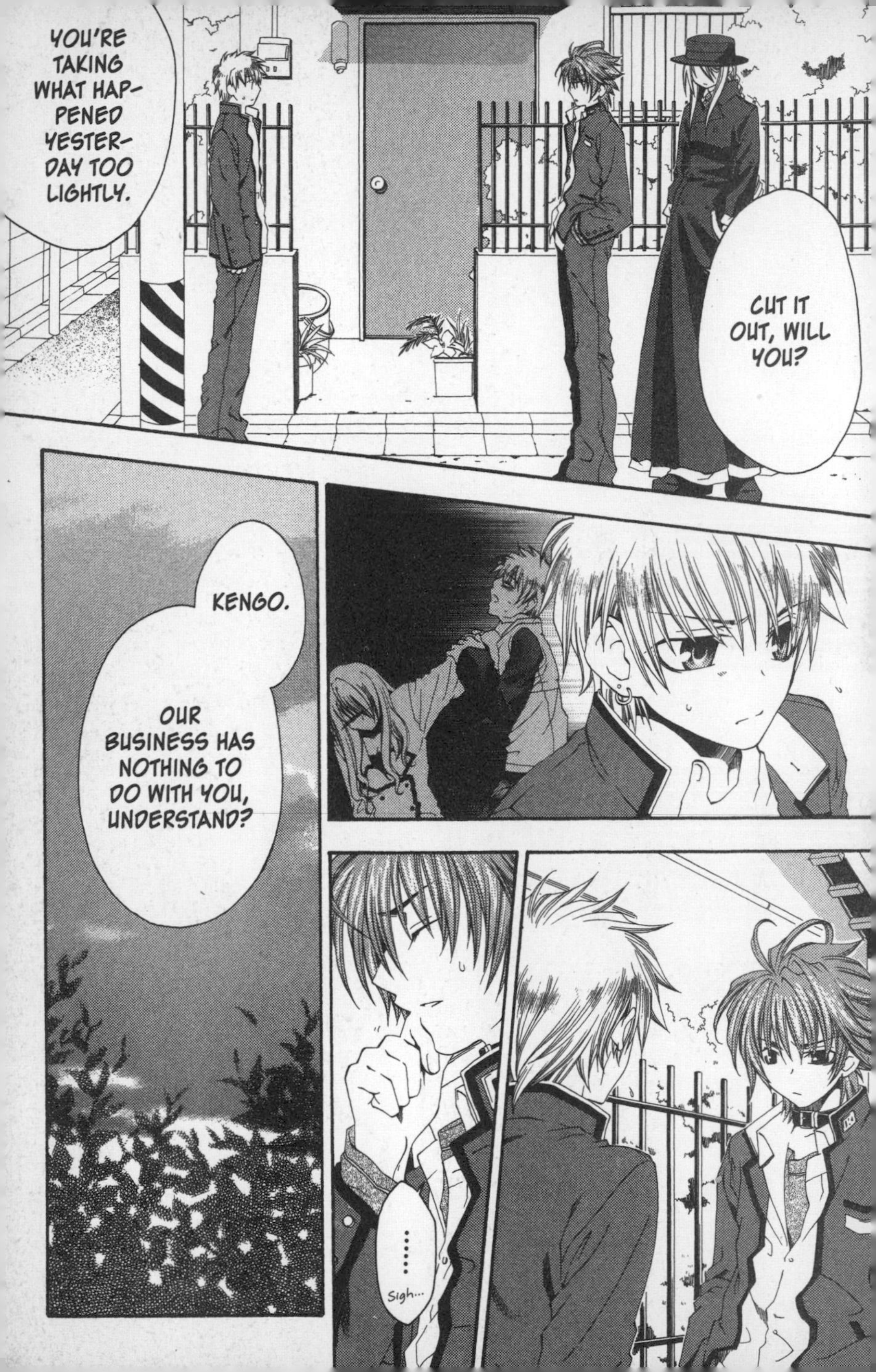
CUT IT OUT, WILL YOU?
YOU'RE TAKING WHAT HAP-PENED YESTER-DAY TOO LIGHTLY.
KENGO.
OUR BUSINESS HAS NOTHING TO DO WITH YOU, UNDERSTAND?
......
Sigh...

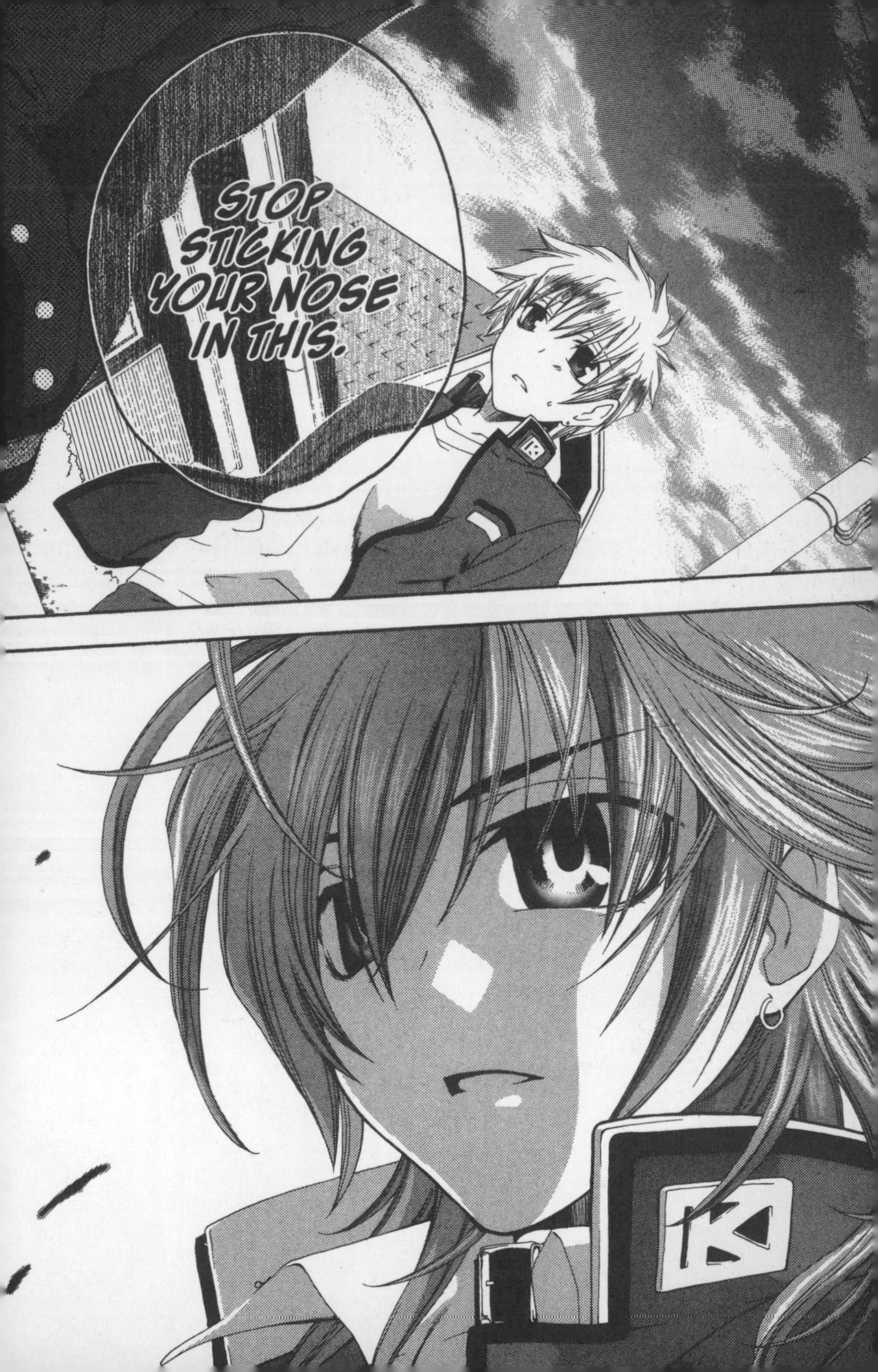
STOP STICKING YOUR NOSE IN THIS.

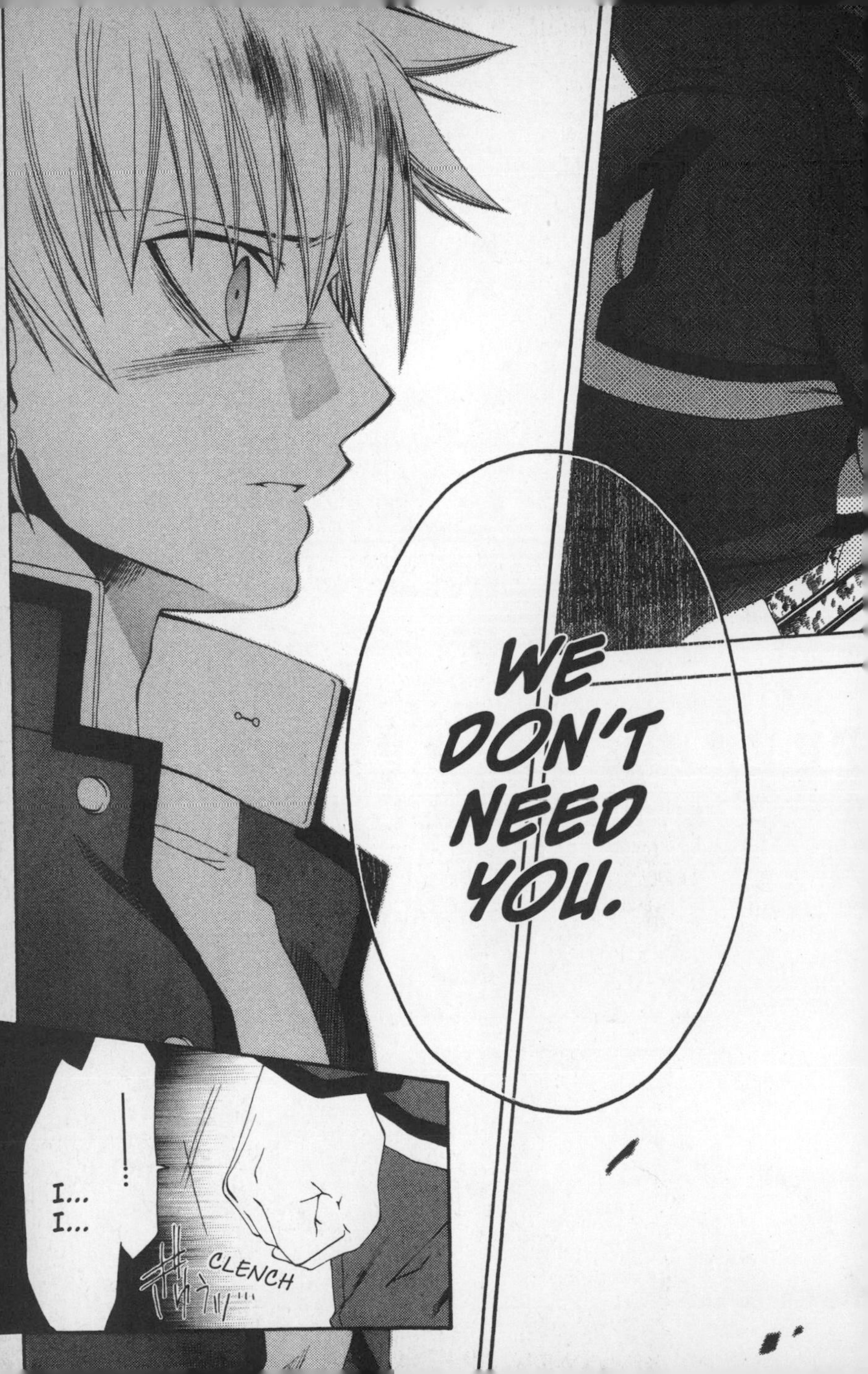
WE DON'T NEED YOU.
...!
I... I...
CLENCH

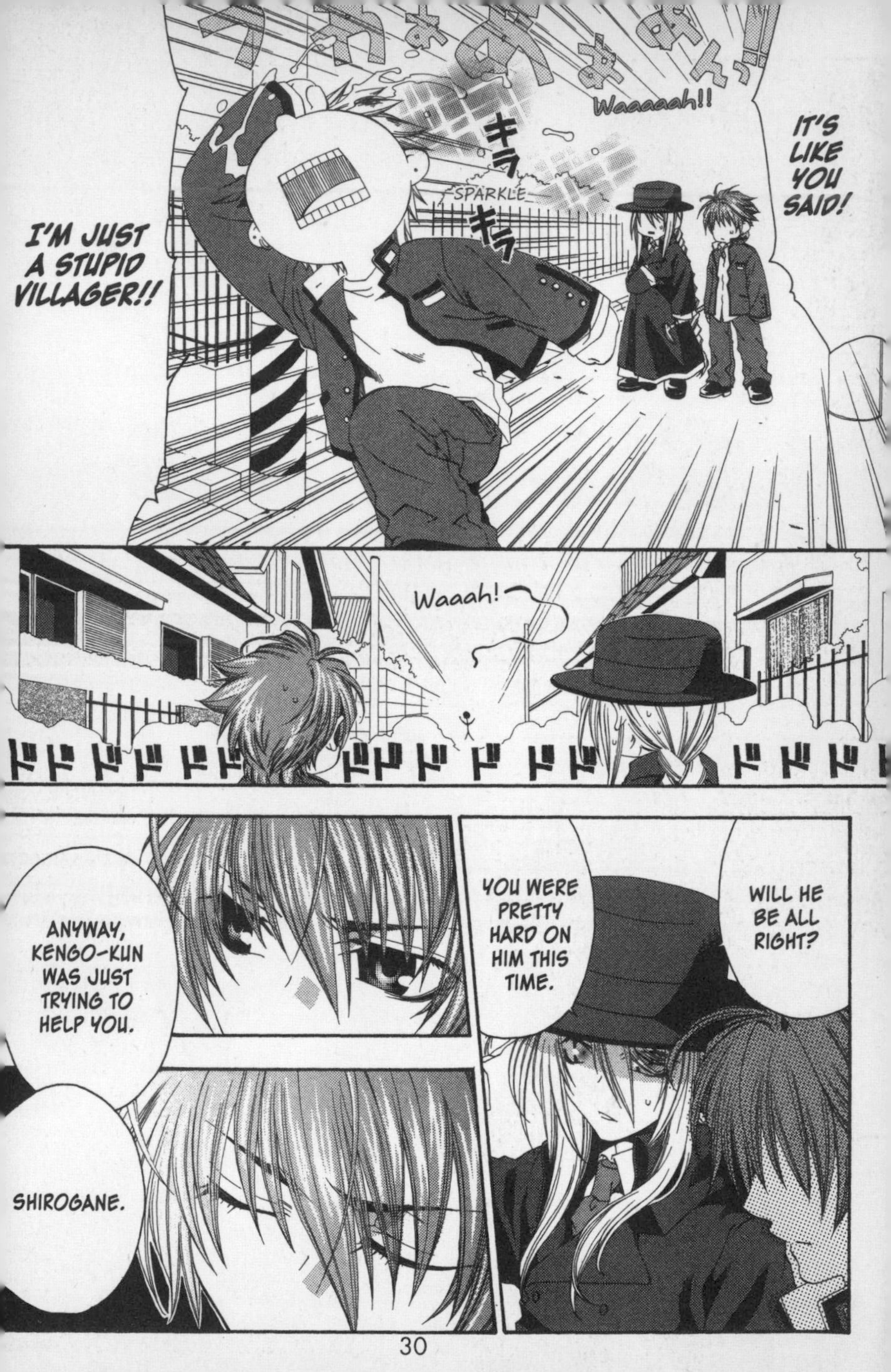
Waaaaah!!
IT'S LIKE YOU SAID!
I'M JUST A STUPID VILLAGER!!
SPARKLE
Waaah!
WILL HE BE ALL RIGHT?
YOU WERE PRETTY HARD ON HIM THIS TIME.
ANYWAY, KENGO-KUN WAS JUST TRYING TO HELP YOU.
SHIROGANE.

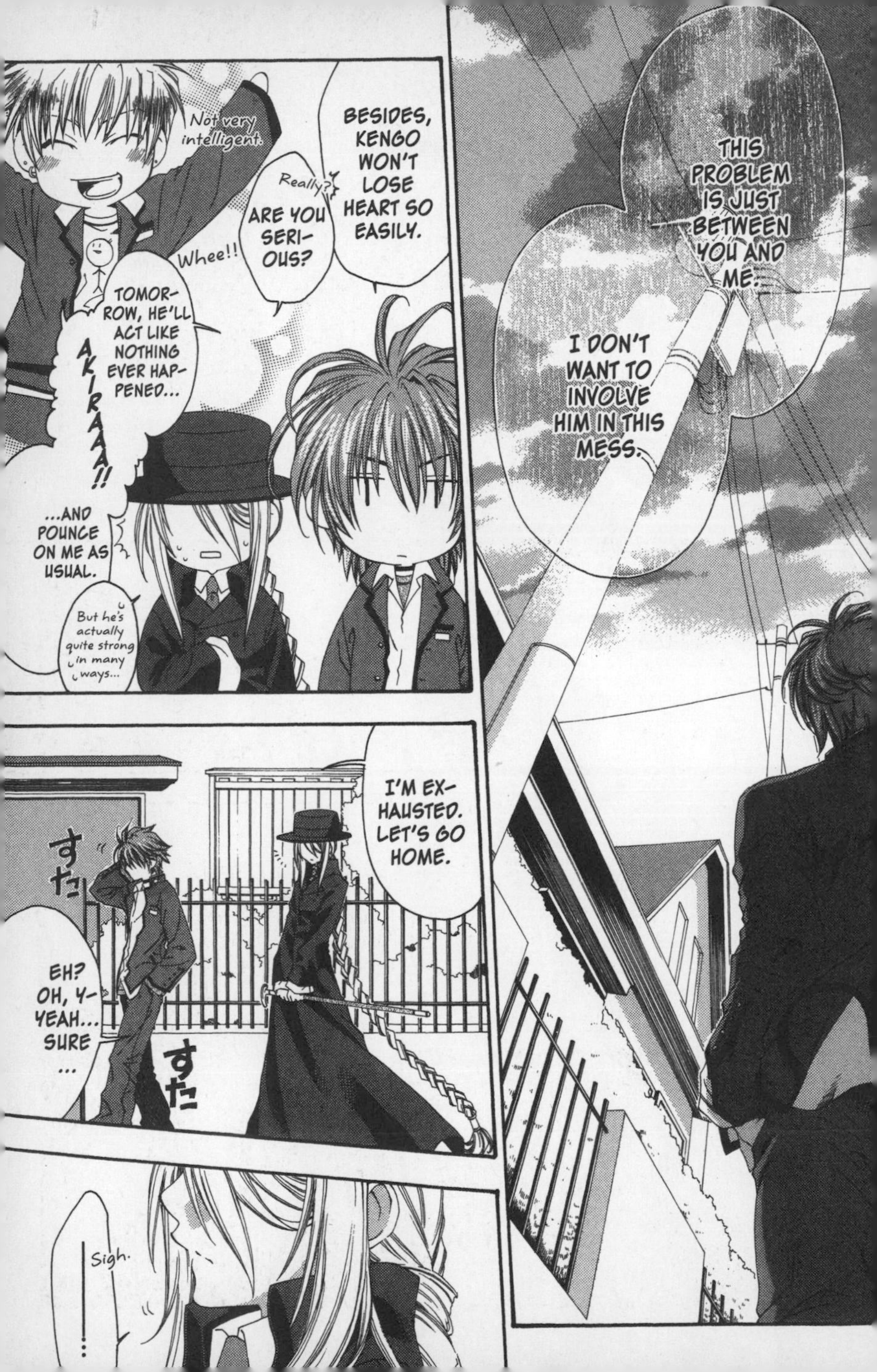
THIS PROBLEM IS JUST BETWEEN YOU AND ME.
I DON'T WANT TO INVOLVE HIM IN THIS MESS.
BESIDES, KENGO WON'T LOSE HEART SO EASILY.
Really?
ARE YOU SERI-OUS?
Not very intelligent.
Whee!!
TOMOR-ROW, HE'LL ACT LIKE NOTHING EVER HAP-PENED...
AKIRAAAA!!
...AND POUNCE ON ME AS USUAL.
But he's actually quite strong in many ways...
I'M EX-HAUSTED. LET'S GO HOME.
EH? OH, Y-YEAH... SURE...
すた
すた
Sigh.
...

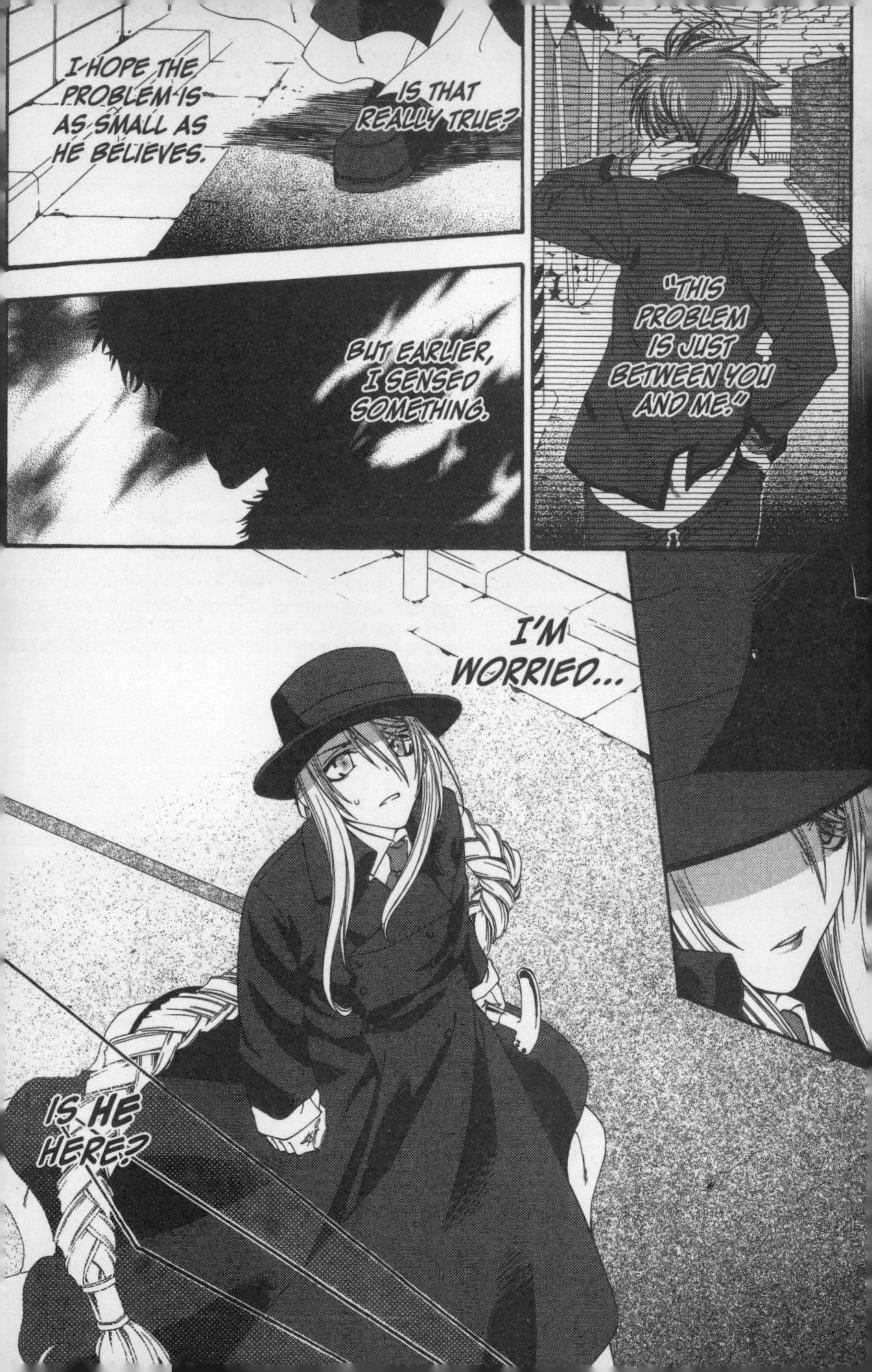

"THIS PROBLEM IS JUST BETWEEN YOU AND ME."
IS THAT REALLY TRUE?
I HOPE THE PROBLEM IS AS SMALL AS HE BELIEVES.
BUT EARLIER, I SENSED SOMETHING.
I'M WORRIED...
IS HE HERE?

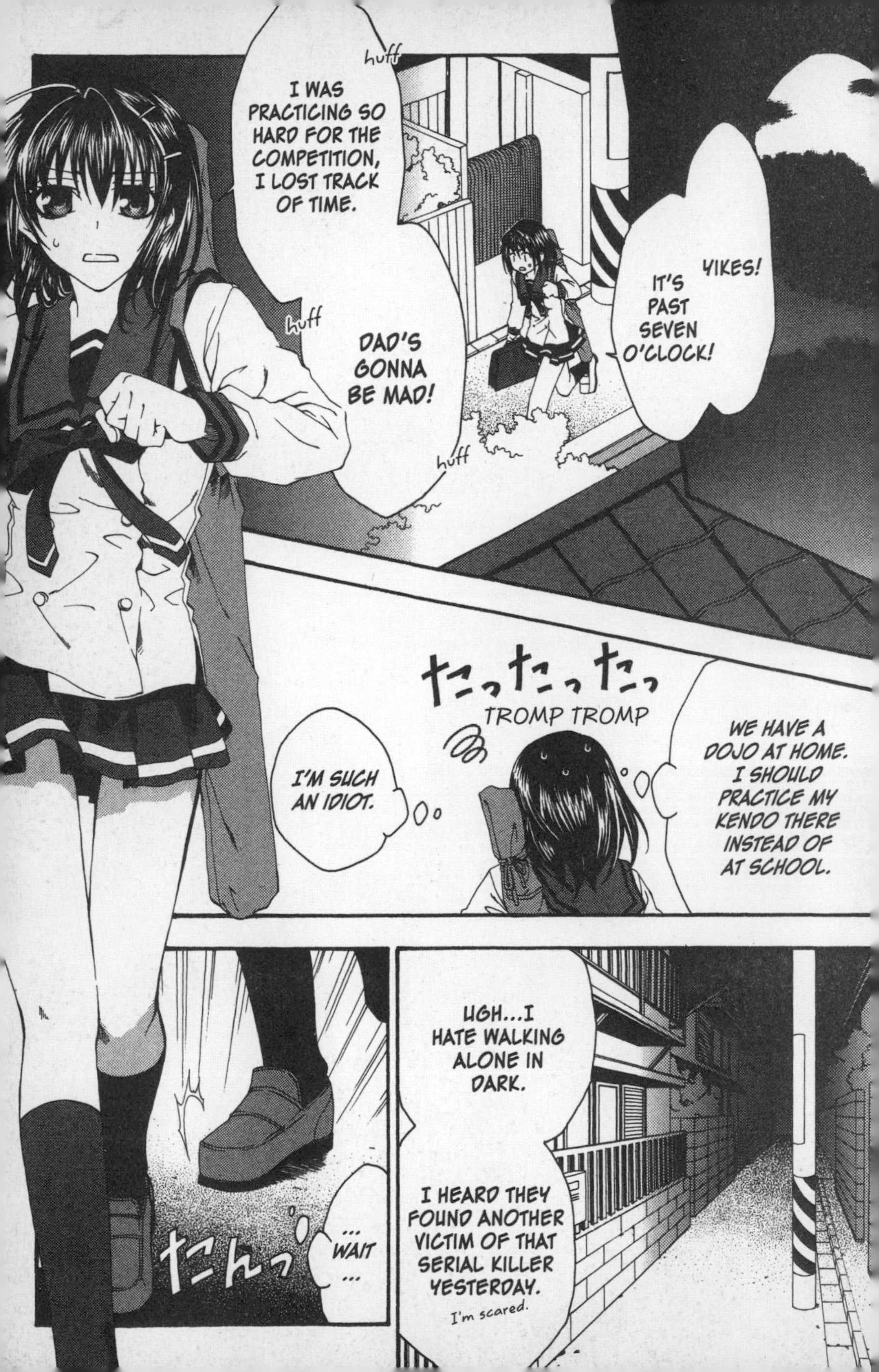
YIKES! IT'S PAST SEVEN O'CLOCK!
huff
I WAS PRACTICING SO HARD FOR THE COMPETITION, I LOST TRACK OF TIME.
huff
DAD'S GONNA BE MAD!
huff
たっ たっ たっ
TROMP TROMP
WE HAVE A DOJO AT HOME. I SHOULD PRACTICE MY KENDO THERE INSTEAD OF AT SCHOOL.
I'M SUCH AN IDIOT.
UGH...I HATE WALKING ALONE IN DARK.
I HEARD THEY FOUND ANOTHER VICTIM OF THAT SERIAL KILLER YESTERDAY.
I'm scared.
...WAIT...
たんっ

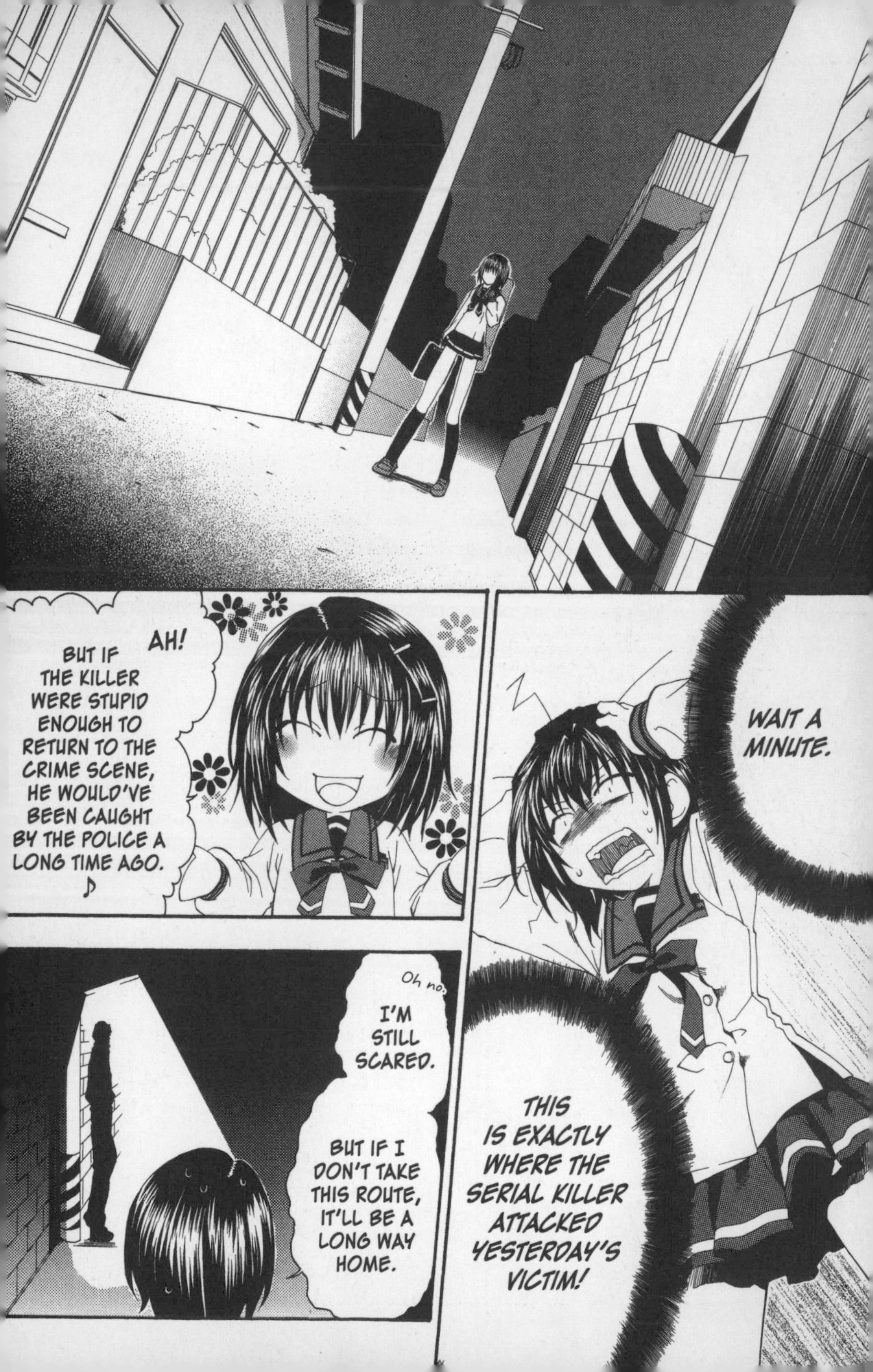
WAIT A MINUTE.
AH!
BUT IF THE KILLER WERE STUPID ENOUGH TO RETURN TO THE CRIME SCENE, HE WOULD'VE BEEN CAUGHT BY THE POLICE A LONG TIME AGO. ♪
THIS IS EXACTLY WHERE THE SERIAL KILLER ATTACKED YESTERDAY'S VICTIM!
Oh no.
I'M STILL SCARED.
BUT IF I DON'T TAKE THIS ROUTE, IT'LL BE A LONG WAY HOME.

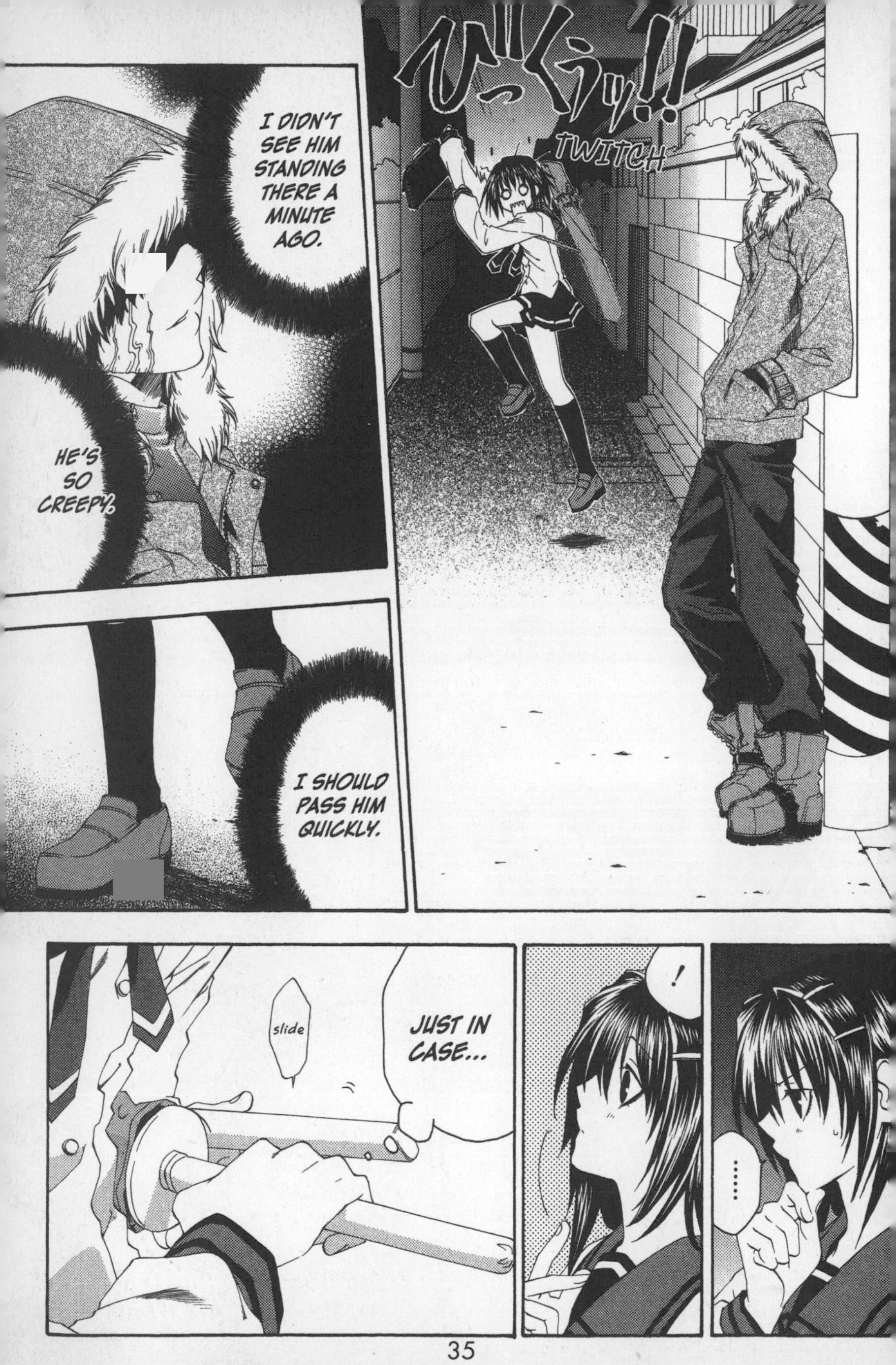
ひっくうッ!!
TWITCH
I DIDN'T SEE HIM STANDING THERE A MINUTE AGO.
HE'S SO CREEPY.
I SHOULD PASS HIM QUICKLY.
!
......
JUST IN CASE...
slide

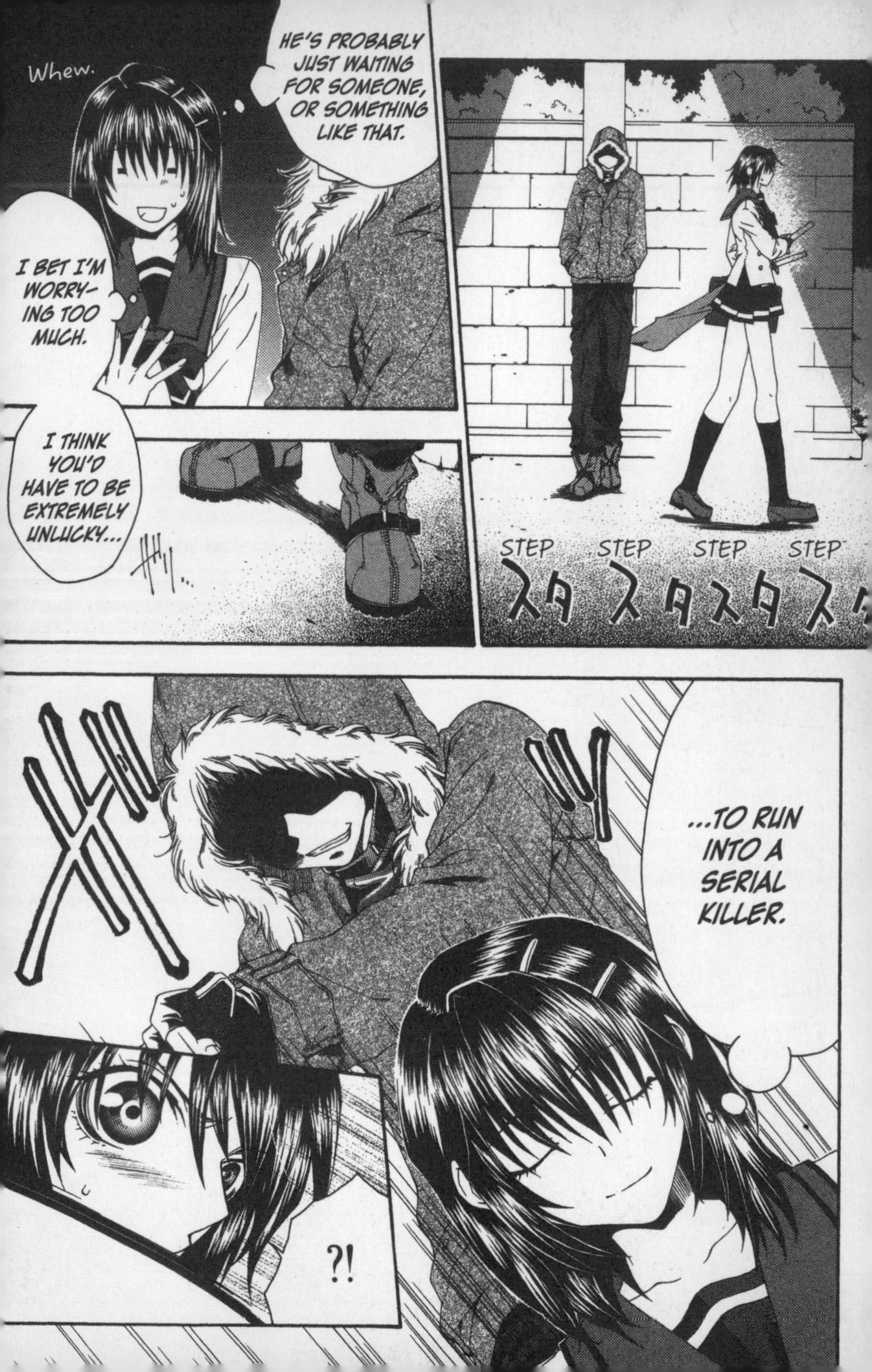
Whew.
HE'S PROBABLY JUST WAITING FOR SOMEONE, OR SOMETHING LIKE THAT.
I BET I'M WORRY-ING TOO MUCH.
STEP STEP STEP STEP
スタスタスタスタ
I THINK YOU'D HAVE TO BE EXTREMELY UNLUCKY...
...TO RUN INTO A SERIAL KILLER.
?!

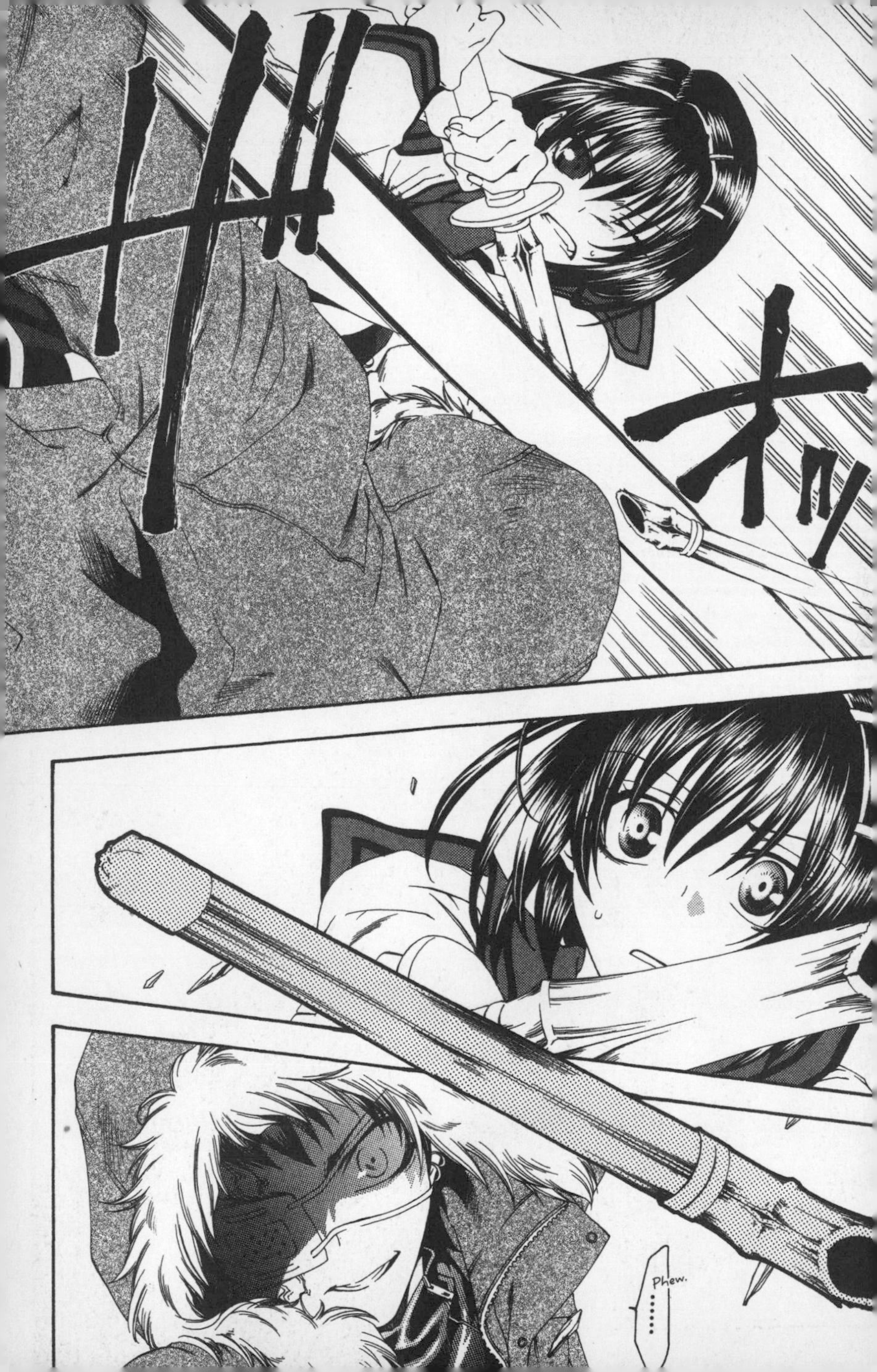
ガキッ
オッ
Phew.
......

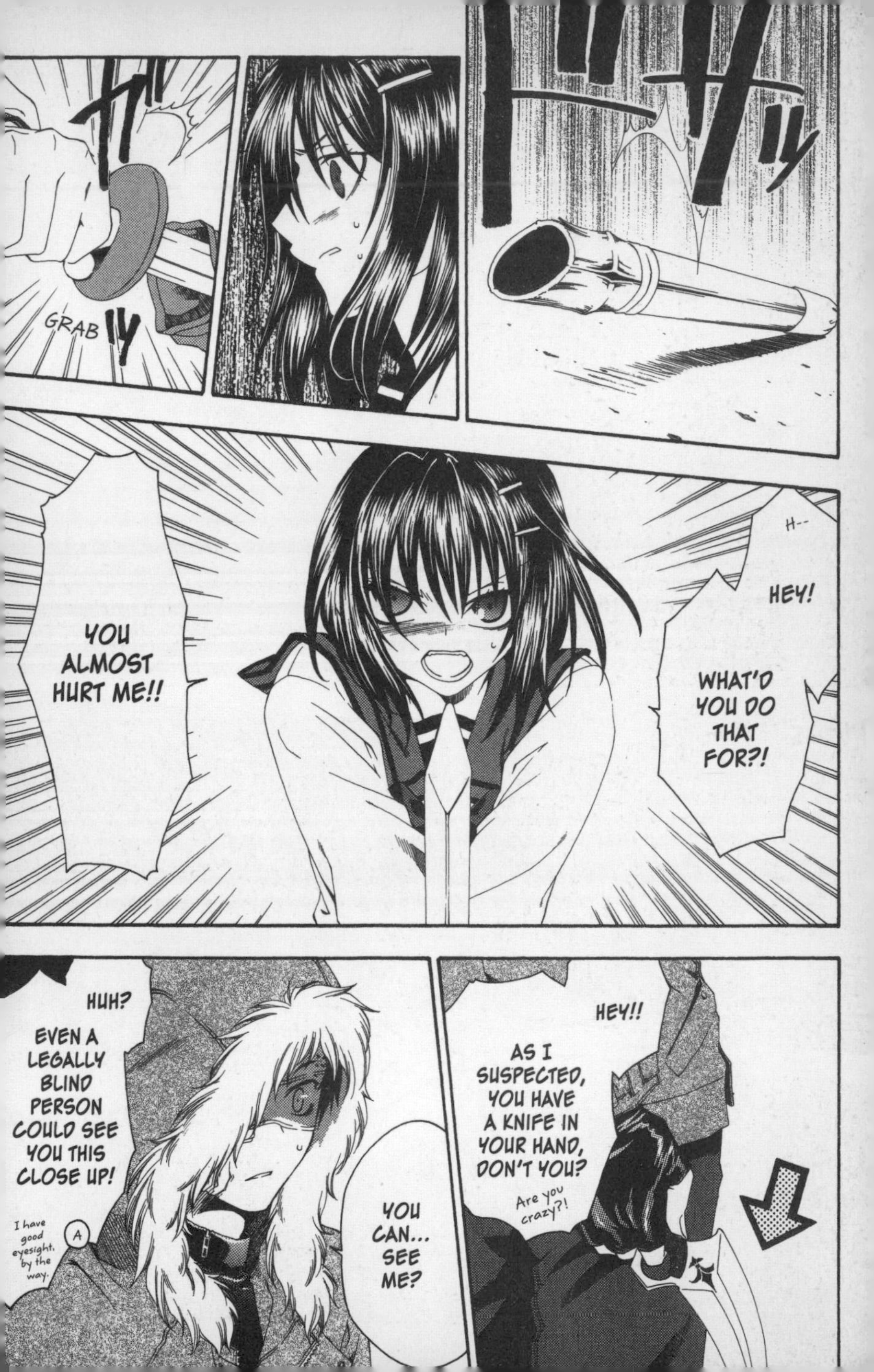
GRAB
H--
HEY!
WHAT'D YOU DO THAT FOR?!
YOU ALMOST HURT ME!!
HEY!!
AS I SUSPECTED, YOU HAVE A KNIFE IN YOUR HAND, DON'T YOU?
Are you crazy?!
YOU CAN... SEE ME?
HUH?
EVEN A LEGALLY BLIND PERSON COULD SEE YOU THIS CLOSE UP!
I have good eyesight, by the way.
A

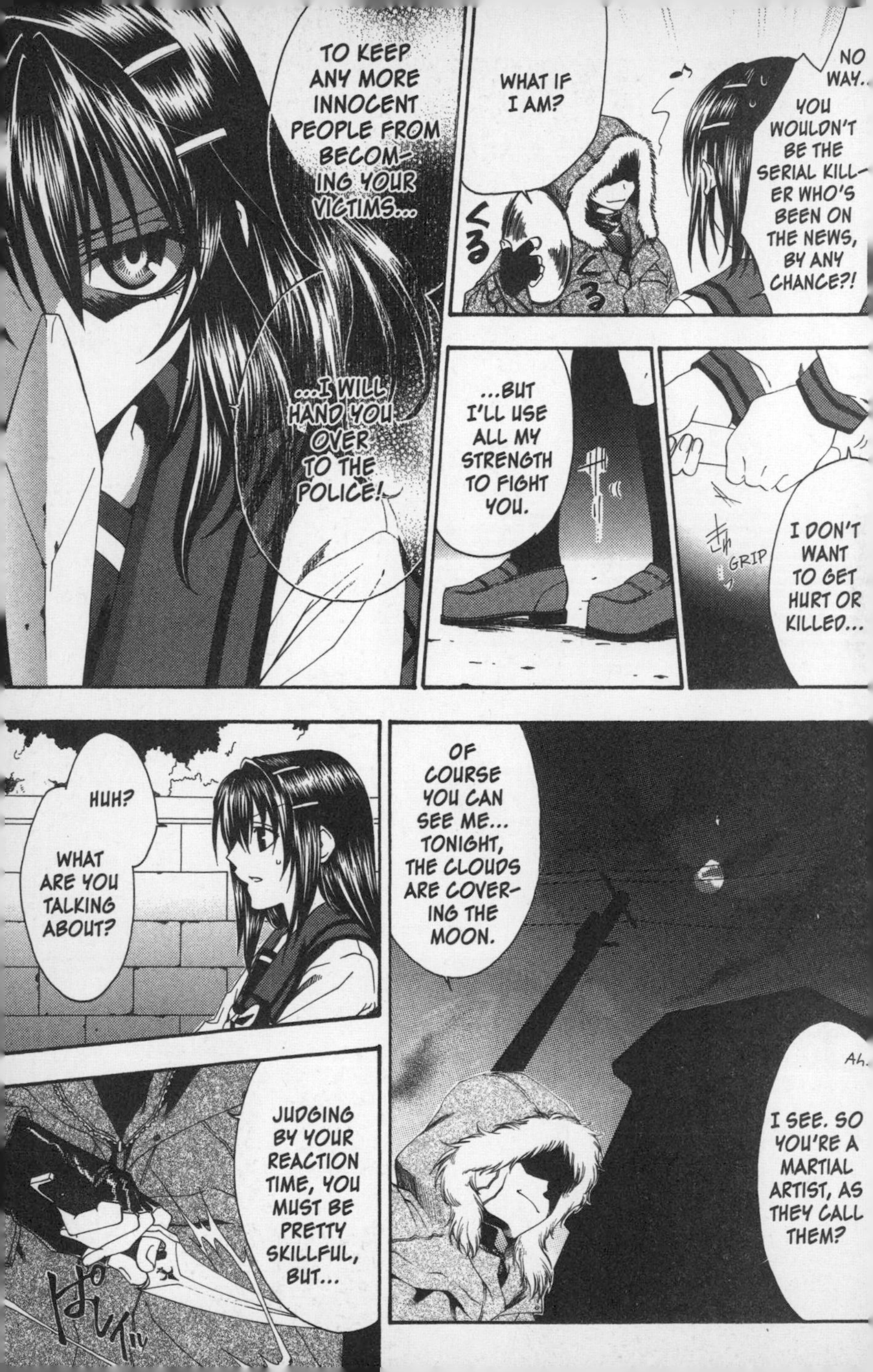
NO WAY... YOU WOULDN'T BE THE SERIAL KILLER WHO'S BEEN ON THE NEWS, BY ANY CHANCE?!
WHAT IF I AM?
I DON'T WANT TO GET HURT OR KILLED...
GRIP
...BUT I'LL USE ALL MY STRENGTH TO FIGHT YOU.
TO KEEP ANY MORE INNOCENT PEOPLE FROM BECOMING YOUR VICTIMS...
...I WILL HAND YOU OVER TO THE POLICE!
Ah.
I SEE. SO YOU'RE A MARTIAL ARTIST, AS THEY CALL THEM?
JUDGING BY YOUR REACTION TIME, YOU MUST BE PRETTY SKILLFUL, BUT...
OF COURSE YOU CAN SEE ME... TONIGHT, THE CLOUDS ARE COVERING THE MOON.
HUH?
WHAT ARE YOU TALKING ABOUT?

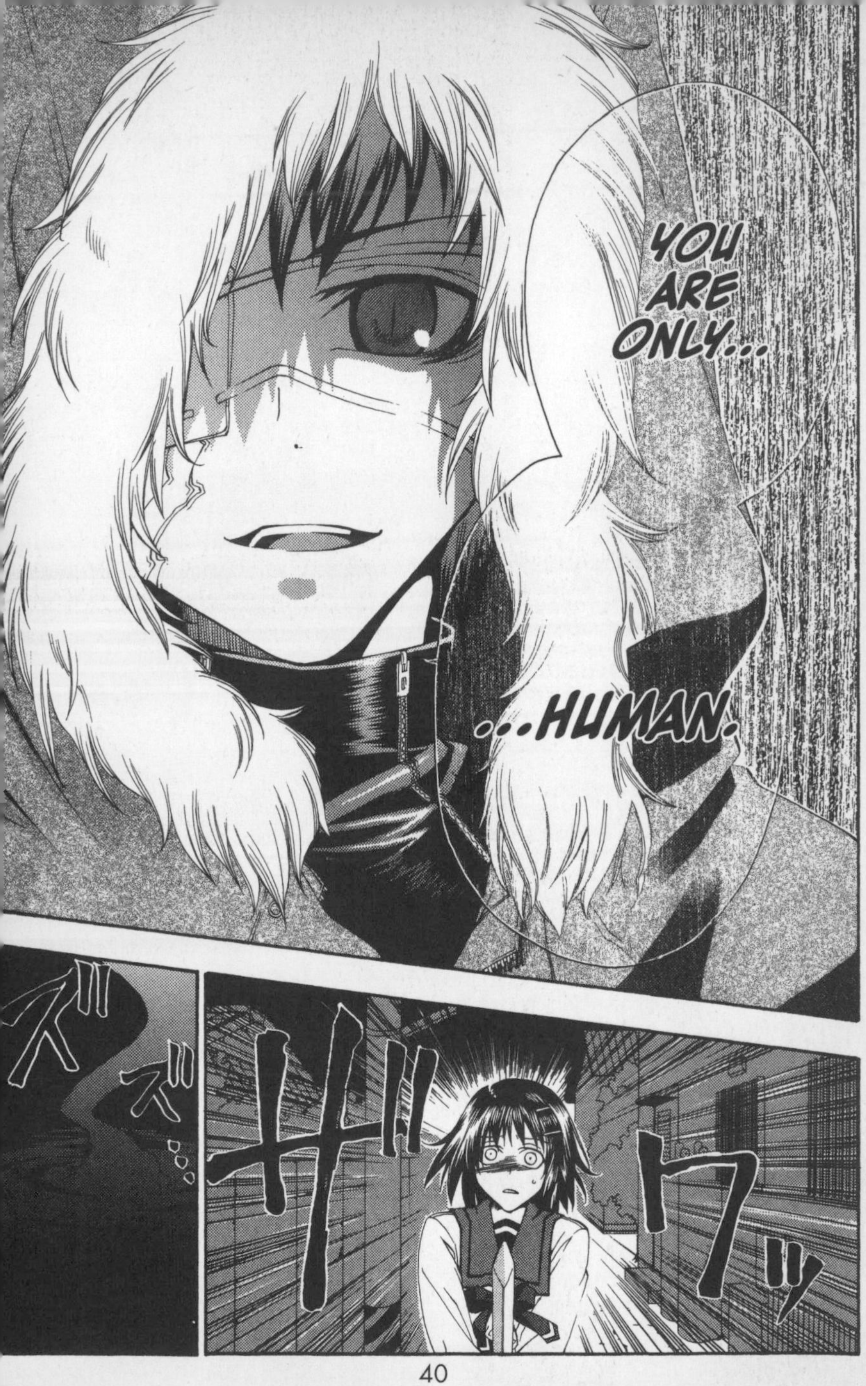

YOU ARE ONLY...
...HUMAN.
ズ
ズ...
ザワッ

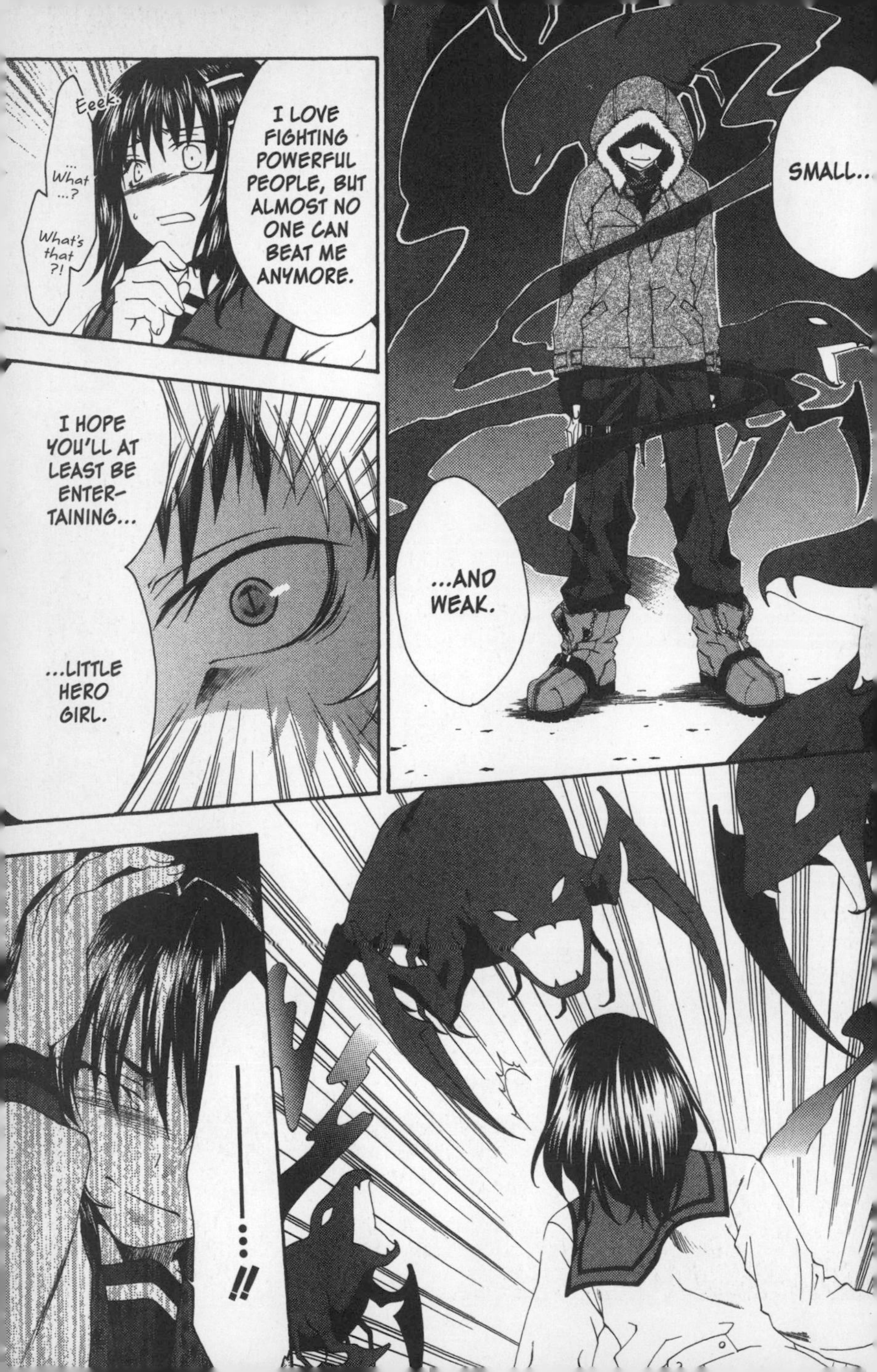
SMALL...
...AND WEAK.
I LOVE FIGHTING POWERFUL PEOPLE, BUT ALMOST NO ONE CAN BEAT ME ANYMORE.
Eeek.
...What...?
What's that?!
I HOPE YOU'LL AT LEAST BE ENTER-TAINING...
...LITTLE HERO GIRL.
––...!!

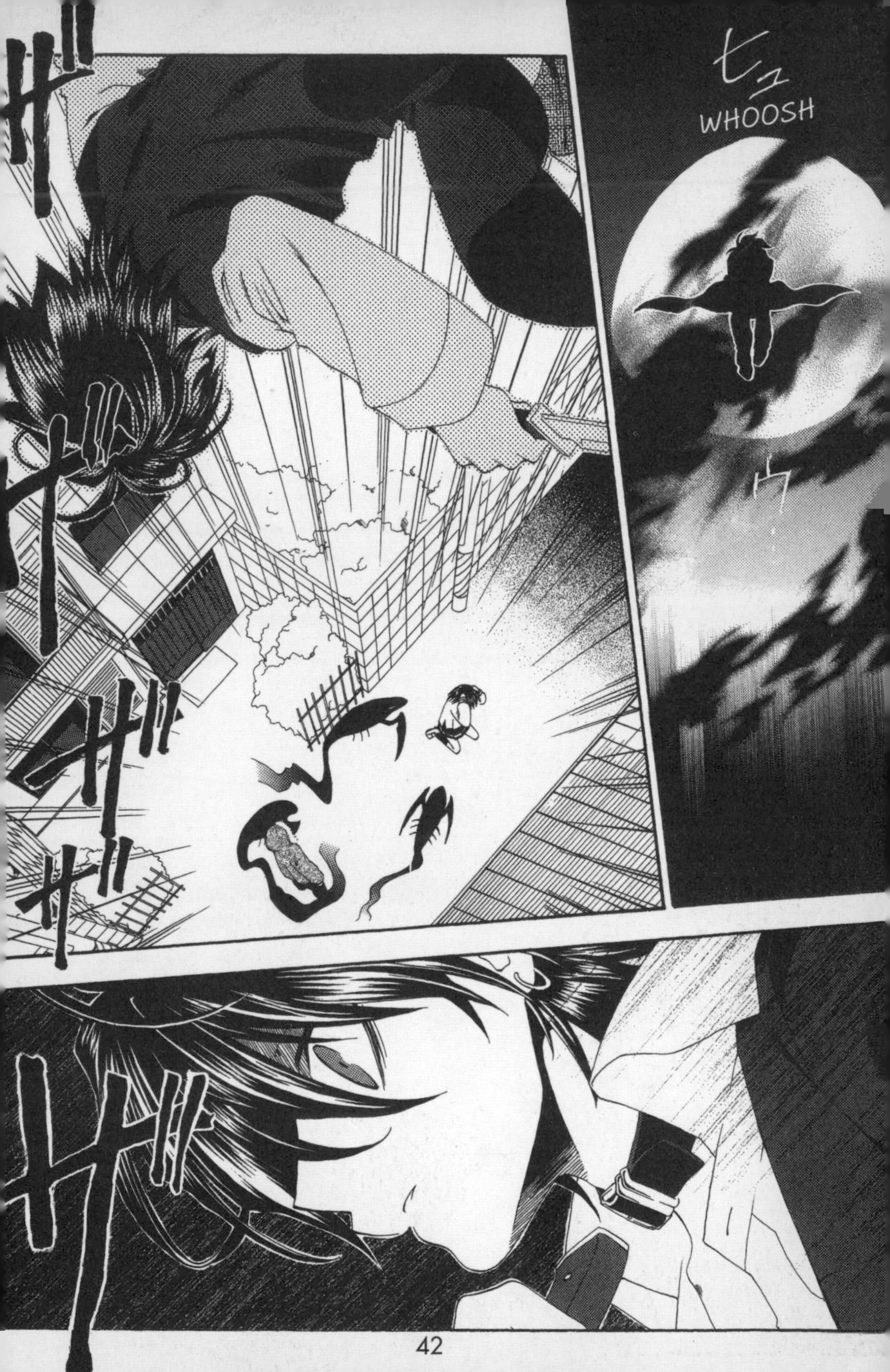
ヒュ
WHOOSH

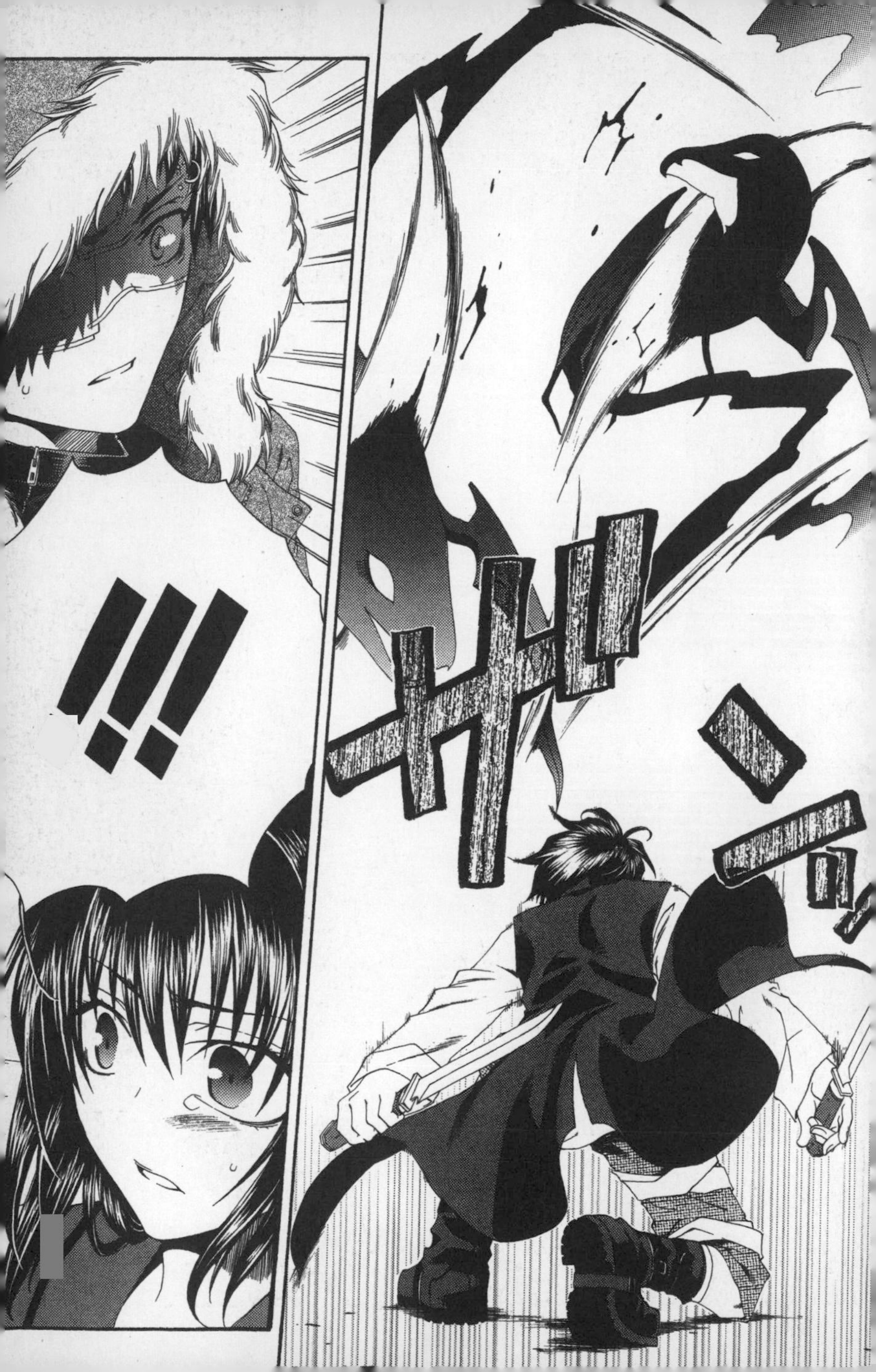
!!!

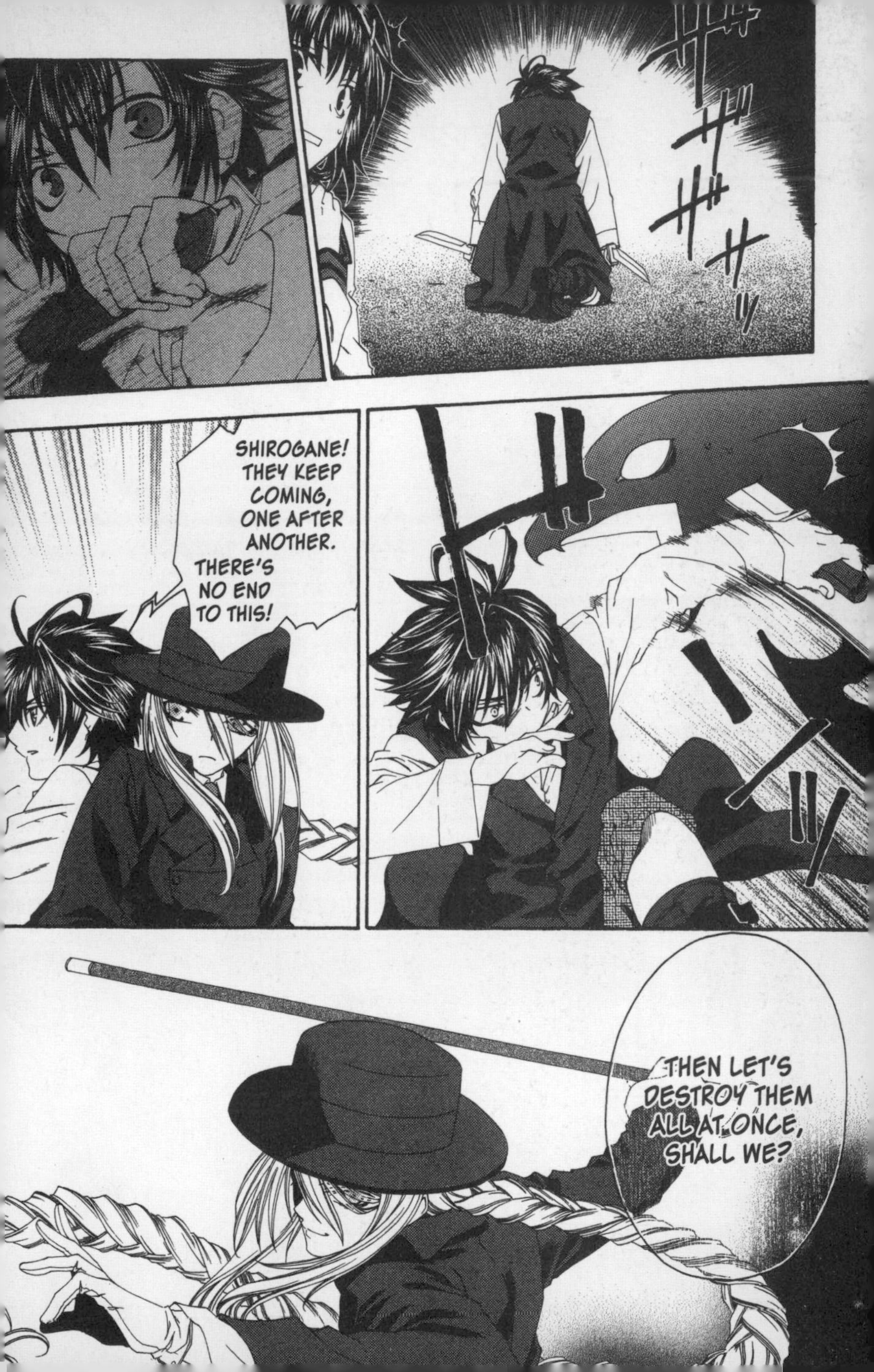
SHIROGANE! THEY KEEP COMING, ONE AFTER ANOTHER.
THERE'S NO END TO THIS!
THEN LET'S DESTROY THEM ALL AT ONCE, SHALL WE?

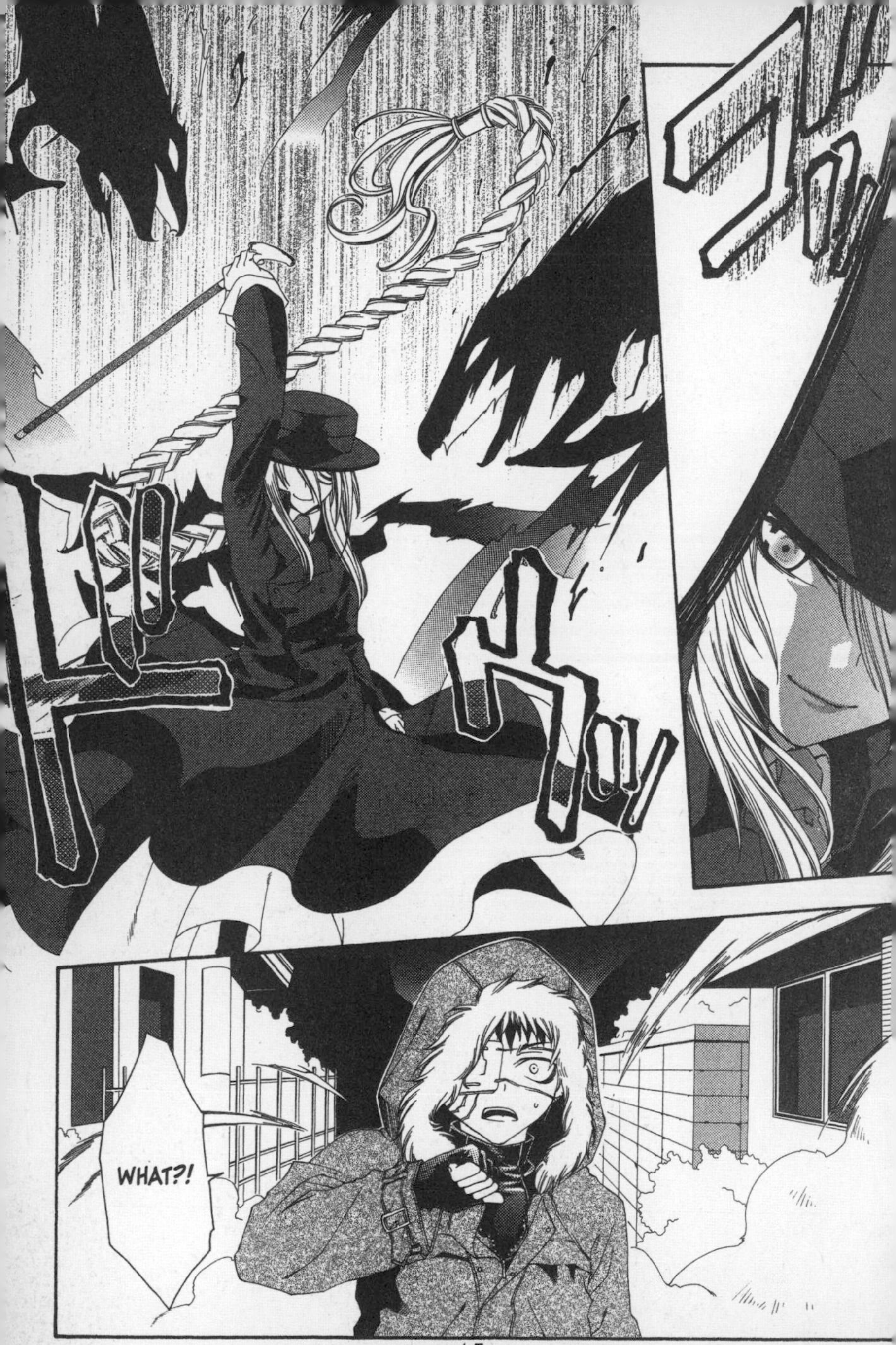
WHAT?!

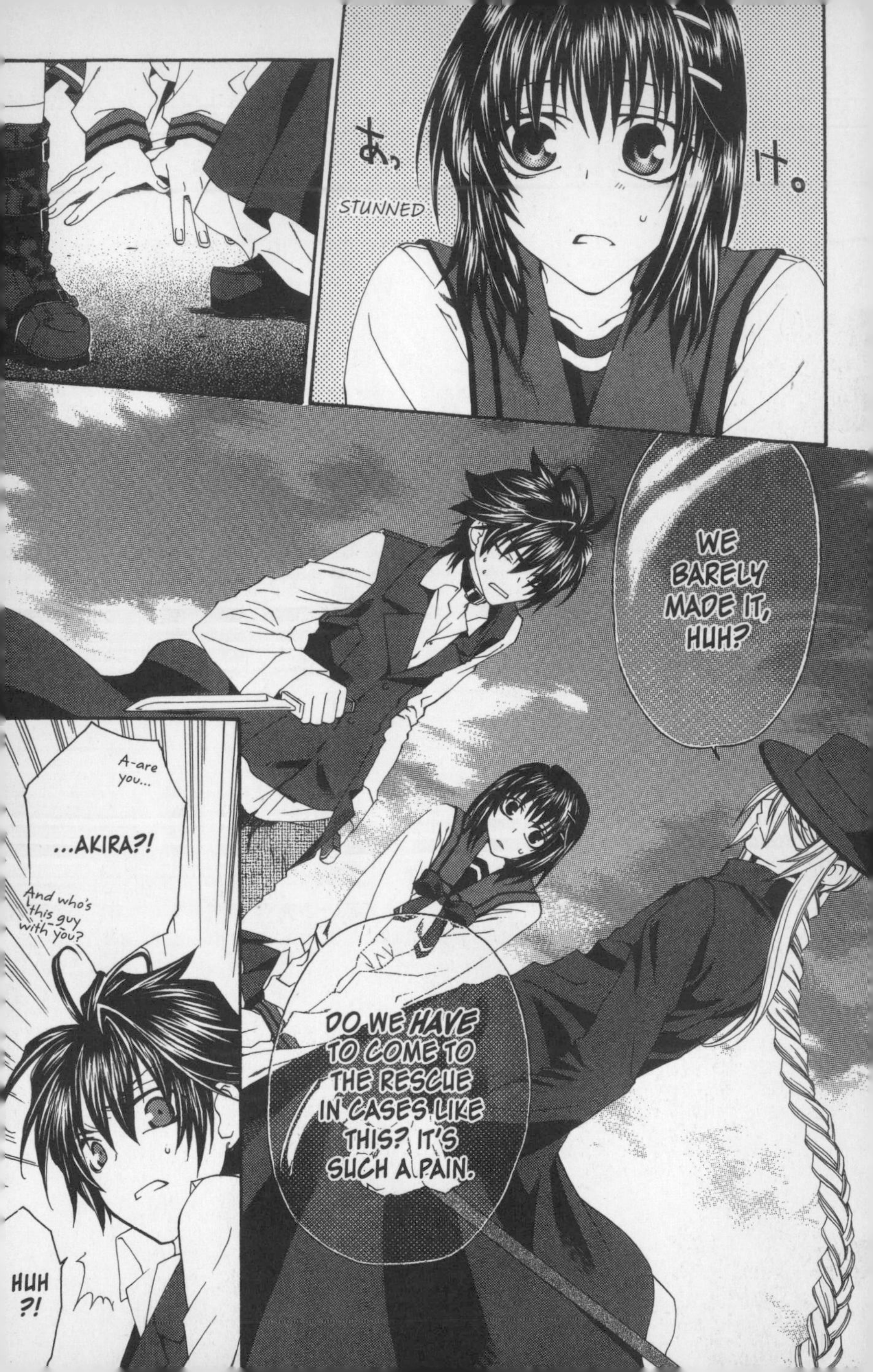

あっけ。
STUNNED
WE BARELY MADE IT, HUH?
DO WE HAVE TO COME TO THE RESCUE IN CASES LIKE THIS? IT'S SUCH A PAIN.
A-are you...
...AKIRA?!
And who's this guy with you?
HUH ?!

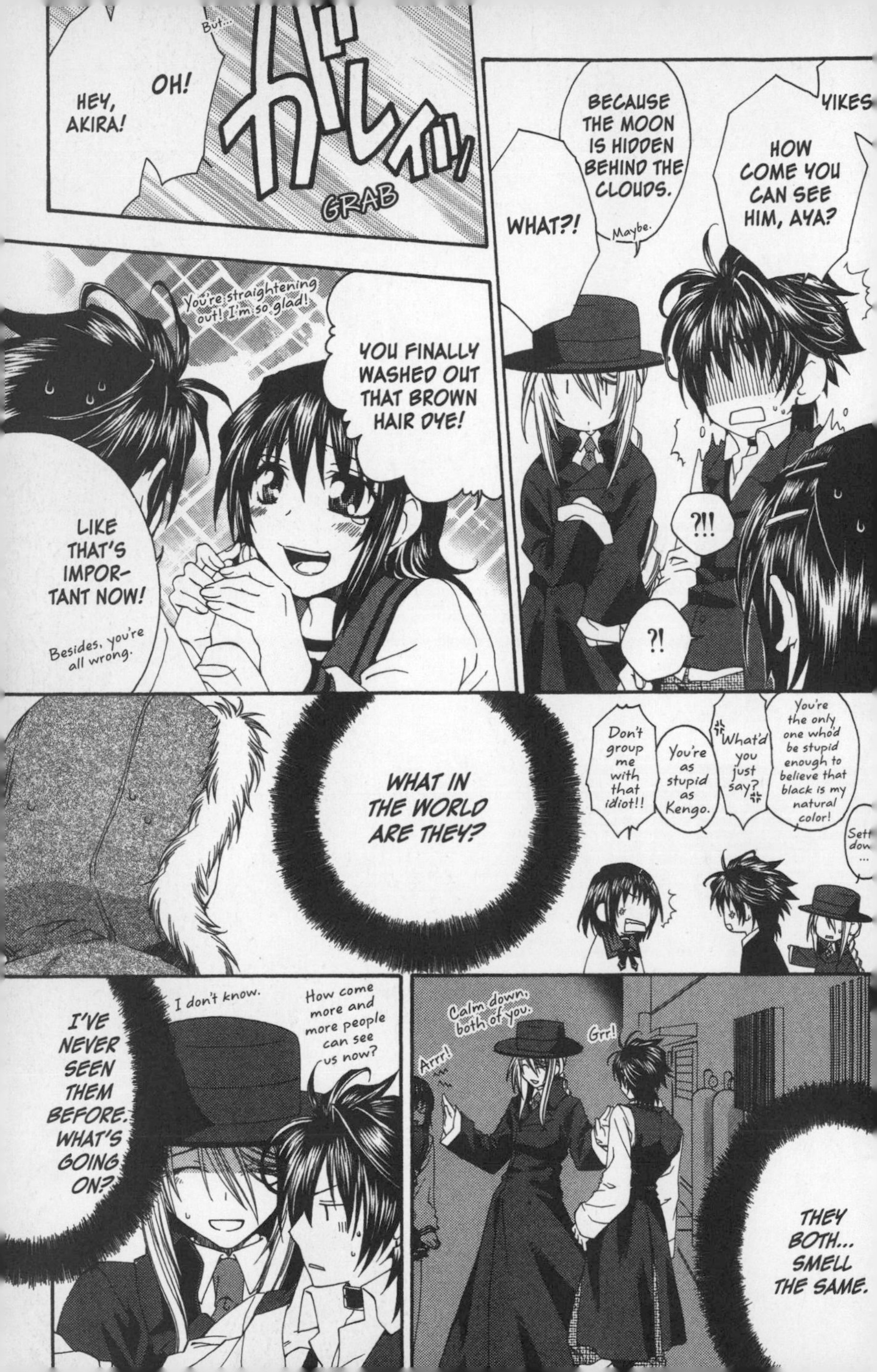
YIKES
HOW COME YOU CAN SEE HIM, AYA?
BECAUSE THE MOON IS HIDDEN BEHIND THE CLOUDS.
Maybe.
WHAT?!
?!!
?!
But..
OH!
HEY, AKIRA!
GRAB
YOU FINALLY WASHED OUT THAT BROWN HAIR DYE!
You're straightening out! I'm so glad!
LIKE THAT'S IMPORTANT NOW!
Besides, you're all wrong.
You're the only one who'd be stupid enough to believe that black is my natural color!
What'd you just say?
You're as stupid as Kengo.
Don't group me with that idiot!!
Sett dow ...
WHAT IN THE WORLD ARE THEY?
THEY BOTH... SMELL THE SAME.
Calm down, both of you.
Grr!
Arrr!
How come more and more people can see us now?
I don't know.
I'VE NEVER SEEN THEM BEFORE. WHAT'S GOING ON?

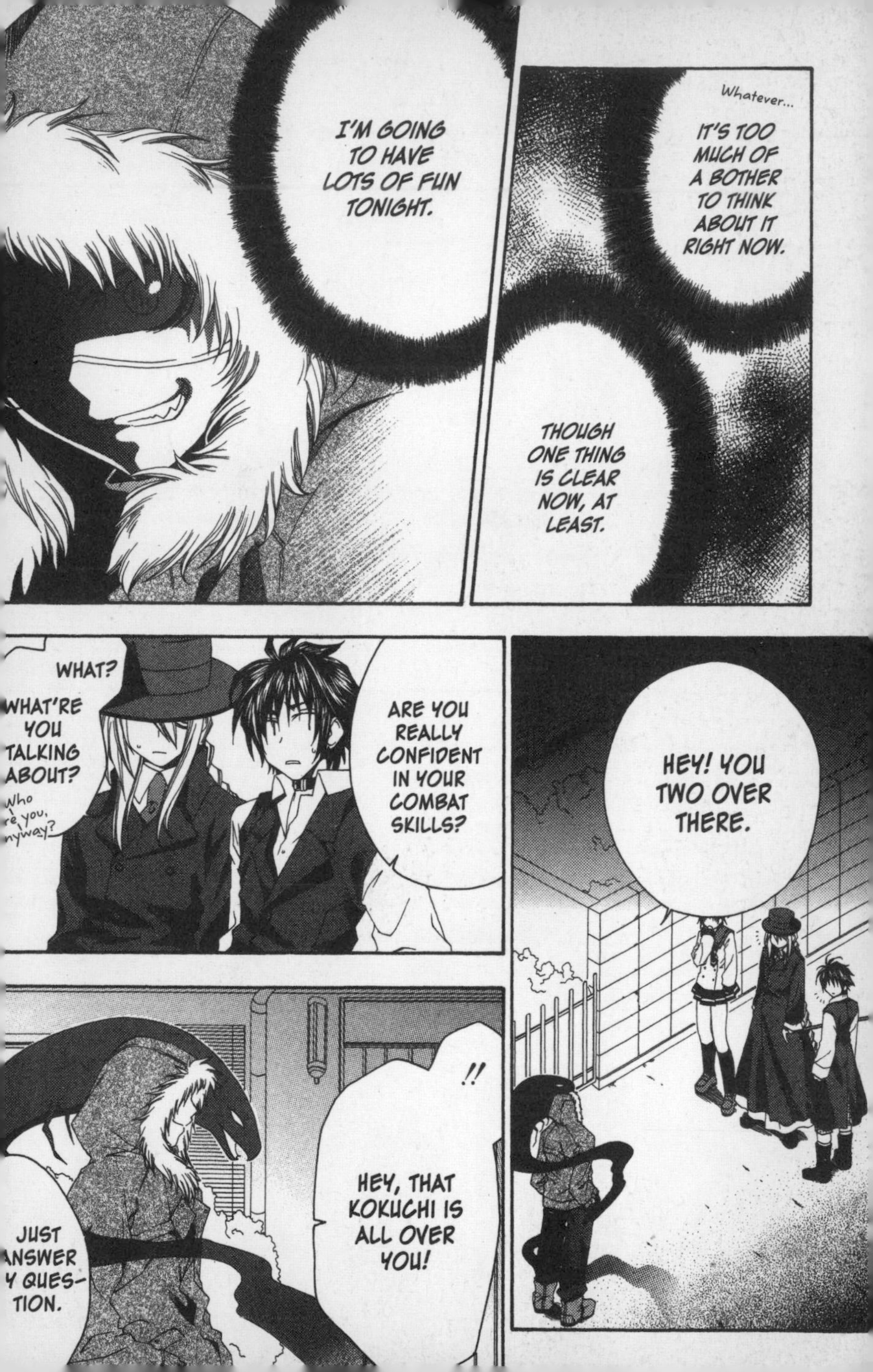
Whatever...
IT'S TOO MUCH OF A BOTHER TO THINK ABOUT IT RIGHT NOW.
THOUGH ONE THING IS CLEAR NOW, AT LEAST.
I'M GOING TO HAVE LOTS OF FUN TONIGHT.
HEY! YOU TWO OVER THERE.
ARE YOU REALLY CONFIDENT IN YOUR COMBAT SKILLS?
WHAT?
WHAT'RE YOU TALKING ABOUT?
Who 're you, nyway?
!!
HEY, THAT KOKUCHI IS ALL OVER YOU!
JUST ANSWER Y QUES- TION.

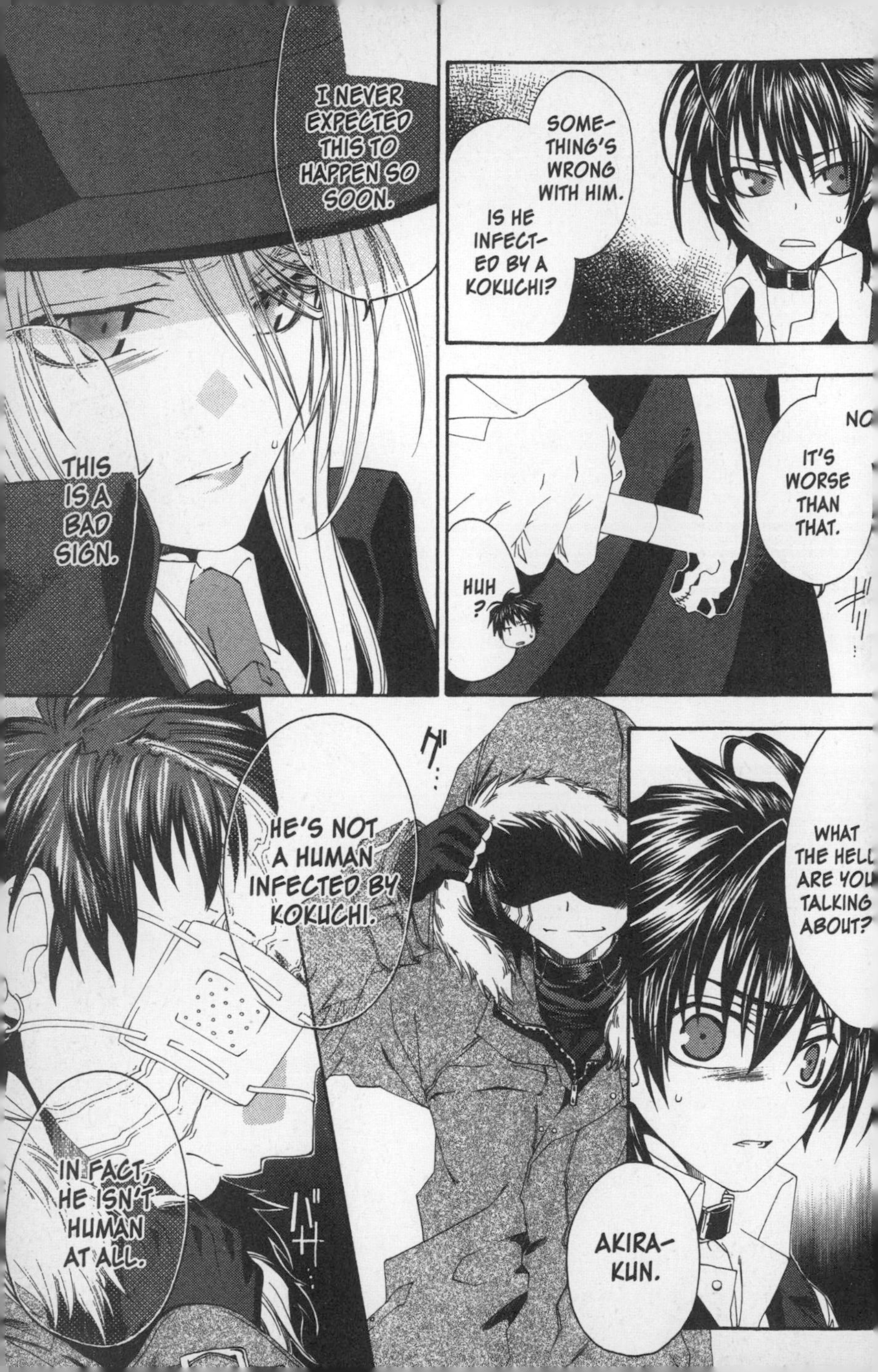
SOME-THING'S WRONG WITH HIM.
IS HE INFECT-ED BY A KOKUCHI?
NO
IT'S WORSE THAN THAT.
HUH?
I NEVER EXPECTED THIS TO HAPPEN SO SOON.
THIS IS A BAD SIGN.
WHAT THE HELL ARE YOU TALKING ABOUT?
AKIRA-KUN.
HE'S NOT A HUMAN INFECTED BY KOKUCHI.
IN FACT, HE ISN'T HUMAN AT ALL.

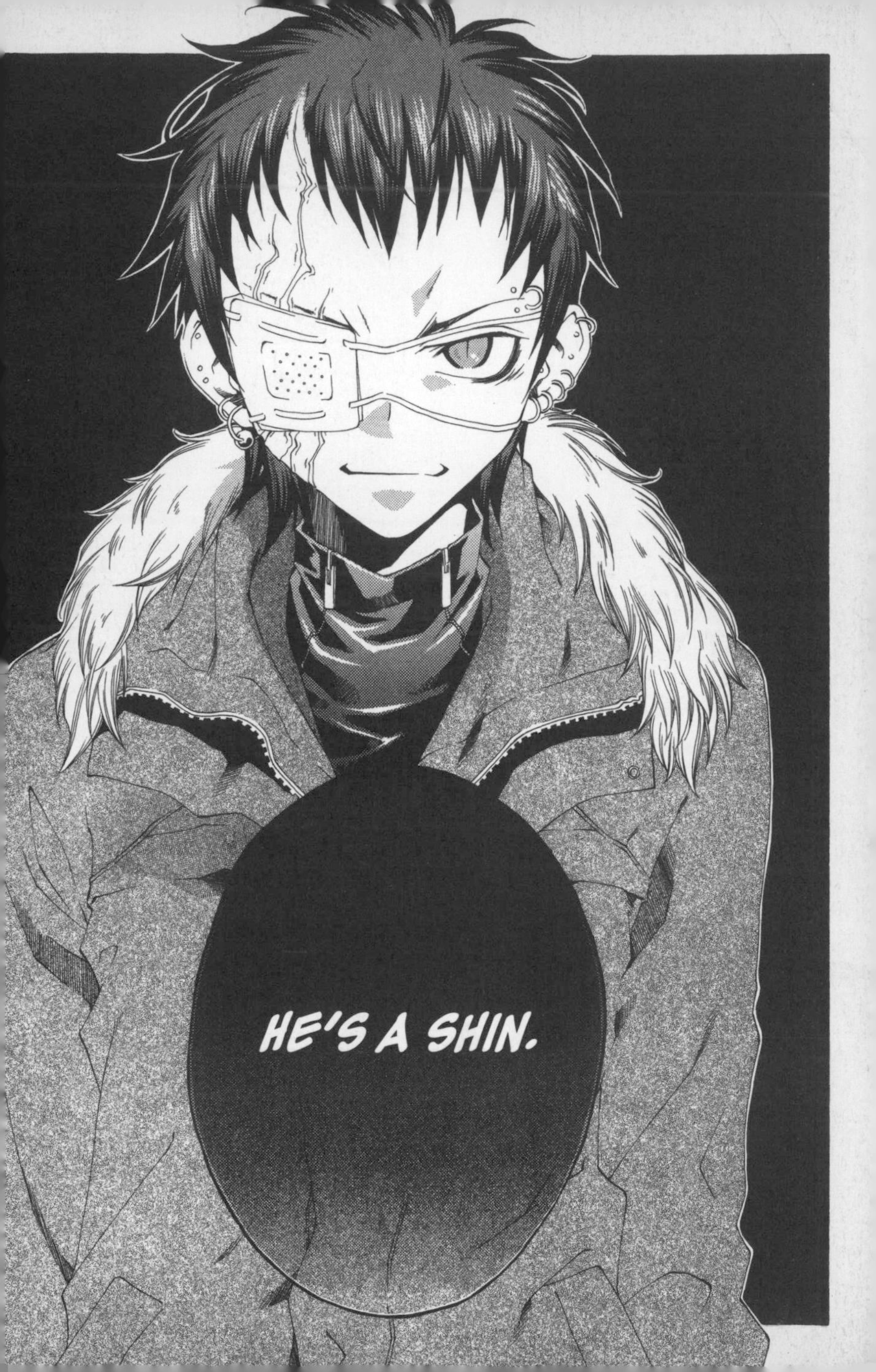
HE'S A SHIN.

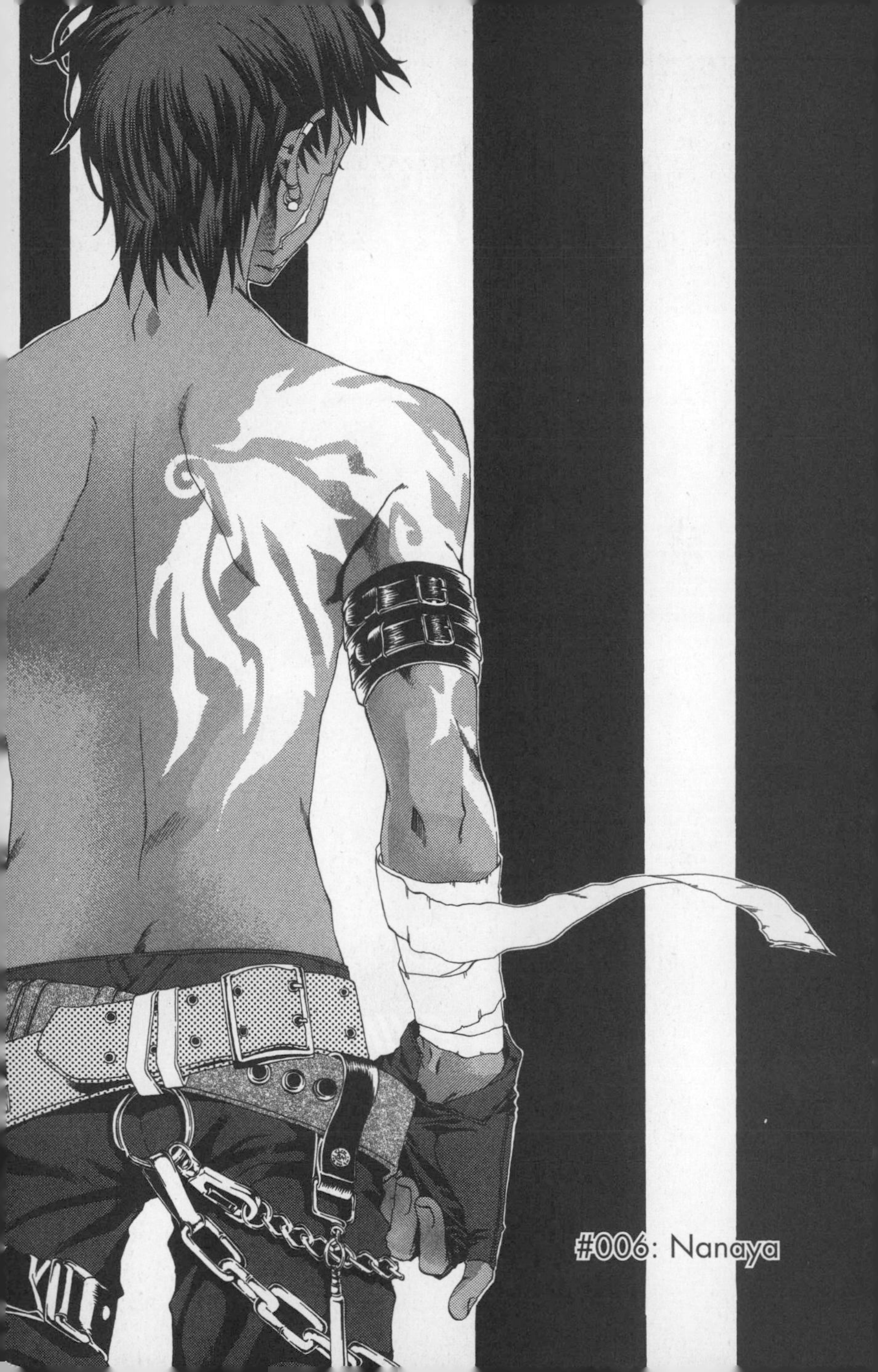

#006: Nanaya

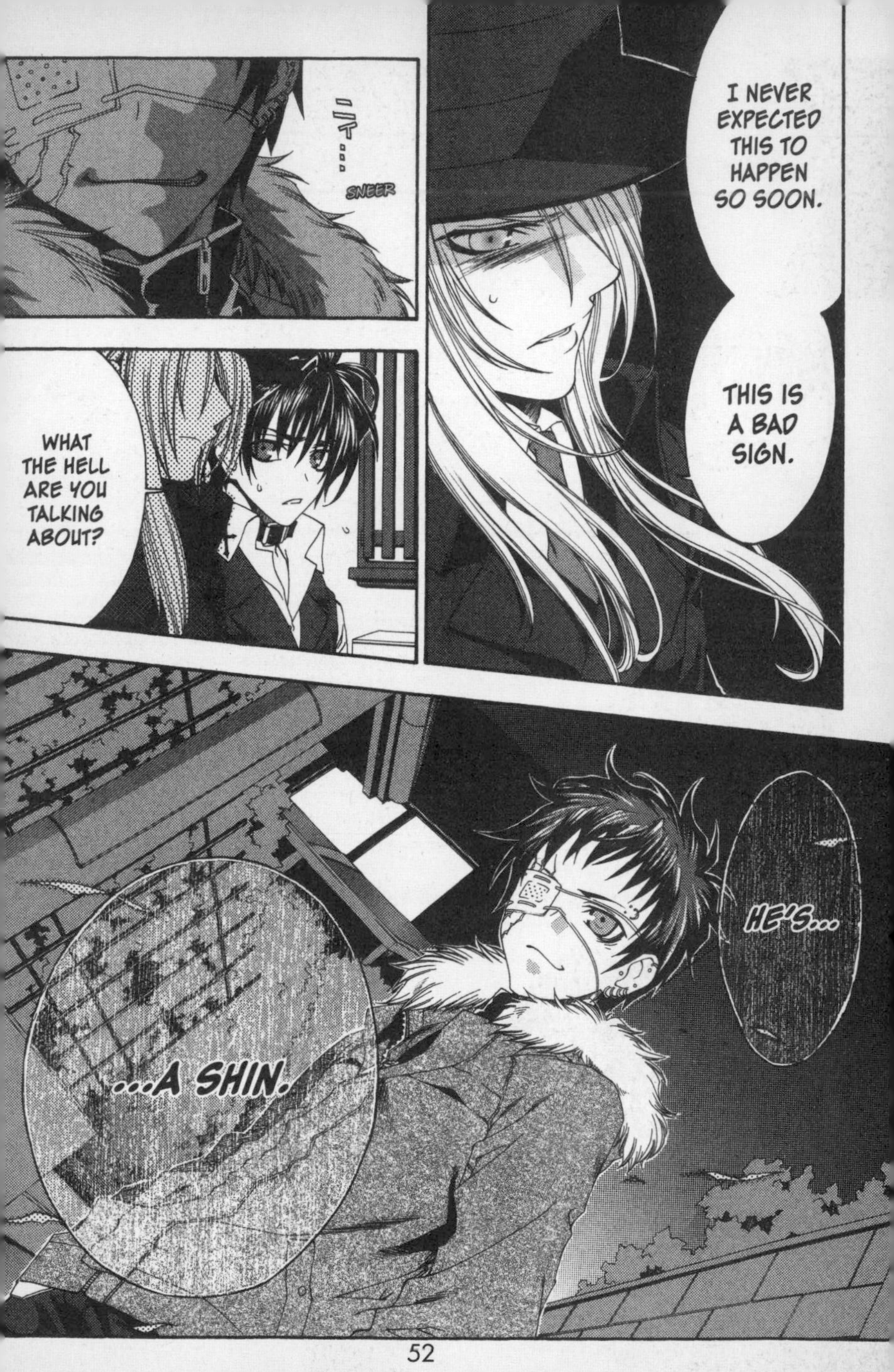
I NEVER EXPECTED THIS TO HAPPEN SO SOON.
THIS IS A BAD SIGN.
ニィ…
SNEER
WHAT THE HELL ARE YOU TALKING ABOUT?
HE'S...
...A SHIN.

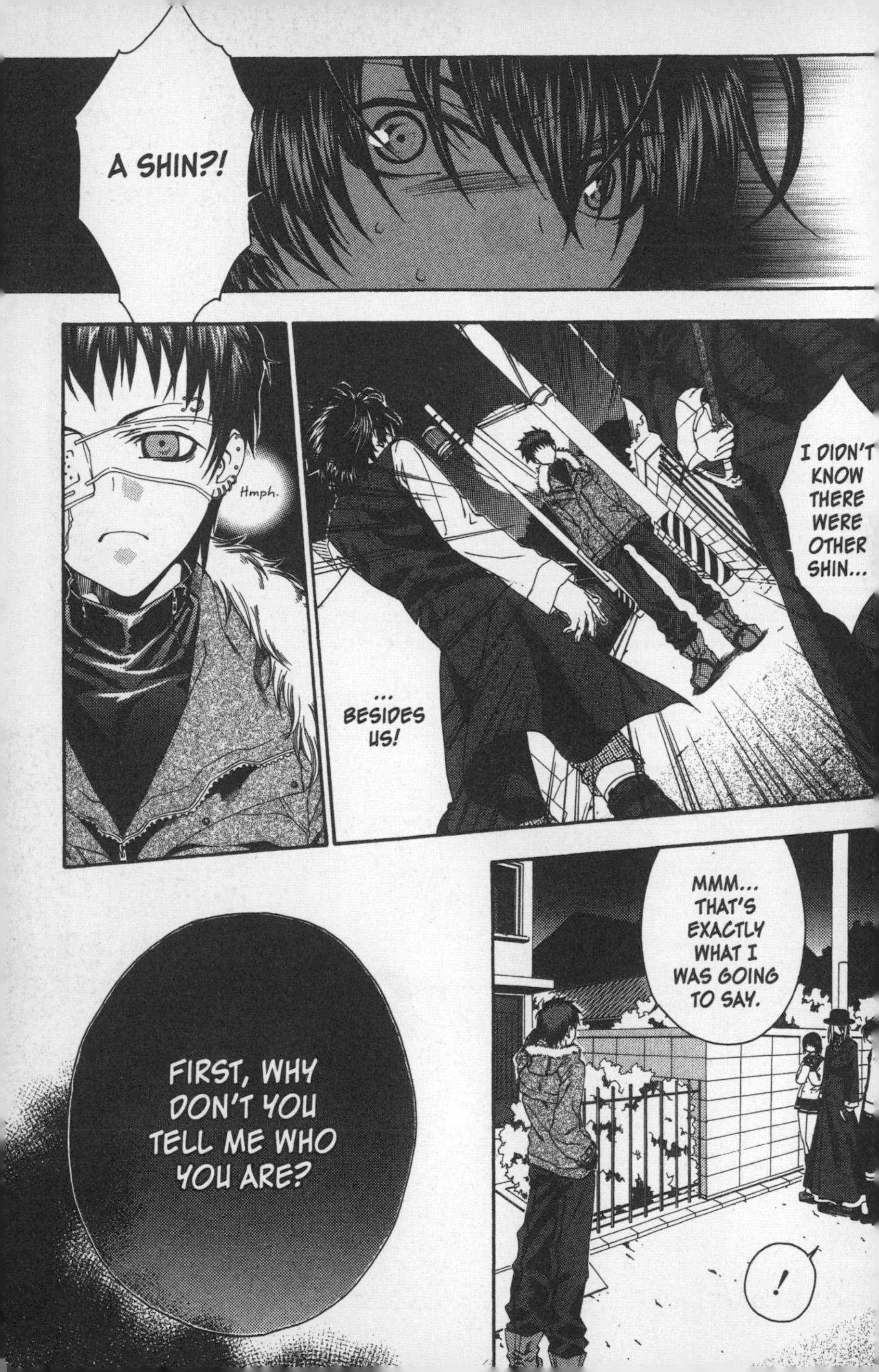
A SHIN?!
I DIDN'T KNOW THERE WERE OTHER SHIN...
... BESIDES US!
Hmph.
MMM... THAT'S EXACTLY WHAT I WAS GOING TO SAY.
!
FIRST, WHY DON'T YOU TELL ME WHO YOU ARE?

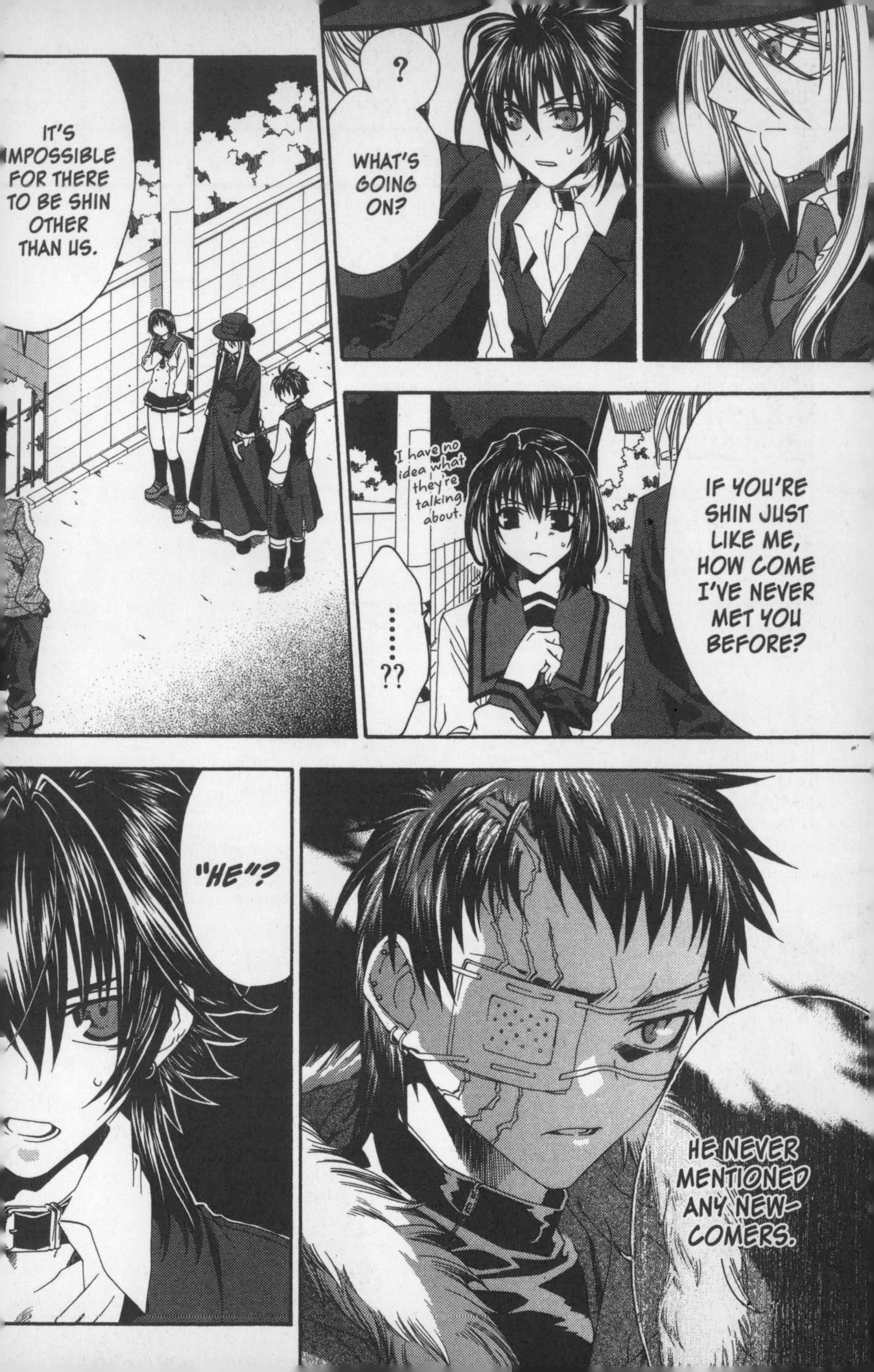
?
WHAT'S GOING ON?
IF YOU'RE SHIN JUST LIKE ME, HOW COME I'VE NEVER MET YOU BEFORE?
I have no idea what they're talking about.
......??
IT'S IMPOSSIBLE FOR THERE TO BE SHIN OTHER THAN US.
HE NEVER MENTIONED ANY NEW-COMERS.
"HE"?

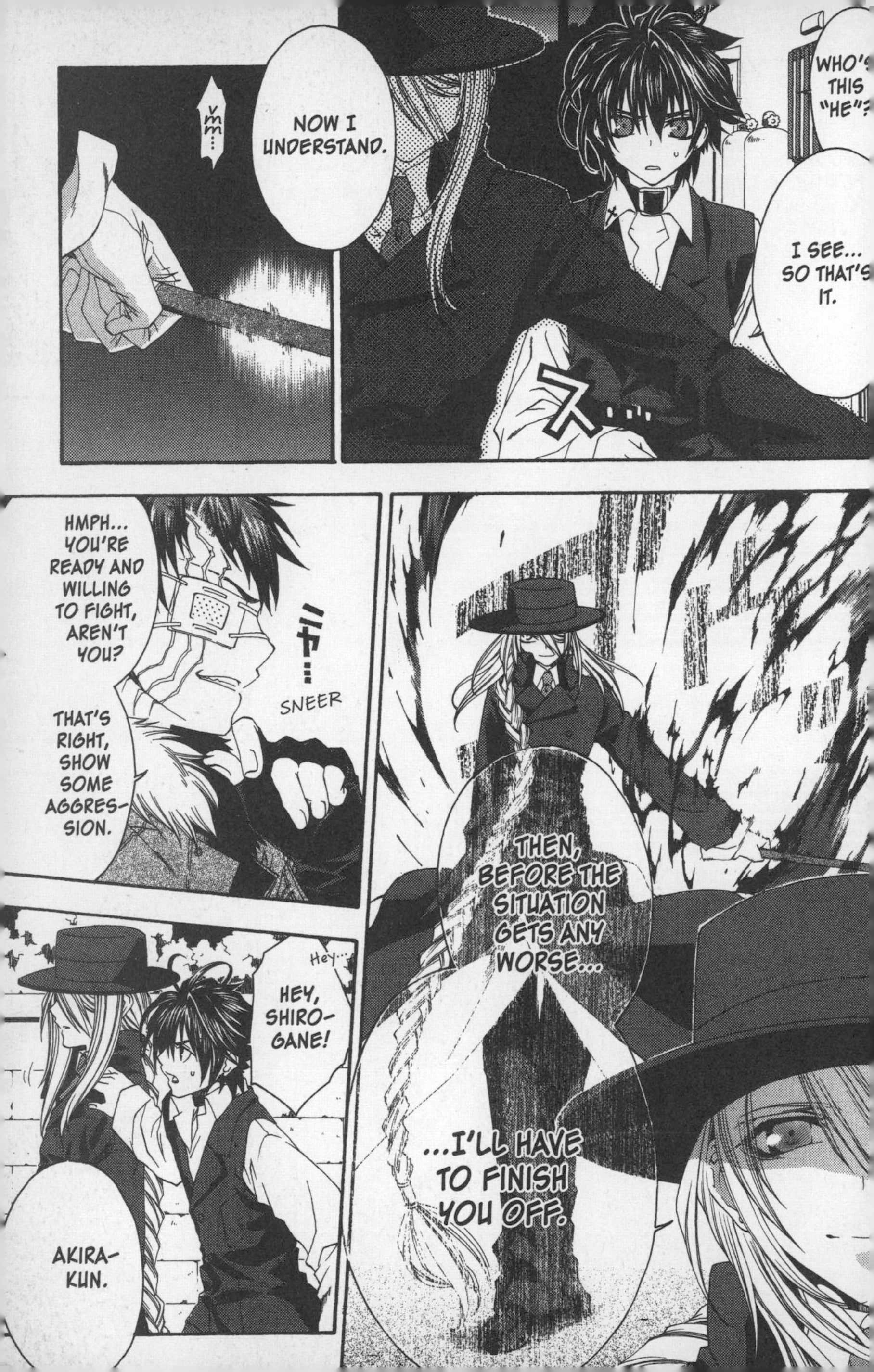
WHO'S THIS "HE"?
I SEE... SO THAT'S IT.
NOW I UNDERSTAND.
vmm...
THEN, BEFORE THE SITUATION GETS ANY WORSE...
...I'LL HAVE TO FINISH YOU OFF.
HMPH... YOU'RE READY AND WILLING TO FIGHT, AREN'T YOU?
SNEER
THAT'S RIGHT, SHOW SOME AGGRES-SION.
Hey...
HEY, SHIRO-GANE!
AKIRA-KUN.

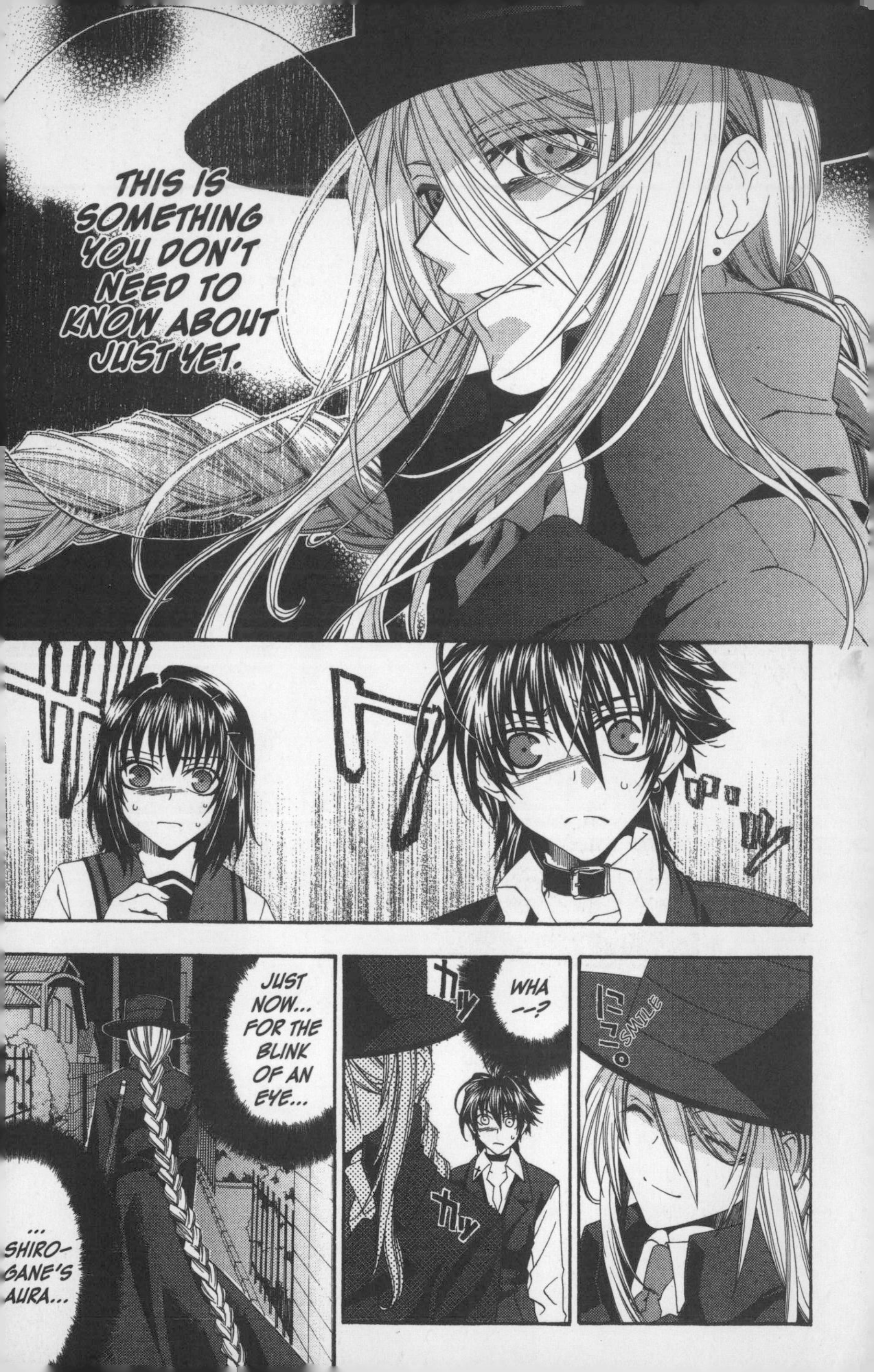
THIS IS SOMETHING YOU DON'T NEED TO KNOW ABOUT JUST YET.
JUST NOW... FOR THE BLINK OF AN EYE...
... SHIRO-GANE'S AURA...
WHA --?
SMILE

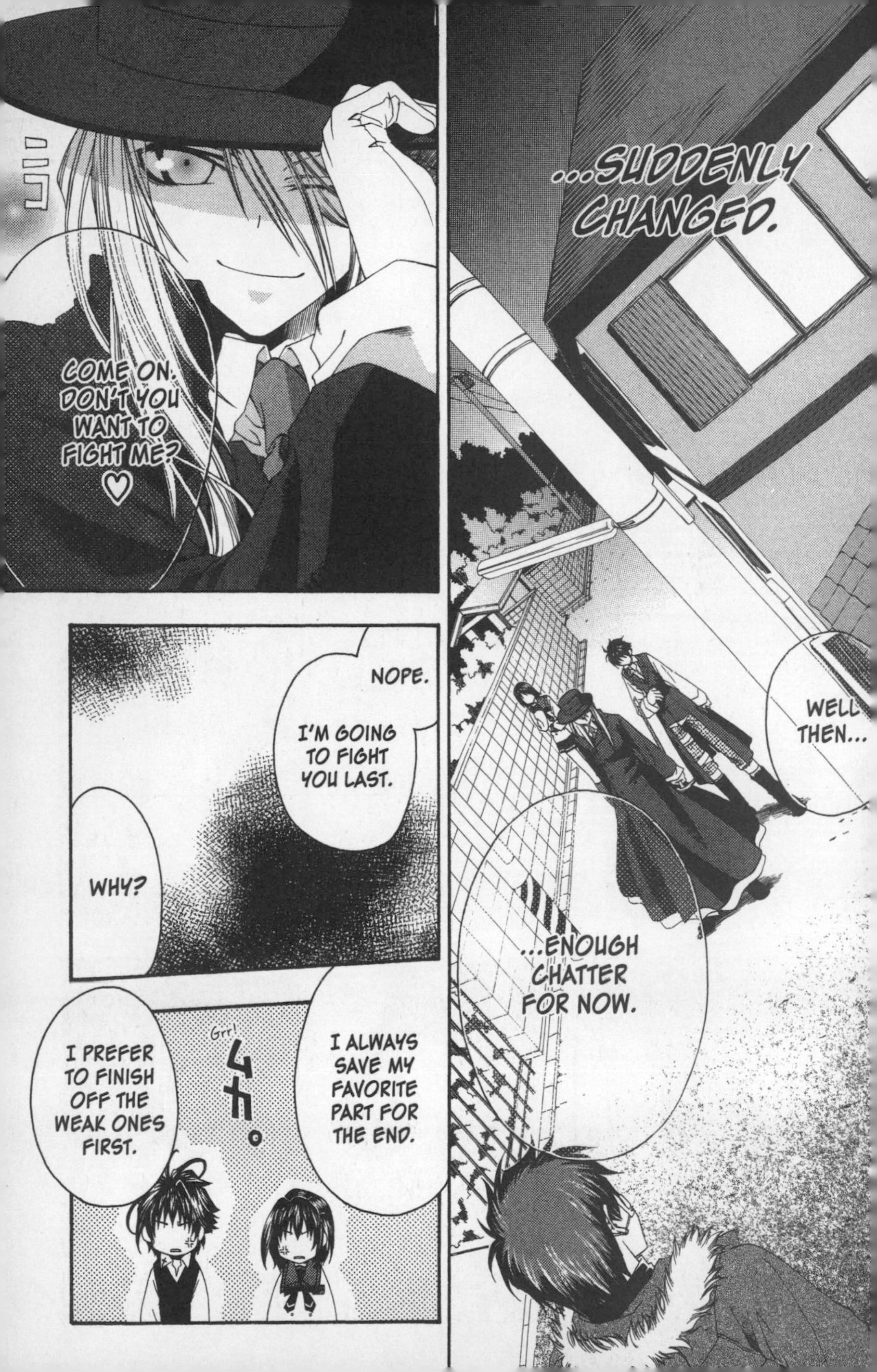
...SUDDENLY CHANGED.
WELL THEN...
...ENOUGH CHATTER FOR NOW.
COME ON. DON'T YOU WANT TO FIGHT ME? ♡
NOPE.
I'M GOING TO FIGHT YOU LAST.
WHY?
I ALWAYS SAVE MY FAVORITE PART FOR THE END.
I PREFER TO FINISH OFF THE WEAK ONES FIRST.
Grr!

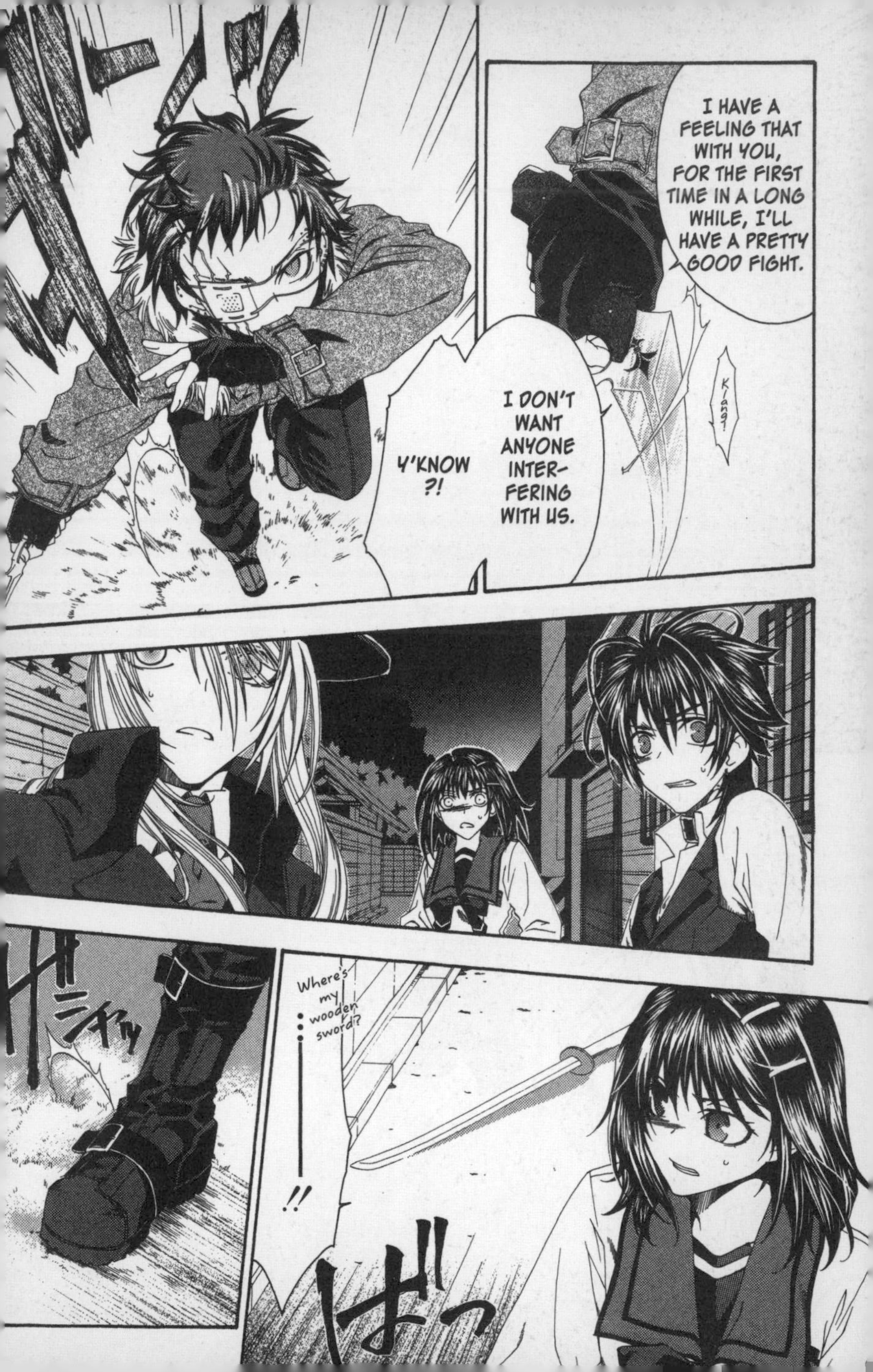
I HAVE A FEELING THAT WITH YOU, FOR THE FIRST TIME IN A LONG WHILE, I'LL HAVE A PRETTY GOOD FIGHT.
Klang!
I DON'T WANT ANYONE INTER-FERING WITH US.
Y'KNOW ?!
Where's my wooden sword?
!!
ばっ
シャッ

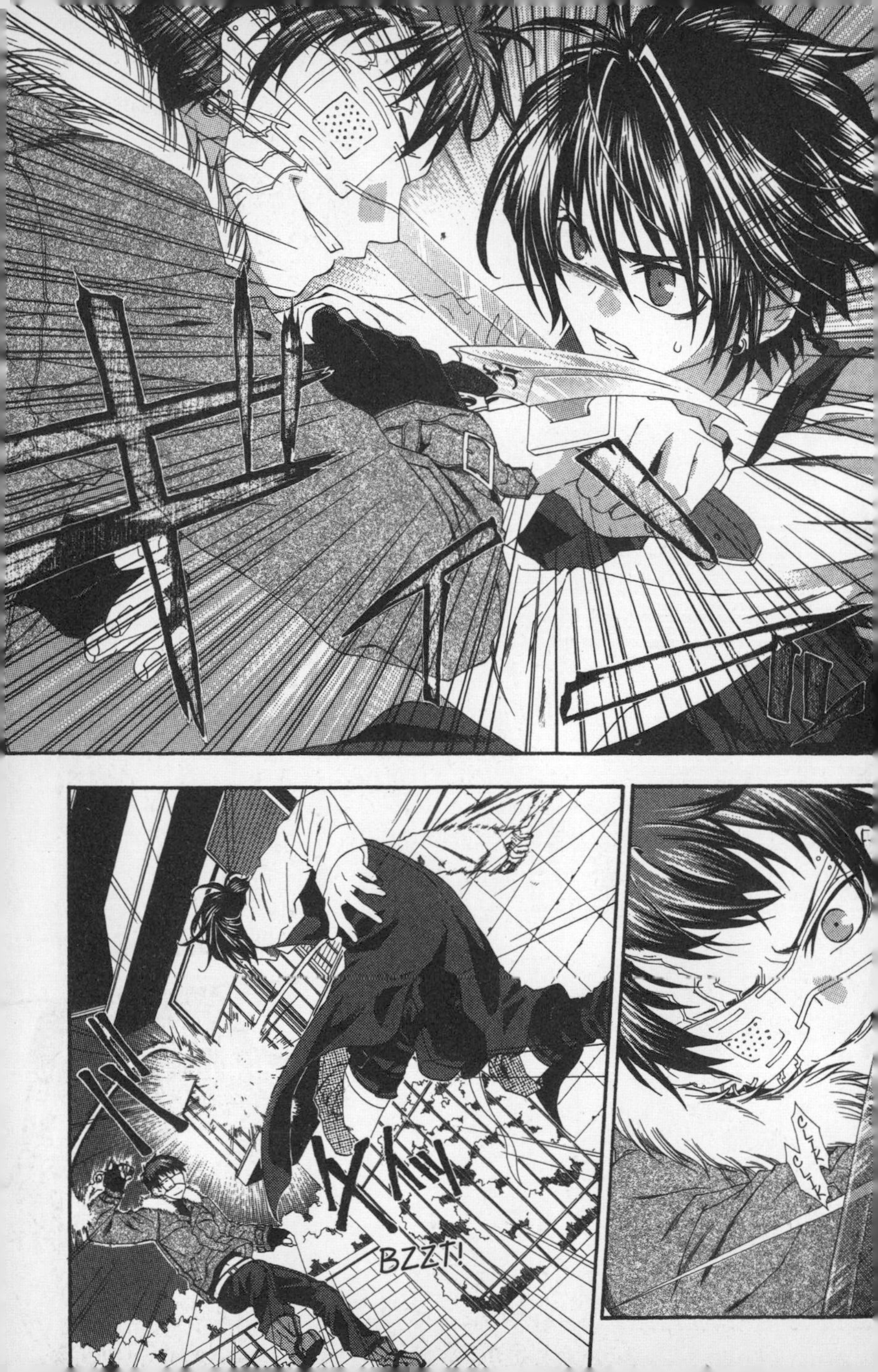
CLIK CLIK
BZZT!

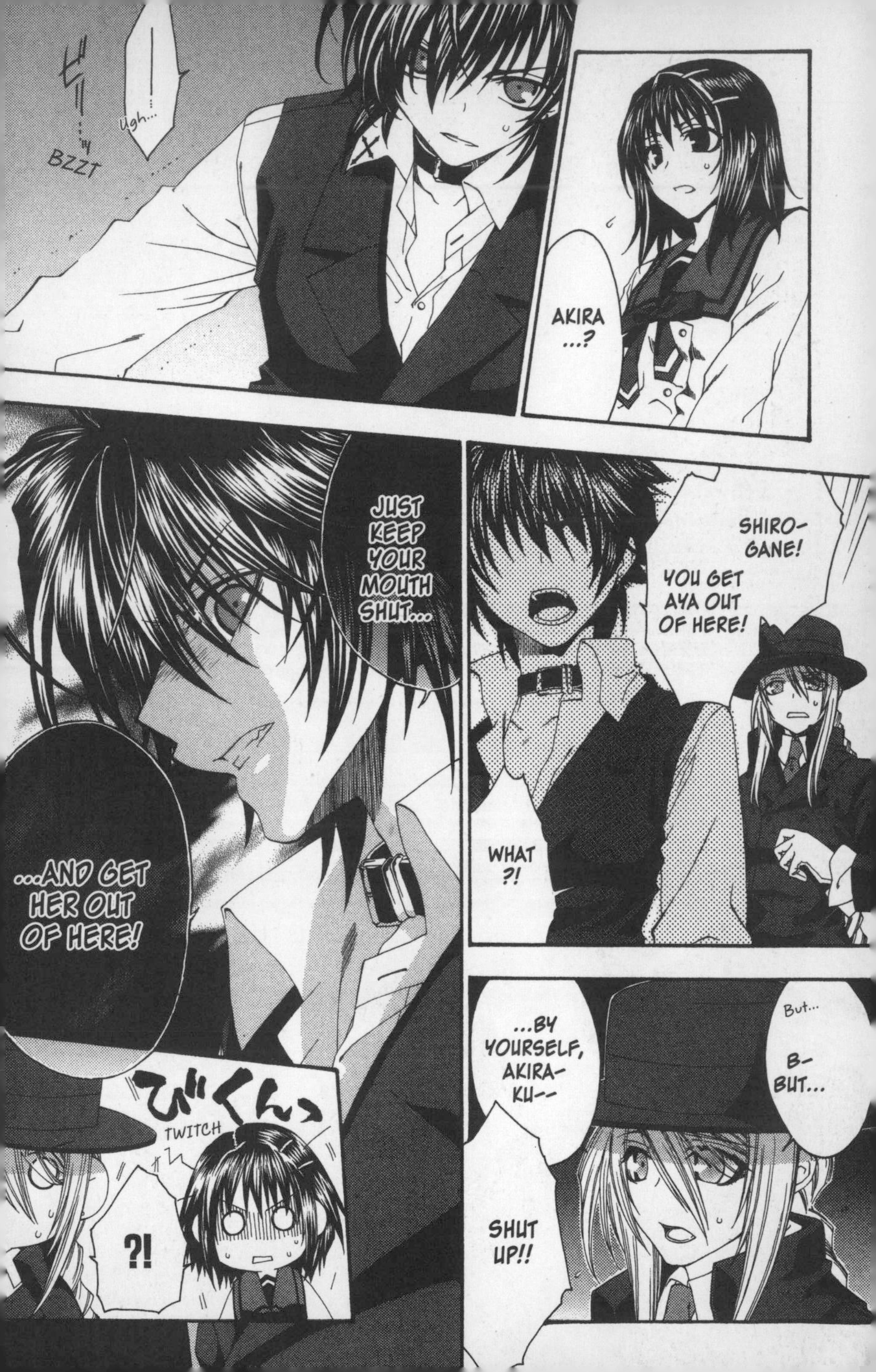
AKIRA ...?
Ugh...
BZZT
SHIRO-GANE!
YOU GET AYA OUT OF HERE!
WHAT ?!
JUST KEEP YOUR MOUTH SHUT...
...AND GET HER OUT OF HERE!
But...
B-BUT...
...BY YOURSELF, AKIRA-KU--
SHUT UP!!
びくんっ
TWITCH
?!

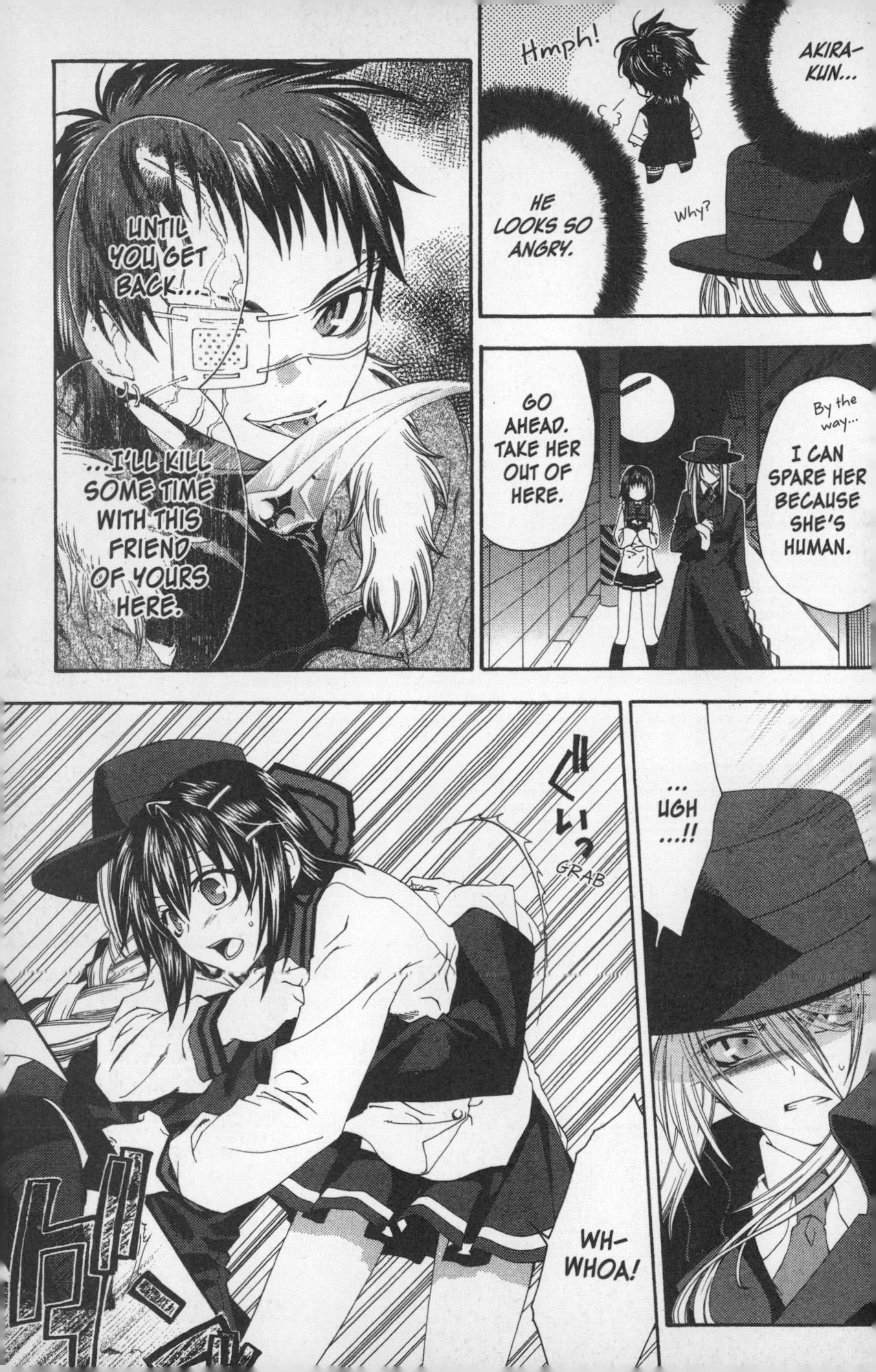
AKIRA-KUN...
Hmph!
Why?
HE LOOKS SO ANGRY.
By the way...
I CAN SPARE HER BECAUSE SHE'S HUMAN.
GO AHEAD. TAKE HER OUT OF HERE.
UNTIL YOU GET BACK...
...I'LL KILL SOME TIME WITH THIS FRIEND OF YOURS HERE.
...UGH ...!!
WH-WHOA!
GRAB

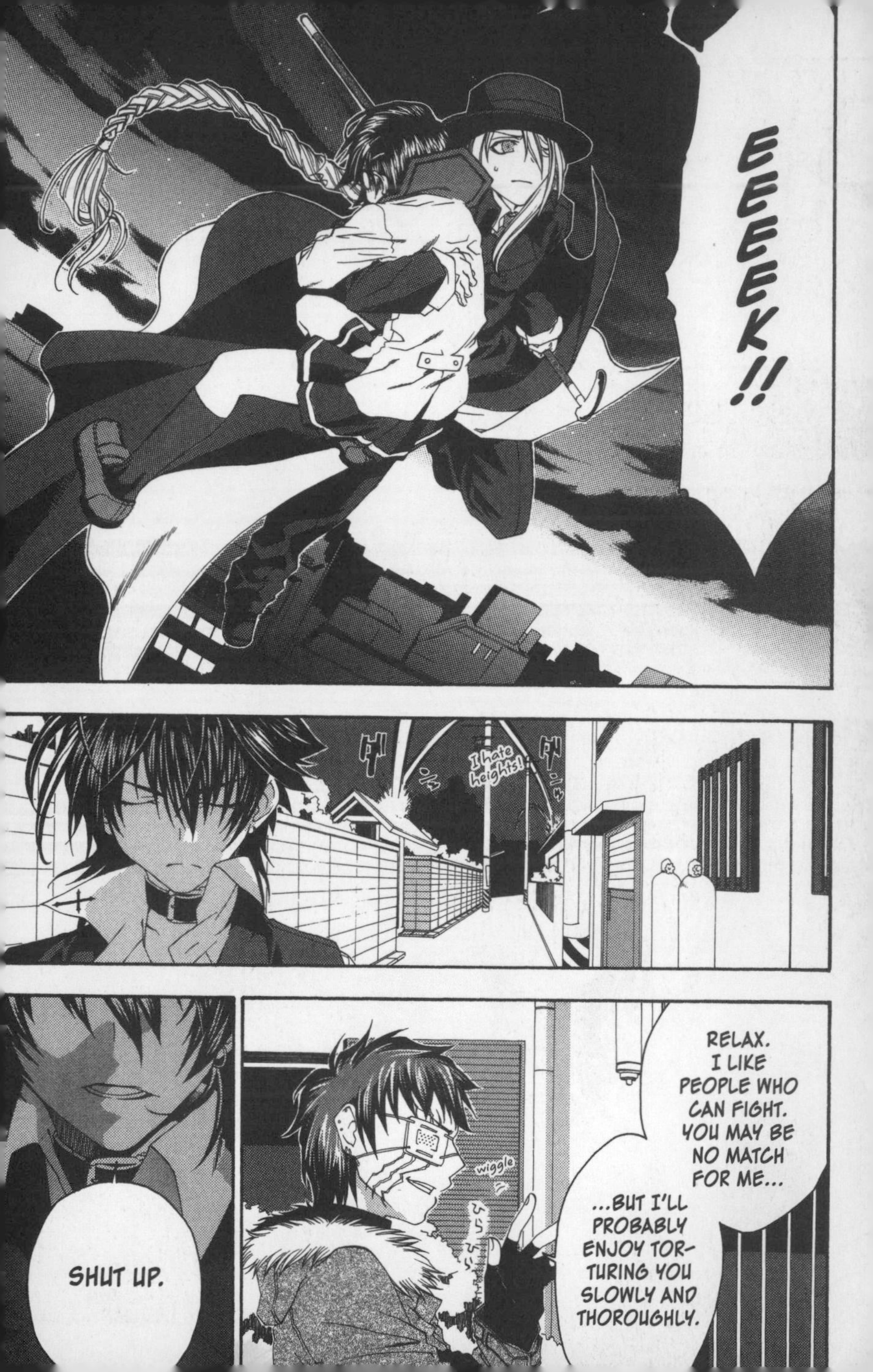
EEEEEK!!
I hate heights!
RELAX. I LIKE PEOPLE WHO CAN FIGHT. YOU MAY BE NO MATCH FOR ME...
...BUT I'LL PROBABLY ENJOY TORTURING YOU SLOWLY AND THOROUGHLY.
wiggle
SHUT UP.

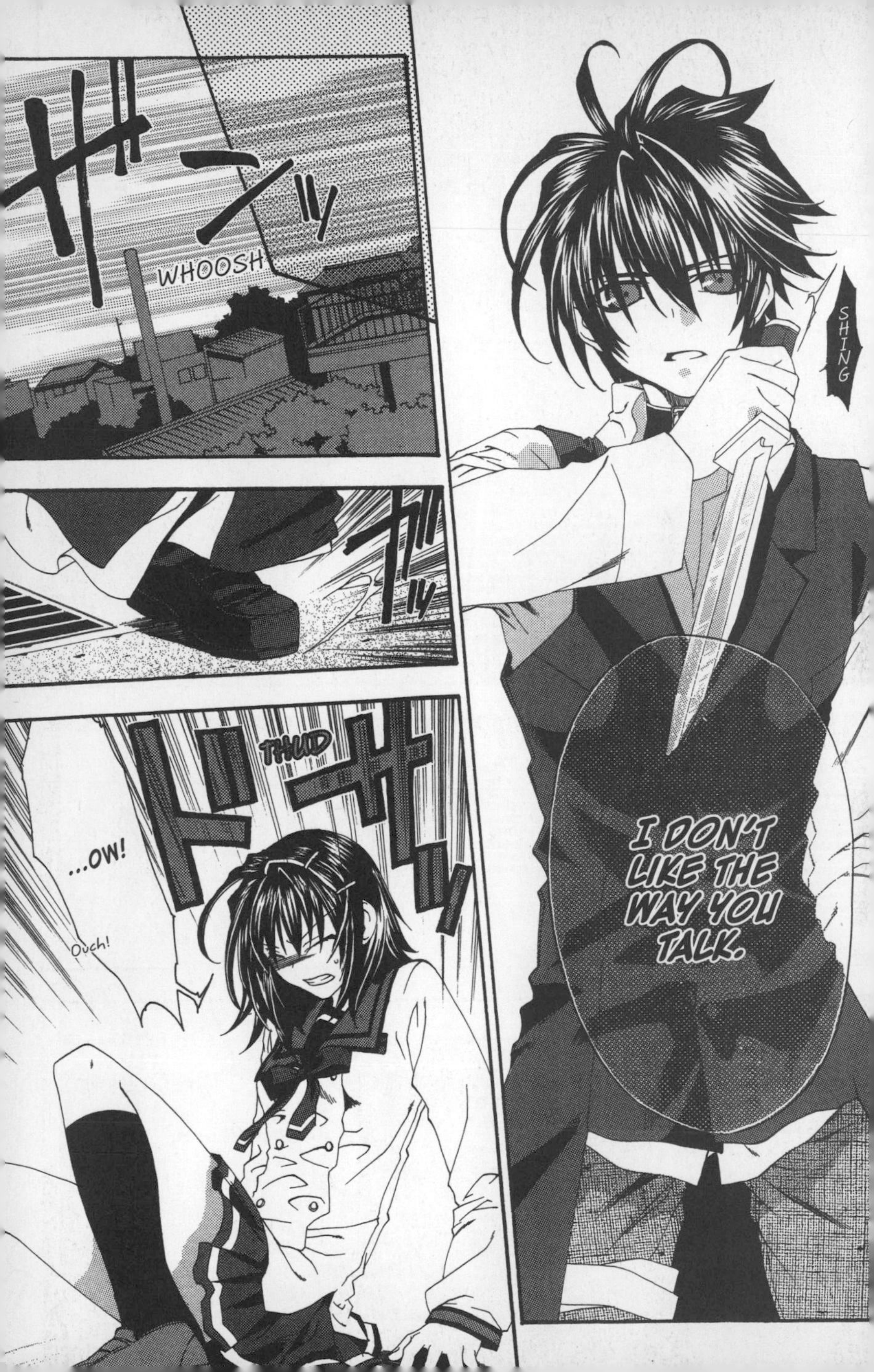
SHING
I DON'T LIKE THE WAY YOU TALK.
WHOOSH
THUD
...OW!
Ouch!

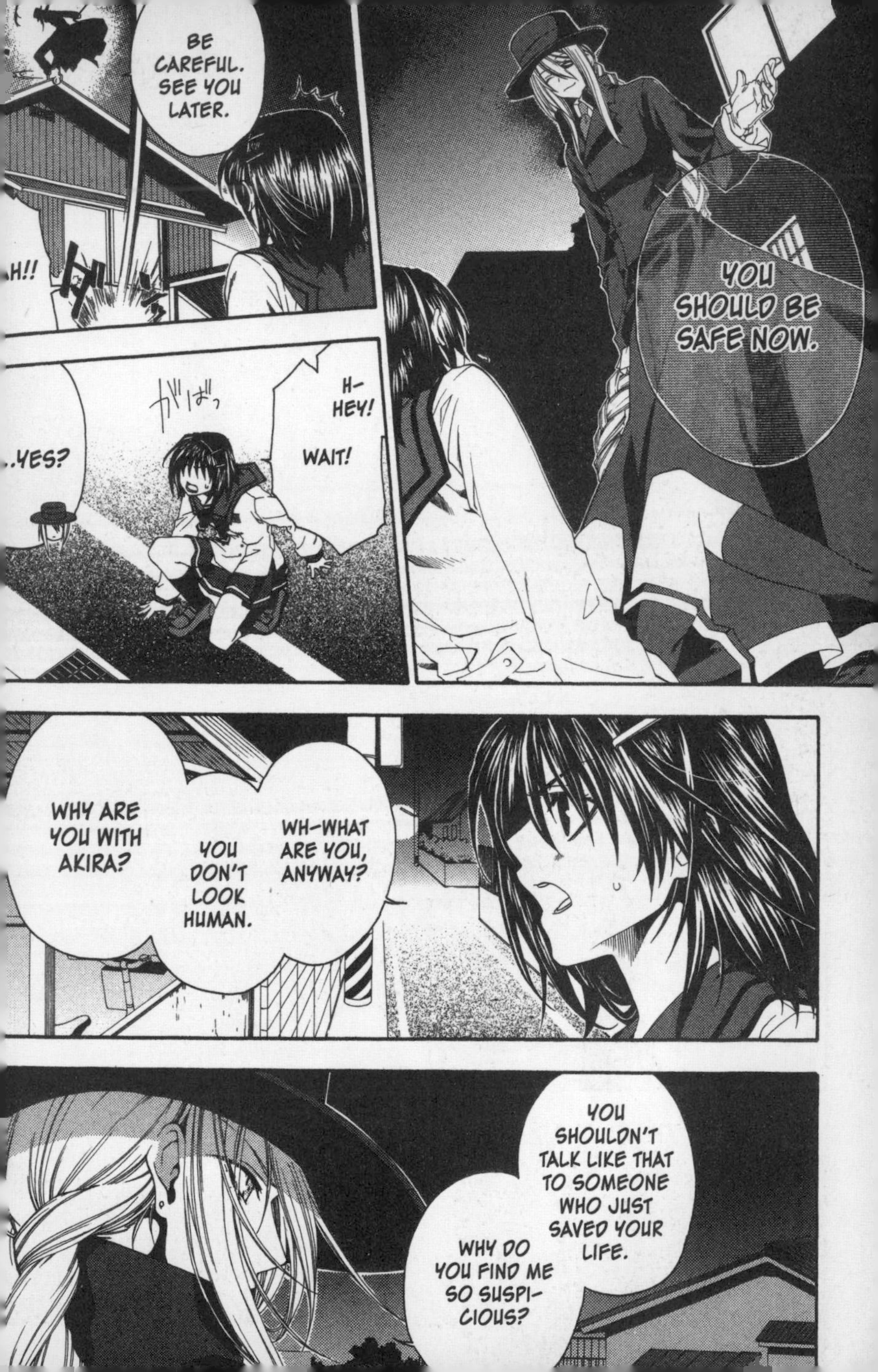

YOU SHOULD BE SAFE NOW.
BE CAREFUL. SEE YOU LATER.
H!!
H-HEY!
WAIT!
がばっ
...YES?
WH-WHAT ARE YOU, ANYWAY?
YOU DON'T LOOK HUMAN.
WHY ARE YOU WITH AKIRA?
YOU SHOULDN'T TALK LIKE THAT TO SOMEONE WHO JUST SAVED YOUR LIFE.
WHY DO YOU FIND ME SO SUSPI-CIOUS?

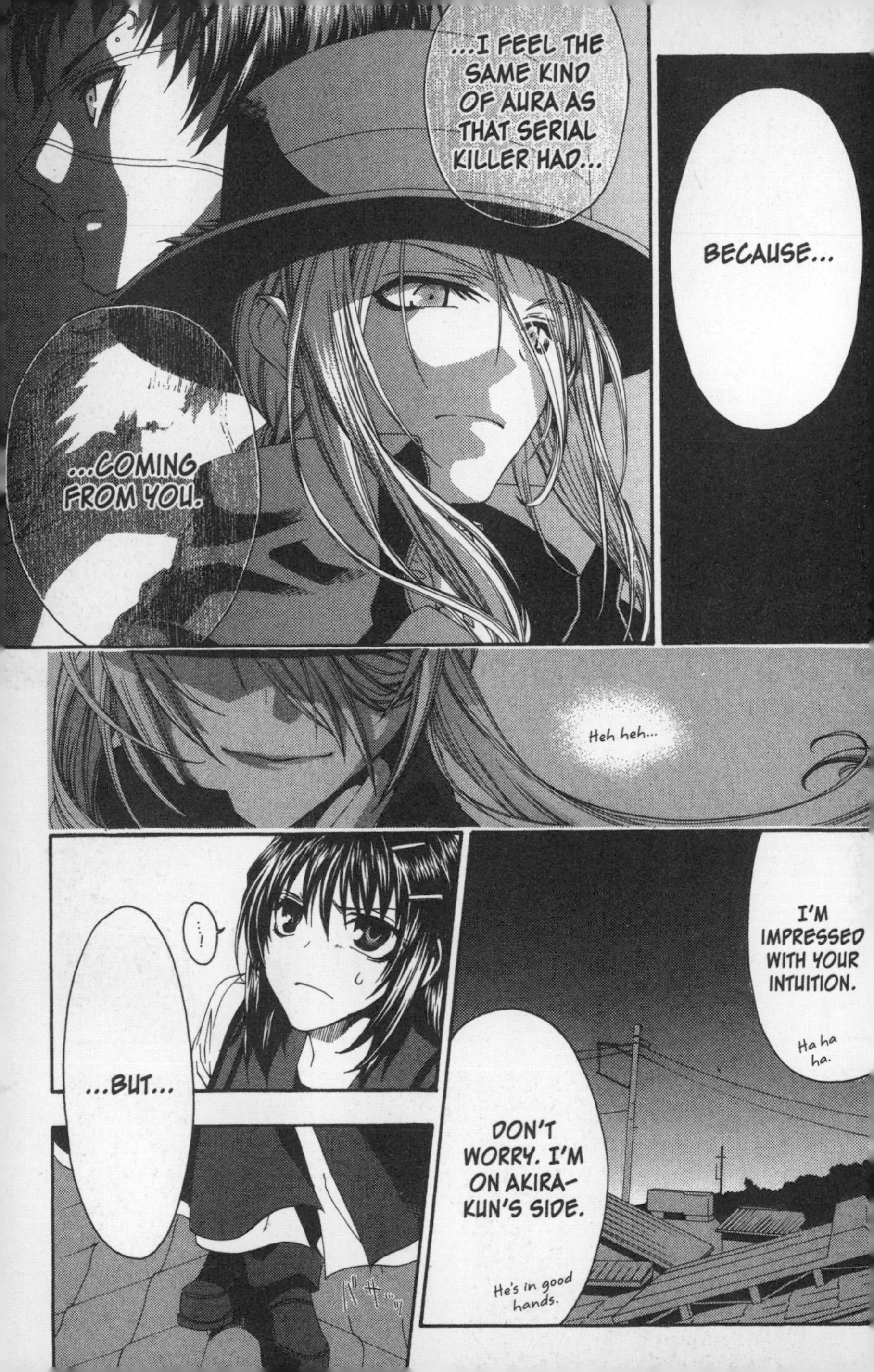
BECAUSE...
...I FEEL THE SAME KIND OF AURA AS THAT SERIAL KILLER HAD...
...COMING FROM YOU.
Heh heh...
I'M IMPRESSED WITH YOUR INTUITION.
Ha ha ha.
...!
DON'T WORRY. I'M ON AKIRA-KUN'S SIDE.
He's in good hands.
...BUT...

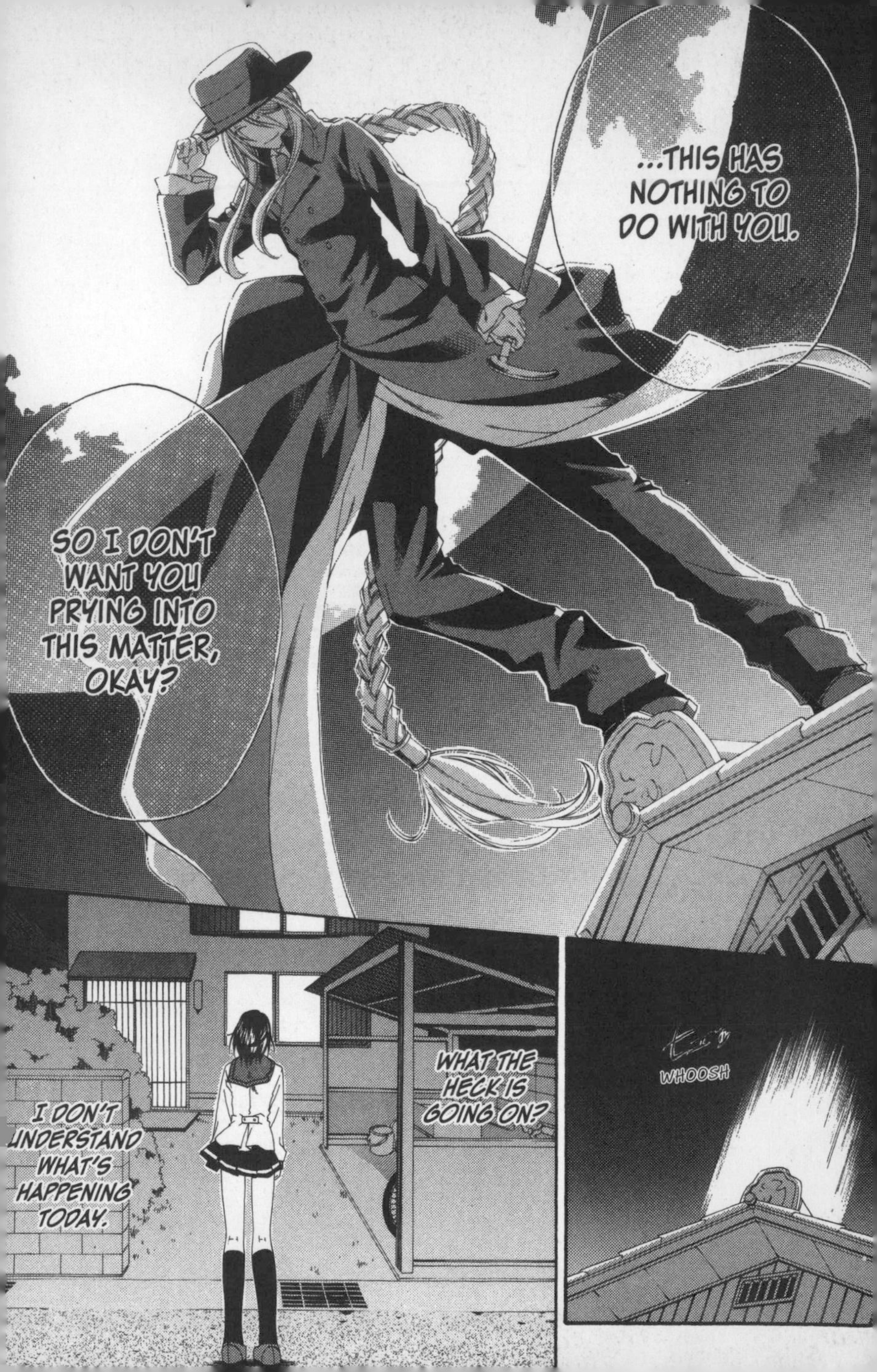
...THIS HAS NOTHING TO DO WITH YOU.
SO I DON'T WANT YOU PRYING INTO THIS MATTER, OKAY?
WHOOSH
WHAT THE HECK IS GOING ON?
I DON'T UNDERSTAND WHAT'S HAPPENING TODAY.

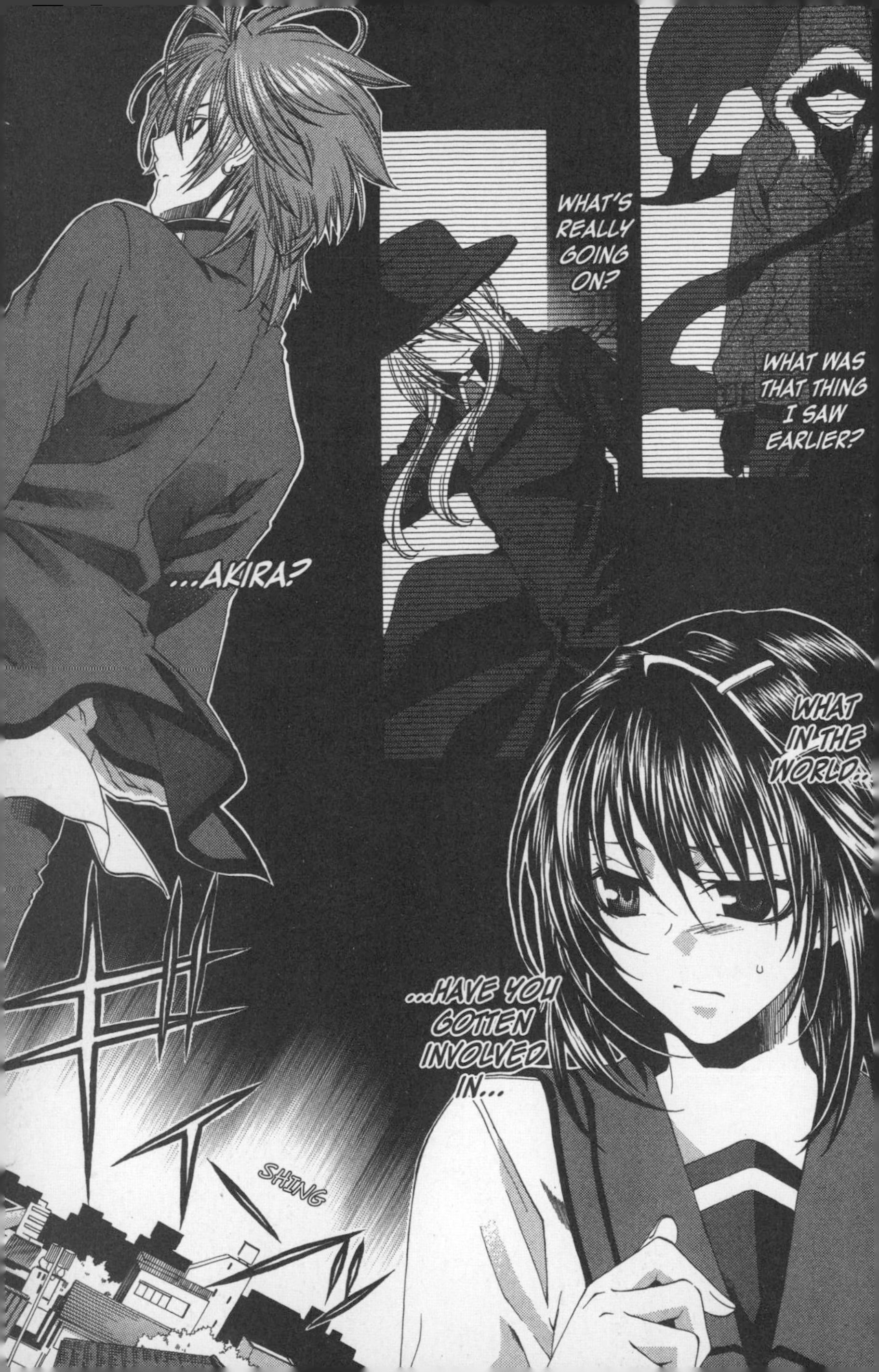
WHAT'S REALLY GOING ON?
WHAT WAS THAT THING I SAW EARLIER?
...AKIRA?
WHAT IN THE WORLD...
...HAVE YOU GOTTEN INVOLVED IN...
SHING

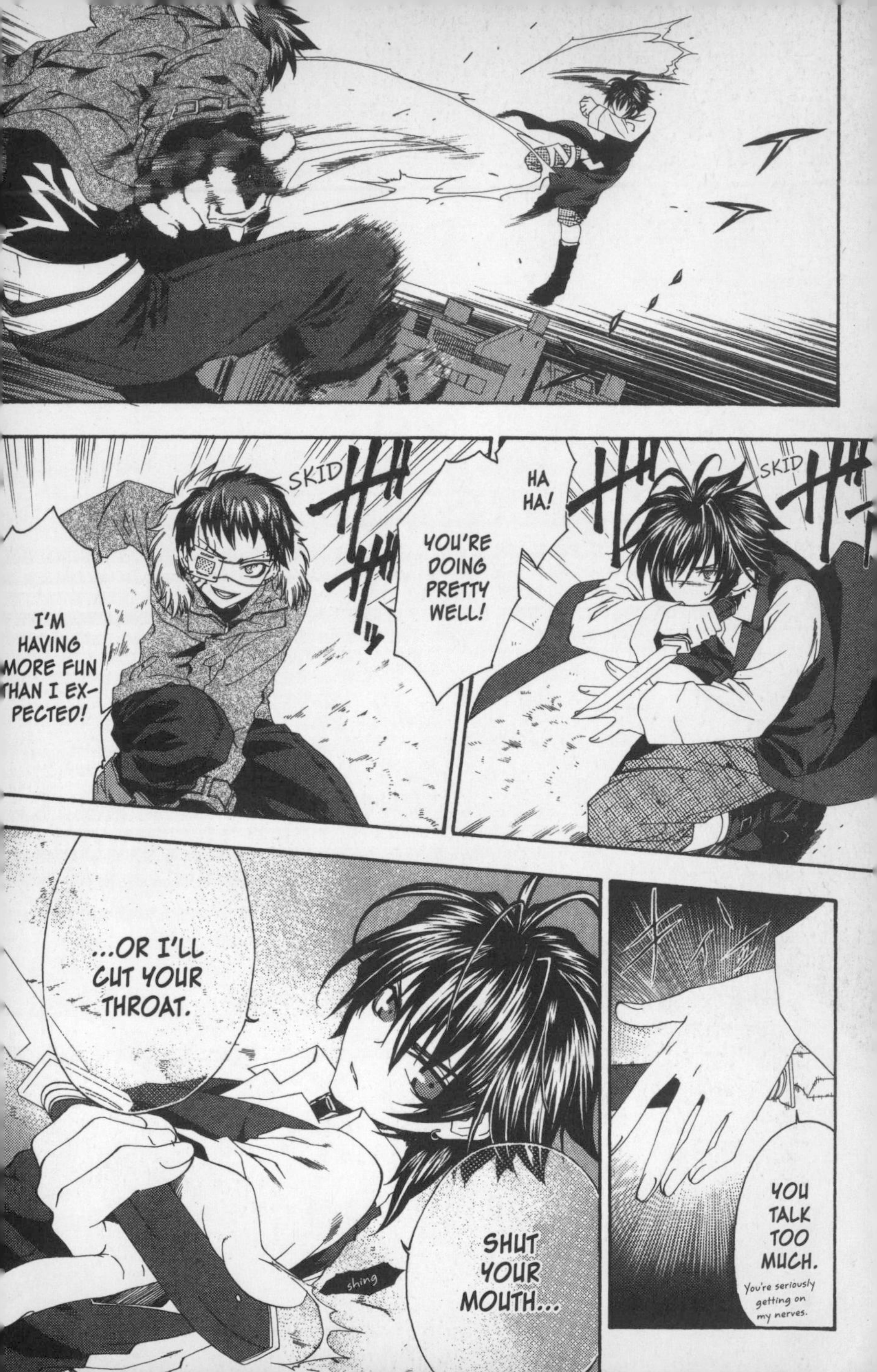
SKID
HA HA!
YOU'RE DOING PRETTY WELL!
SKID
I'M HAVING MORE FUN THAN I EXPECTED!
YOU TALK TOO MUCH.
You're seriously getting on my nerves.
SHUT YOUR MOUTH...
shing
...OR I'LL CUT YOUR THROAT.

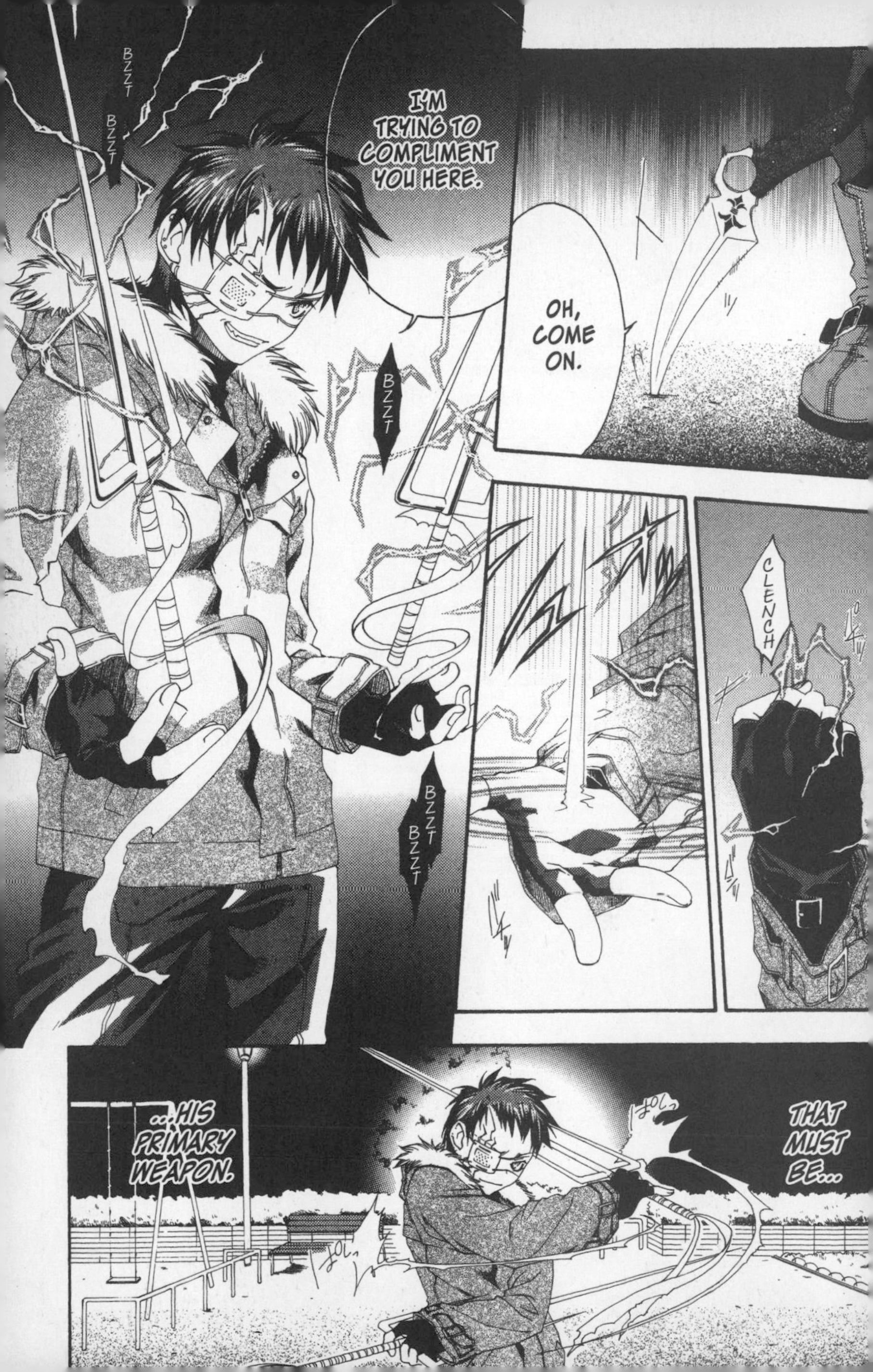
OH, COME ON.
I'M TRYING TO COMPLIMENT YOU HERE.
BZZT BZZT
BZZT
BZZT BZZT
CLENCH
THAT MUST BE...
...HIS PRIMARY WEAPON.

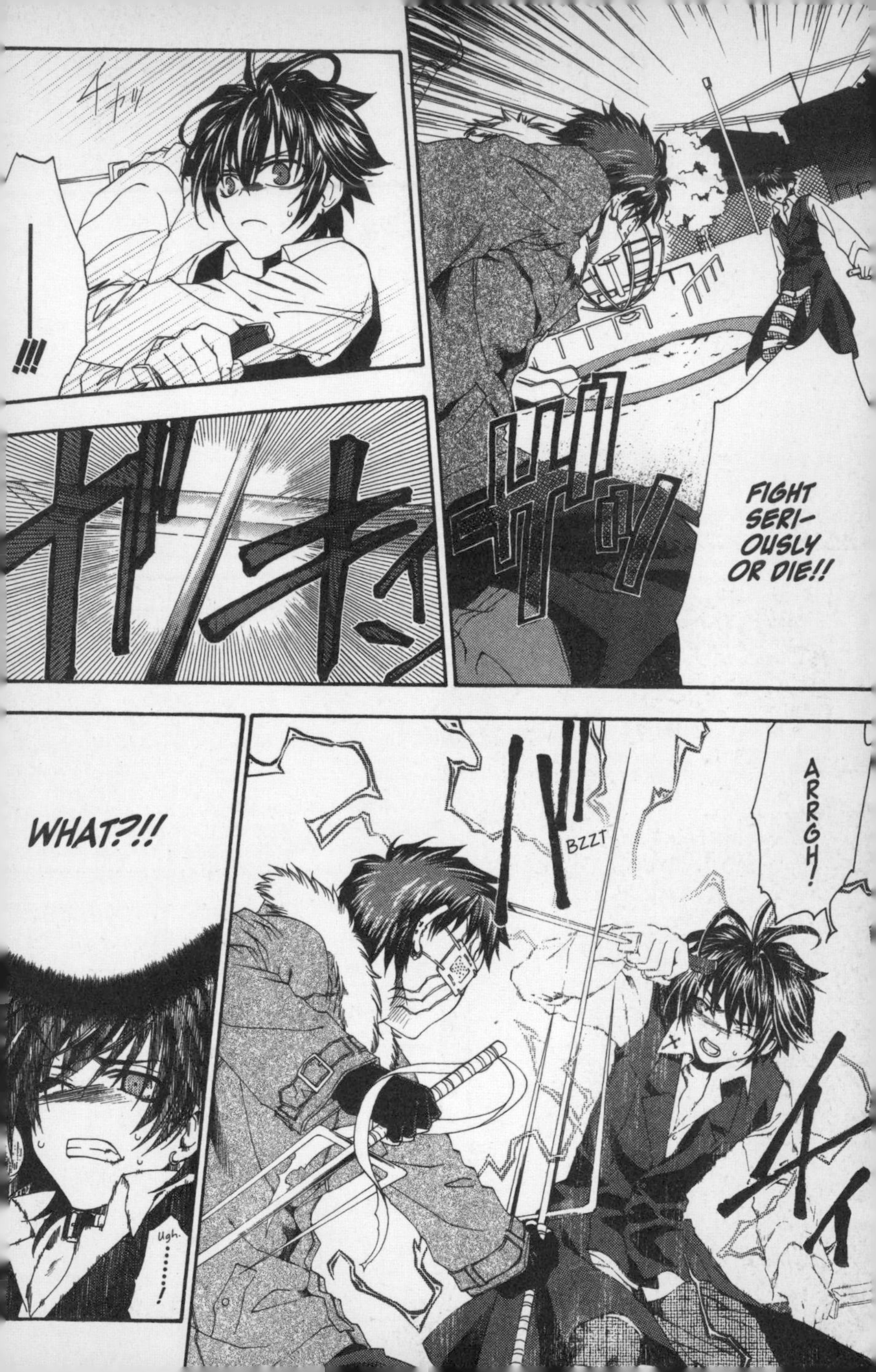
FIGHT SERIOUSLY OR DIE!!
!!!
ARRGH!
BZZT
WHAT?!!
Ugh. ......!

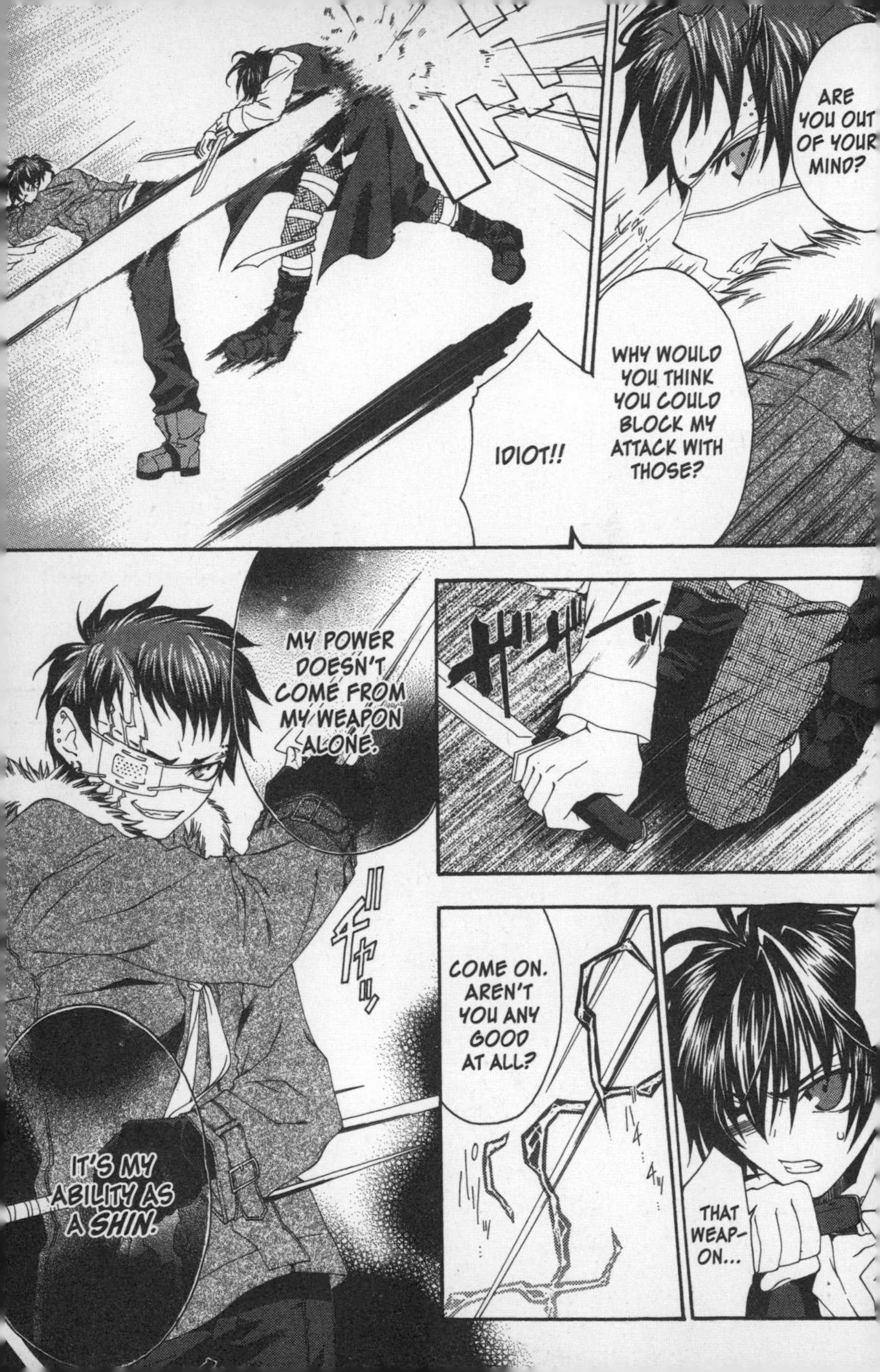
ARE YOU OUT OF YOUR MIND?
WHY WOULD YOU THINK YOU COULD BLOCK MY ATTACK WITH THOSE?
IDIOT!!
MY POWER DOESN'T COME FROM MY WEAPON ALONE.
COME ON. AREN'T YOU ANY GOOD AT ALL?
THAT WEAP-ON...
IT'S MY ABILITY AS A SHIN.

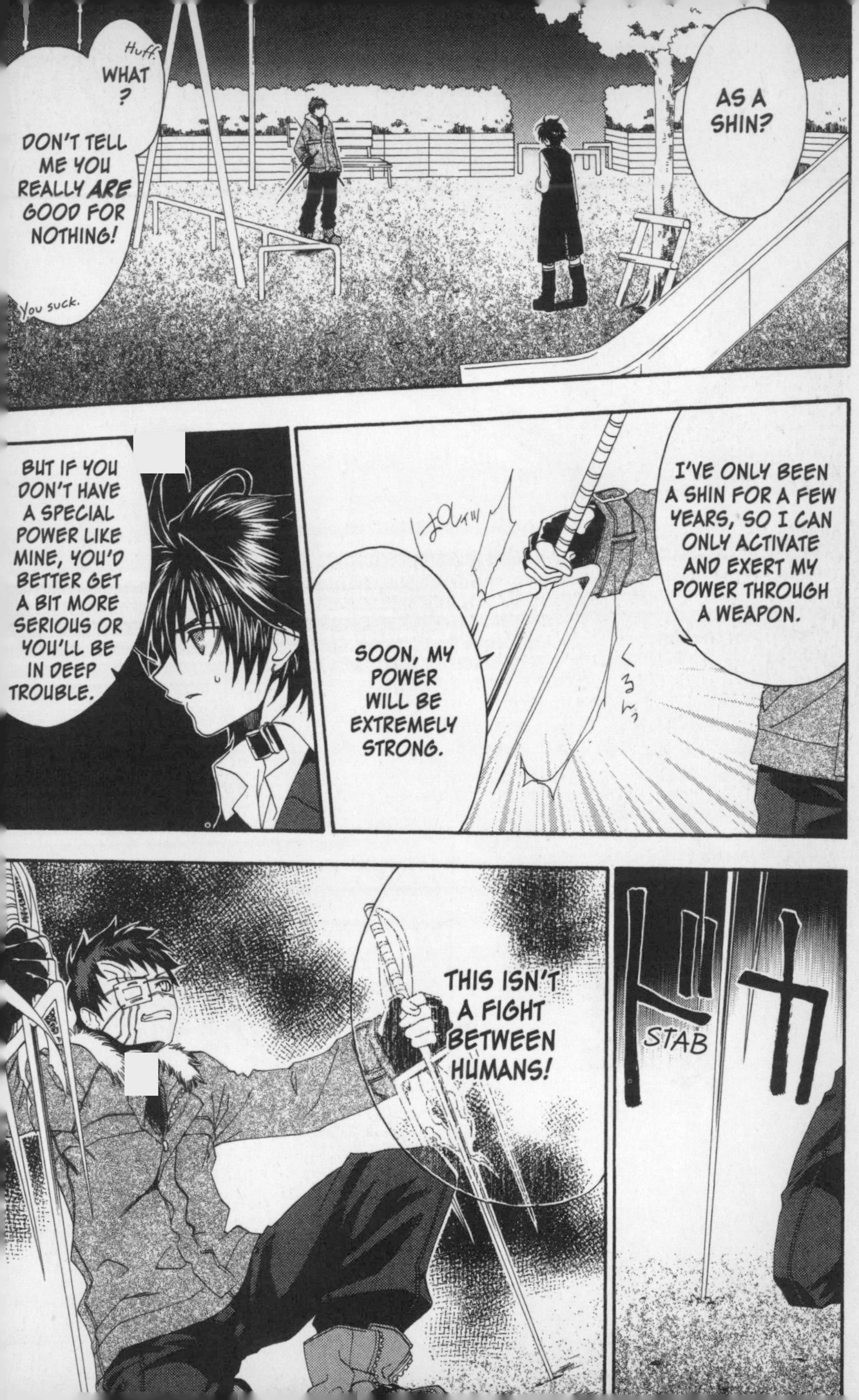
AS A SHIN?
Huff.
WHAT?
DON'T TELL ME YOU REALLY ARE GOOD FOR NOTHING!
You suck.
I'VE ONLY BEEN A SHIN FOR A FEW YEARS, SO I CAN ONLY ACTIVATE AND EXERT MY POWER THROUGH A WEAPON.
SOON, MY POWER WILL BE EXTREMELY STRONG.
BUT IF YOU DON'T HAVE A SPECIAL POWER LIKE MINE, YOU'D BETTER GET A BIT MORE SERIOUS OR YOU'LL BE IN DEEP TROUBLE.
STAB
THIS ISN'T A FIGHT BETWEEN HUMANS!

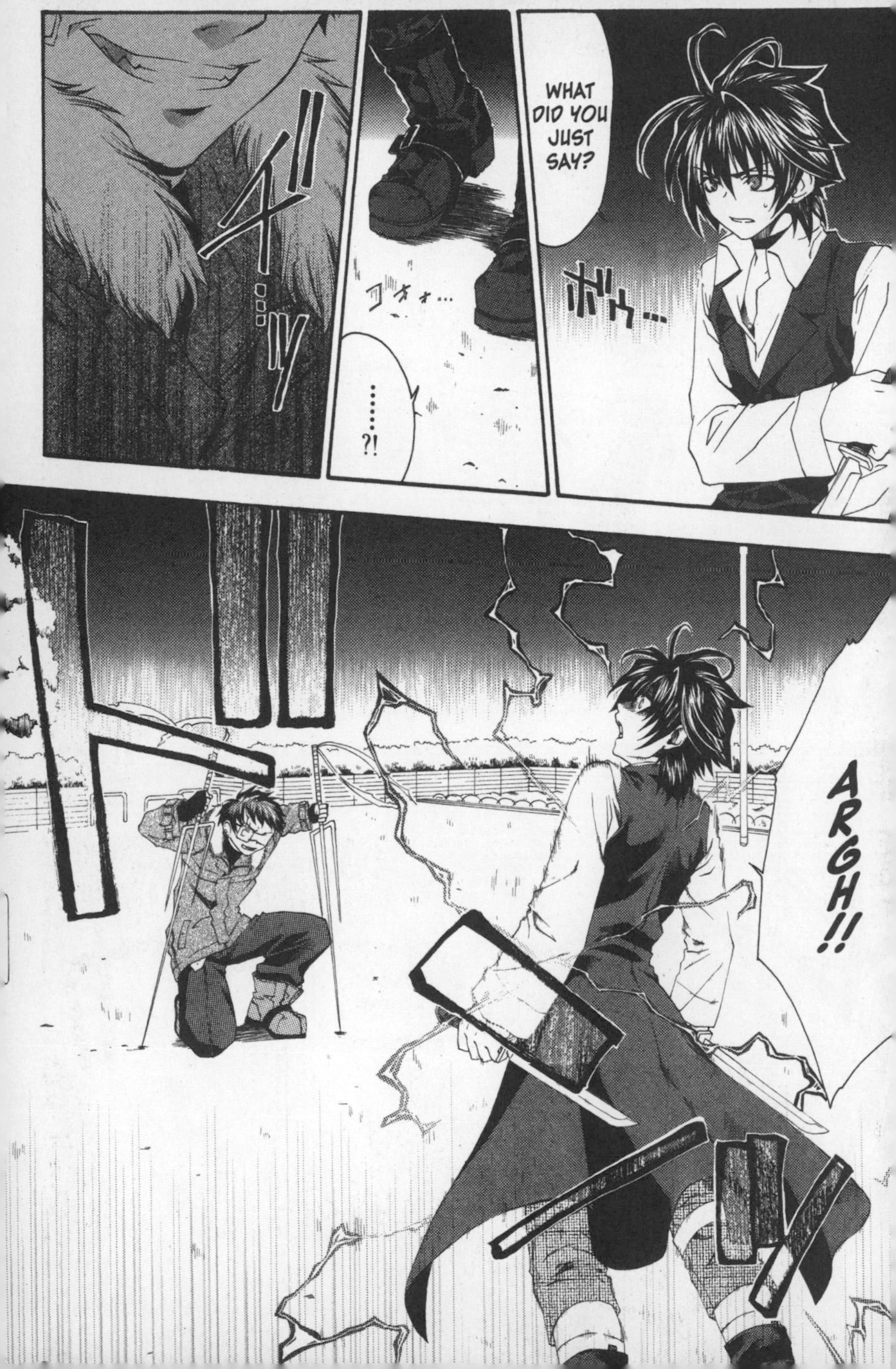
WHAT DID YOU JUST SAY?
......?!
ARGH!!

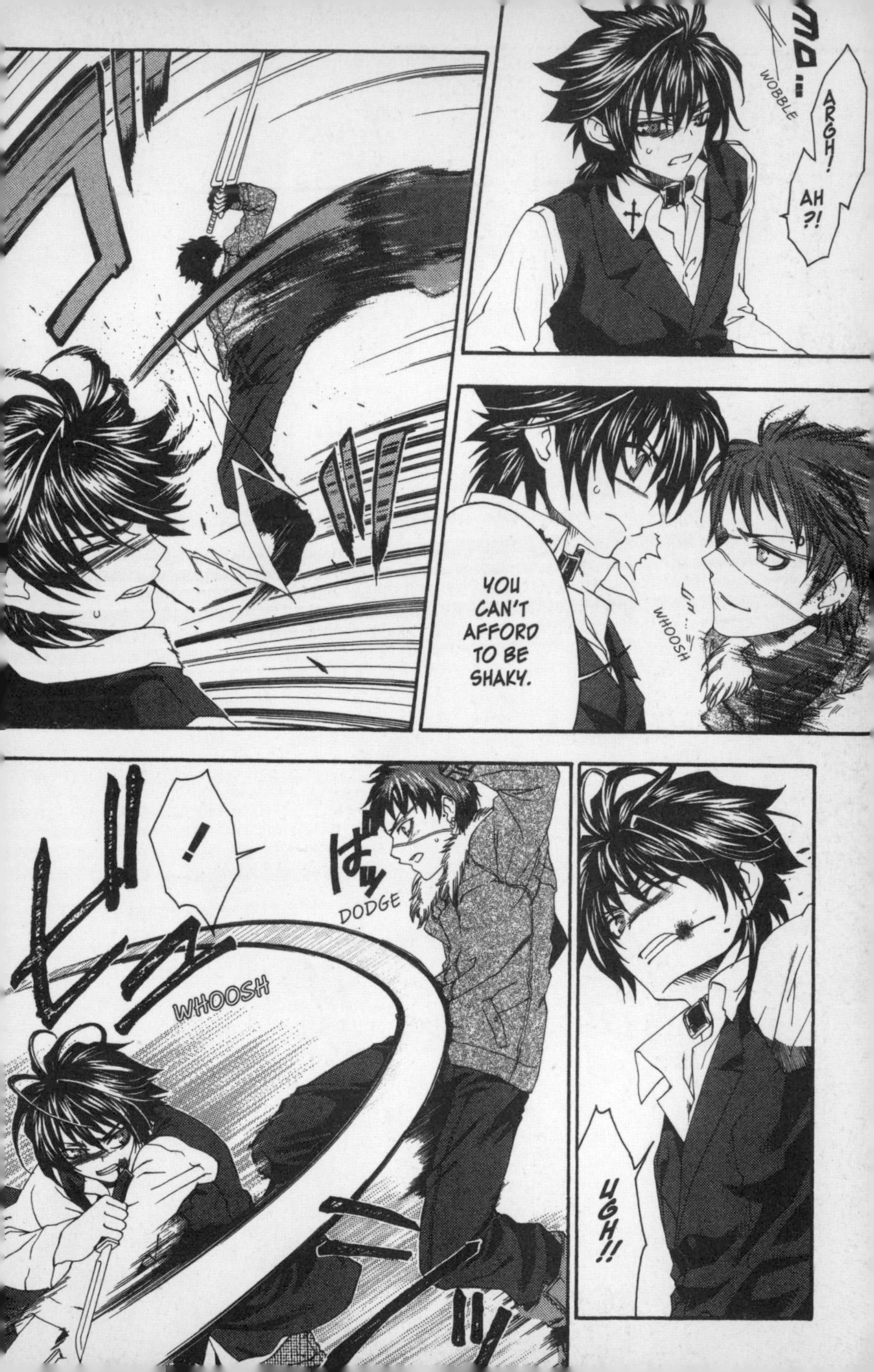

WOBBLE
ARGH!
AH?!
WHOOSH
YOU CAN'T AFFORD TO BE SHAKY.
UGH!!
DODGE
!
WHOOSH

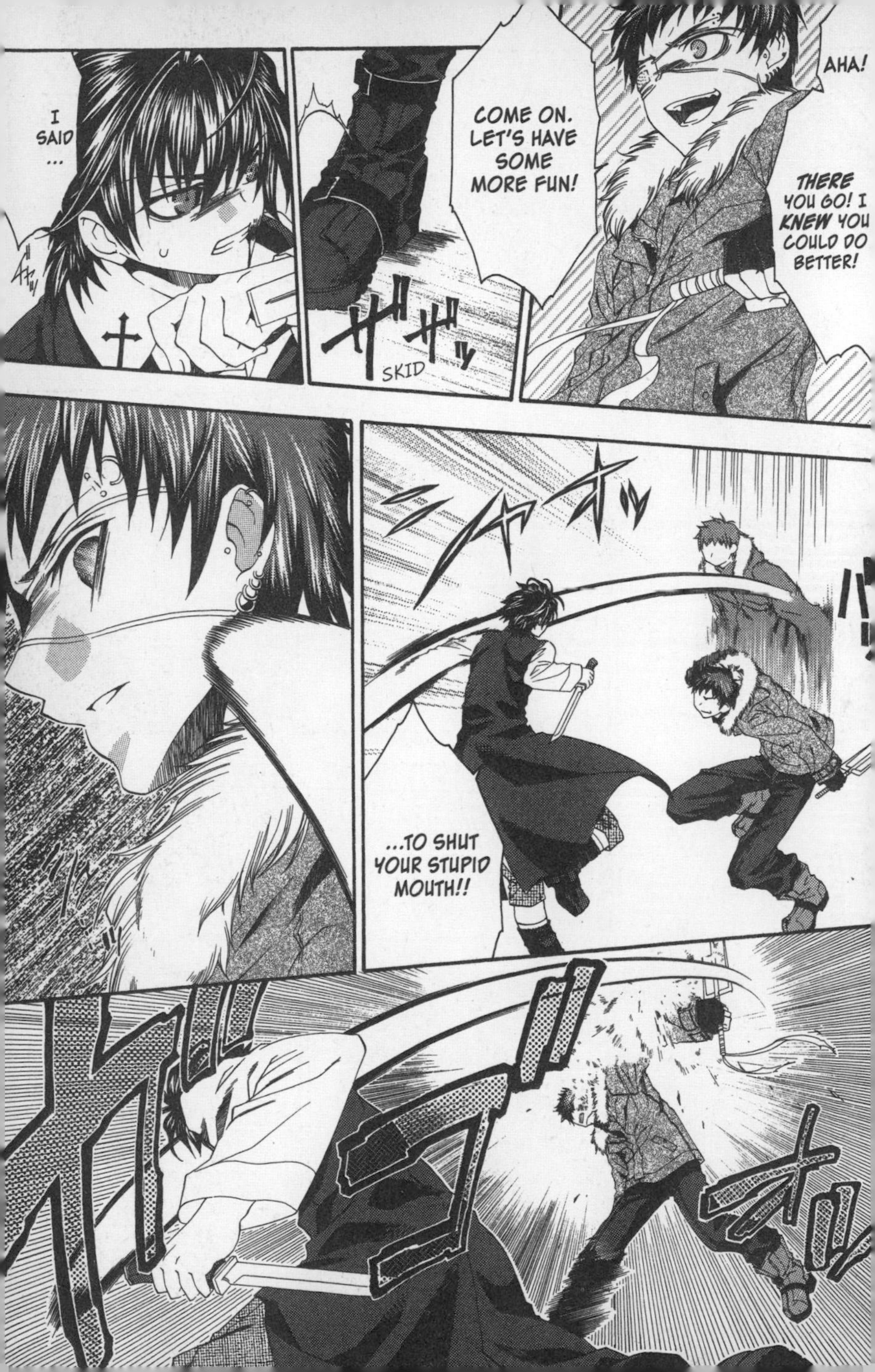
AHA!
THERE YOU GO! I KNEW YOU COULD DO BETTER!
COME ON. LET'S HAVE SOME MORE FUN!
SKID
I SAID ...
...TO SHUT YOUR STUPID MOUTH!!

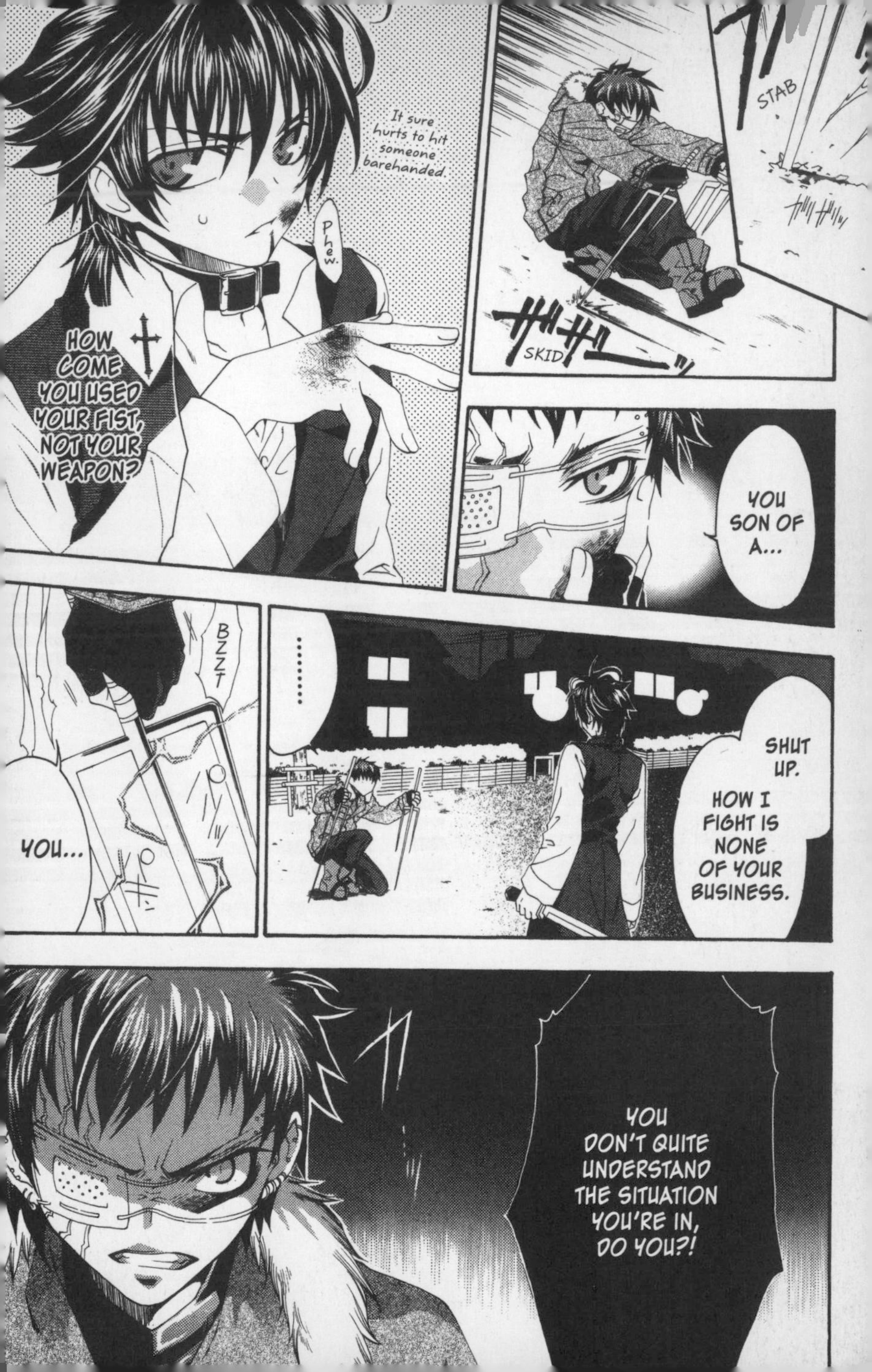
STAB
SKID
It sure hurts to hit someone barehanded.
Phew.
HOW COME YOU USED YOUR FIST, NOT YOUR WEAPON?
YOU SON OF A...
BZZT
YOU...
......
SHUT UP.
HOW I FIGHT IS NONE OF YOUR BUSINESS.
YOU DON'T QUITE UNDERSTAND THE SITUATION YOU'RE IN, DO YOU?!

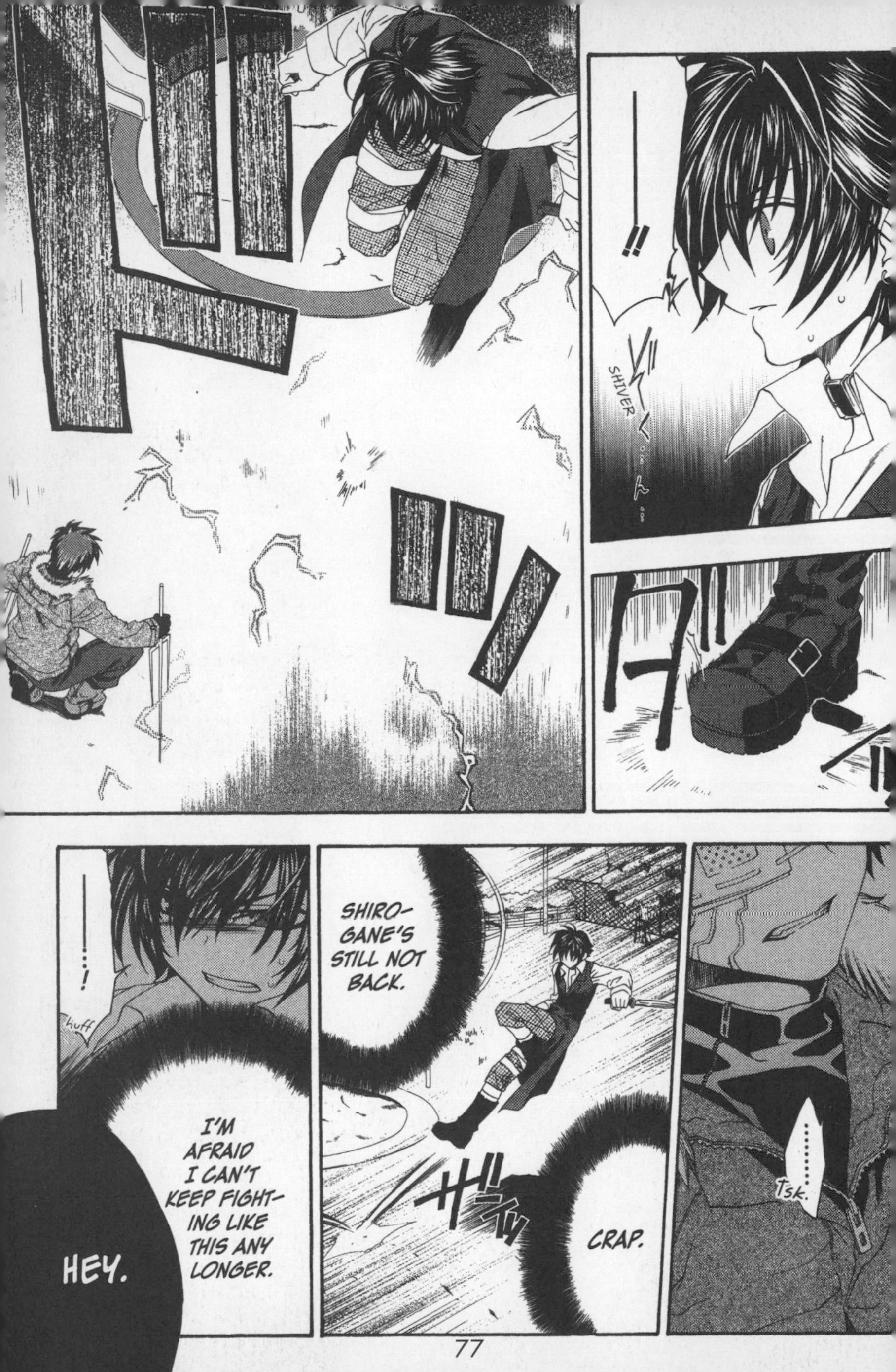
SHIVER
!!
…!
huff
SHIRO-GANE'S STILL NOT BACK.
Tsk.
CRAP.
I'M AFRAID I CAN'T KEEP FIGHT-ING LIKE THIS ANY LONGER.
HEY.

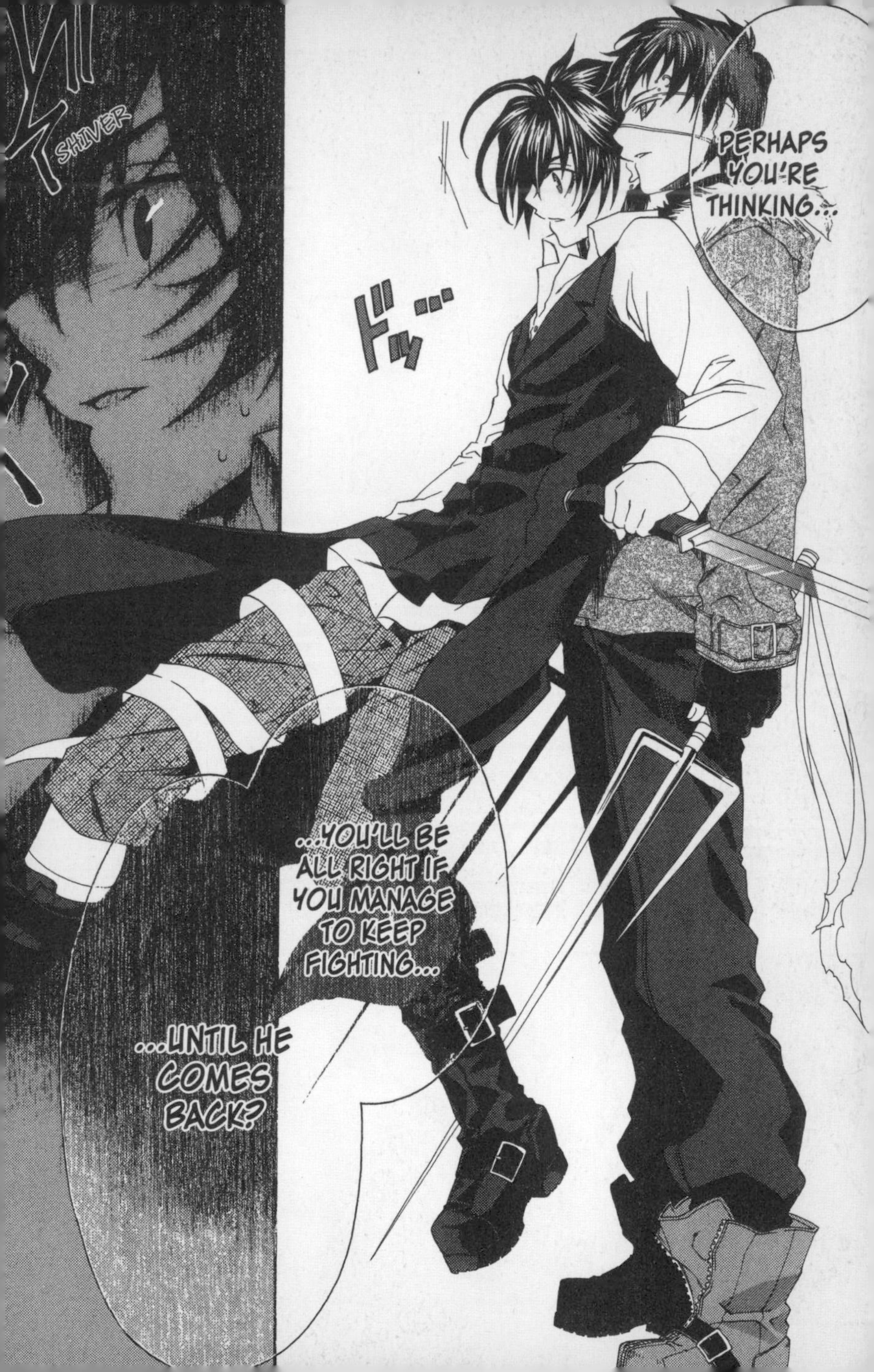
PERHAPS YOU'RE THINKING...
ドッ...
SHIVER
...YOU'LL BE ALL RIGHT IF YOU MANAGE TO KEEP FIGHTING...
...UNTIL HE COMES BACK?

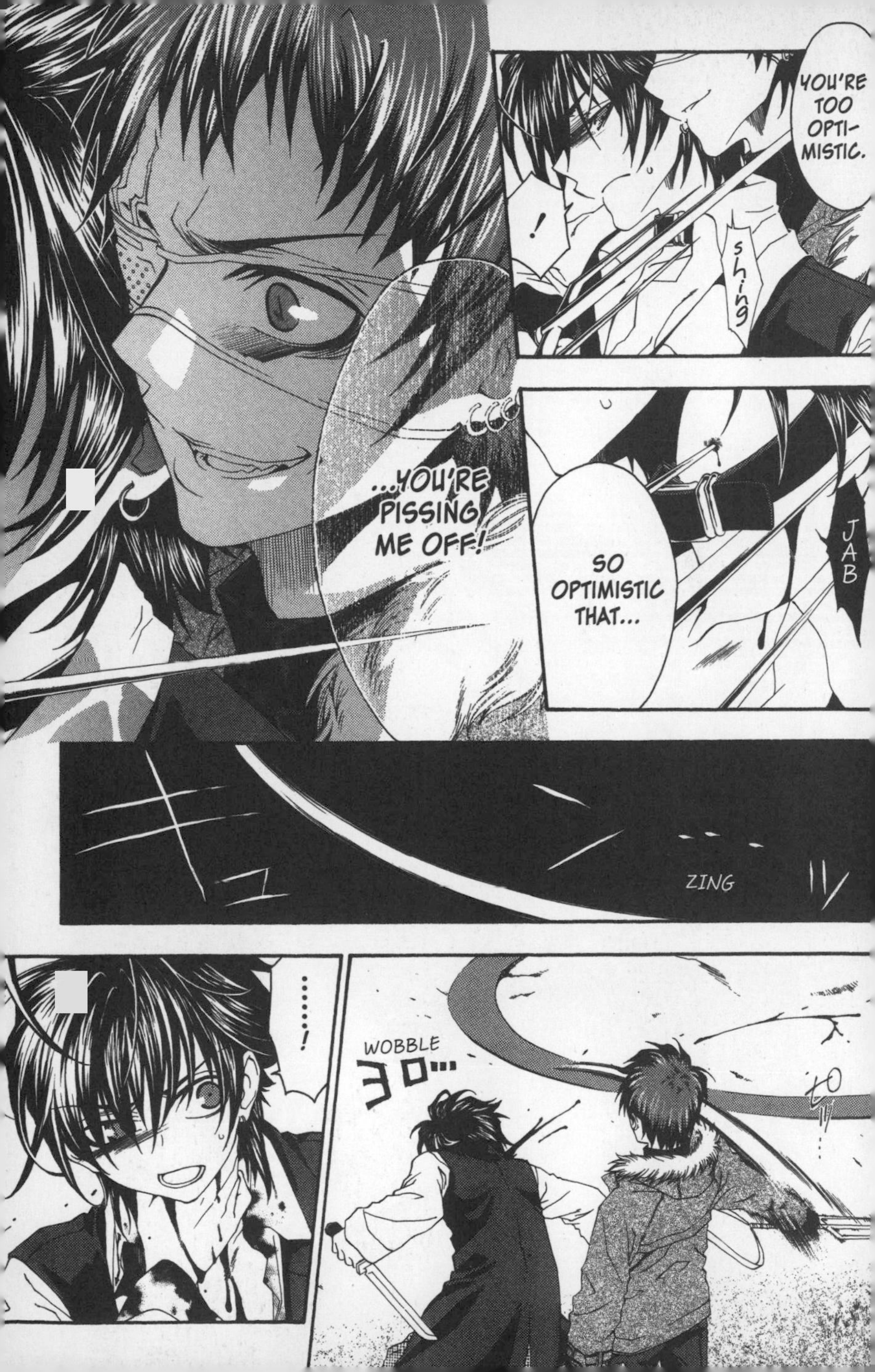
YOU'RE TOO OPTI- MISTIC.
!
shing
SO OPTIMISTIC THAT...
JAB
...YOU'RE PISSING ME OFF!
ZING
WOBBLE
......!

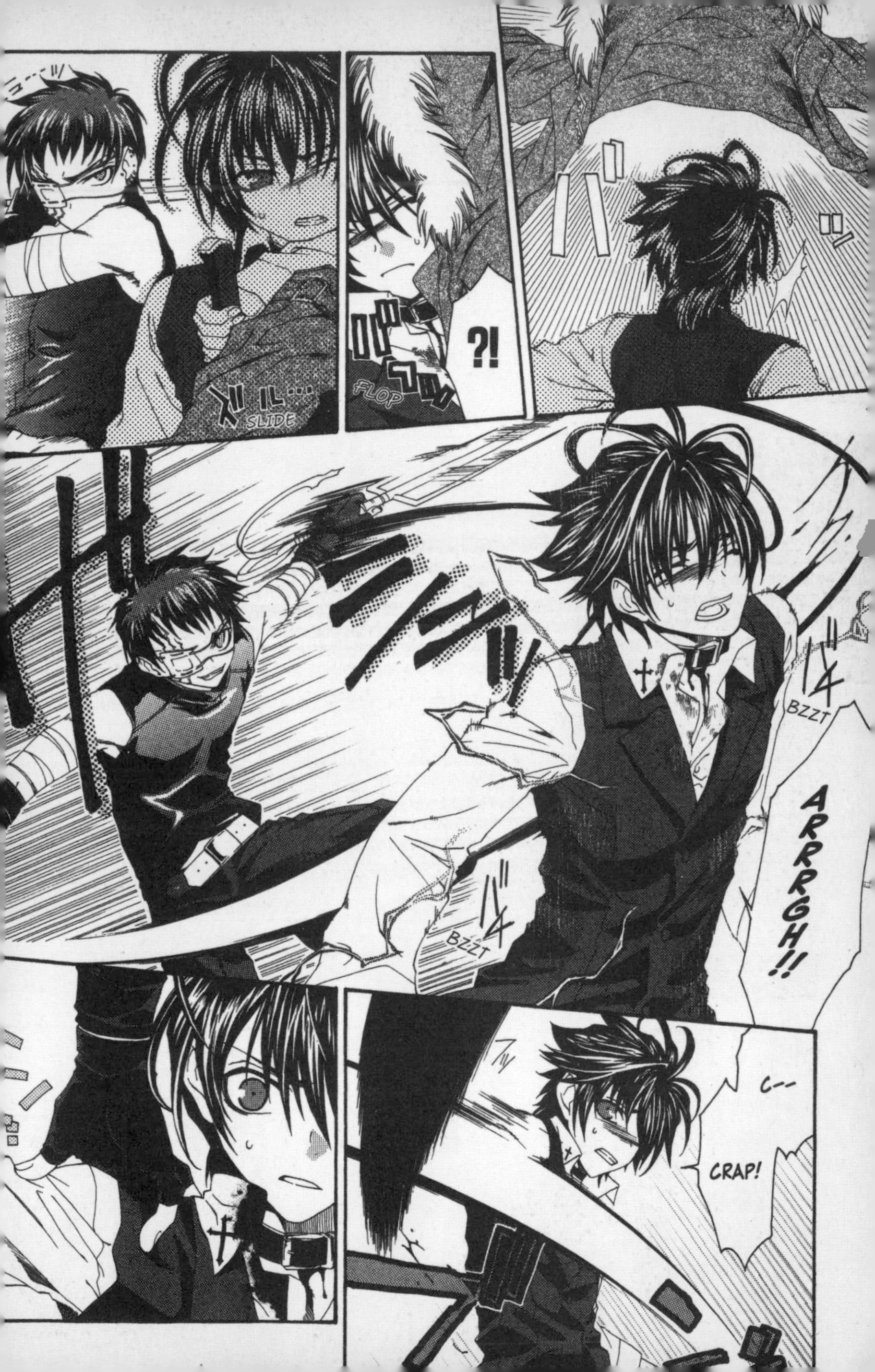

?!
FLOP
SLIDE
BZZT
ARRRGH!!
BZZT
C--
CRAP!

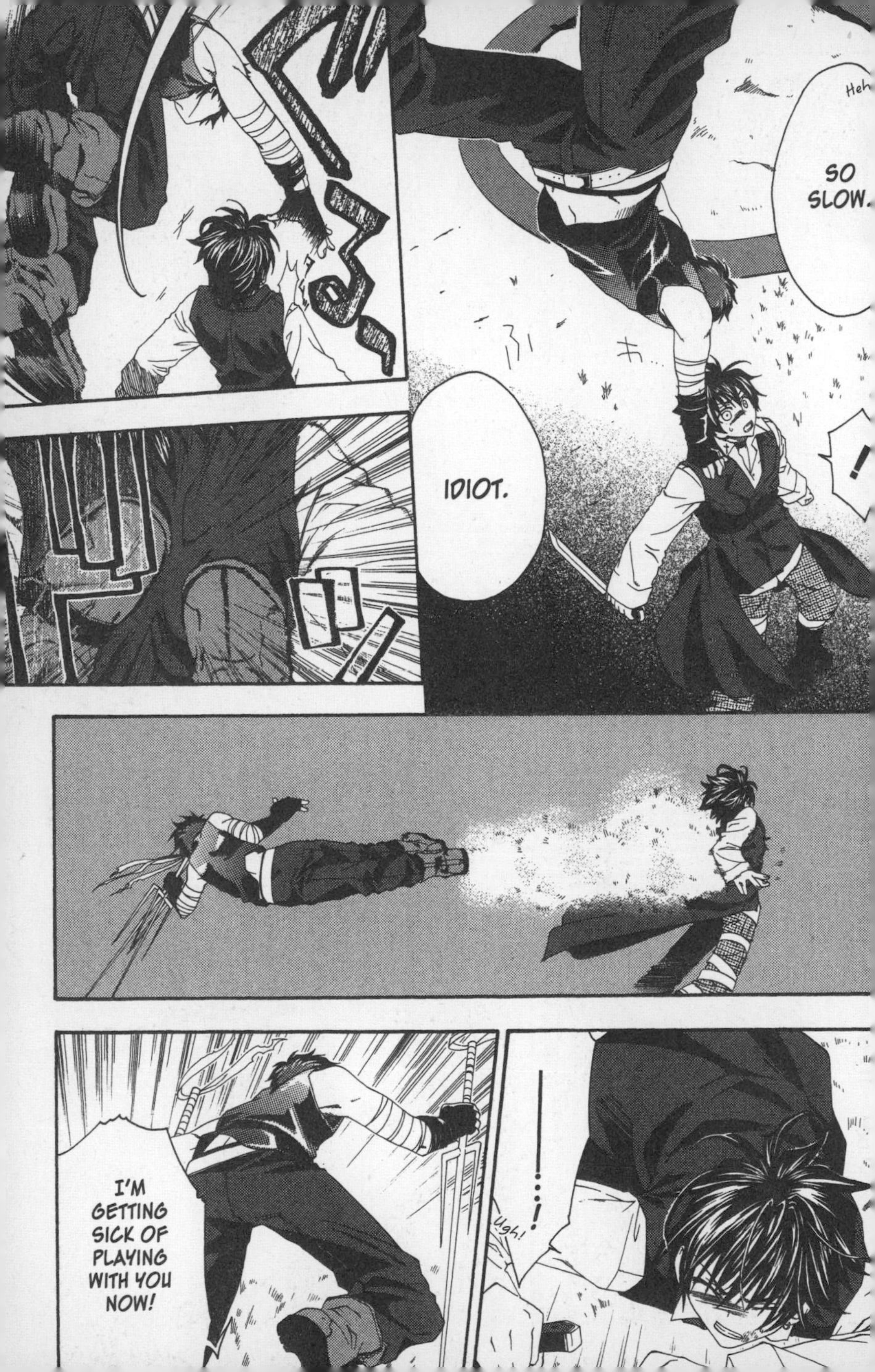
Heh
SO SLOW.
IDIOT.
!
I'M GETTING SICK OF PLAYING WITH YOU NOW!
Ugh!
...!

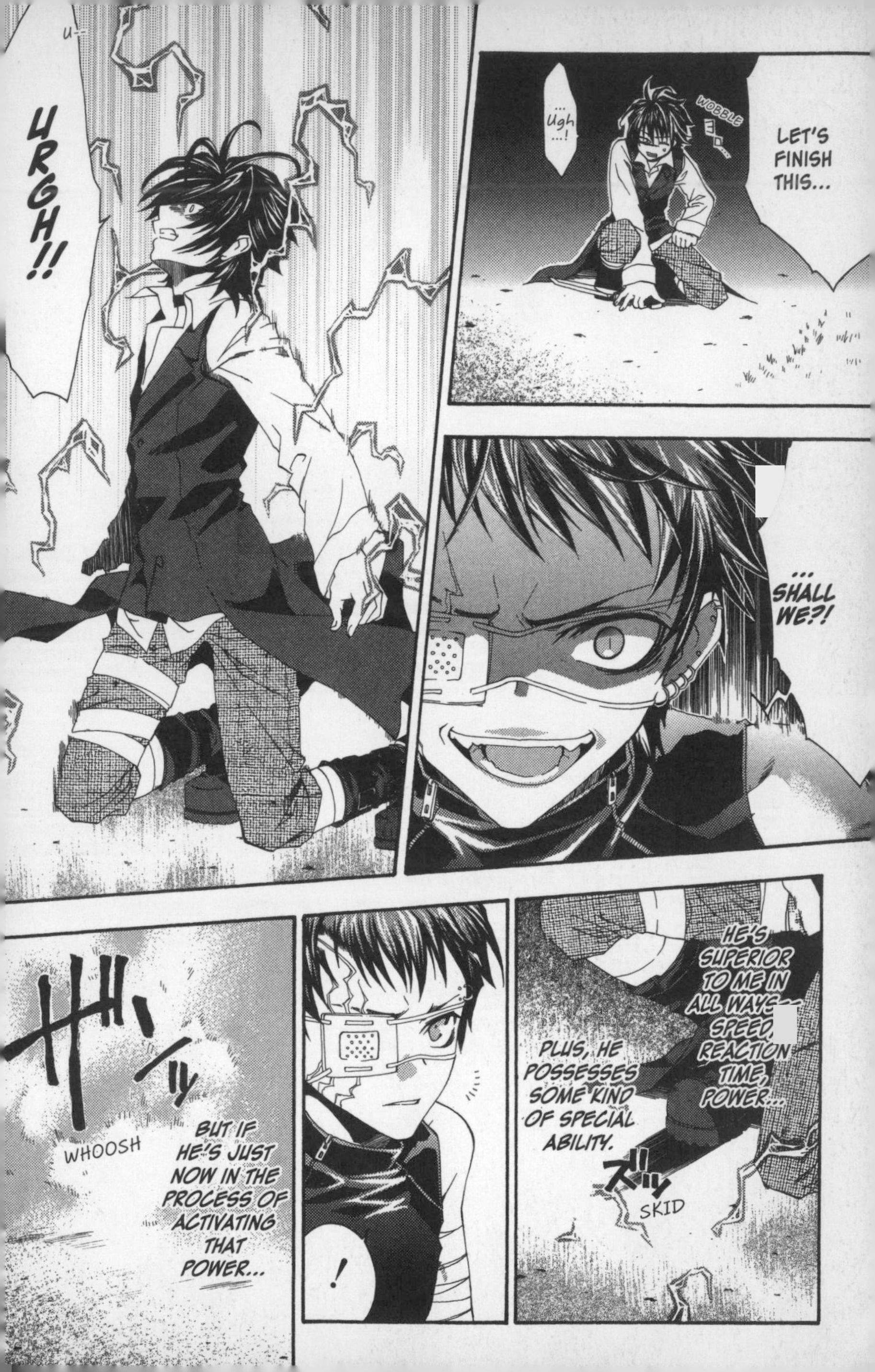

LET'S FINISH THIS...
WOBBLE
...Ugh...!
...SHALL WE?!
U--
URGH!!
HE'S SUPERIOR TO ME IN ALL WAYS... SPEED, REACTION TIME, POWER...
PLUS, HE POSSESSES SOME KIND OF SPECIAL ABILITY.
SKID
!
WHOOSH
BUT IF HE'S JUST NOW IN THE PROCESS OF ACTIVATING THAT POWER...

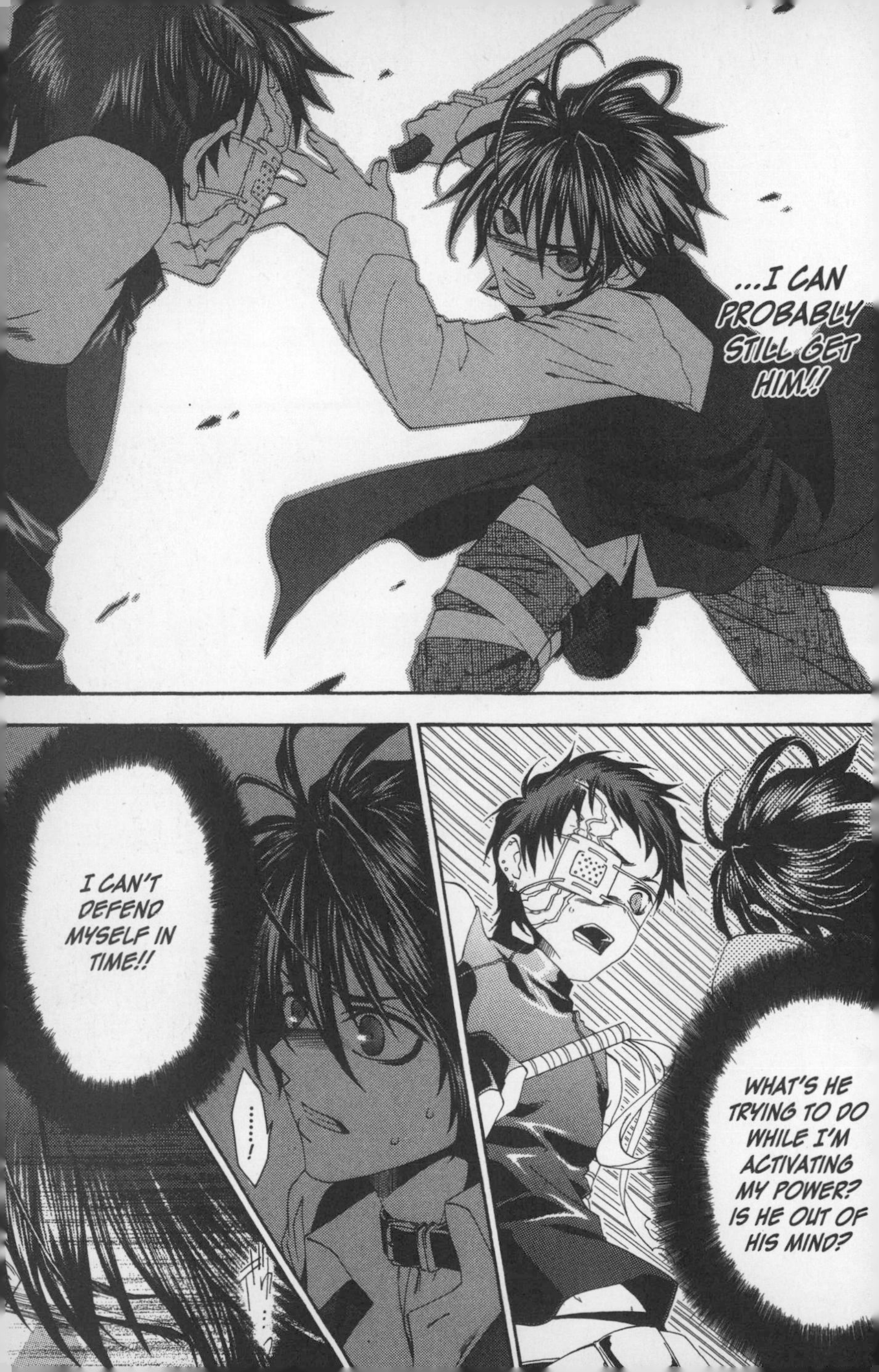
...I CAN PROBABLY STILL GET HIM!!
WHAT'S HE TRYING TO DO WHILE I'M ACTIVATING MY POWER? IS HE OUT OF HIS MIND?
I CAN'T DEFEND MYSELF IN TIME!!
......!

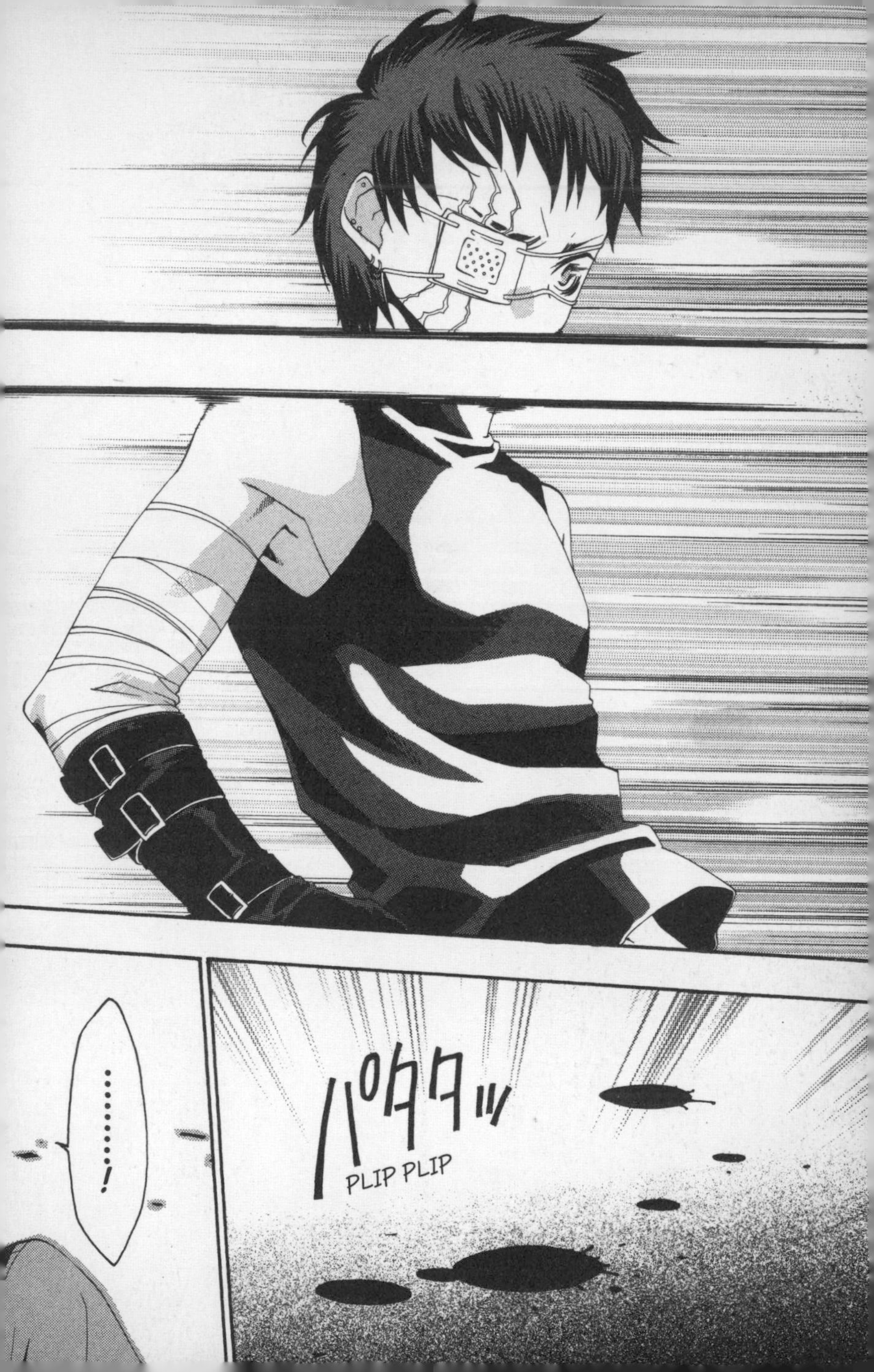

......!
パタタッ
PLIP PLIP

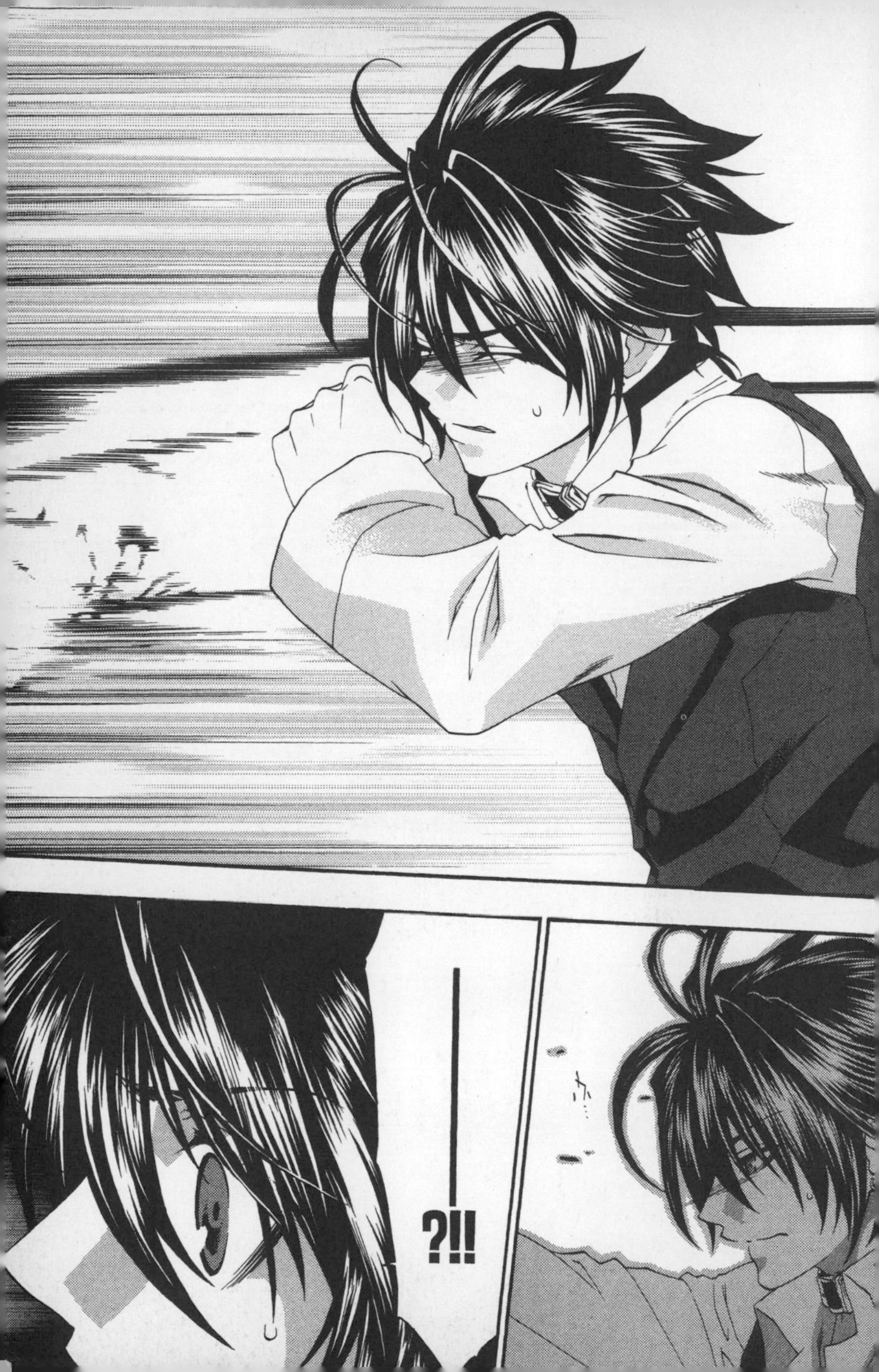
?!!

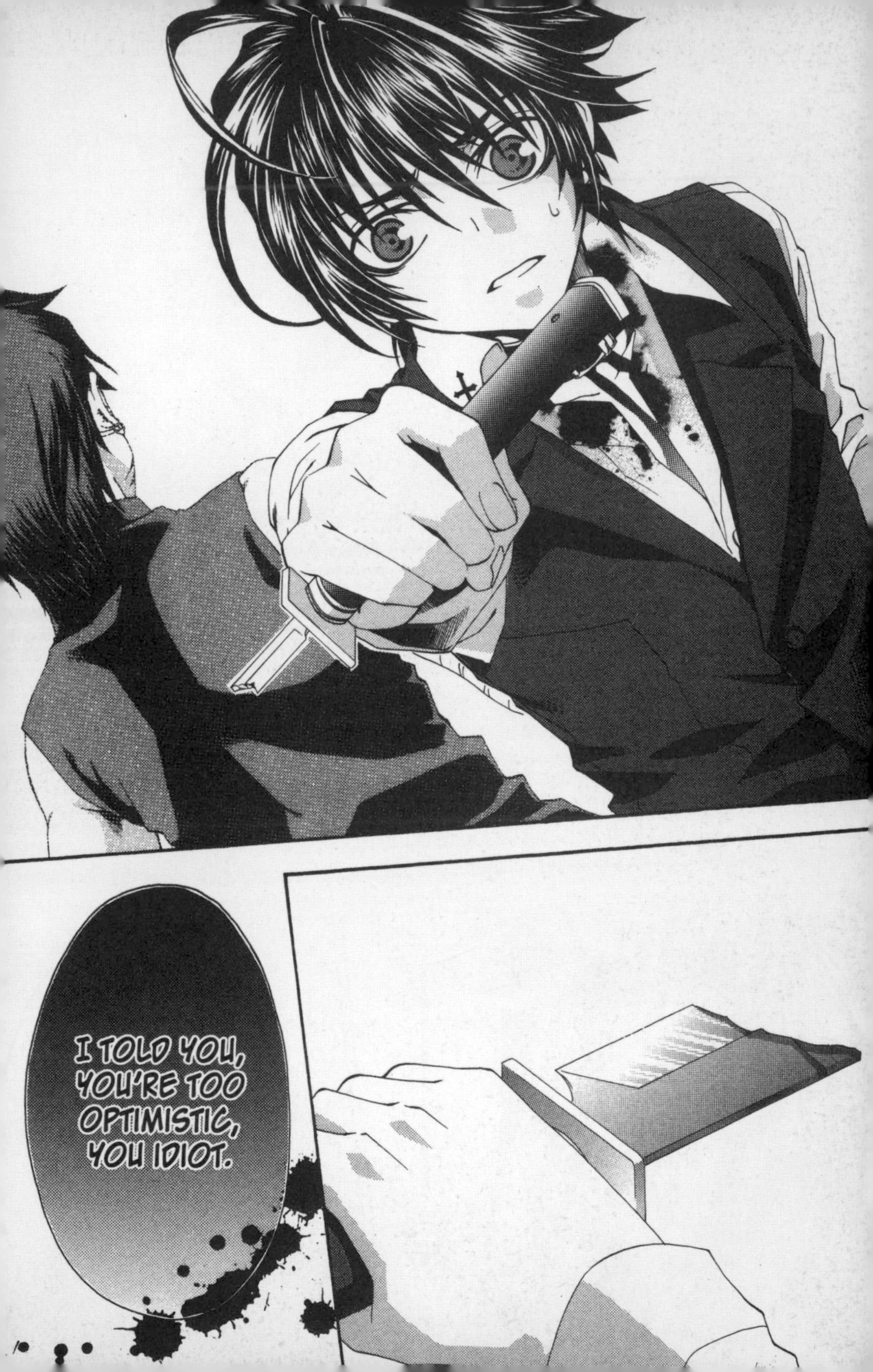
I TOLD YOU, YOU'RE TOO OPTIMISTIC, YOU IDIOT.

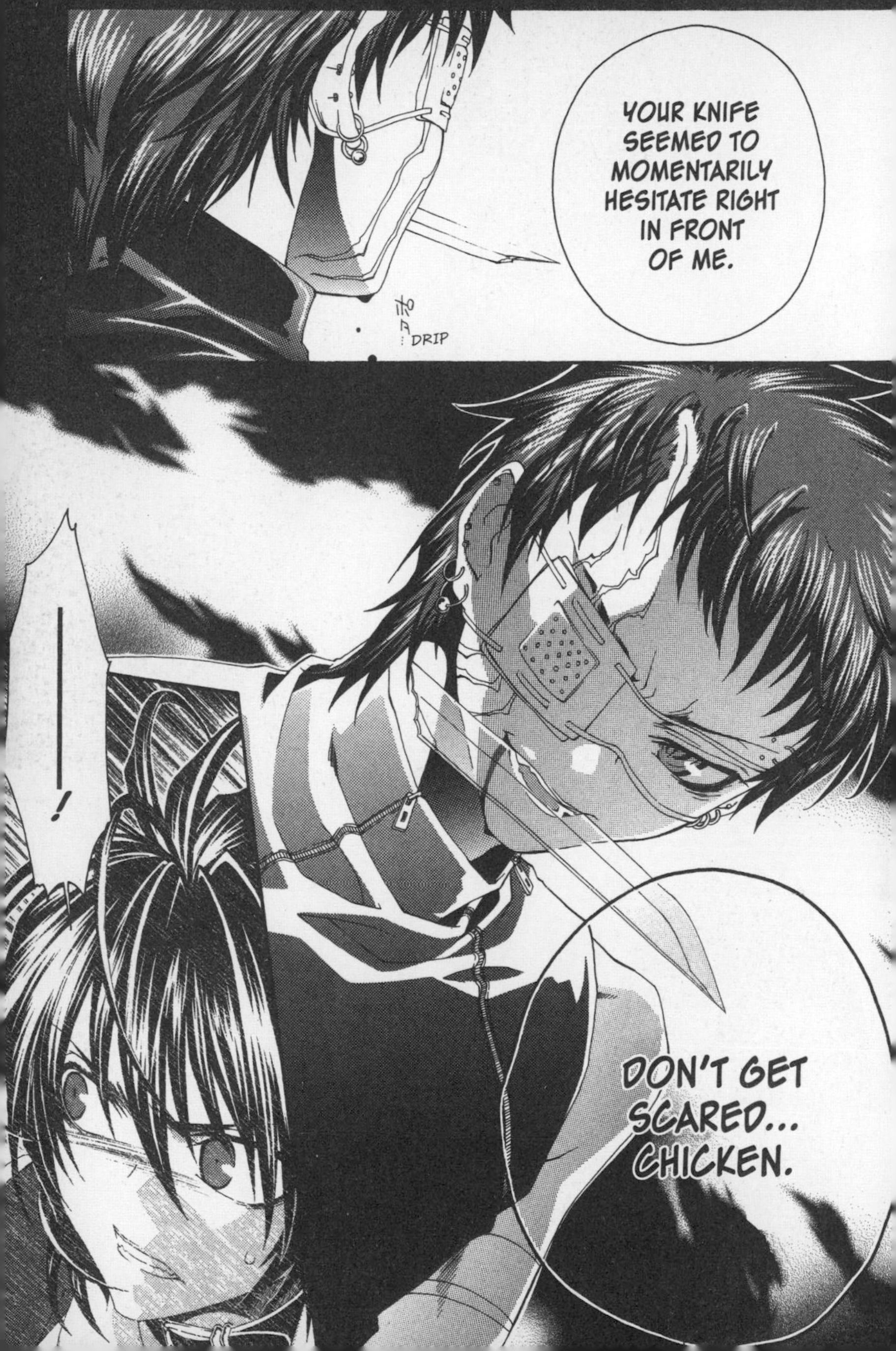
YOUR KNIFE SEEMED TO MOMENTARILY HESITATE RIGHT IN FRONT OF ME.
DRIP
--!
DON'T GET SCARED... CHICKEN.

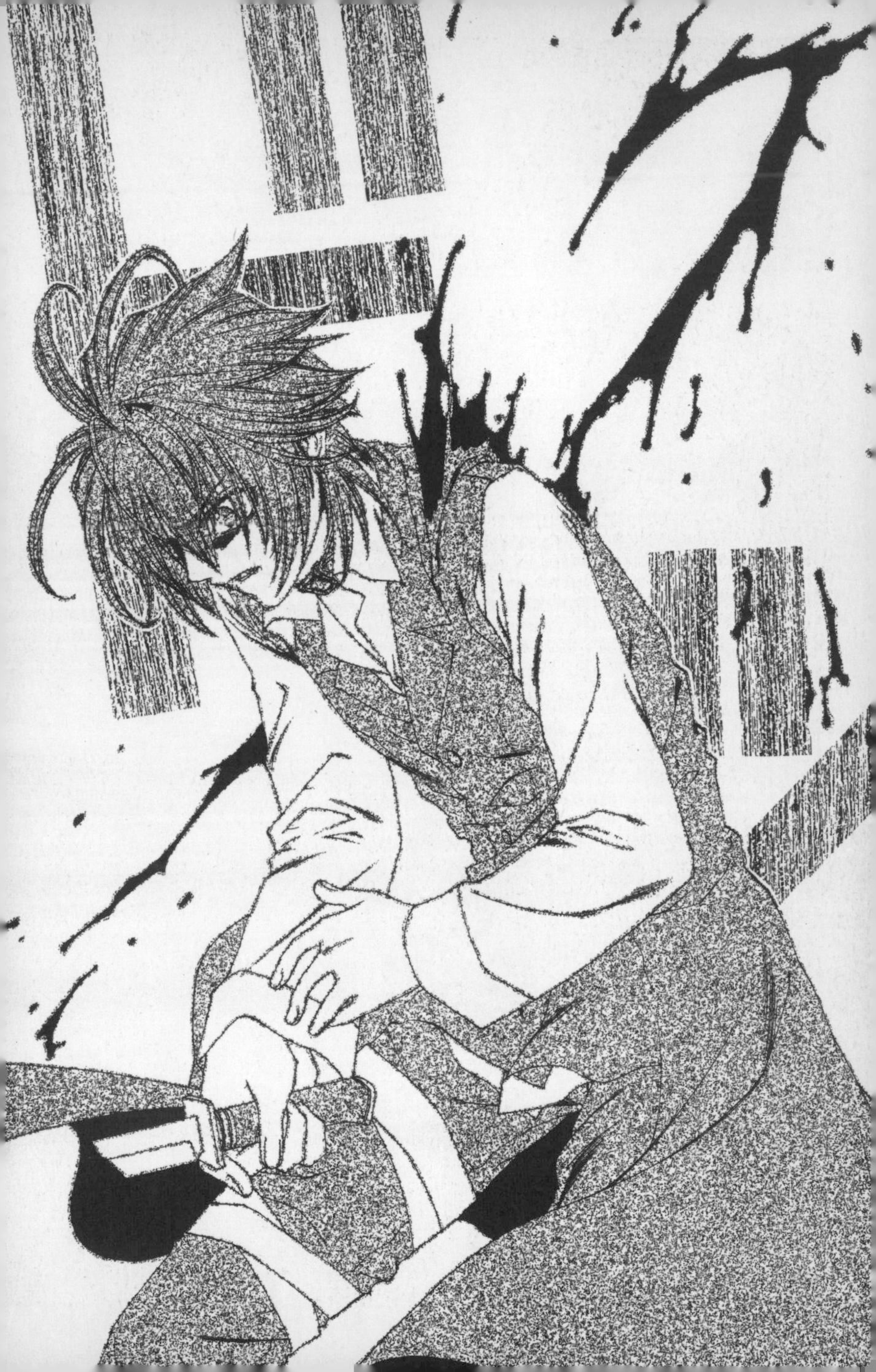

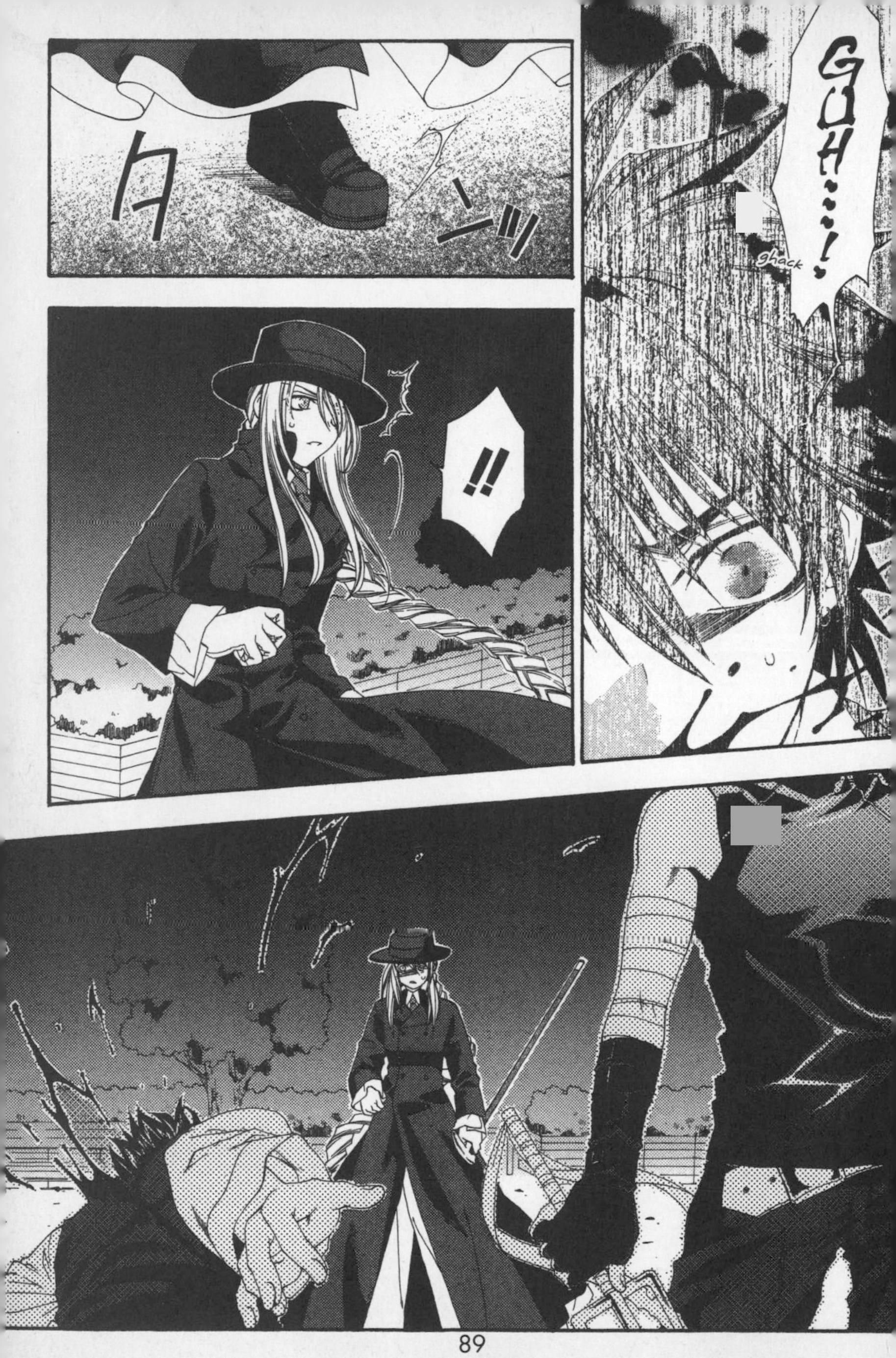
GUH...!
ghack
!!

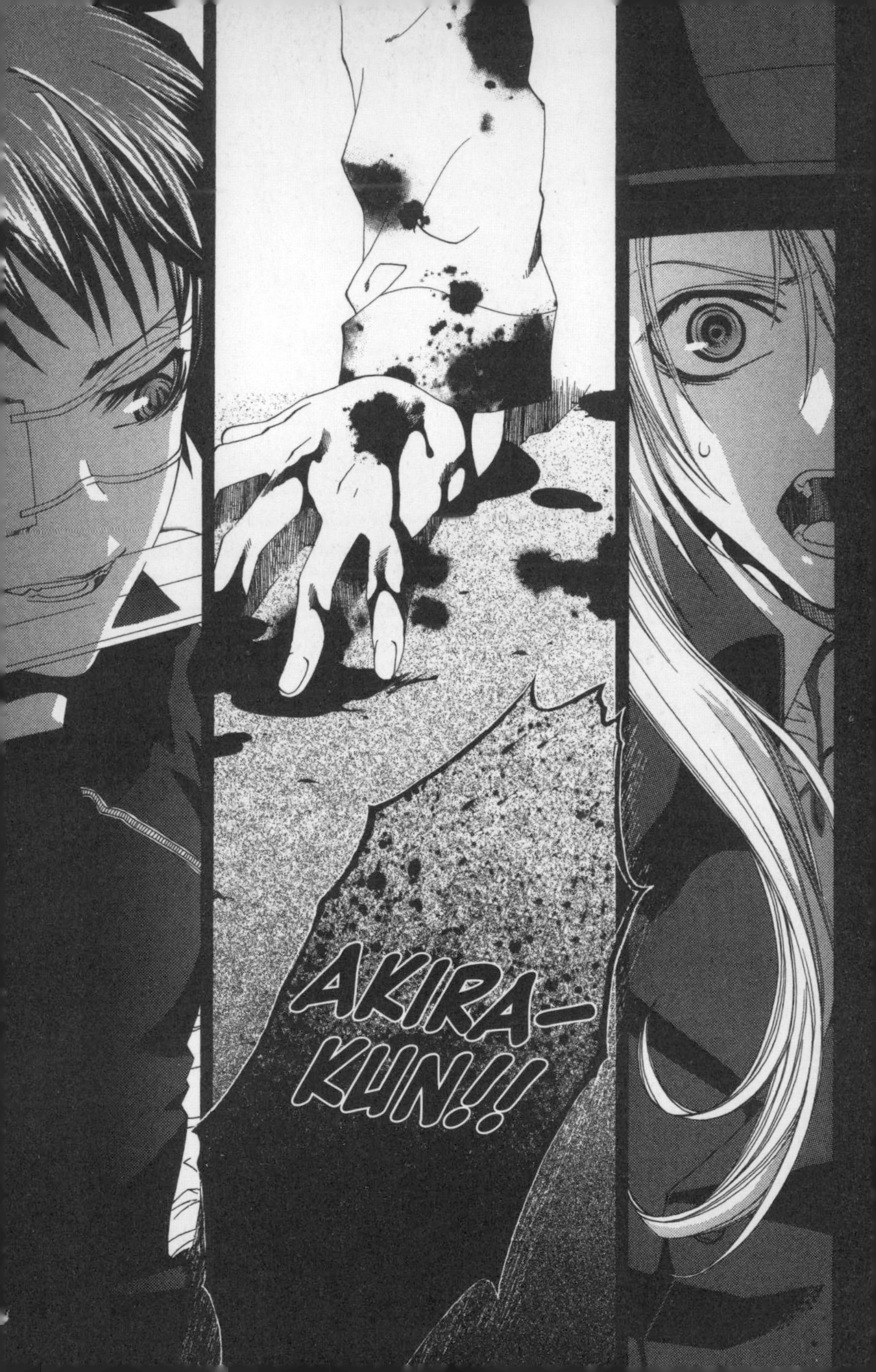
AKIRA-KUN!!

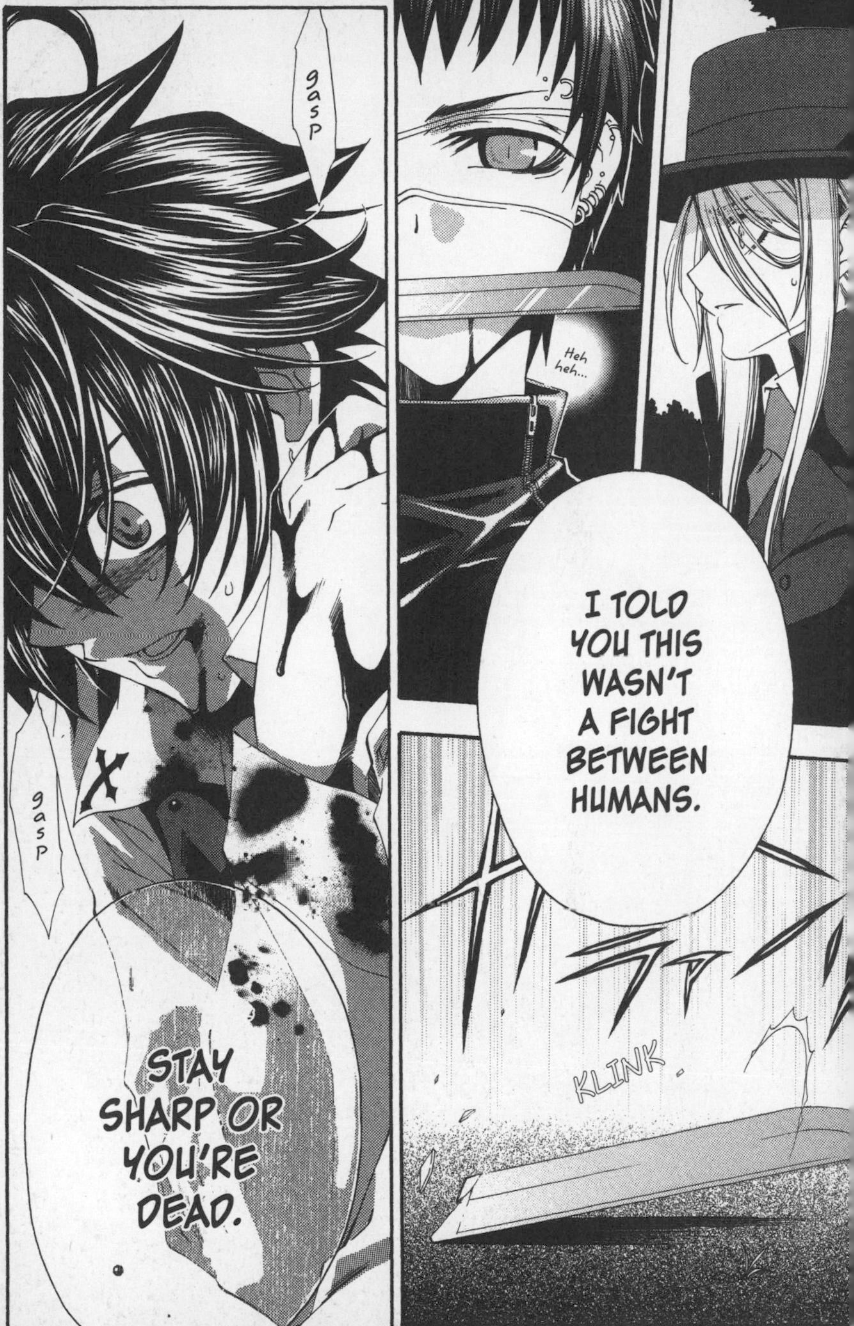
Heh heh...
I TOLD YOU THIS WASN'T A FIGHT BETWEEN HUMANS.
KLINK
gasp
gasp
STAY SHARP OR YOU'RE DEAD.

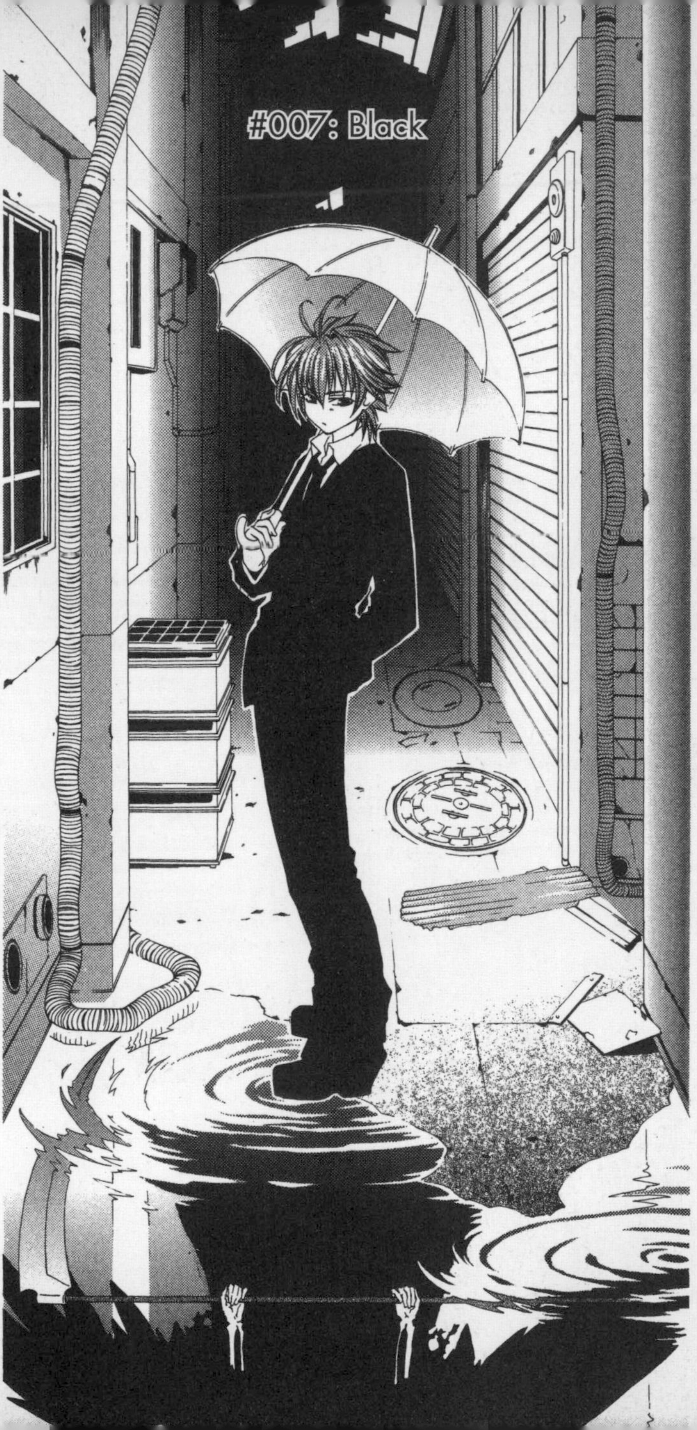
#007: Black

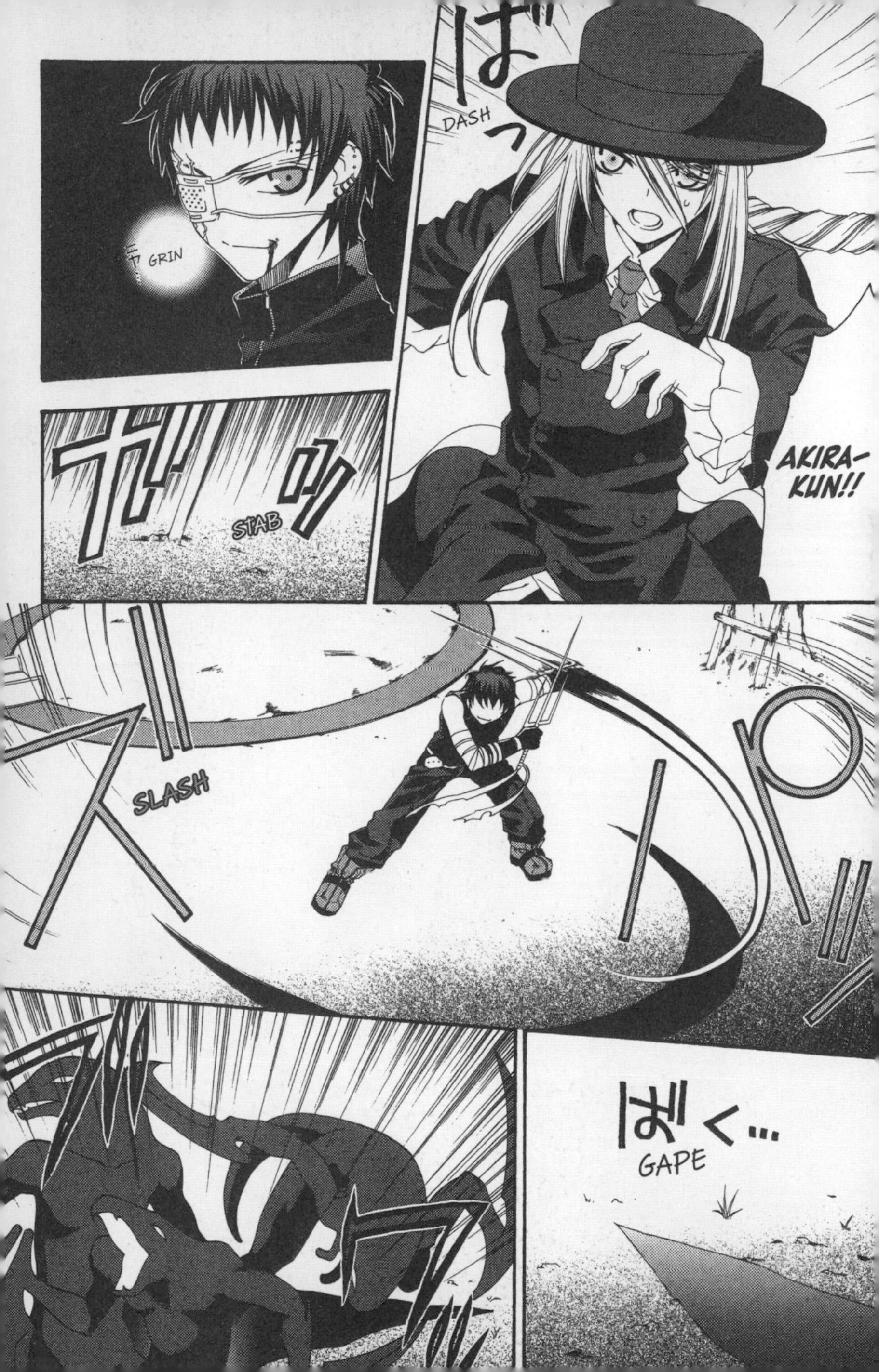
ばっ
DASH
AKIRA-KUN!!
ニヤ
GRIN
ガリッ
STAB
ズパッ
SLASH
ぱく…
GAPE

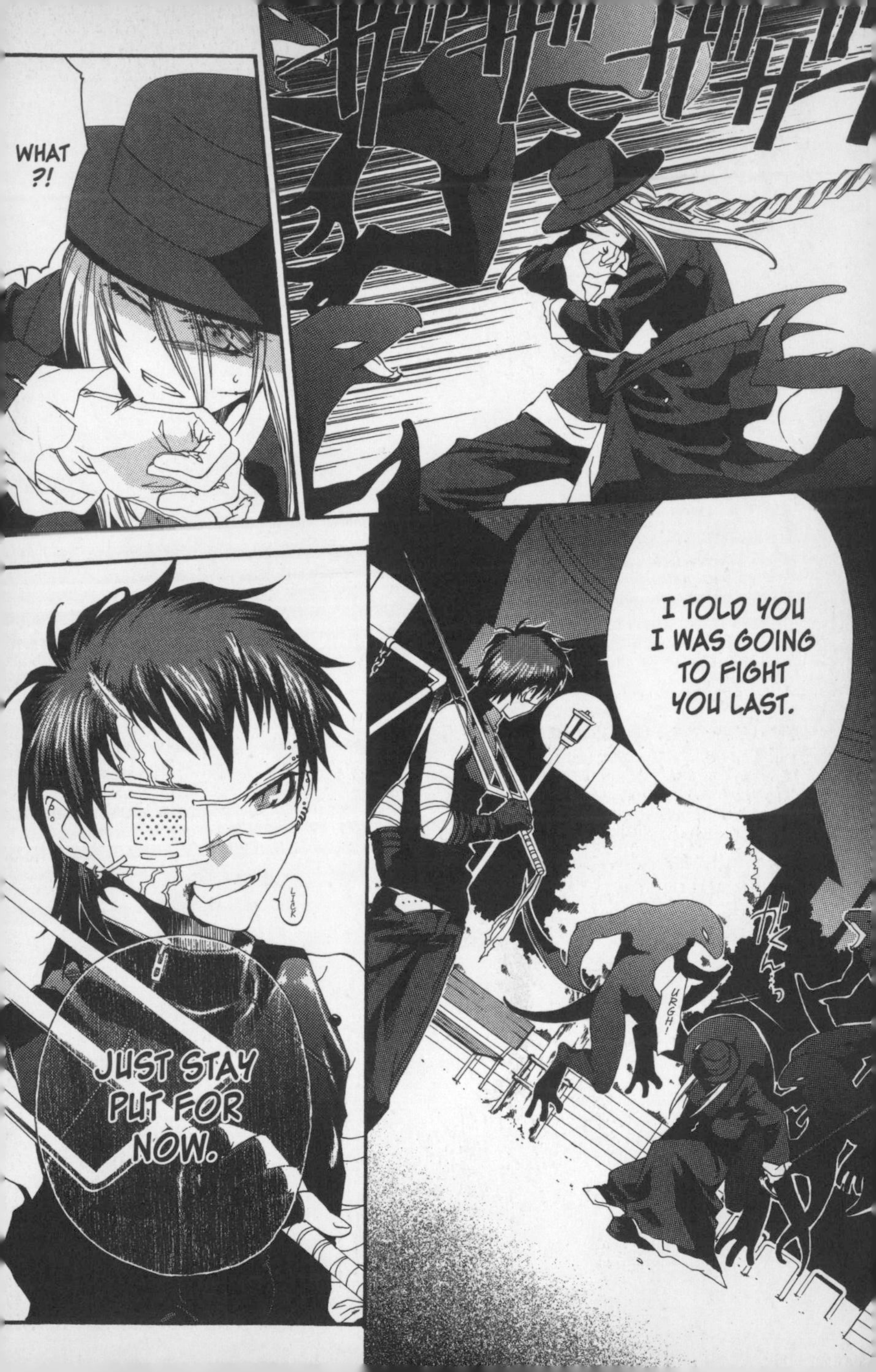
WHAT ?!
I TOLD YOU I WAS GOING TO FIGHT YOU LAST.
URGH!
LICK
JUST STAY PUT FOR NOW.

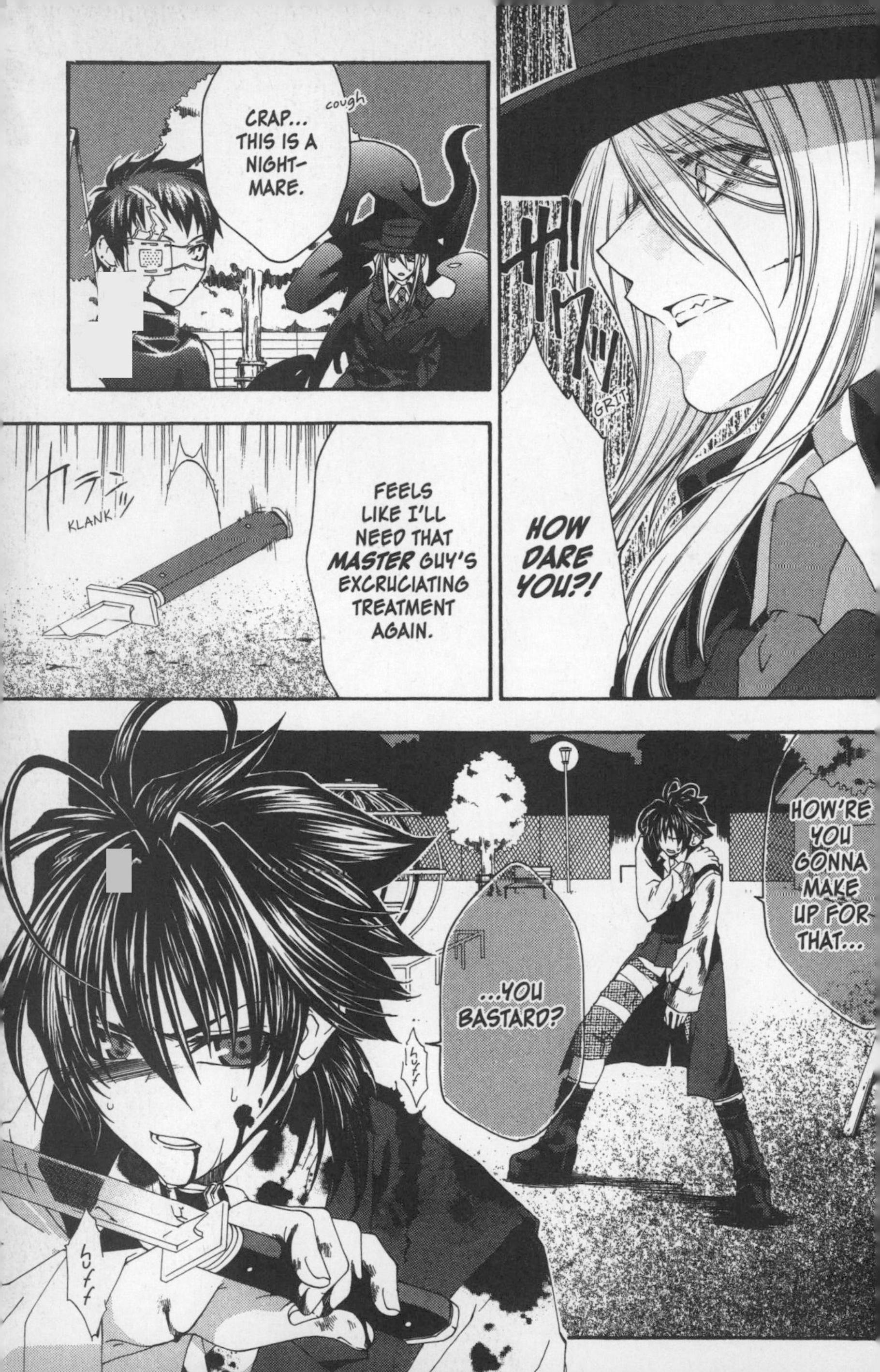
GRIT
HOW DARE YOU?!
cough
CRAP... THIS IS A NIGHT-MARE.
KLANK
FEELS LIKE I'LL NEED THAT MASTER GUY'S EXCRUCIATING TREATMENT AGAIN.
HOW'RE YOU GONNA MAKE UP FOR THAT...
...YOU BASTARD?

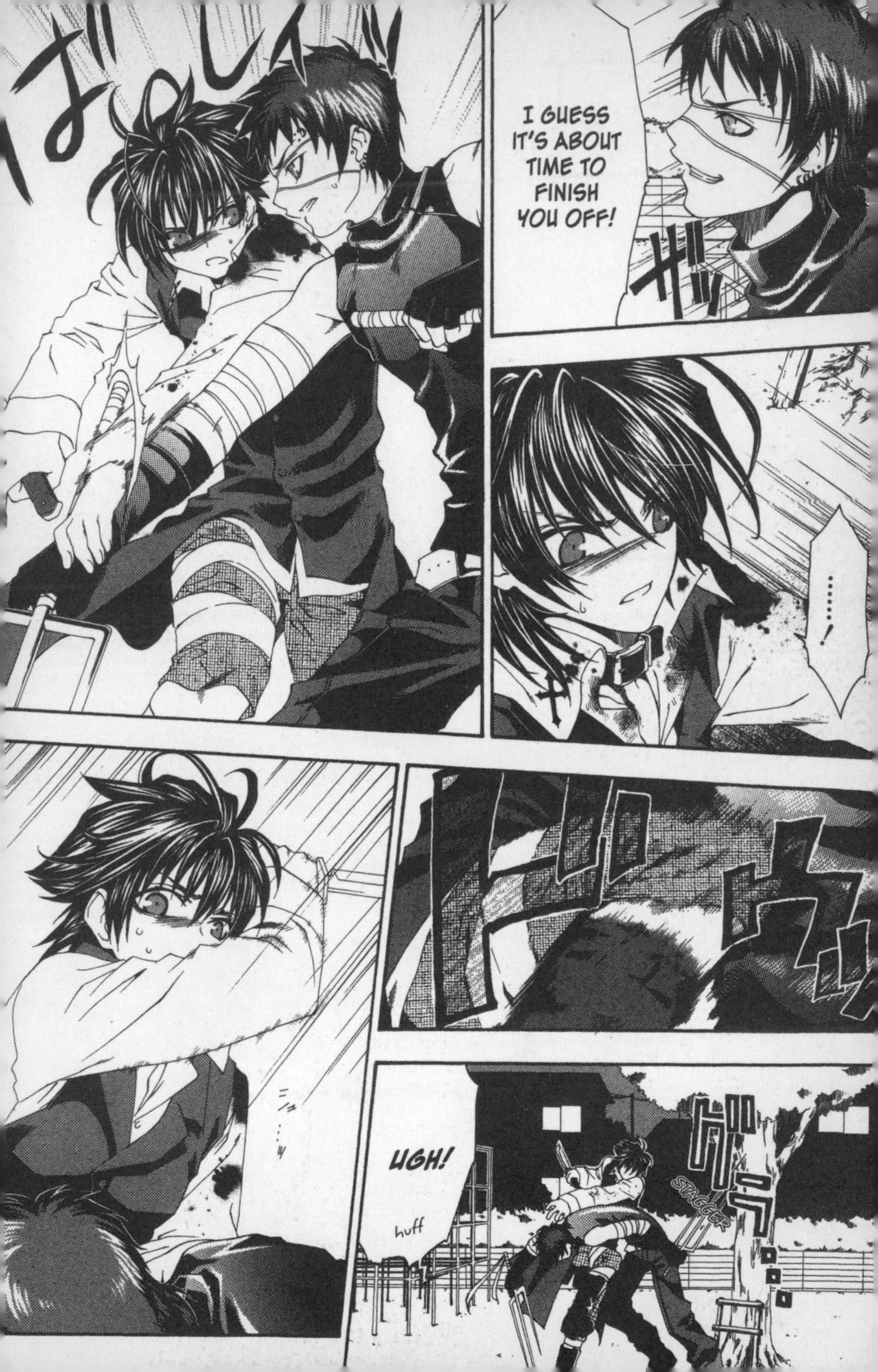
I GUESS IT'S ABOUT TIME TO FINISH YOU OFF!
......!
UGH!
huff
STAGGER

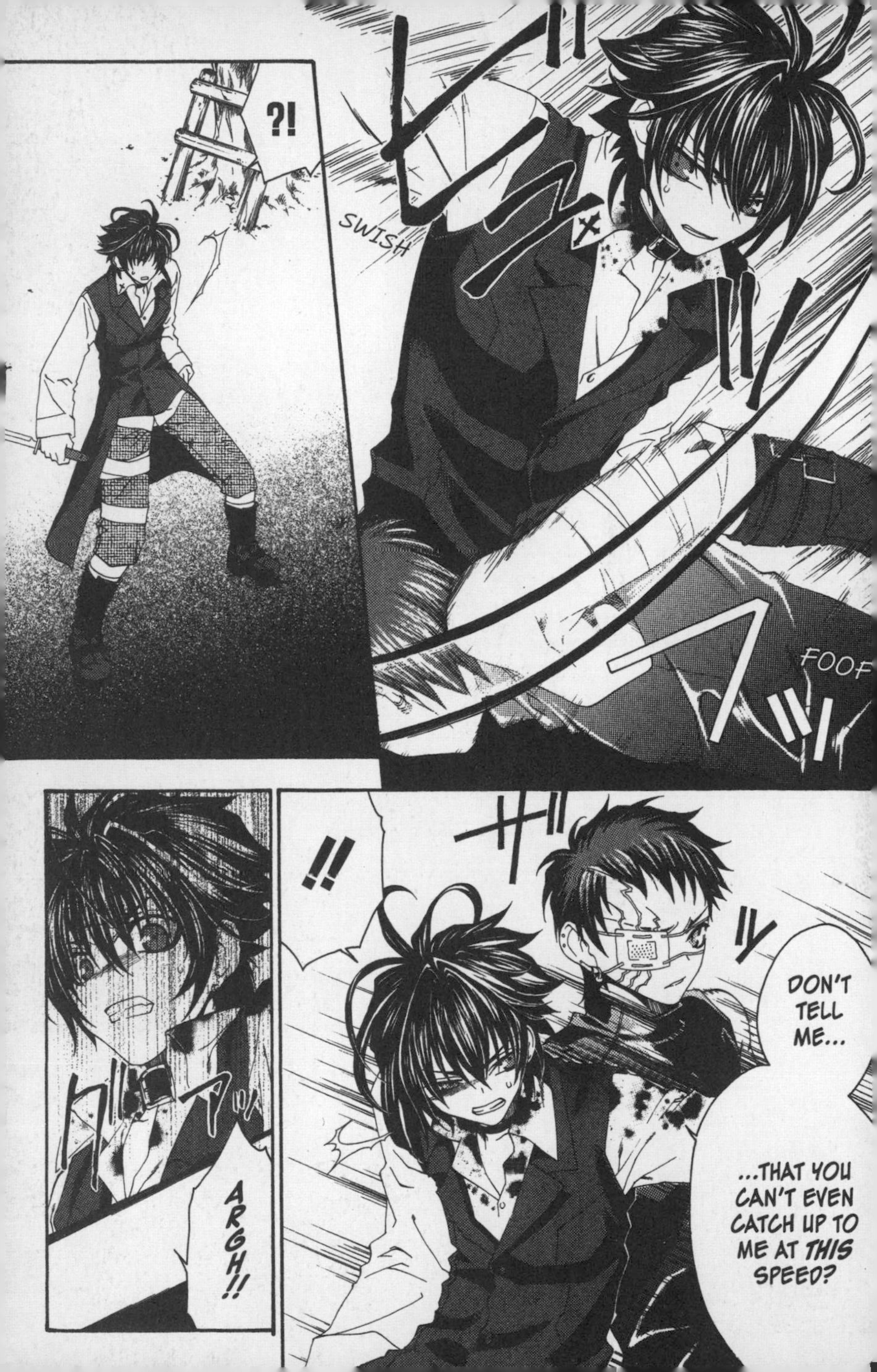
SWISH
FOOF
?!
!!
DON'T TELL ME...
...THAT YOU CAN'T EVEN CATCH UP TO ME AT *THIS* SPEED?
ARGH!!

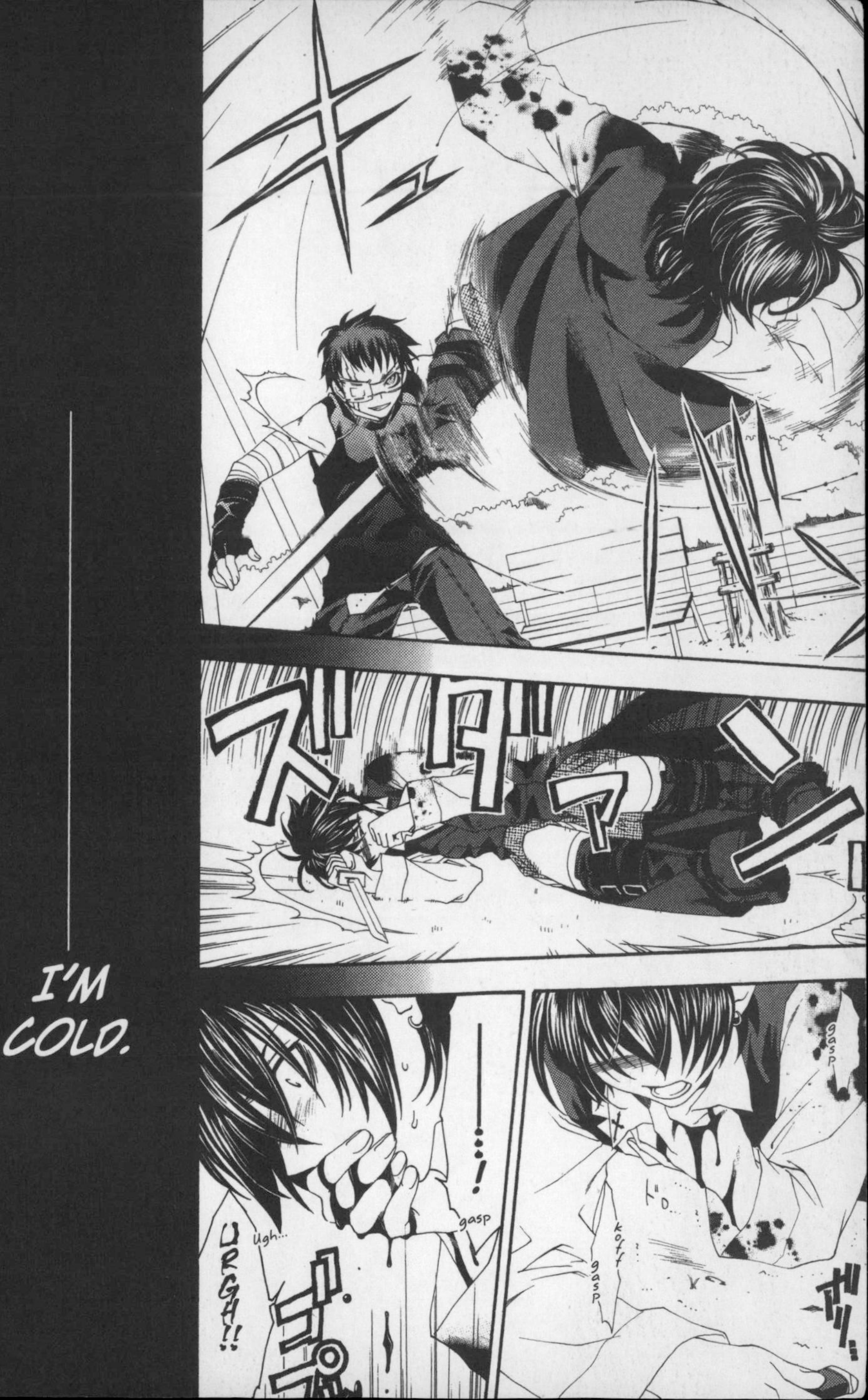
gasp
koff
gasp
...!
gasp
Ugh...
URGH!!
I'M COLD.

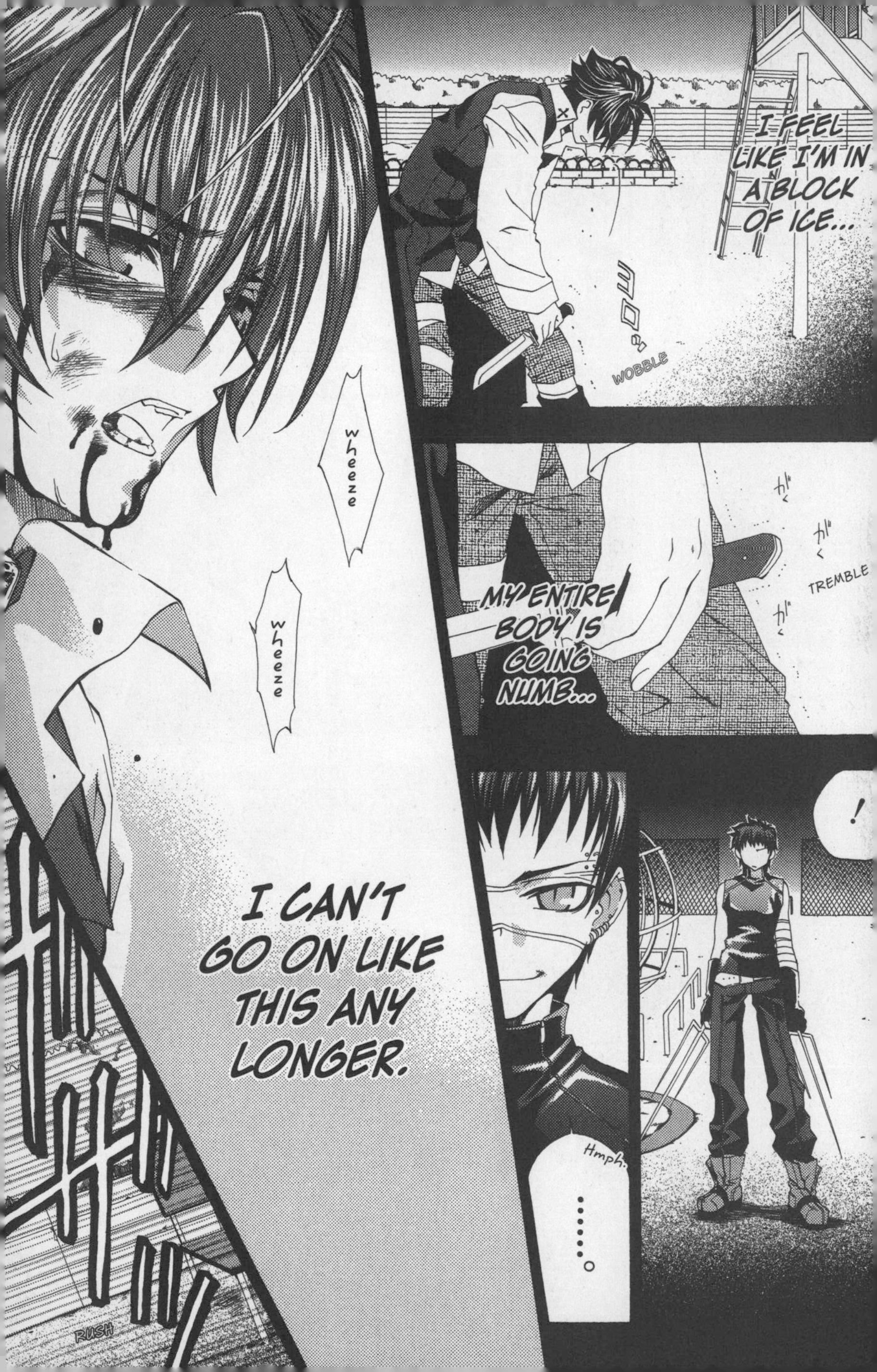

I FEEL LIKE I'M IN A BLOCK OF ICE...
ヨロッ
WOBBLE
ガくガくガく
TREMBLE
MY ENTIRE BODY IS GOING NUMB...
!
Hmph.
......。
wheeze
wheeze
I CAN'T GO ON LIKE THIS ANY LONGER.
RUSH

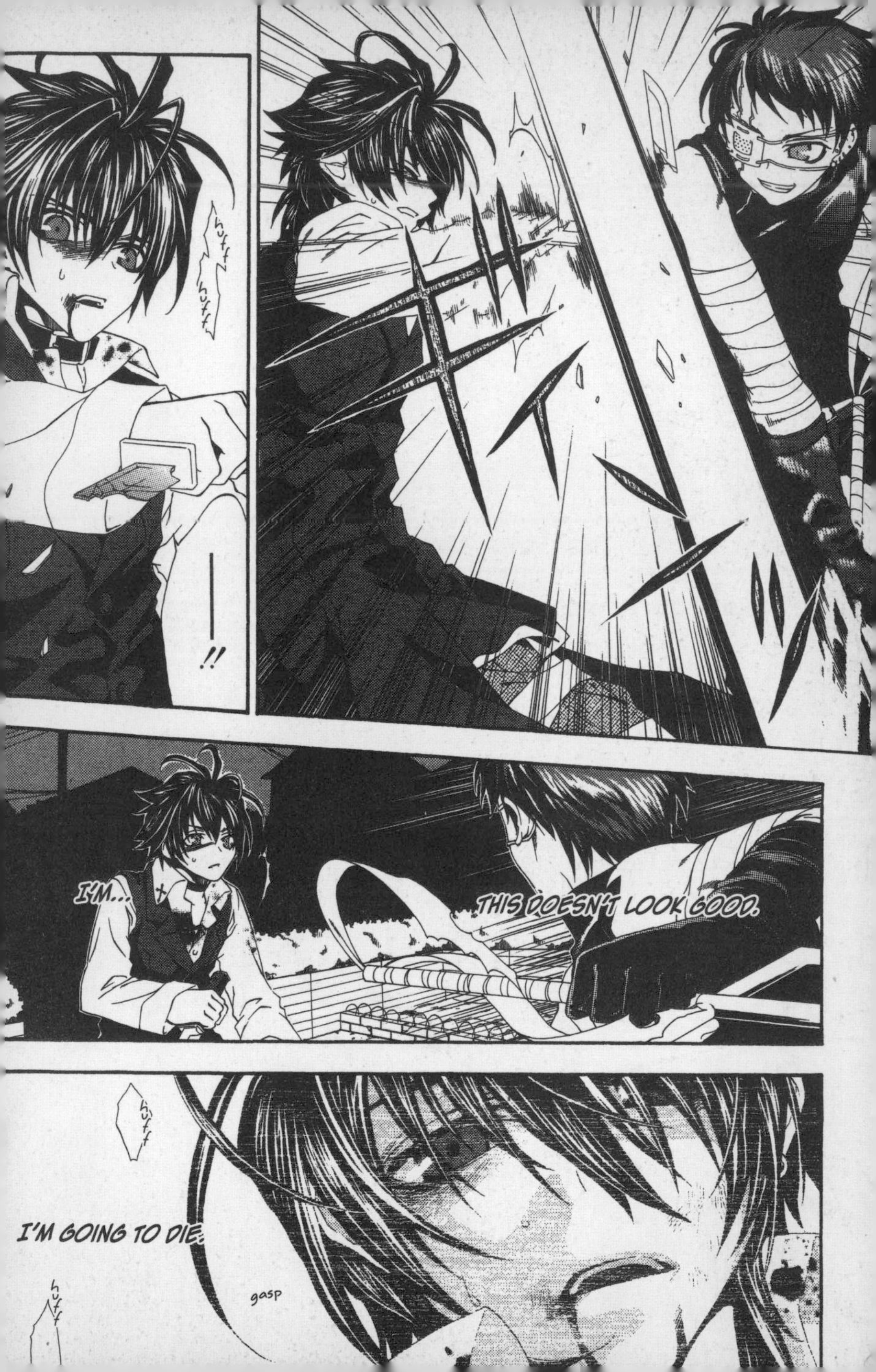

huff huff
!!
THIS DOESN'T LOOK GOOD.
I'M...
huff
I'M GOING TO DIE.
gasp
huff

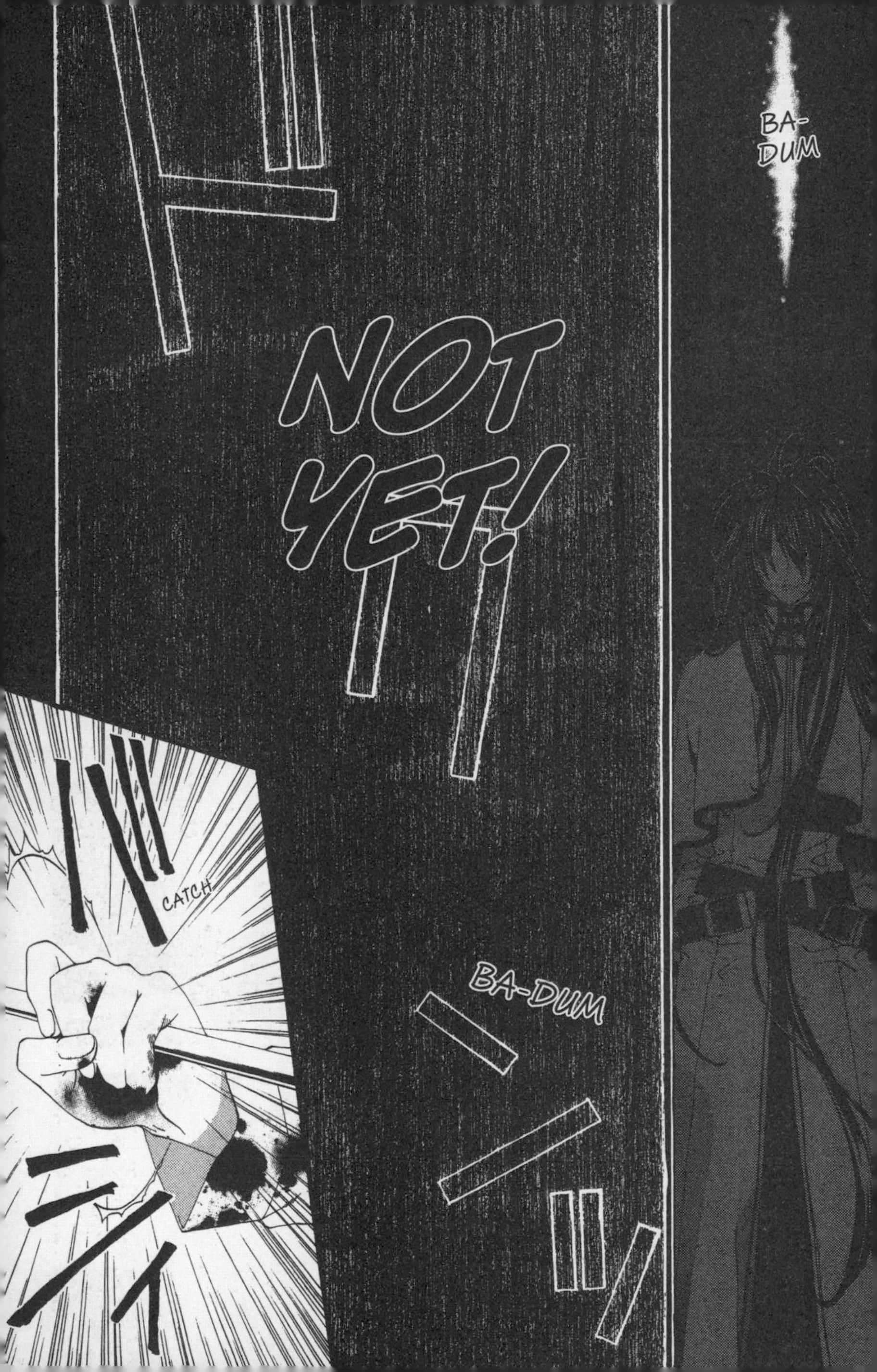
BA-DUM
NOT YET!
BA-DUM
CATCH

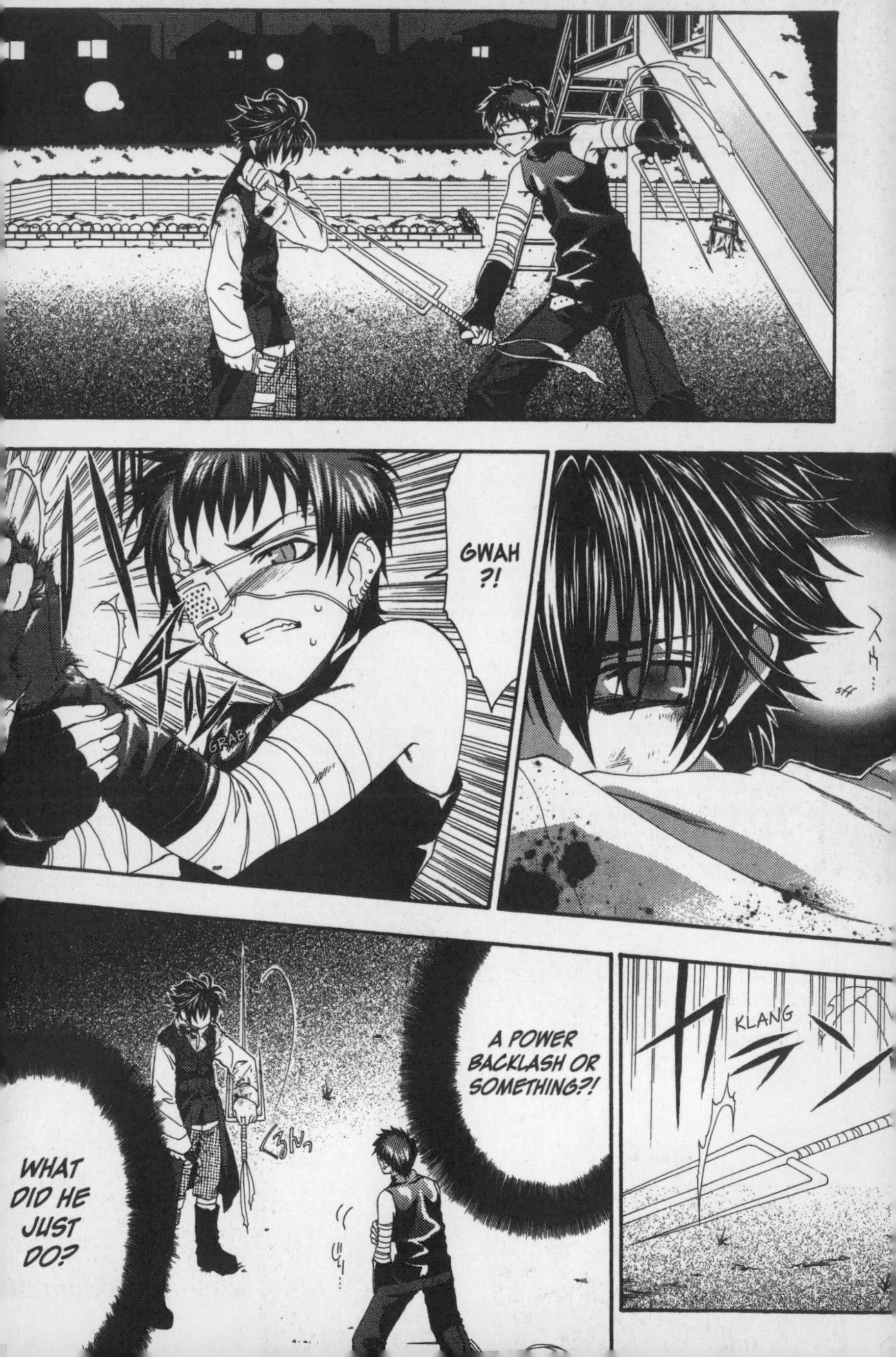
sff
GWAH ?!
GRAB
KLANG
A POWER BACKLASH OR SOMETHING?!
WHAT DID HE JUST DO?

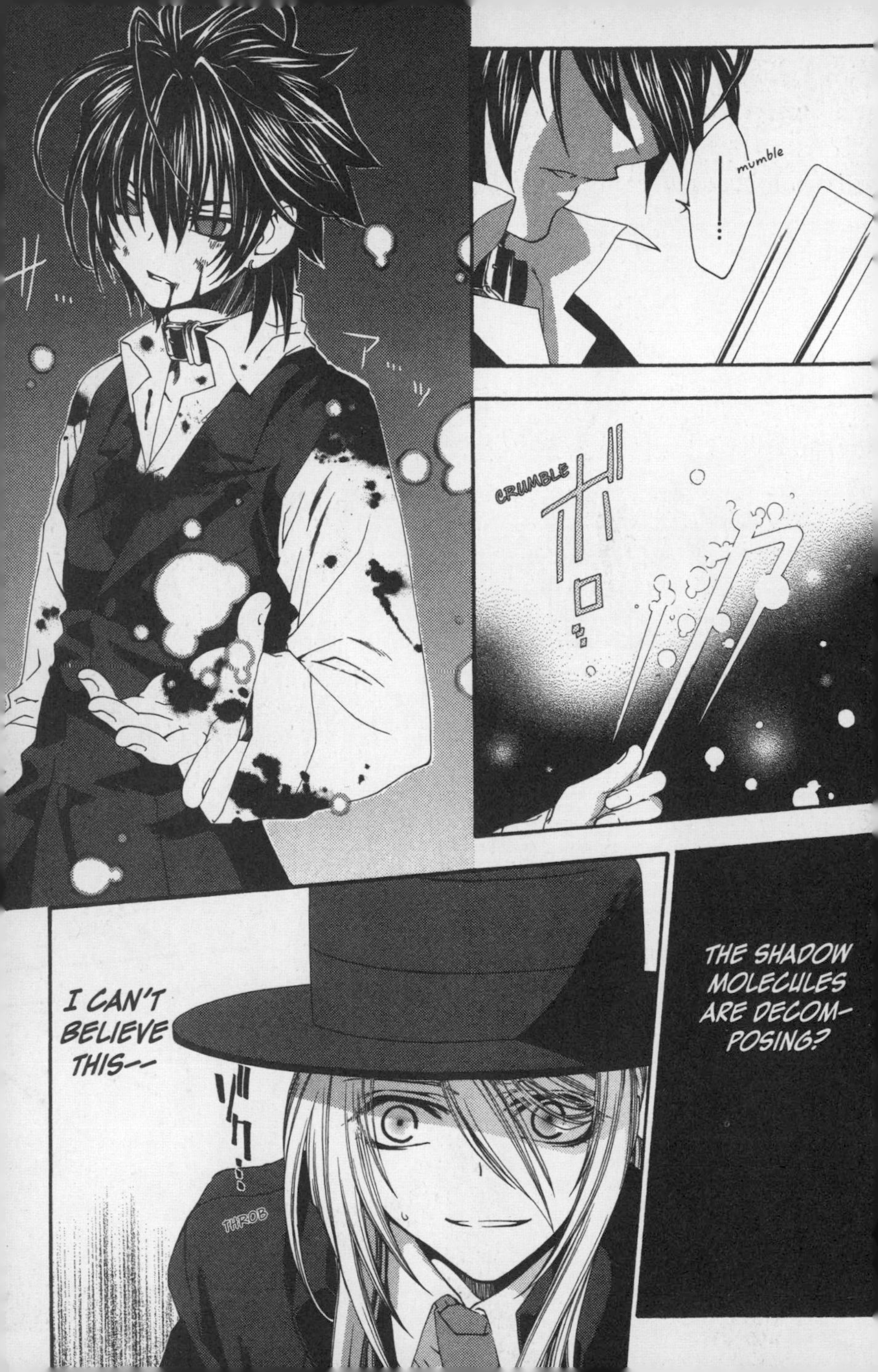
mumble
CRUMBLE
THE SHADOW MOLECULES ARE DECOMPOSING?
I CAN'T BELIEVE THIS--
THROB

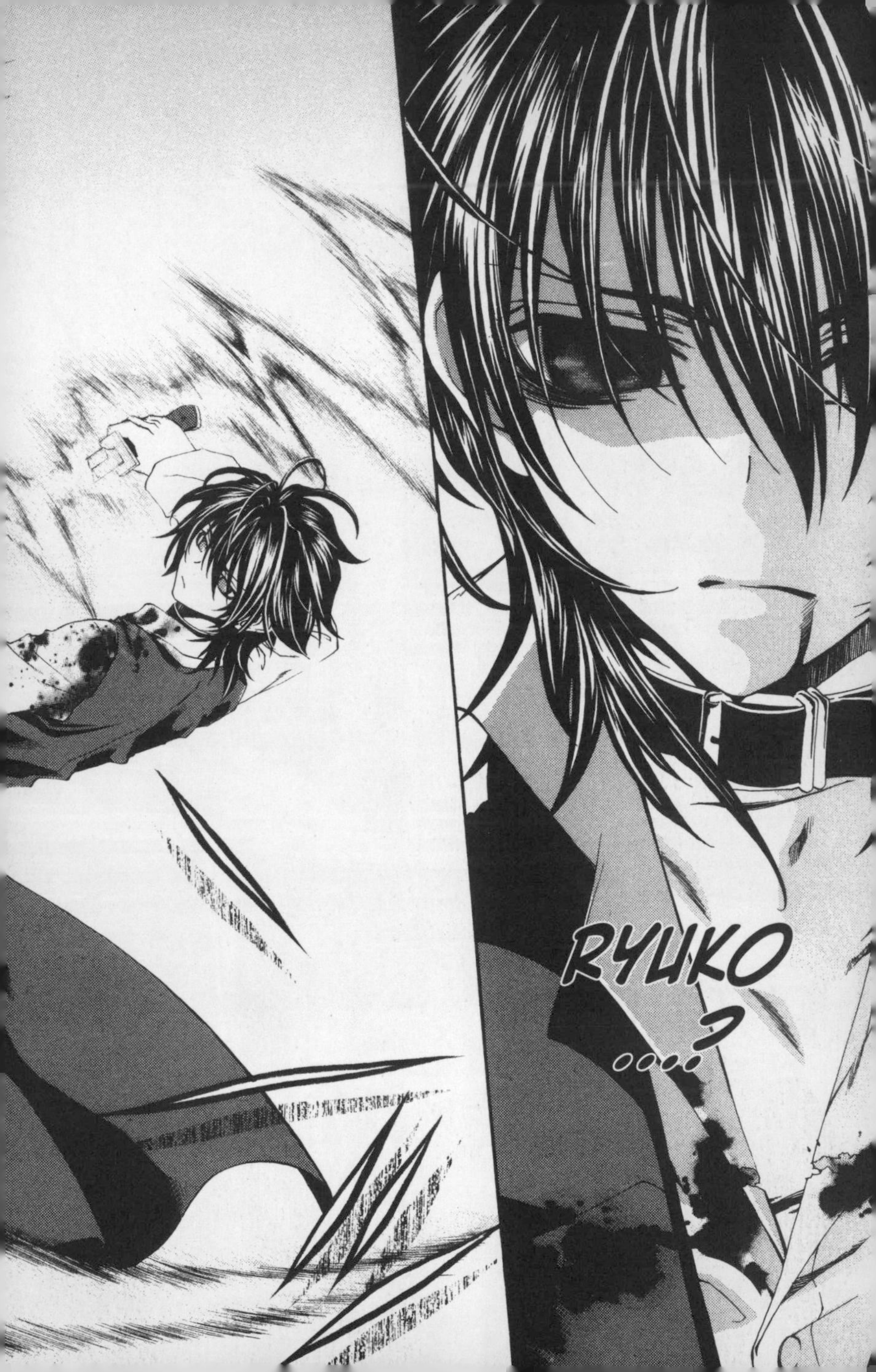
RYUKO ....?

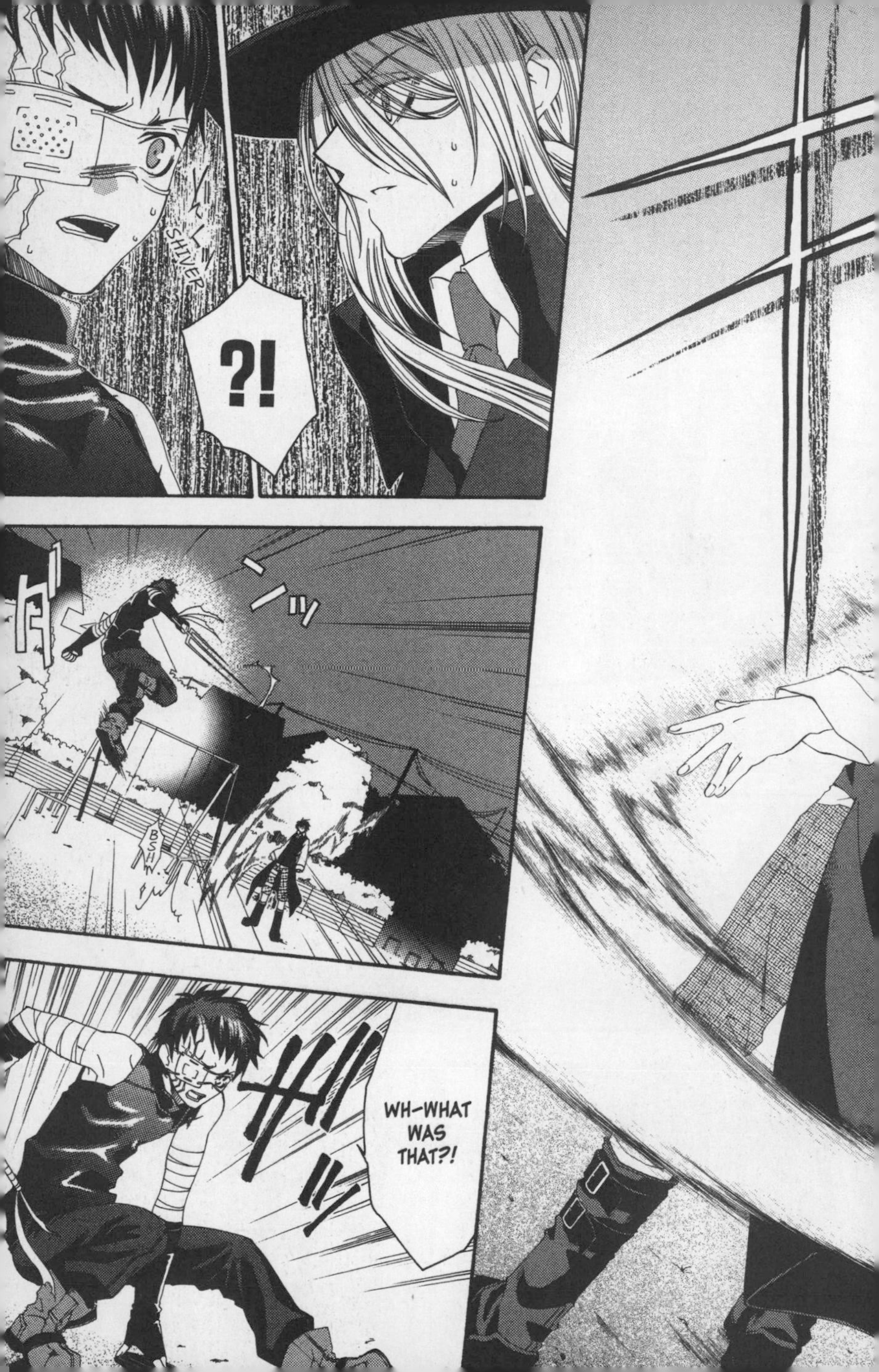
SHIVER
?!
BSH
WH-WHAT WAS THAT?!

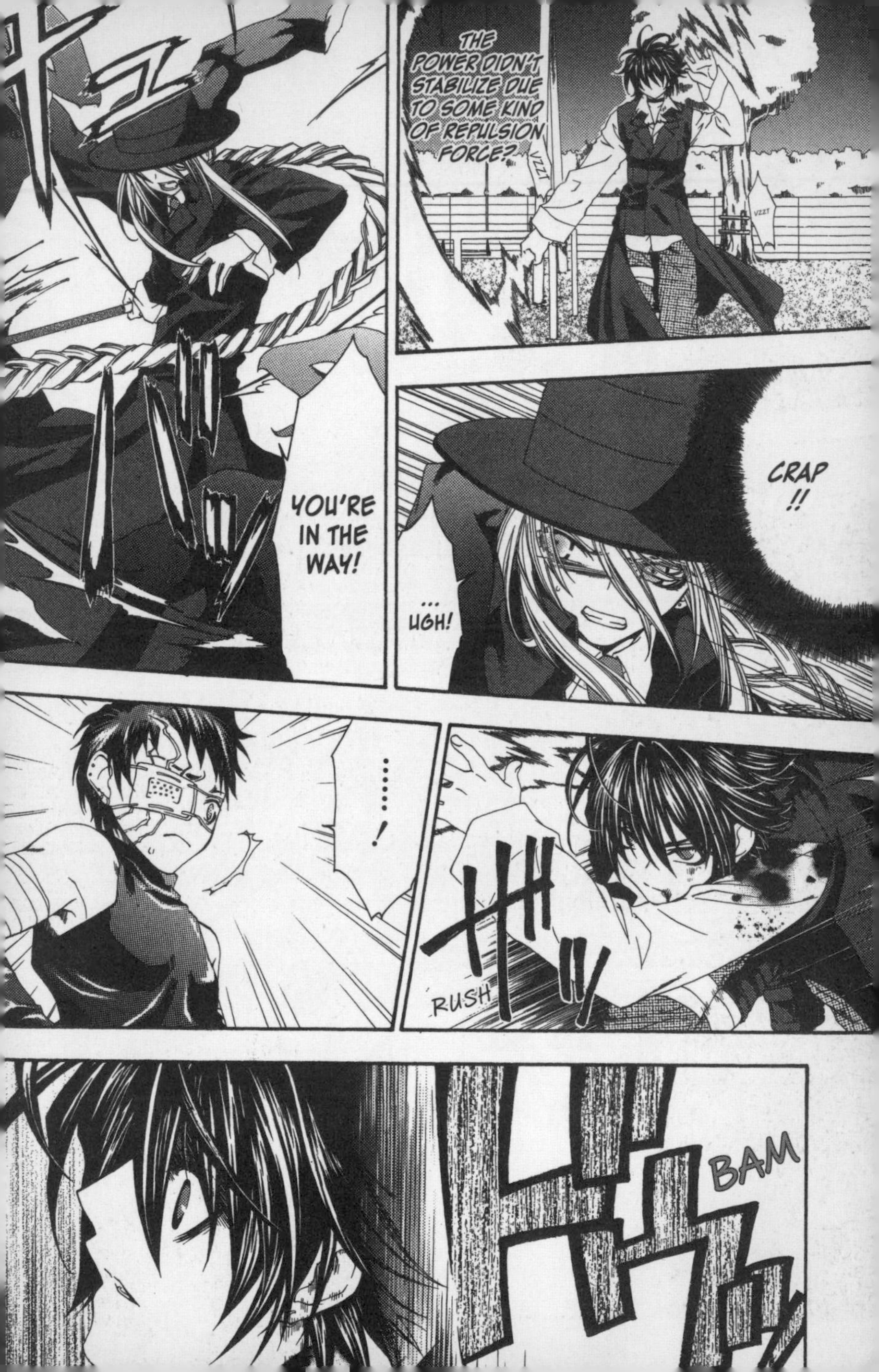
THE POWER DIDN'T STABILIZE DUE TO SOME KIND OF REPULSION FORCE?
VZZT
VZZT
YOU'RE IN THE WAY!
CRAP!!
...UGH!
......!
RUSH
BAM

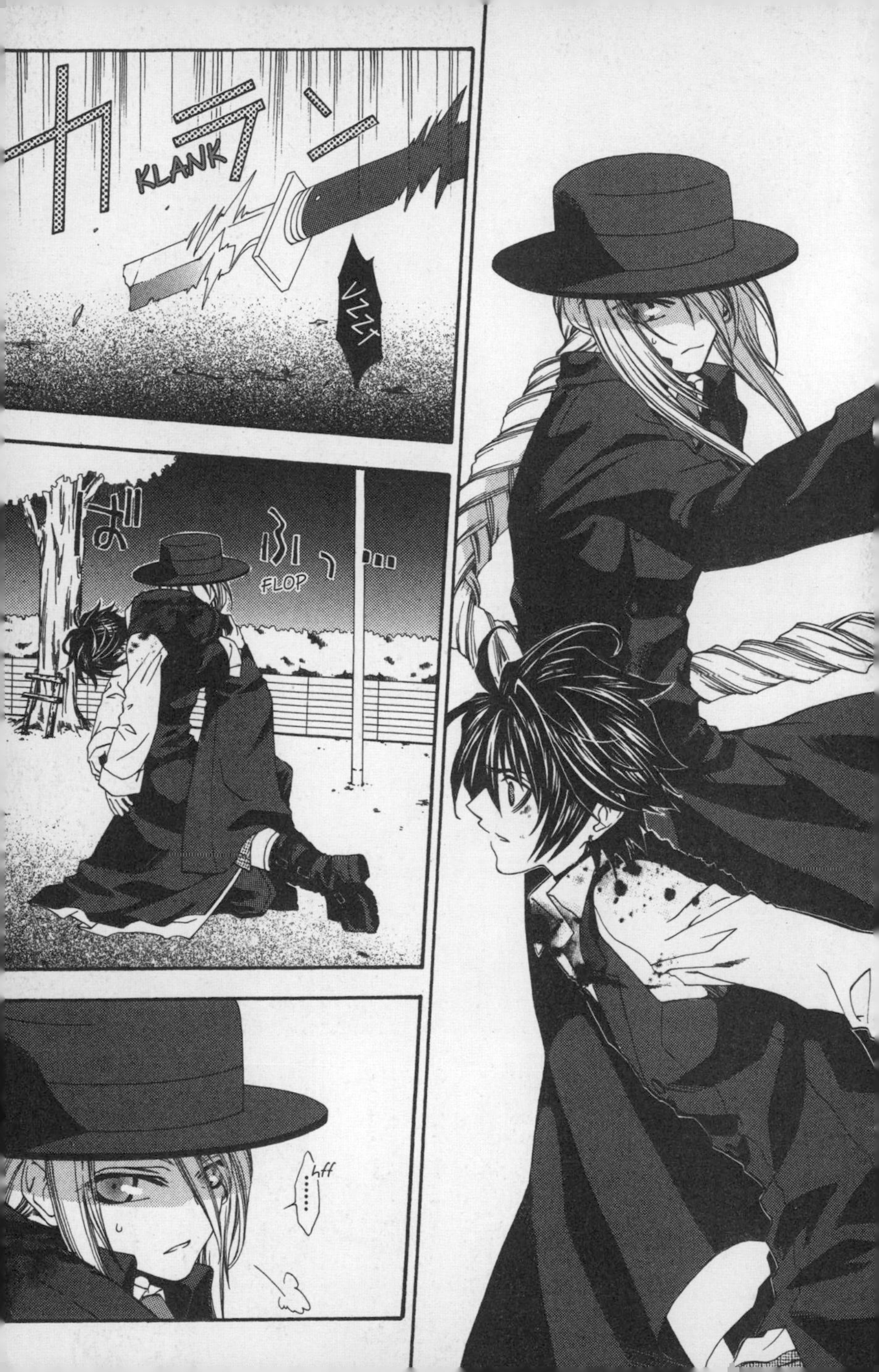

カラン
KLANK
VZZT
ばふっ…
FLOP
hff
……

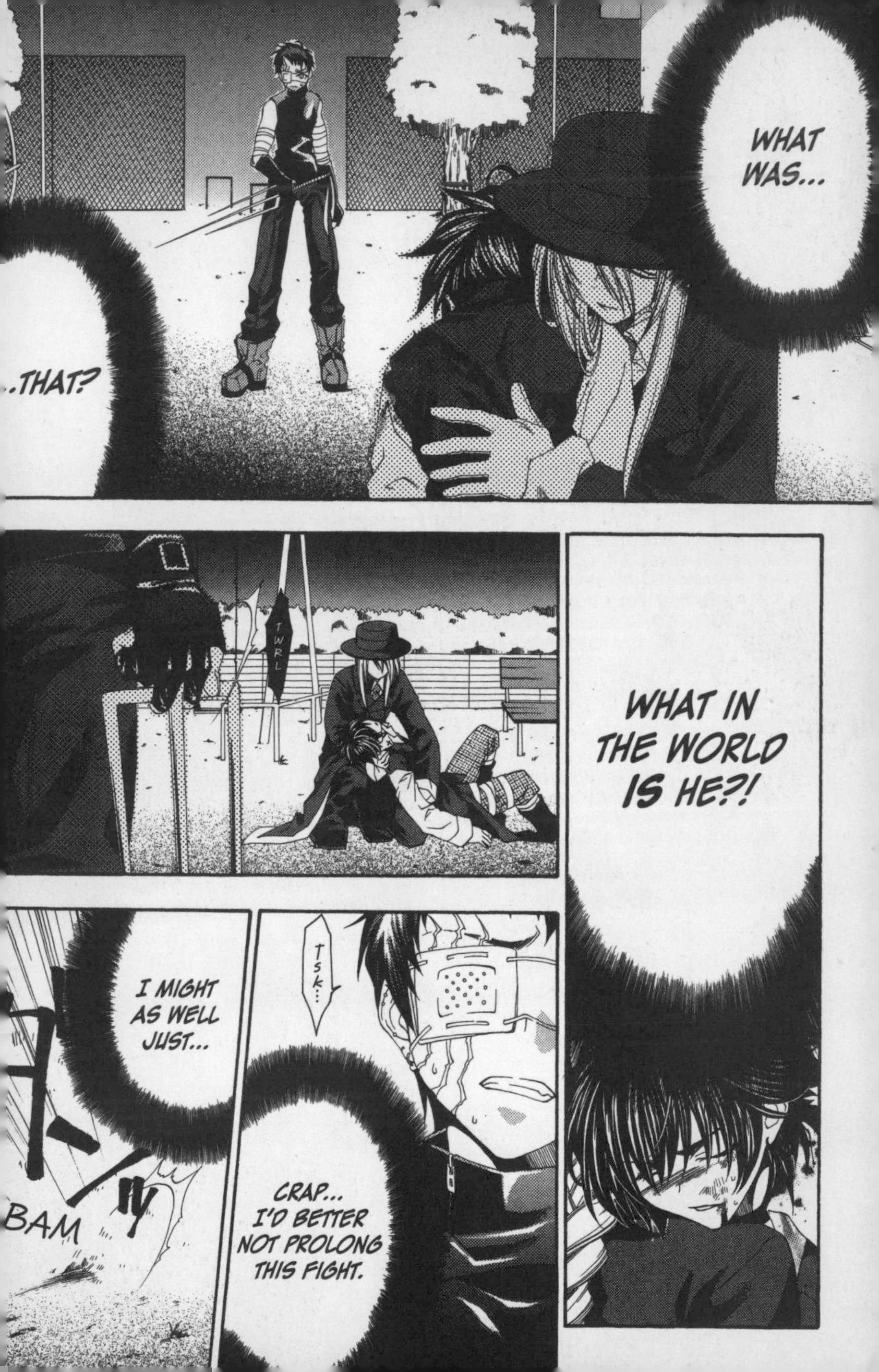
WHAT WAS...
..THAT?
WHAT IN THE WORLD IS HE?!
TWRL
TSK...
I MIGHT AS WELL JUST...
CRAP... I'D BETTER NOT PROLONG THIS FIGHT.
BAM

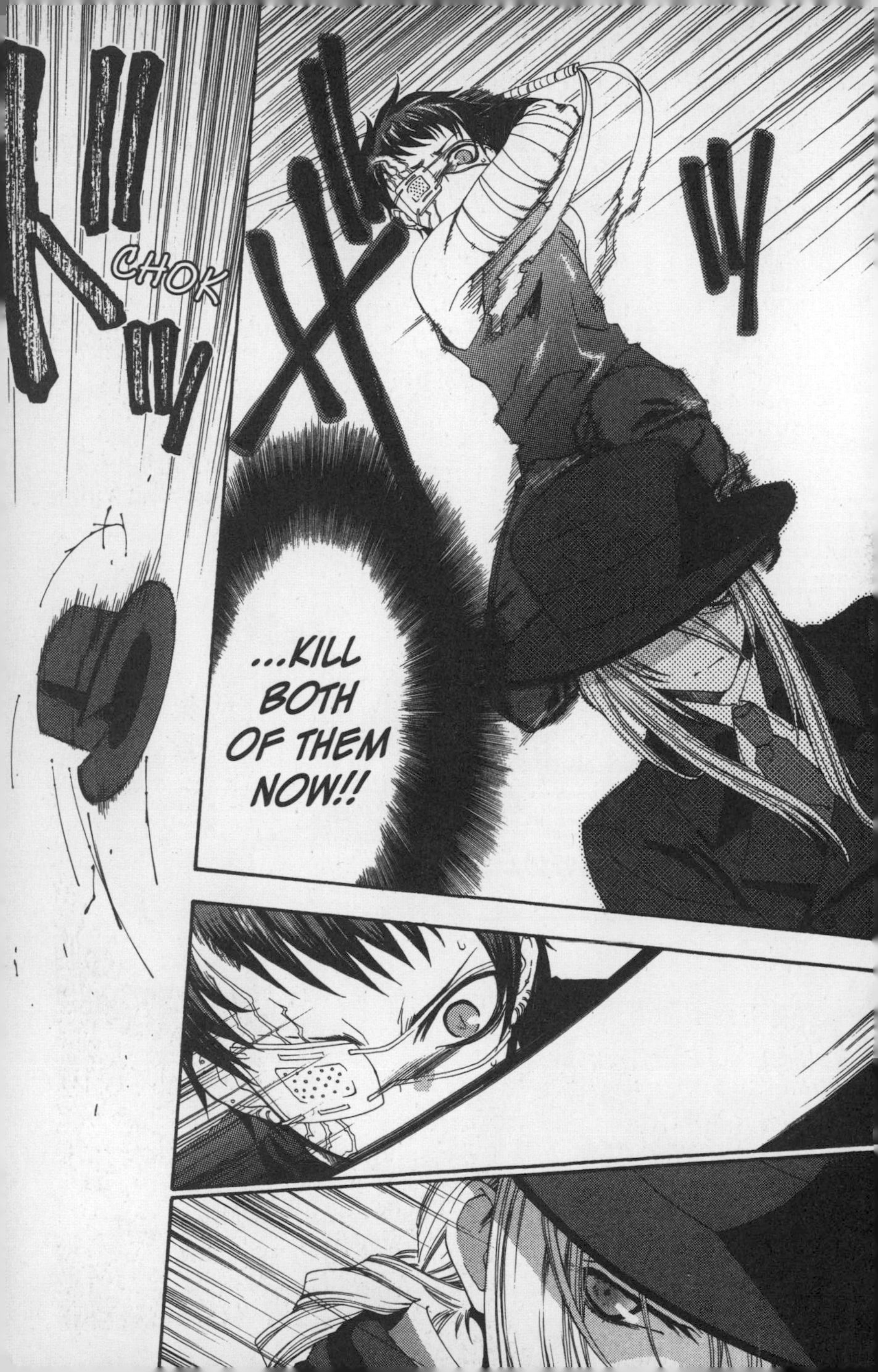
CHOK
...KILL BOTH OF THEM NOW!!

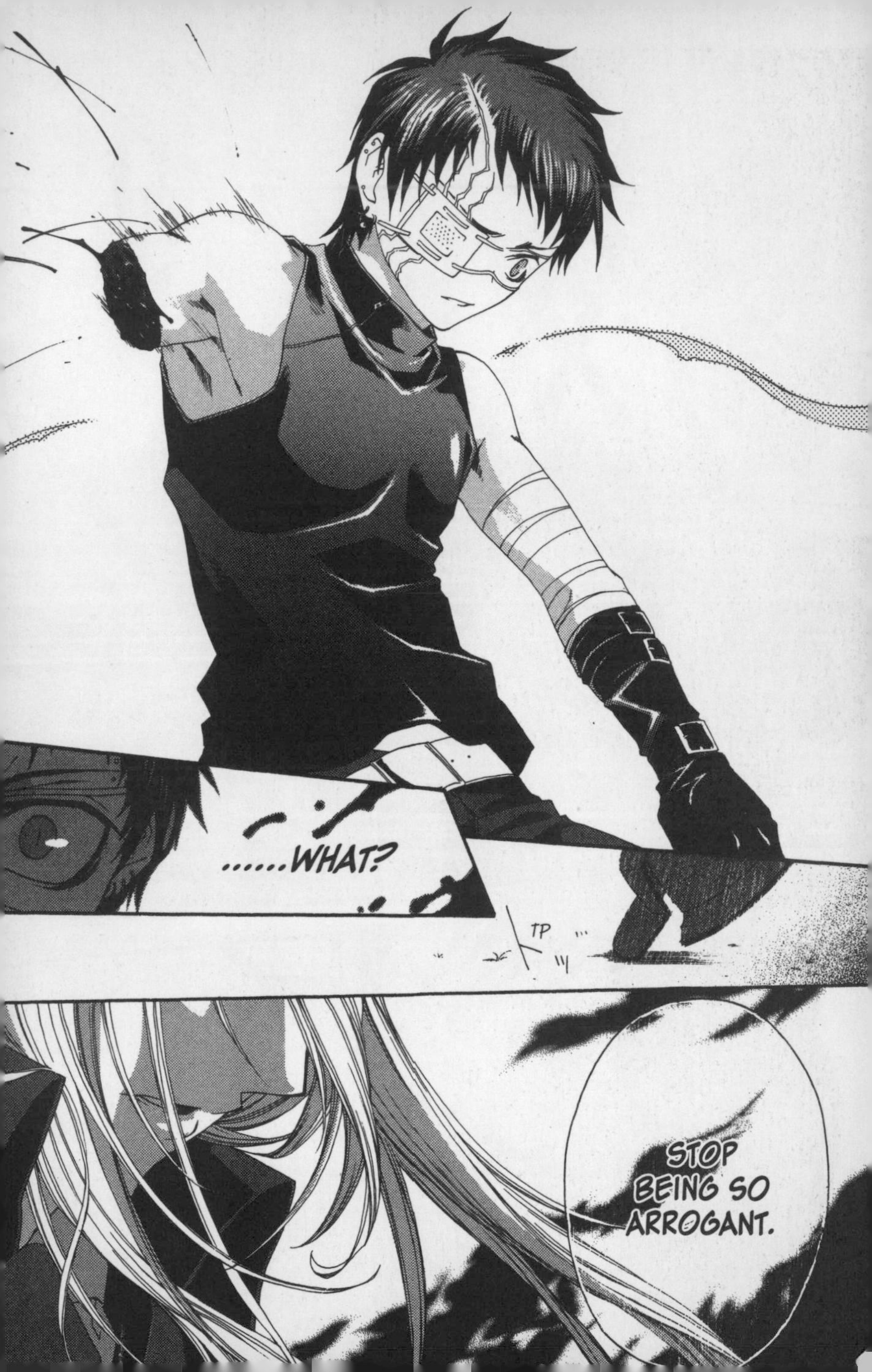

......WHAT?
TP
STOP BEING SO ARROGANT.

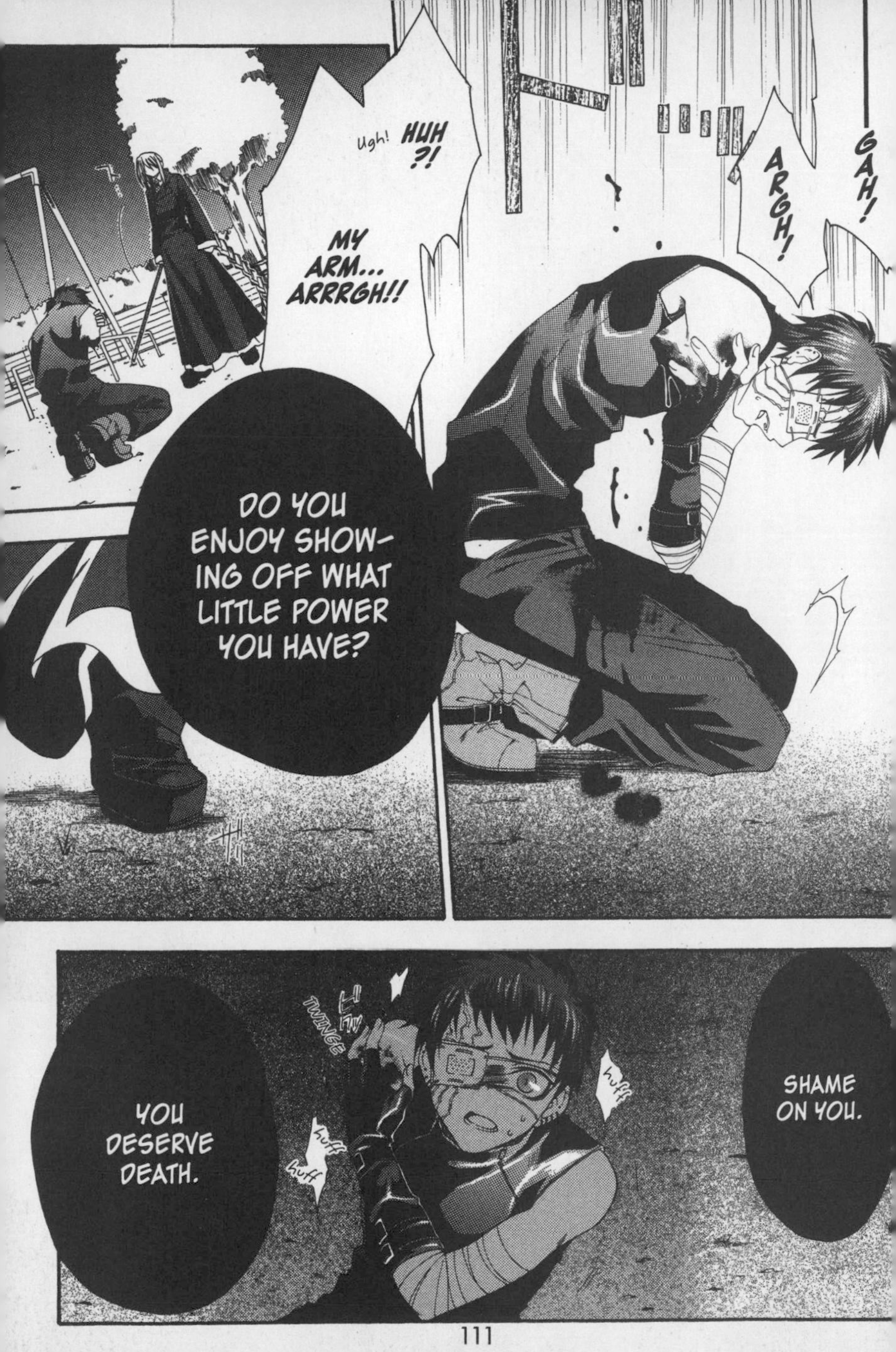
GAH!
ARGH!
HUH?!
Ugh!
MY ARM... ARRRGH!!
DO YOU ENJOY SHOWING OFF WHAT LITTLE POWER YOU HAVE?
SHAME ON YOU.
huff
TWINGE
huff
huff
YOU DESERVE DEATH.

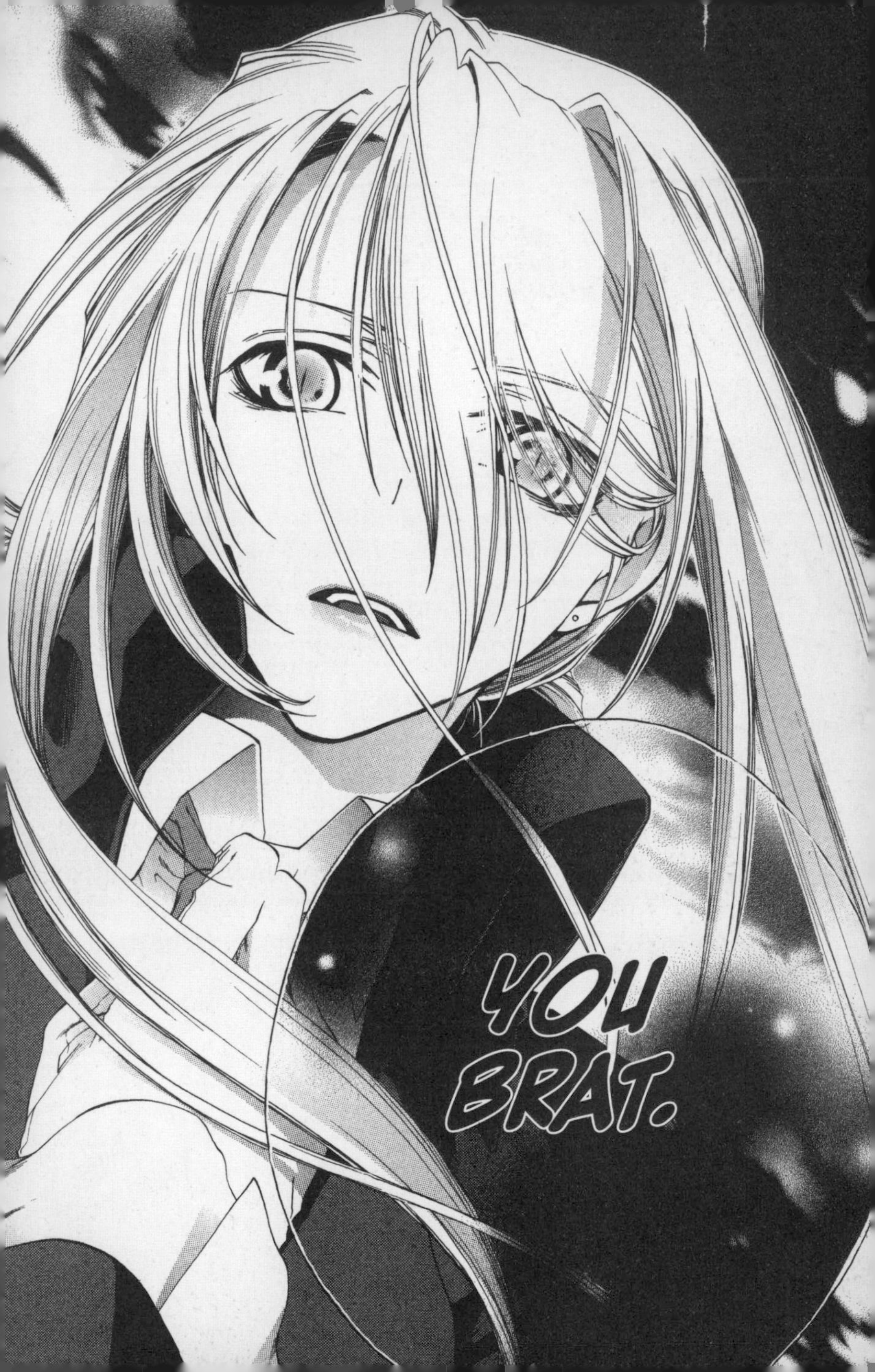
YOU
BRAT.

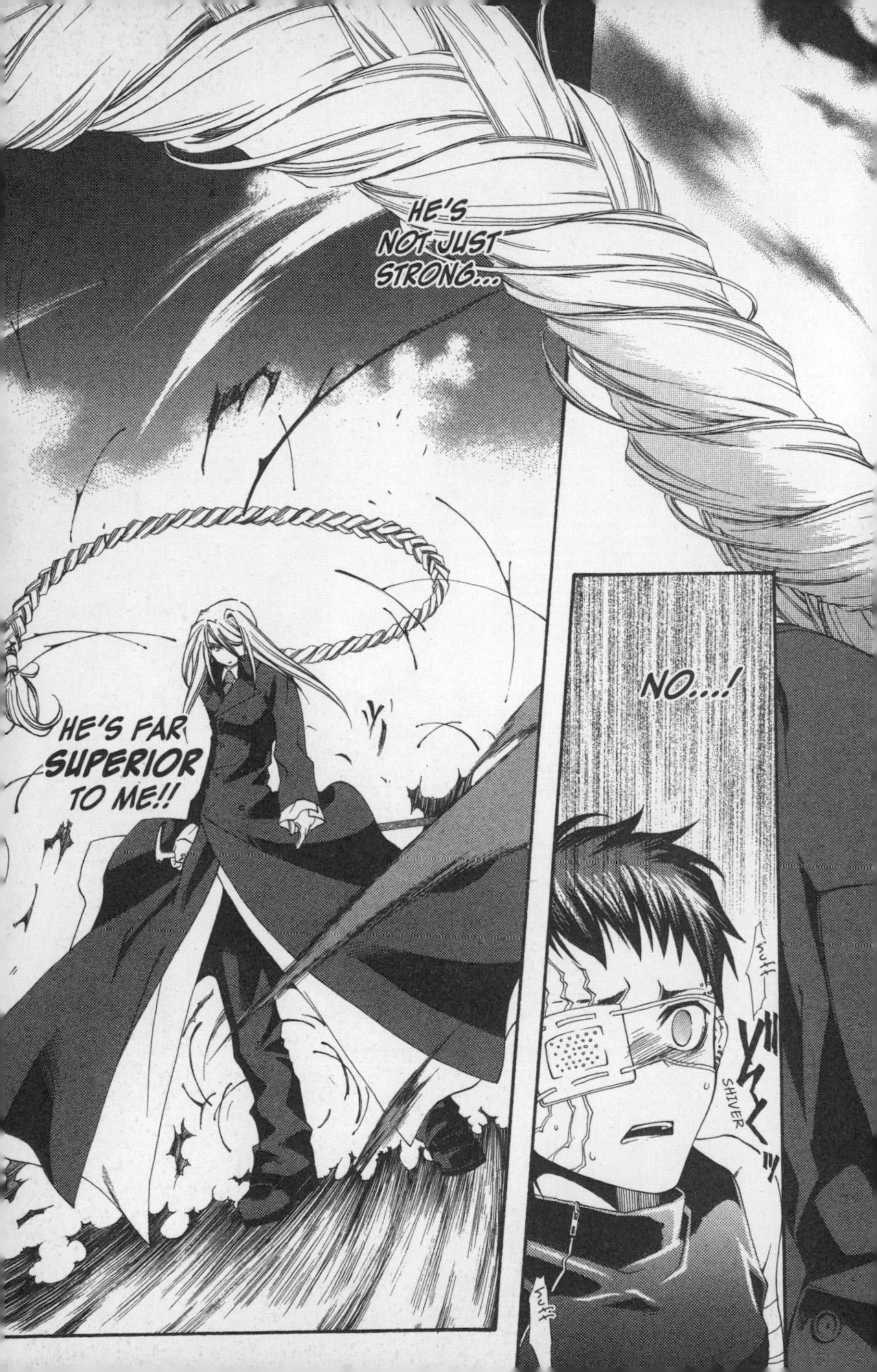
HE'S NOT JUST STRONG...
NO...!
huff
SHIVER
huff
HE'S FAR SUPERIOR TO ME!!

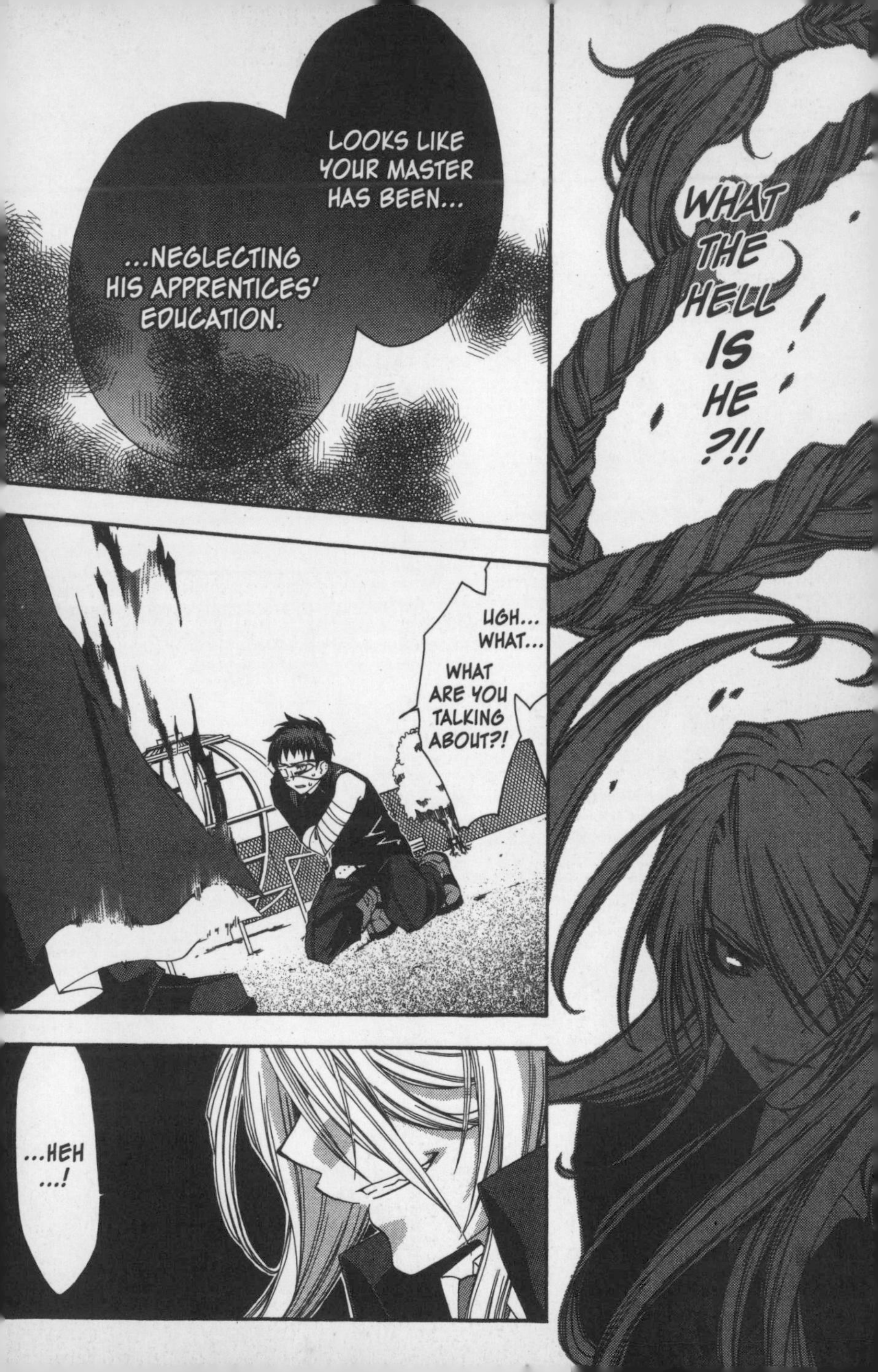
WHAT THE HELL IS HE ?!!
LOOKS LIKE YOUR MASTER HAS BEEN...
...NEGLECTING HIS APPRENTICES' EDUCATION.
UGH... WHAT...
WHAT ARE YOU TALKING ABOUT?!
...HEH ...!

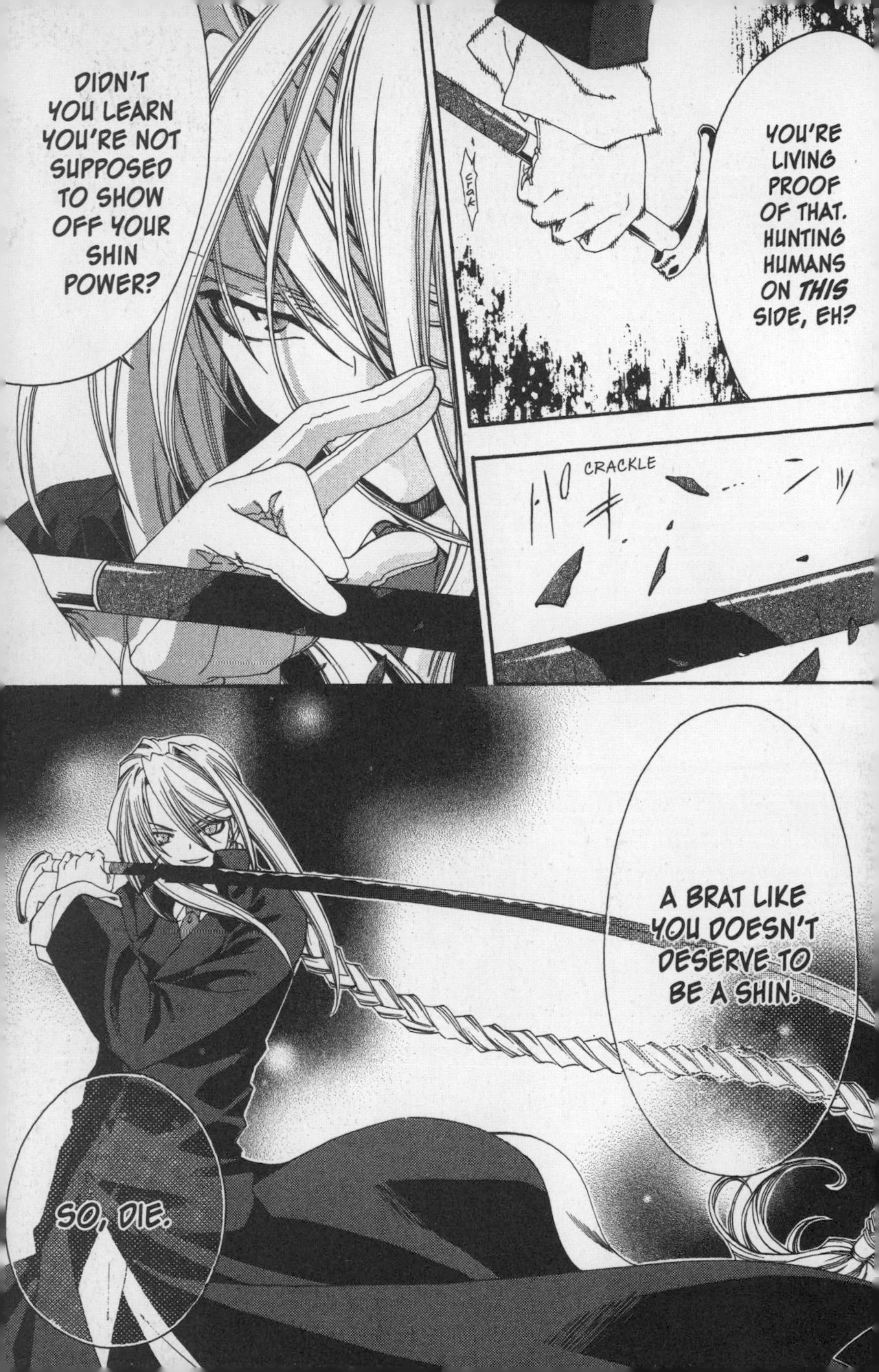
YOU'RE LIVING PROOF OF THAT. HUNTING HUMANS ON *THIS* SIDE, EH?
crak
DIDN'T YOU LEARN YOU'RE NOT SUPPOSED TO SHOW OFF YOUR SHIN POWER?
CRACKLE
A BRAT LIKE YOU DOESN'T DESERVE TO BE A SHIN.
SO, DIE.

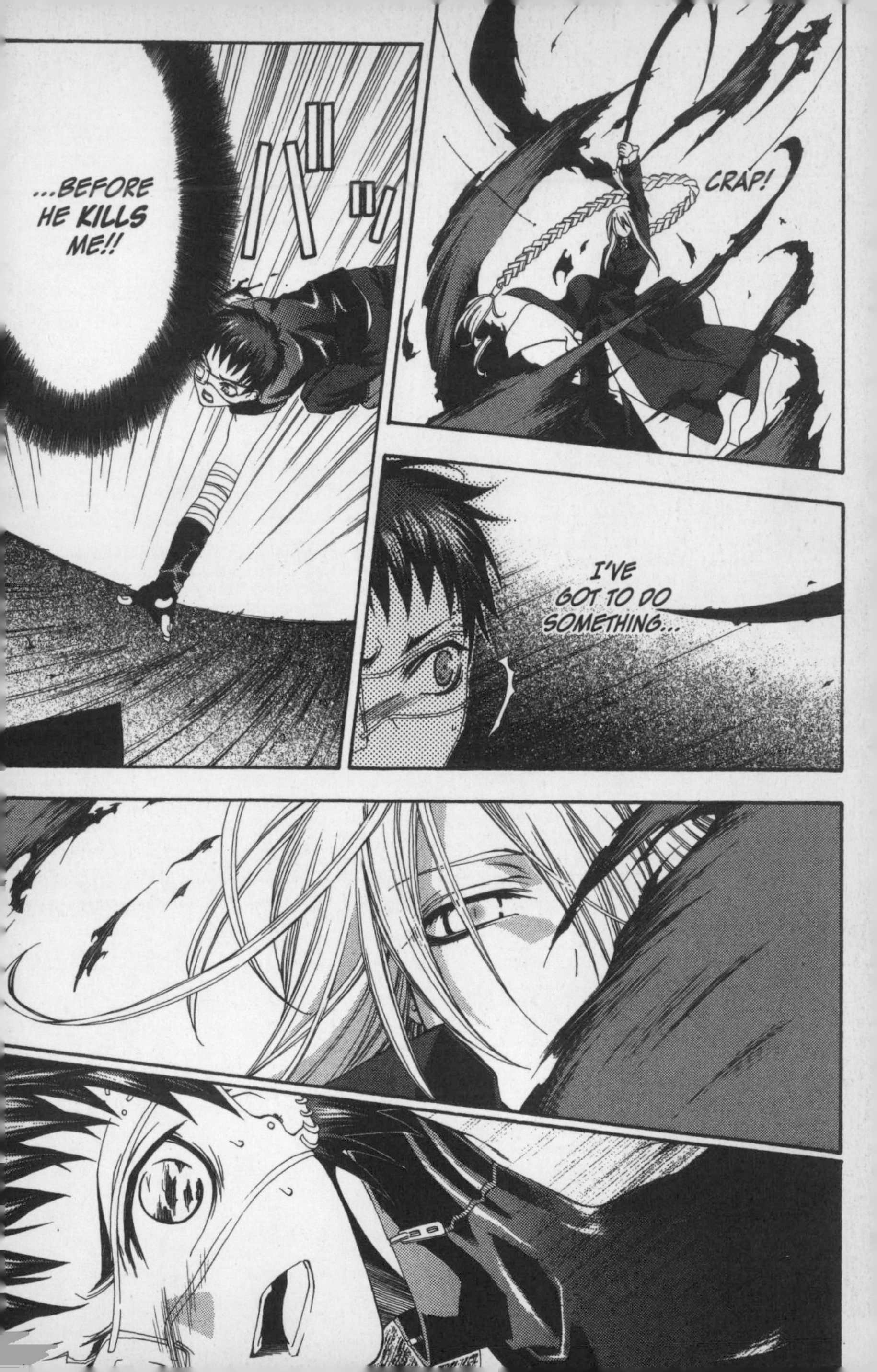
CRAP!
...BEFORE HE KILLS ME!!
I'VE GOT TO DO SOMETHING...

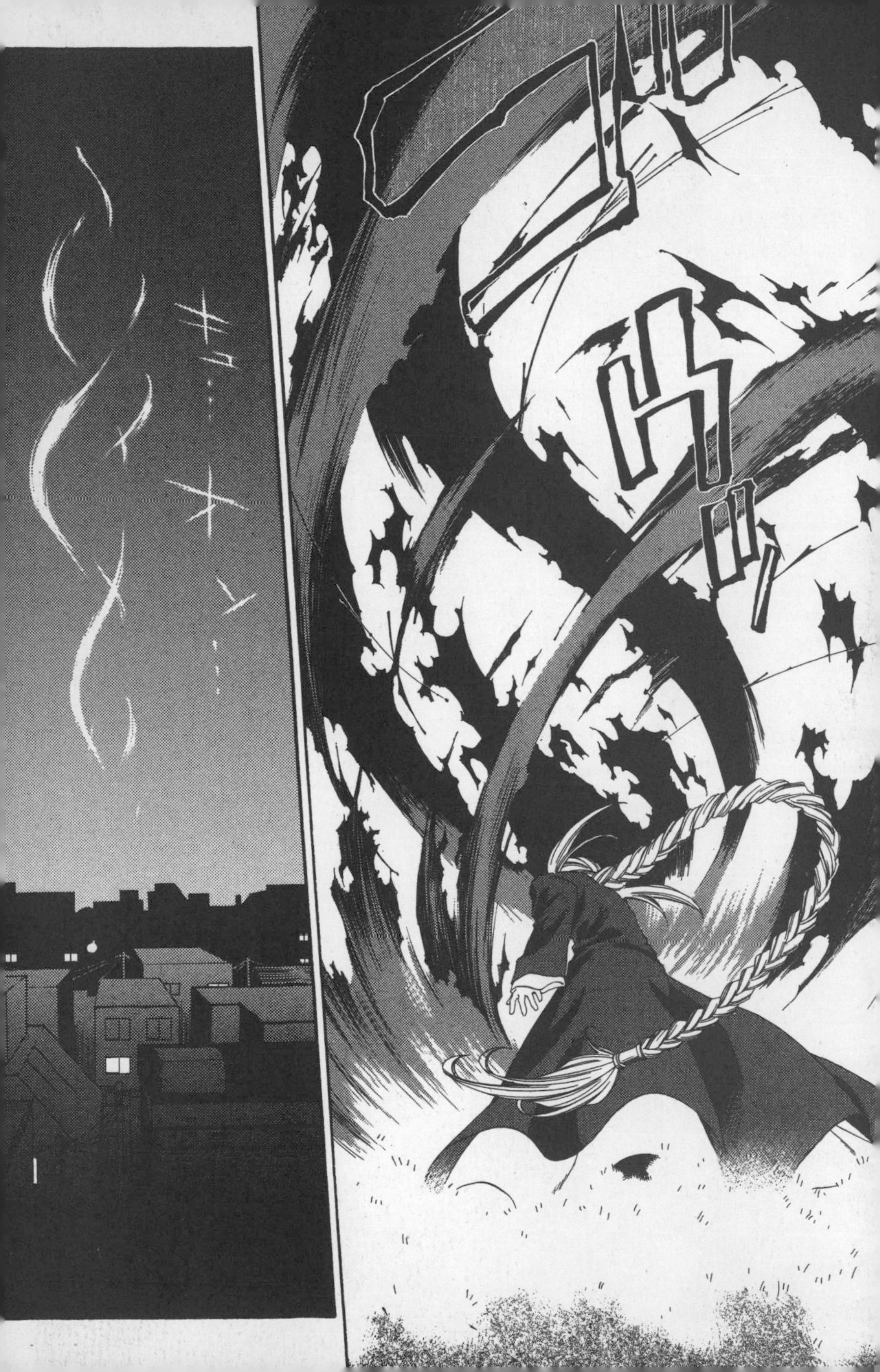
キュ…オン…

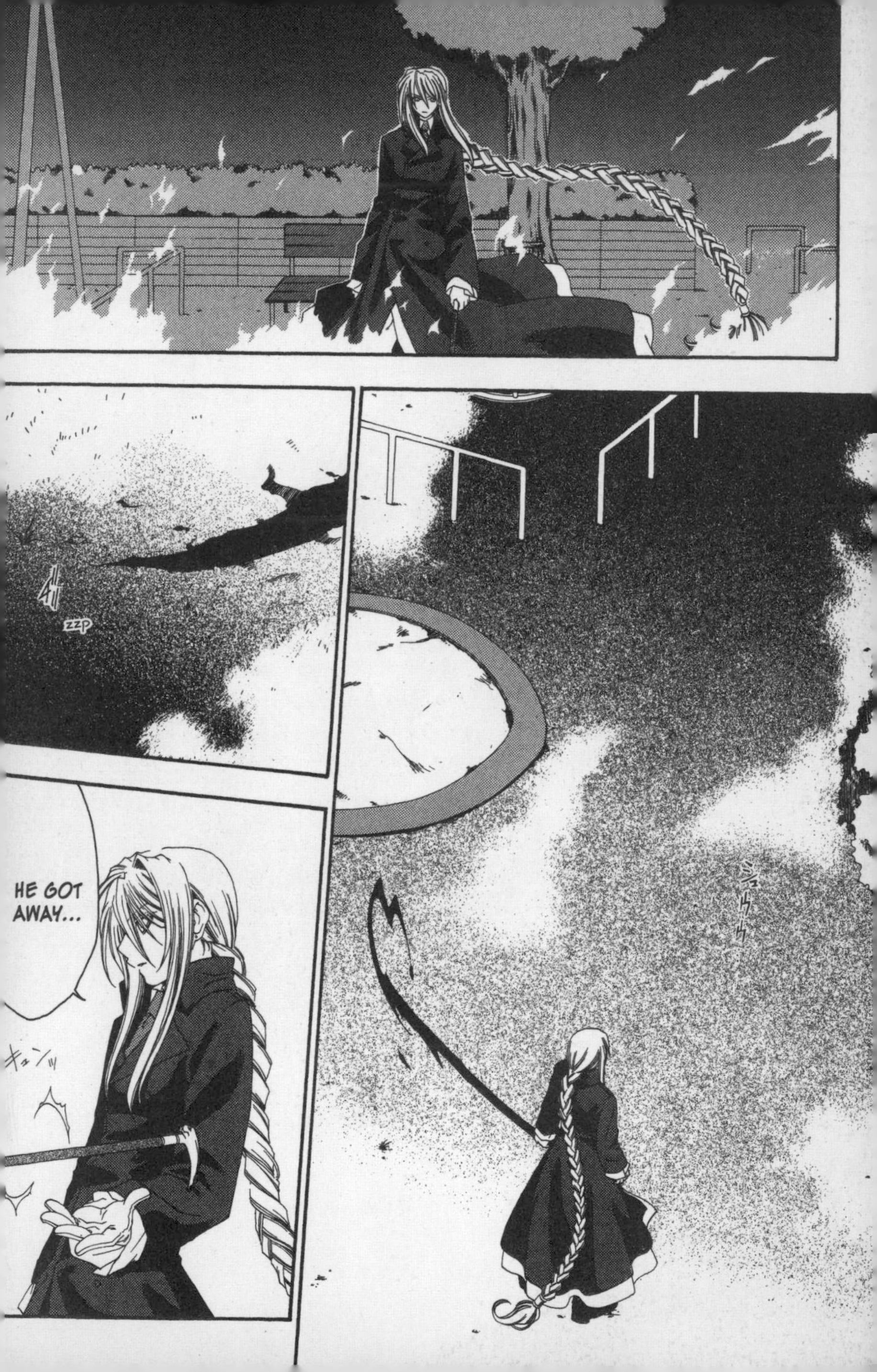
zzp
HE GOT AWAY...

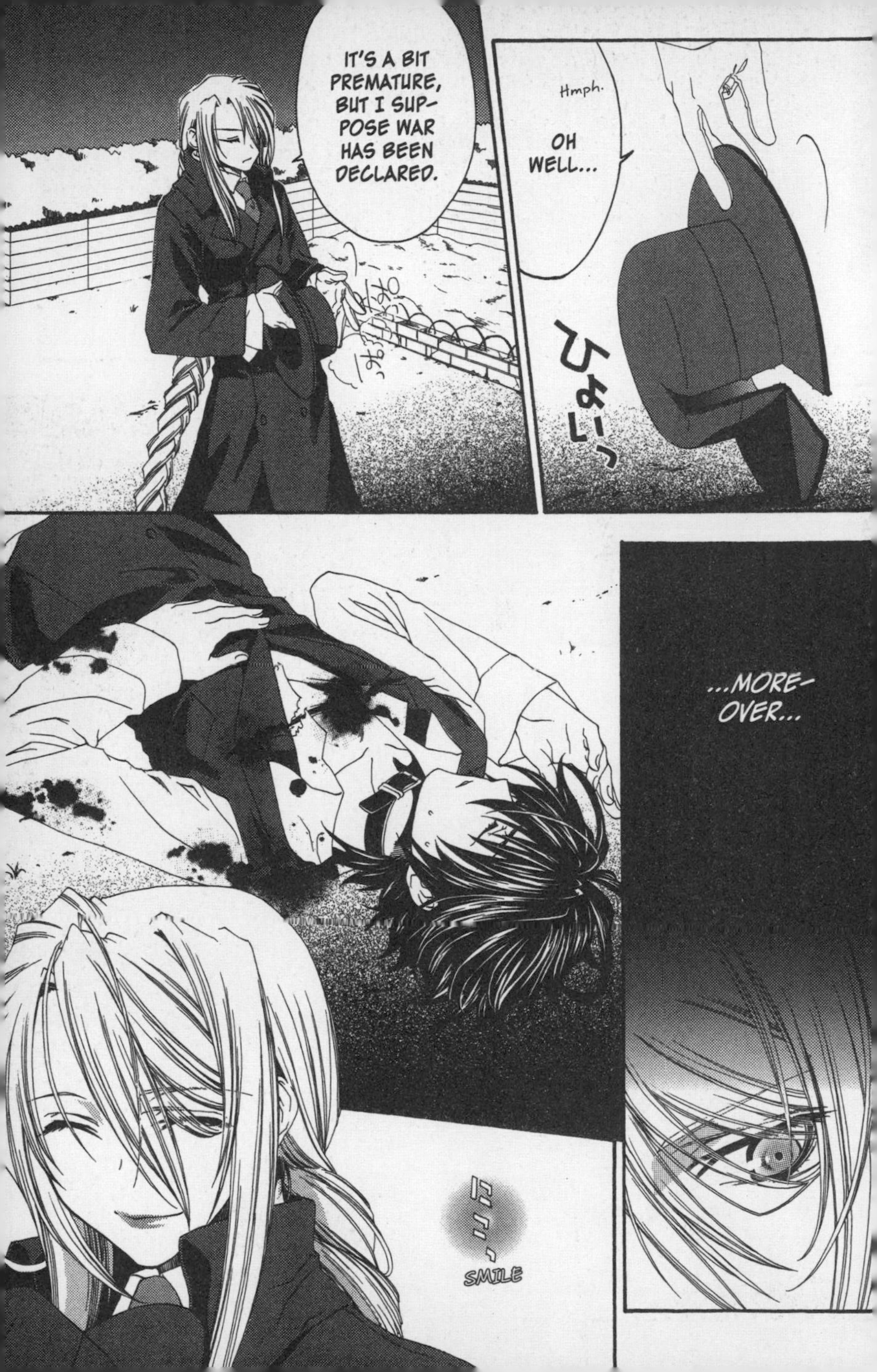
Hmph.
OH WELL...
ひょいっ
IT'S A BIT PREMATURE, BUT I SUPPOSE WAR HAS BEEN DECLARED.
...MORE-OVER...
SMILE

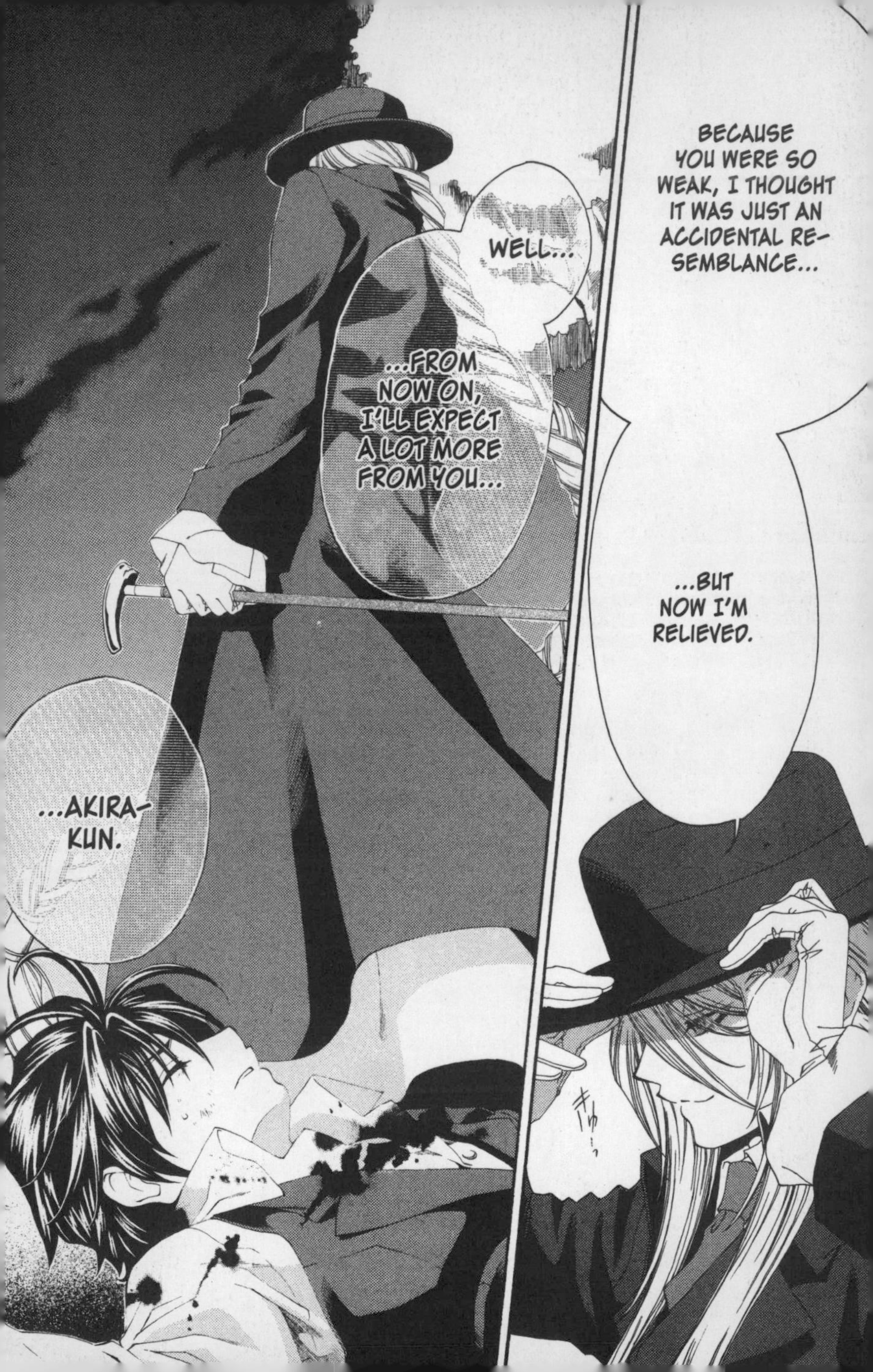
BECAUSE YOU WERE SO WEAK, I THOUGHT IT WAS JUST AN ACCIDENTAL RE-SEMBLANCE...
...BUT NOW I'M RELIEVED.
WELL...
...FROM NOW ON, I'LL EXPECT A LOT MORE FROM YOU...
...AKIRA-KUN.

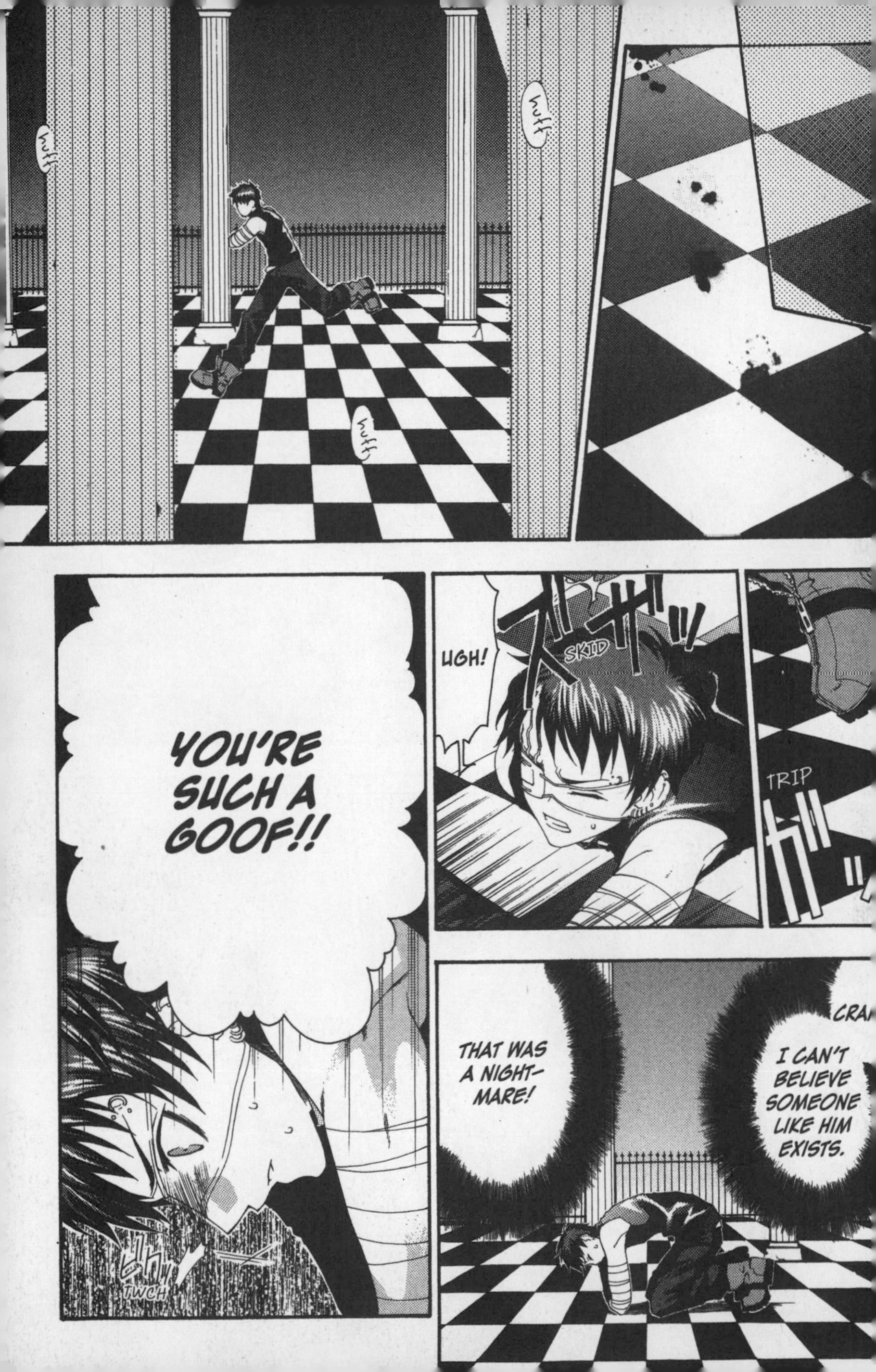
huff
huff
huff
UGH!
SKID
TRIP
YOU'RE SUCH A GOOF!!
TWCH
CRA
I CAN'T BELIEVE SOMEONE LIKE HIM EXISTS.
THAT WAS A NIGHT-MARE!

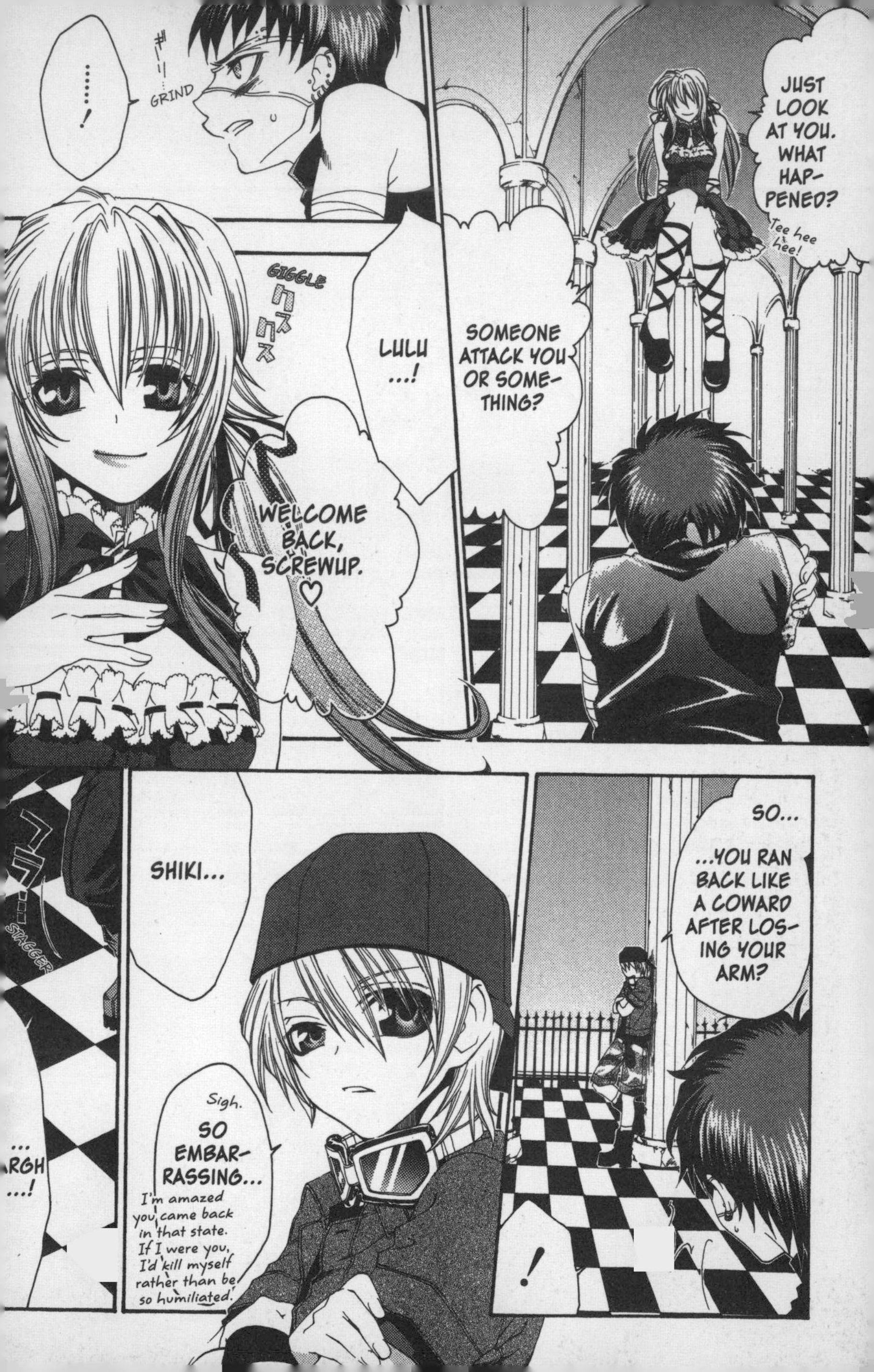
JUST LOOK AT YOU. WHAT HAPPENED?
Tee hee hee!
SOMEONE ATTACK YOU OR SOMETHING?
LULU ...!
GRIND
...!
GIGGLE
WELCOME BACK, SCREWUP. ♡
SO...
...YOU RAN BACK LIKE A COWARD AFTER LOSING YOUR ARM?
!
SHIKI...
Sigh.
SO EMBARRASSING...
I'm amazed you came back in that state. If I were you, I'd kill myself rather than be so humiliated.
STAGGER
...
RGH
...!

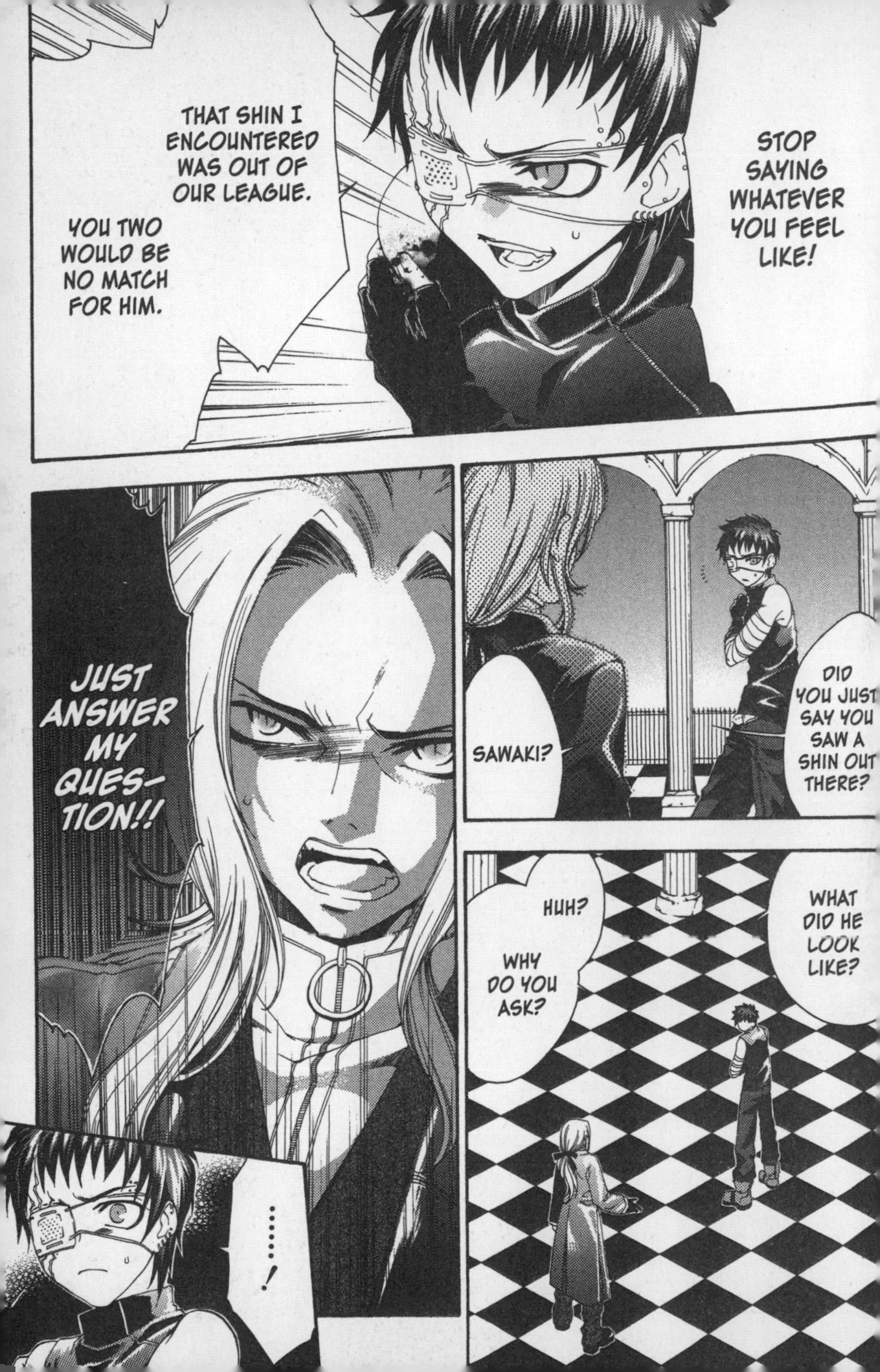
STOP SAYING WHATEVER YOU FEEL LIKE!
THAT SHIN I ENCOUNTERED WAS OUT OF OUR LEAGUE.
YOU TWO WOULD BE NO MATCH FOR HIM.
DID YOU JUST SAY YOU SAW A SHIN OUT THERE?
SAWAKI?
WHAT DID HE LOOK LIKE?
HUH?
WHY DO YOU ASK?
JUST ANSWER MY QUES-TION!!
......!

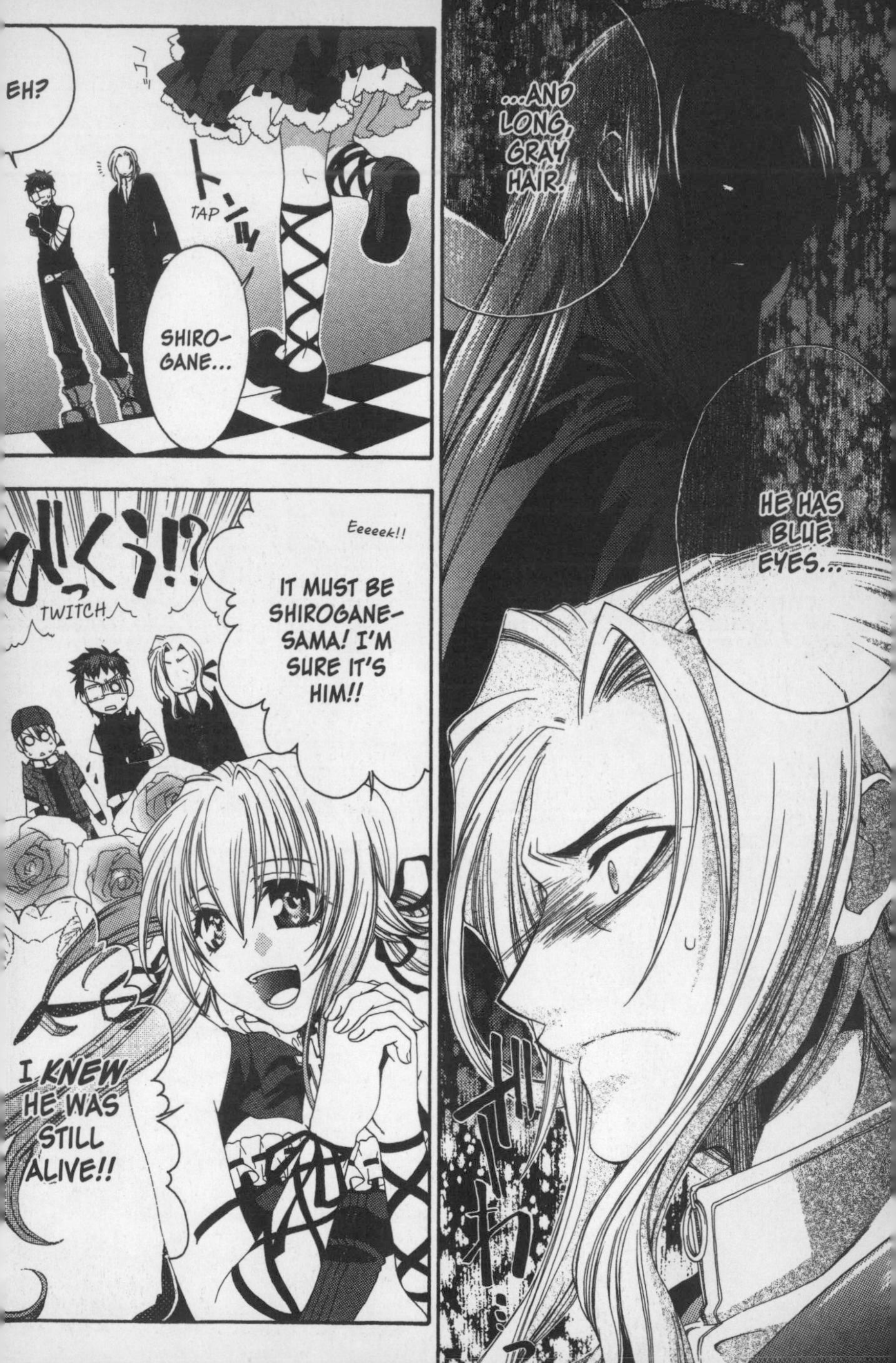
...AND LONG, GRAY HAIR.
HE HAS BLUE EYES...
EH?
TAP
SHIRO-GANE...
Eeeeek!!
IT MUST BE SHIROGANE-SAMA! I'M SURE IT'S HIM!!
TWITCH
I KNEW HE WAS STILL ALIVE!!

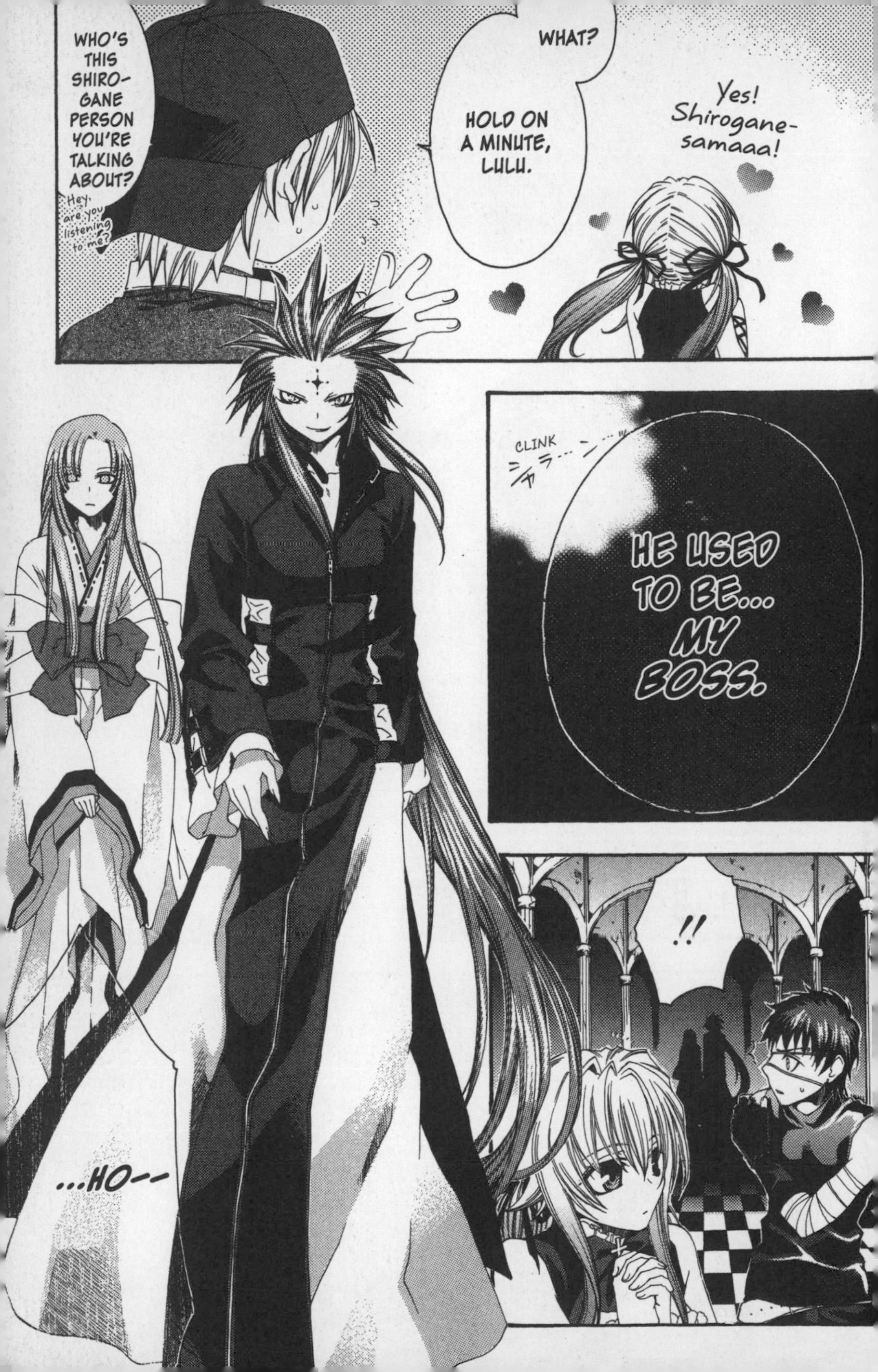

Yes! Shirogane-samaaa!
WHAT?
HOLD ON A MINUTE, LULU.
WHO'S THIS SHIROGANE PERSON YOU'RE TALKING ABOUT?
Hey, are you listening to me?
CLINK
シャラ…ン…
HE USED TO BE... MY BOSS.
!!
...HO--

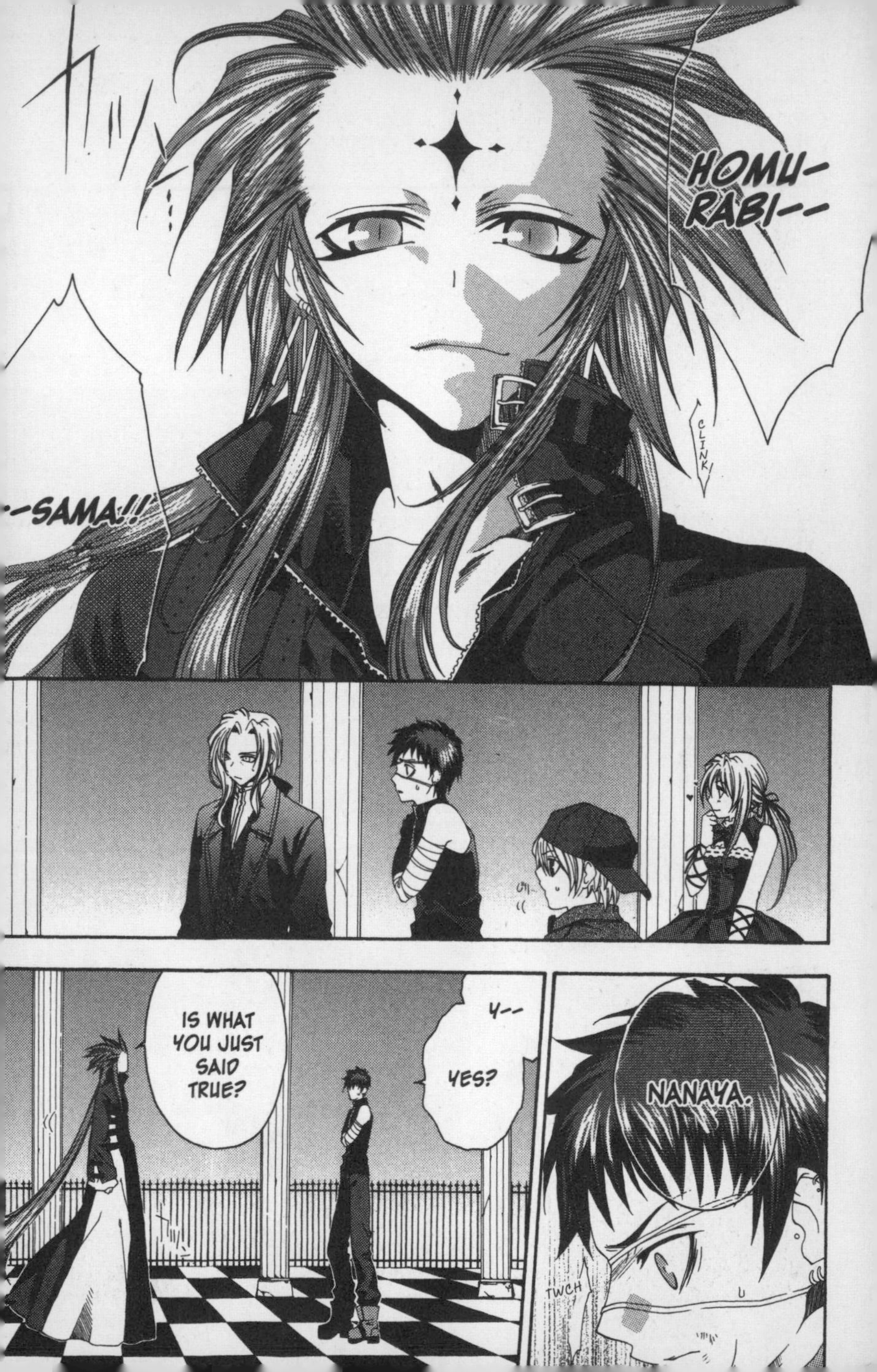
HOMU-RABI--
--SAMA!!
CLINK
NANAYA.
TWCH
Y--
YES?
IS WHAT YOU JUST SAID TRUE?

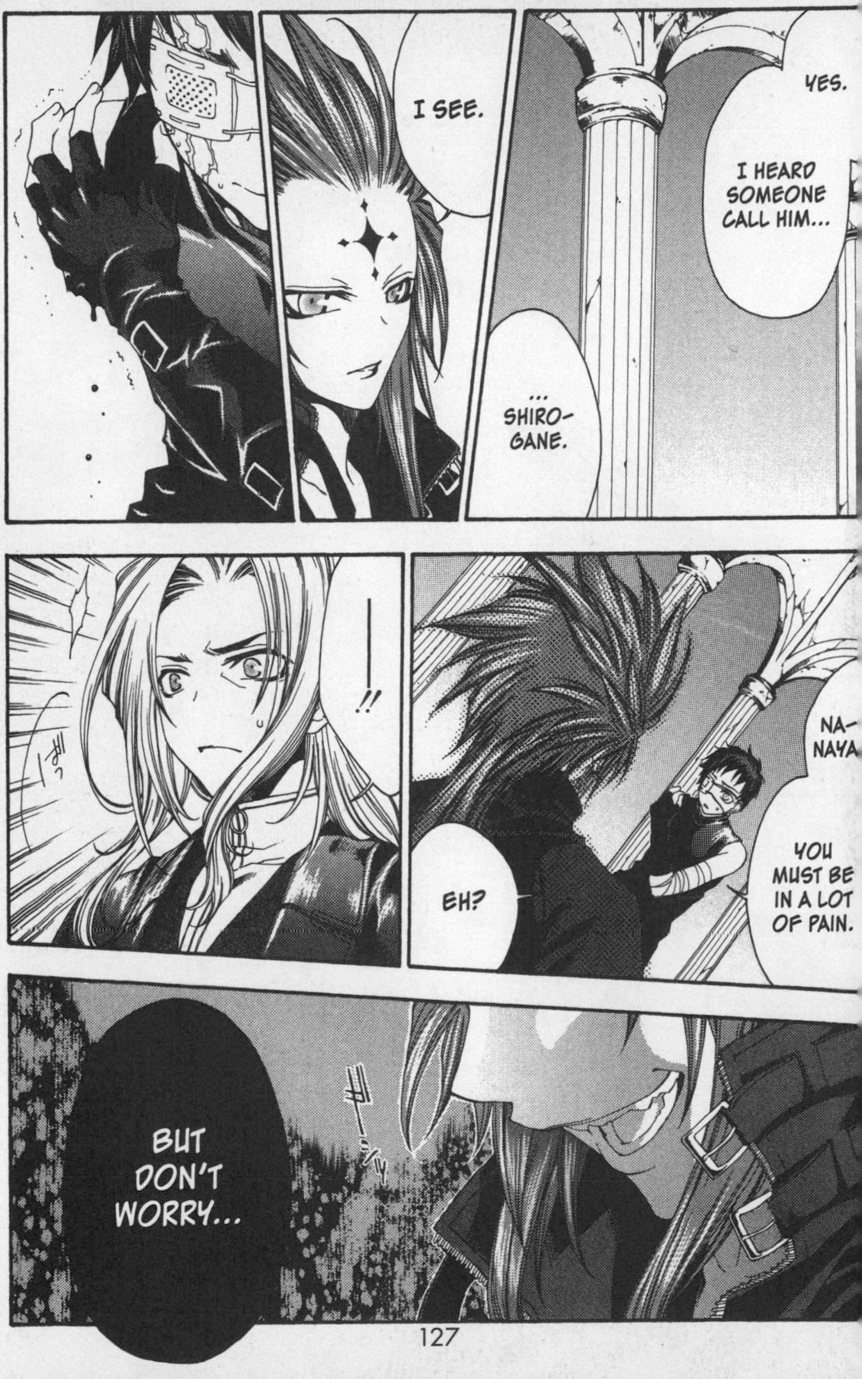
YES.
I HEARD SOMEONE CALL HIM...
... SHIRO-GANE.
I SEE.
NA-NAYA
YOU MUST BE IN A LOT OF PAIN.
EH?
—!!
BUT DON'T WORRY...

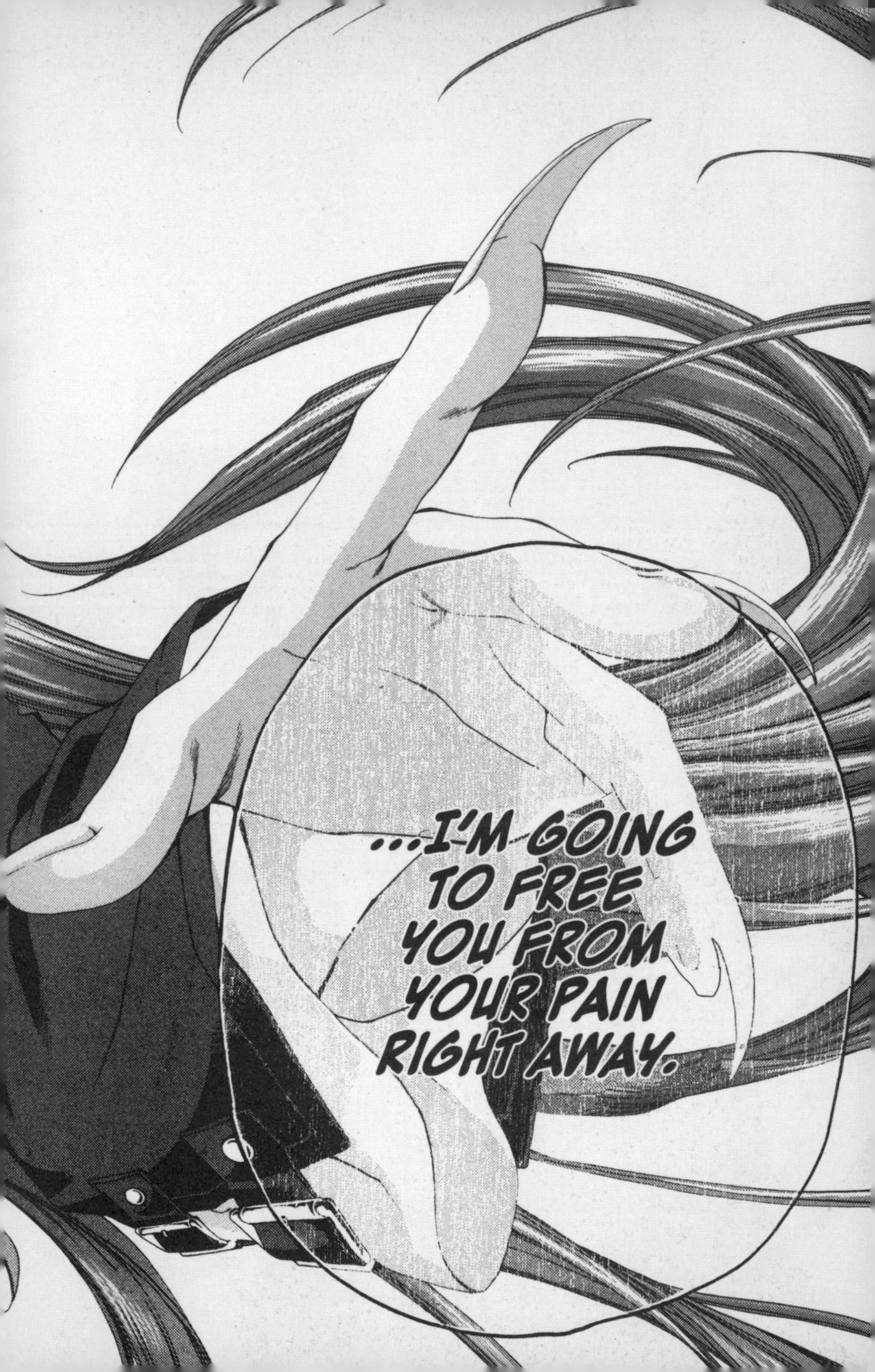
...I'M GOING TO FREE YOU FROM YOUR PAIN RIGHT AWAY.

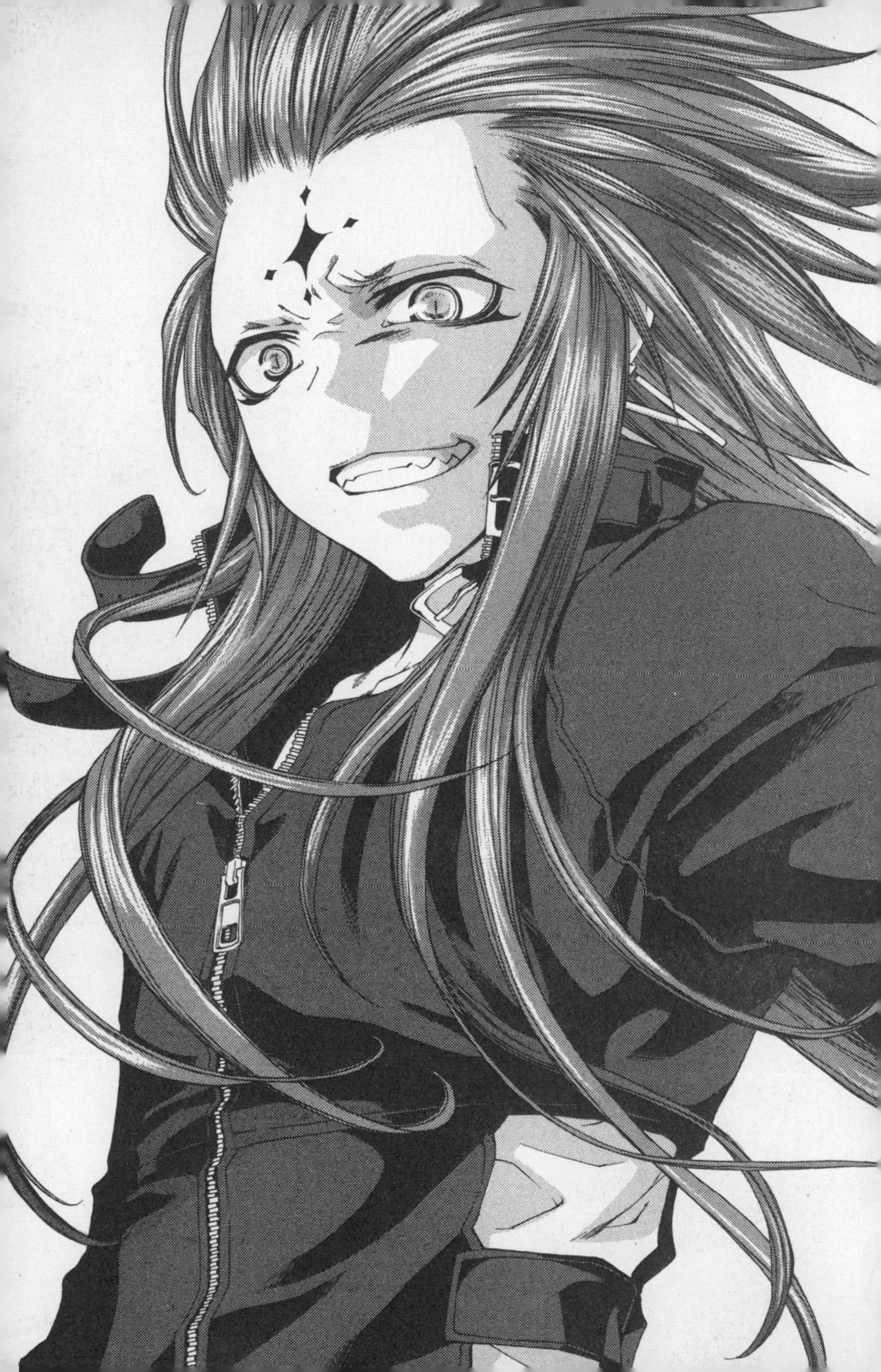

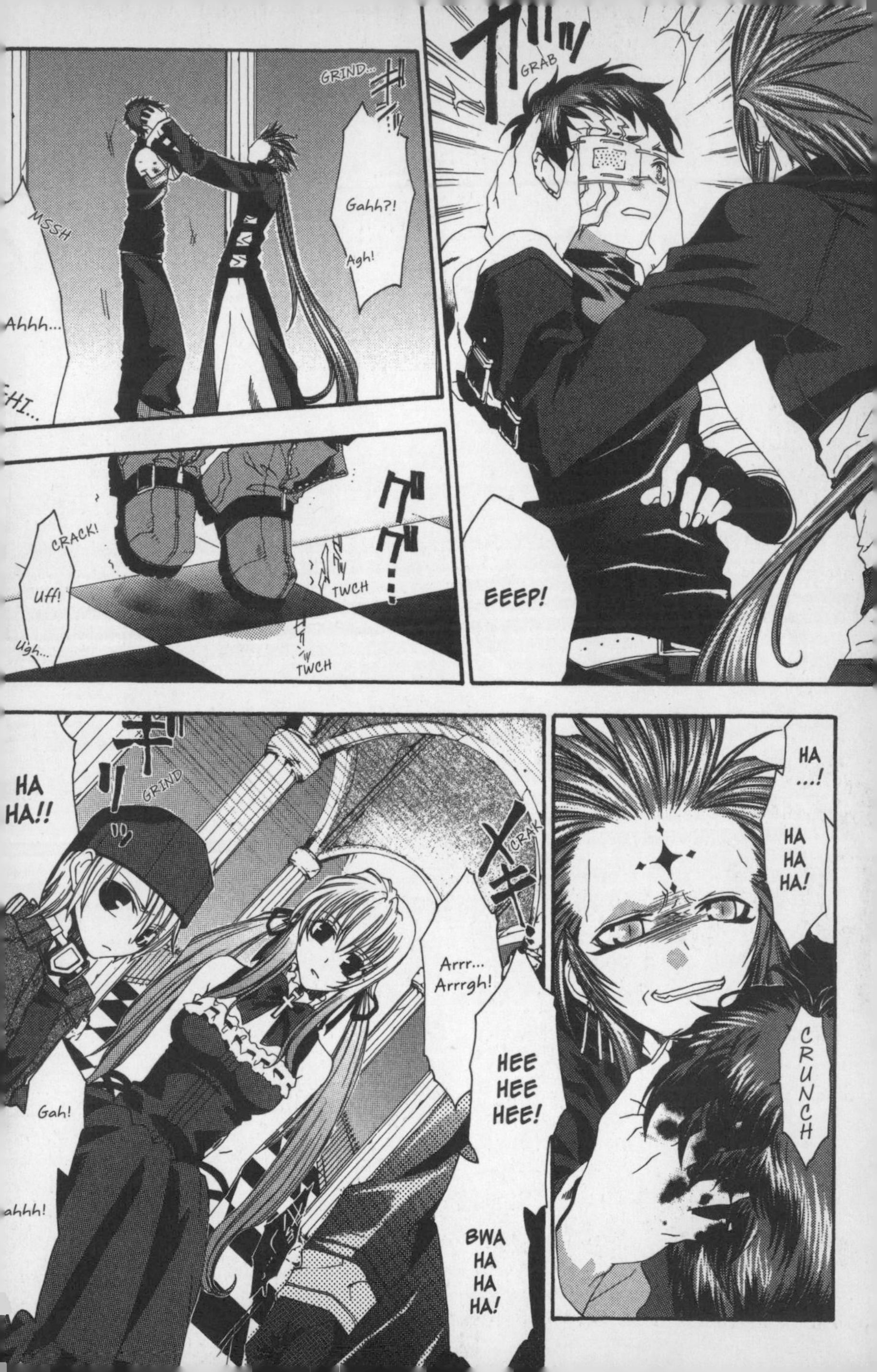
GRAB
EEEP!
GRIND...
Gahh?!
Agh!
MSSH
Ahhh...
HI...
TWCH
TWCH
CRACK!
Uff!
Ugh...
HA ...!
HA HA HA HA!
CRUNCH
BWA HA HA HA HA!
HEE HEE HEE!
CRAK
Arrr... Arrrgh!
GRIND
HA HA!!
Gah!
ahhh!

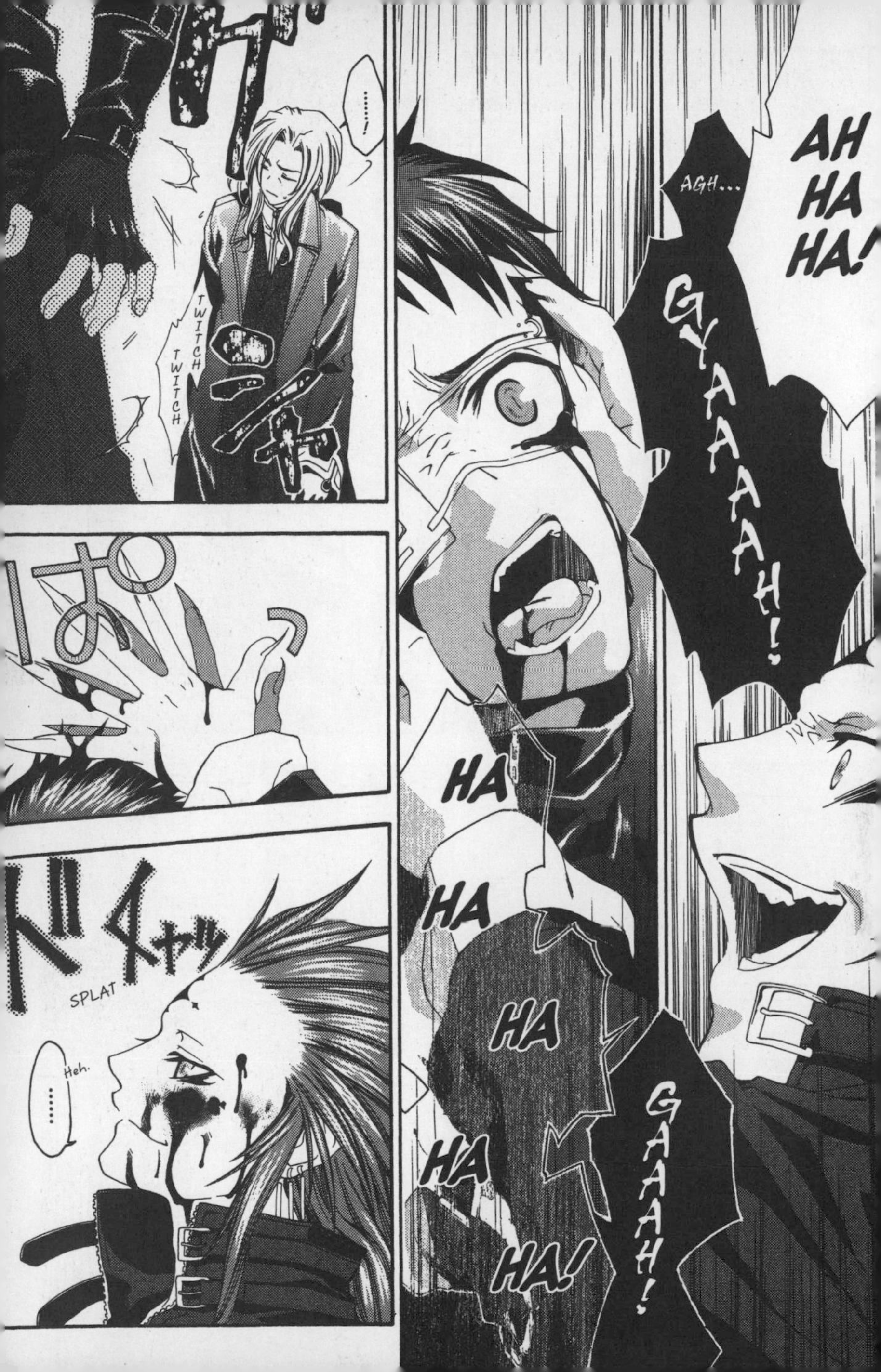
AH HA HA HA!
AGH...
GYAAAAAAH!
HA HA HA HA HA!
GAAAAH!
......!
TWITCH TWITCH
SPLAT
Heh.
......

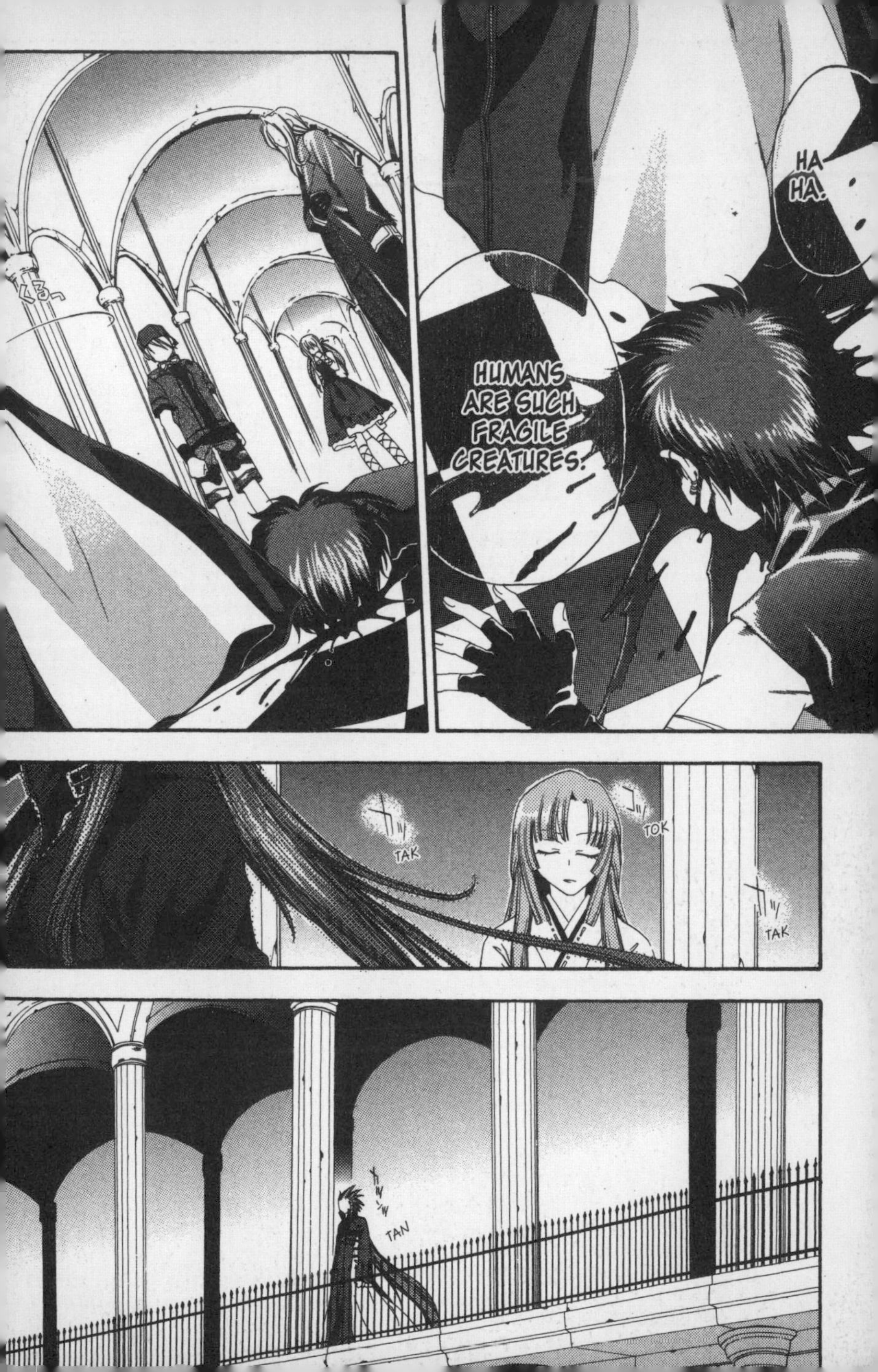

HA HA.
HUMANS ARE SUCH FRAGILE CREATURES.
くるっ
TOK
TAK
TAK
TAN

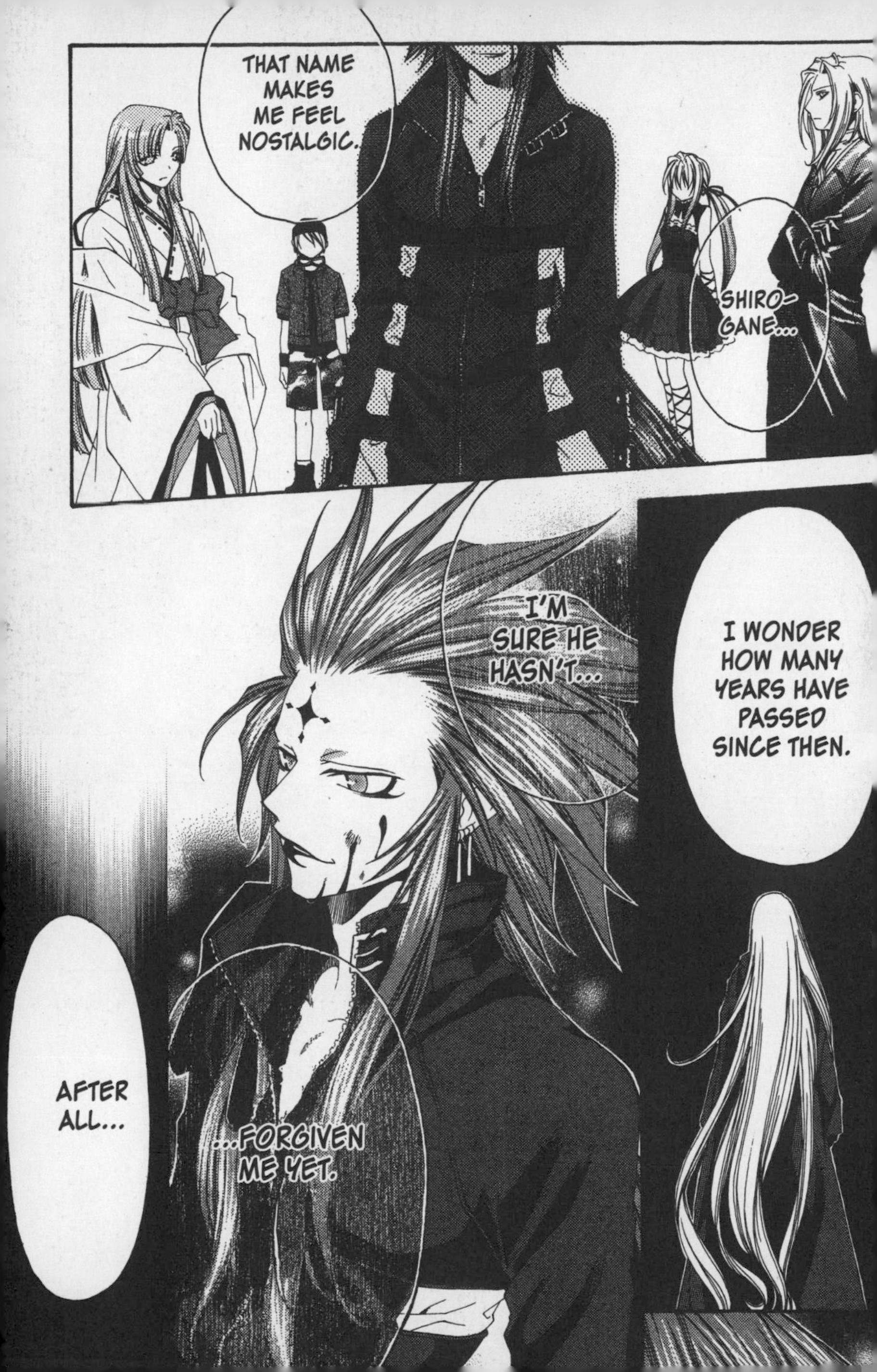
THAT NAME MAKES ME FEEL NOSTALGIC.
SHIRO-GANE...
I WONDER HOW MANY YEARS HAVE PASSED SINCE THEN.
I'M SURE HE HASN'T...
AFTER ALL...
...FORGIVEN ME YET.

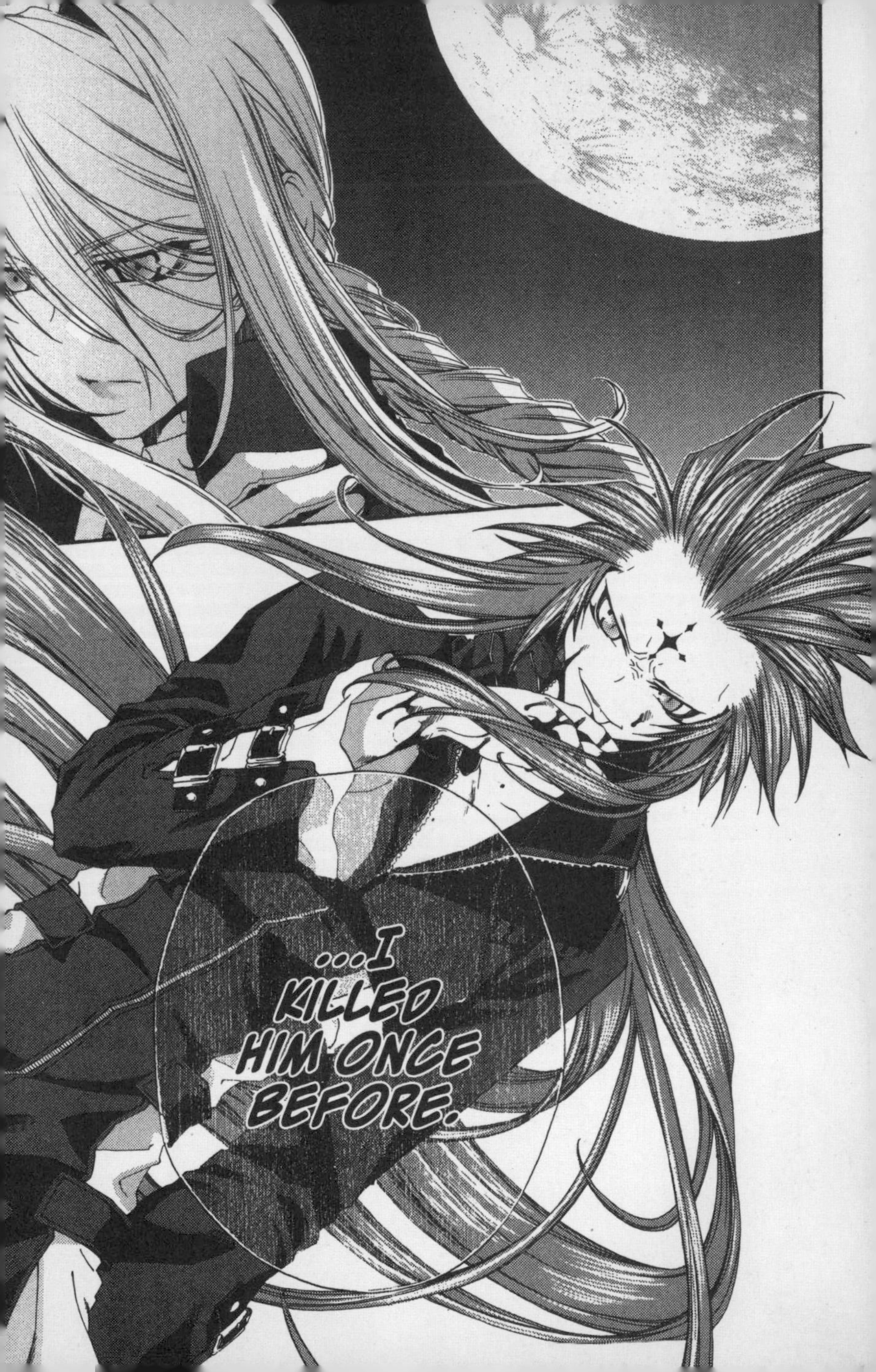
...I KILLED HIM ONCE BEFORE.

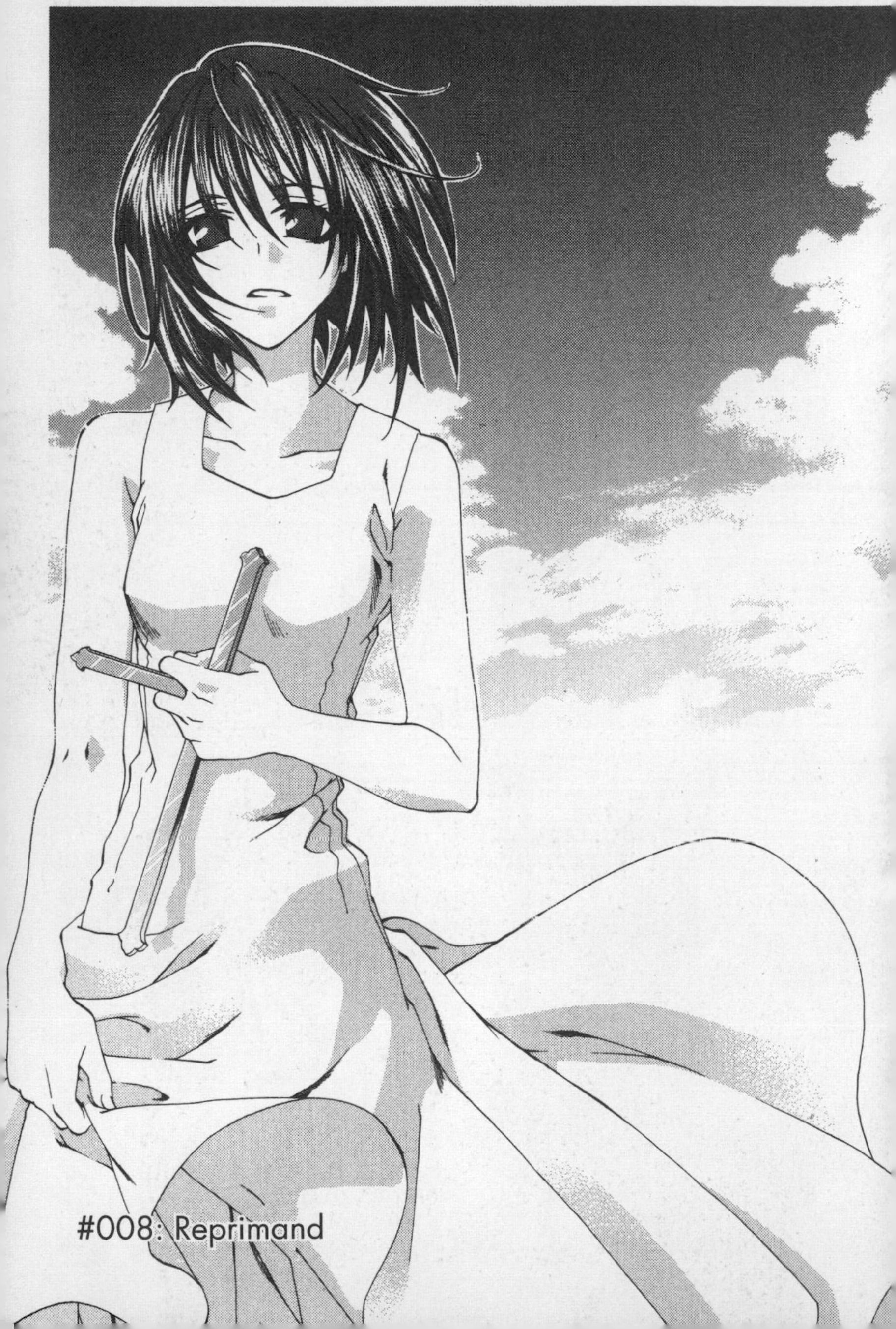

#008: Reprimand

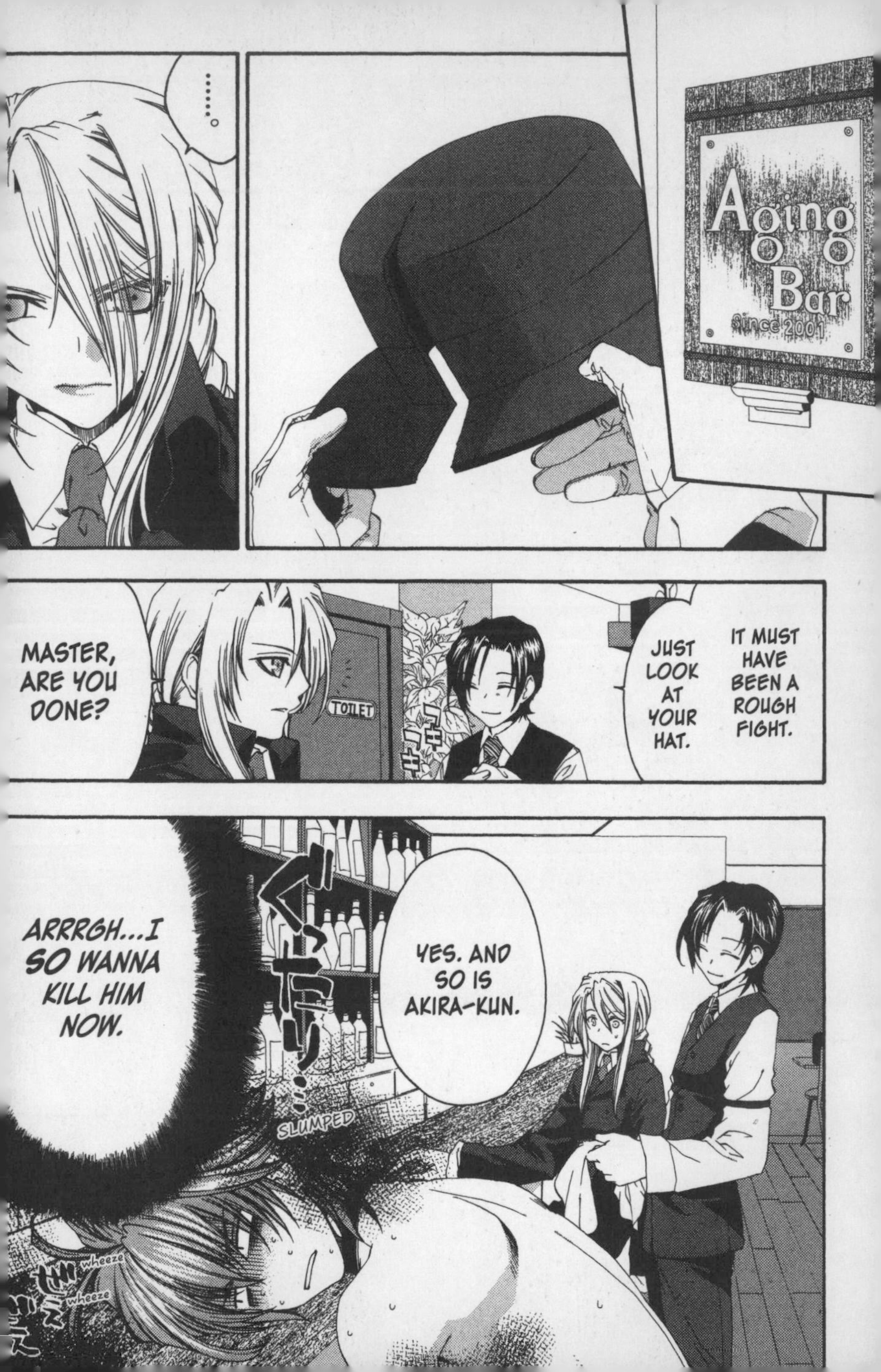
Aging Bar
since 2001
......
IT MUST HAVE BEEN A ROUGH FIGHT.
JUST LOOK AT YOUR HAT.
TOILET
MASTER, ARE YOU DONE?
YES. AND SO IS AKIRA-KUN.
SLUMPED
ARRRGH...I SO WANNA KILL HIM NOW.
wheeze
wheeze

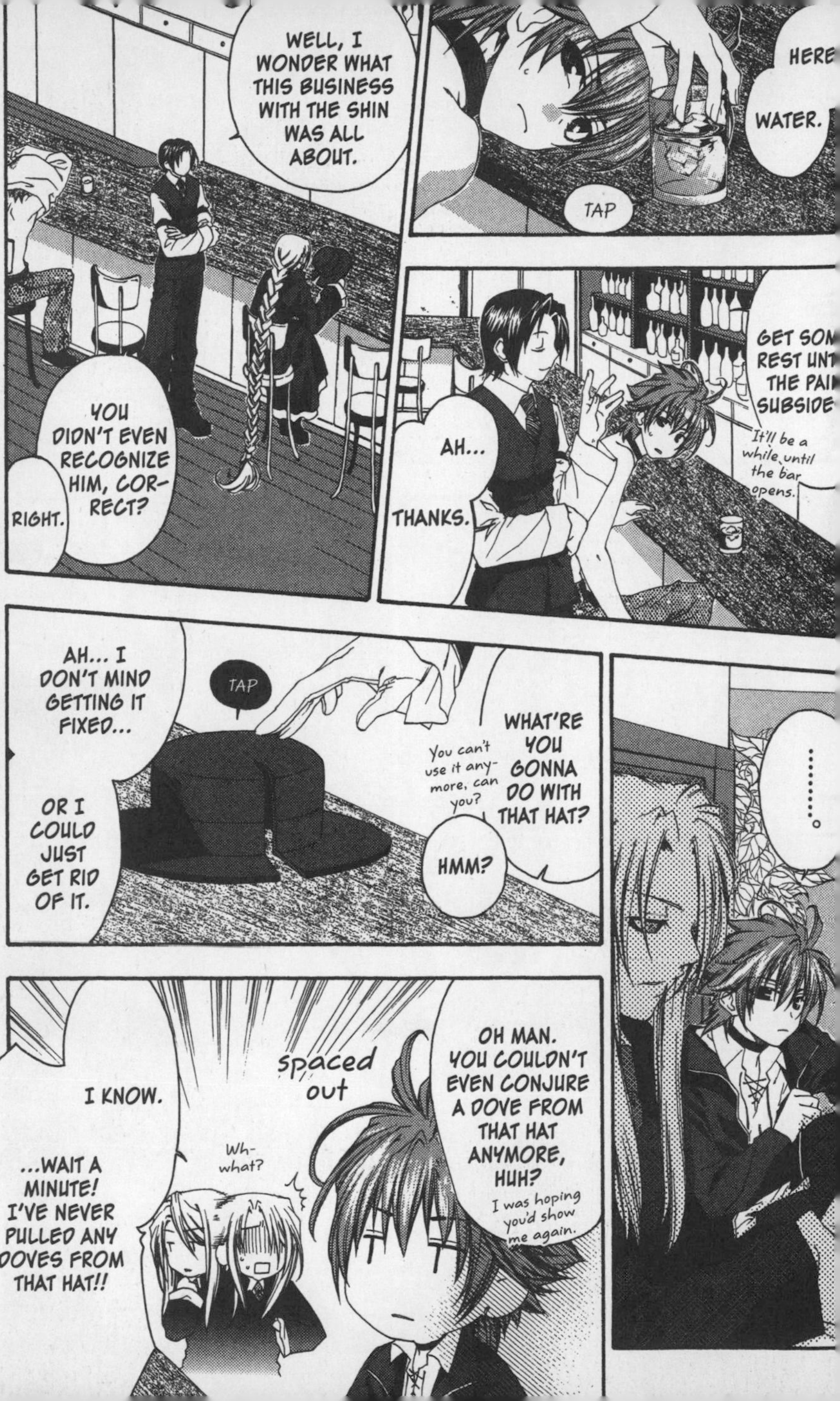
HERE
WATER.
TAP
GET SOM REST UNT THE PAI SUBSIDE
It'll be a while until the bar opens.
AH...
THANKS.
WELL, I WONDER WHAT THIS BUSINESS WITH THE SHIN WAS ALL ABOUT.
YOU DIDN'T EVEN RECOGNIZE HIM, COR-RECT?
RIGHT.
....
WHAT'RE YOU GONNA DO WITH THAT HAT?
You can't use it any-more, can you?
HMM?
TAP
AH... I DON'T MIND GETTING IT FIXED...
OR I COULD JUST GET RID OF IT.
OH MAN. YOU COULDN'T EVEN CONJURE A DOVE FROM THAT HAT ANYMORE, HUH?
I was hoping you'd show me again.
spaced out
I KNOW.
Wh-what?
...WAIT A MINUTE! I'VE NEVER PULLED ANY DOVES FROM THAT HAT!!

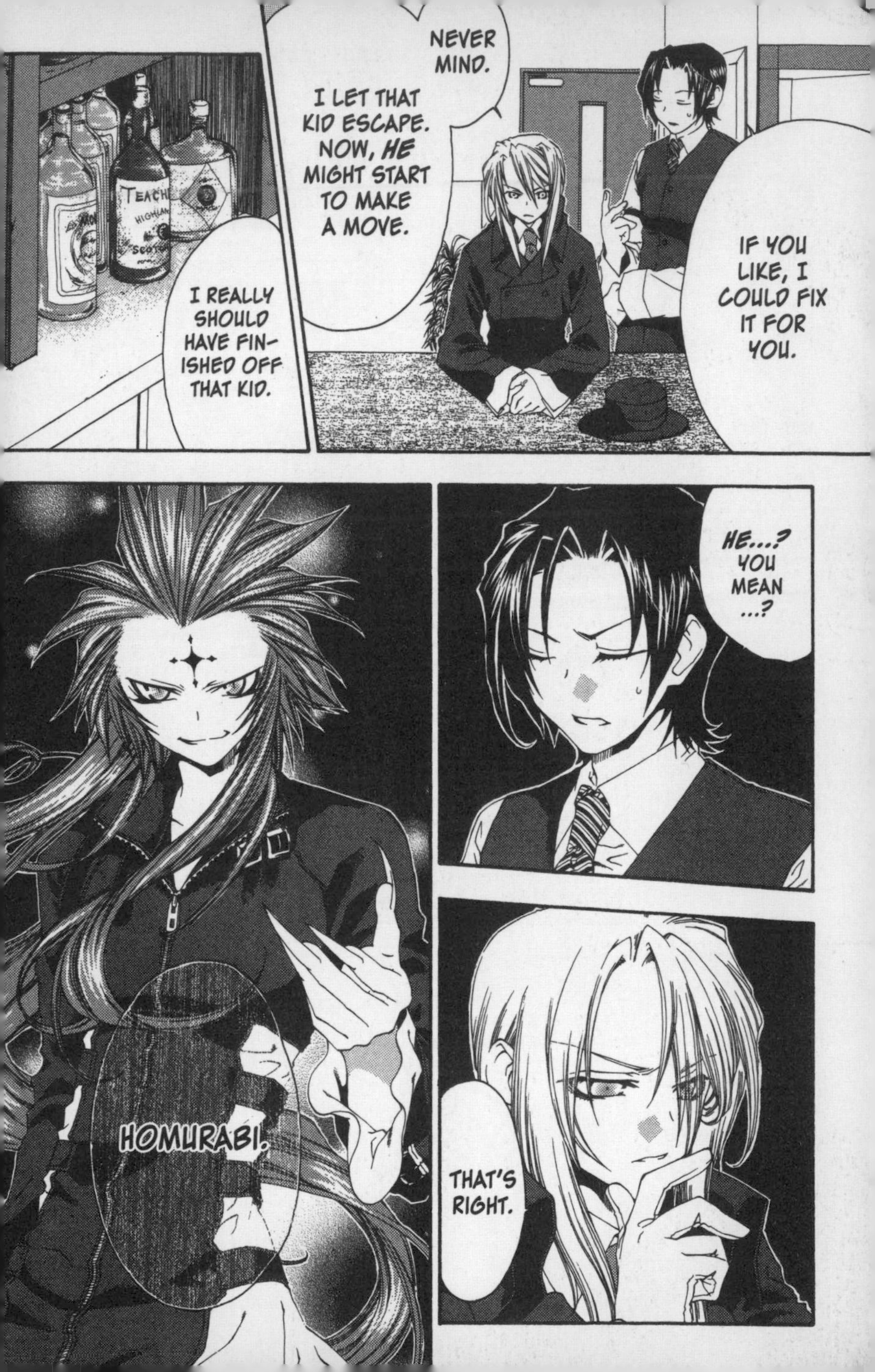
IF YOU LIKE, I COULD FIX IT FOR YOU.
NEVER MIND.
I LET THAT KID ESCAPE. NOW, *HE* MIGHT START TO MAKE A MOVE.
I REALLY SHOULD HAVE FIN-ISHED OFF THAT KID.
HE...? YOU MEAN ...?
THAT'S RIGHT.
HOMURABI.

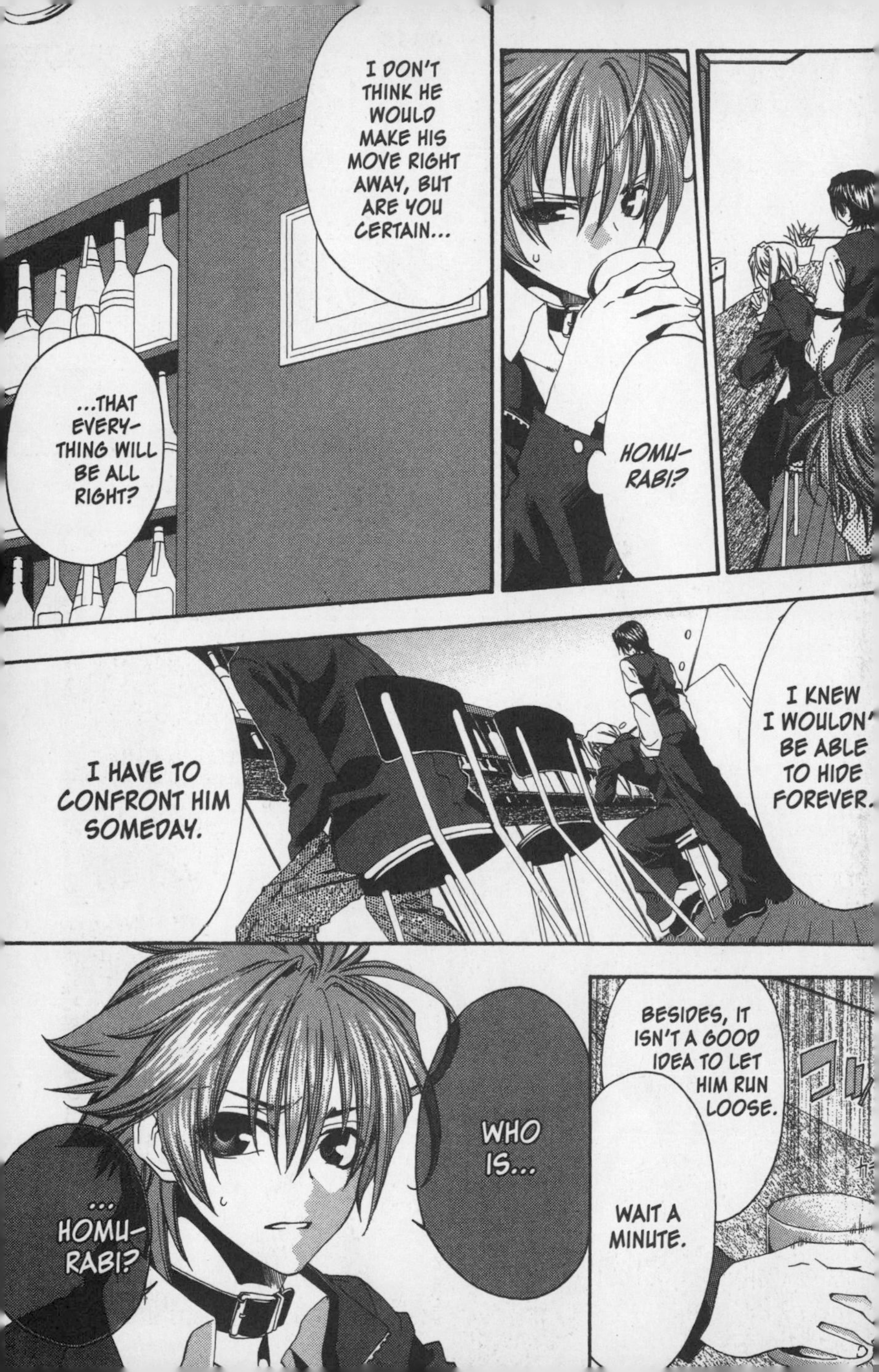
I DON'T THINK HE WOULD MAKE HIS MOVE RIGHT AWAY, BUT ARE YOU CERTAIN...
...THAT EVERY-THING WILL BE ALL RIGHT?
HOMU-RABI?
I KNEW I WOULDN' BE ABLE TO HIDE FOREVER.
I HAVE TO CONFRONT HIM SOMEDAY.
BESIDES, IT ISN'T A GOOD IDEA TO LET HIM RUN LOOSE.
WAIT A MINUTE.
WHO IS...
...HOMU-RABI?

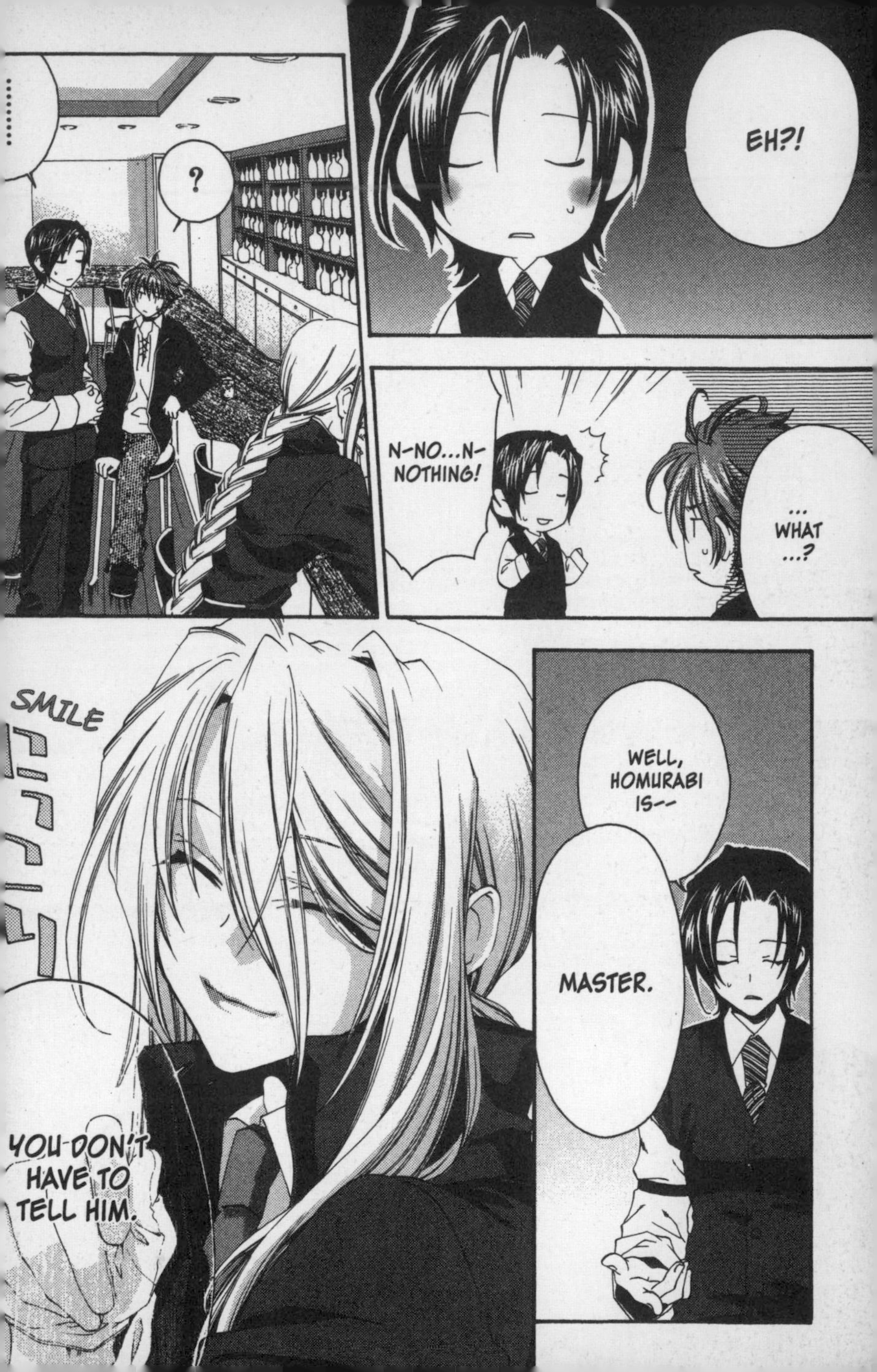
EH?!
... WHAT ...?
N-NO...N-NOTHING!
......
?
WELL, HOMURABI IS--
MASTER.
SMILE
YOU DON'T HAVE TO TELL HIM.

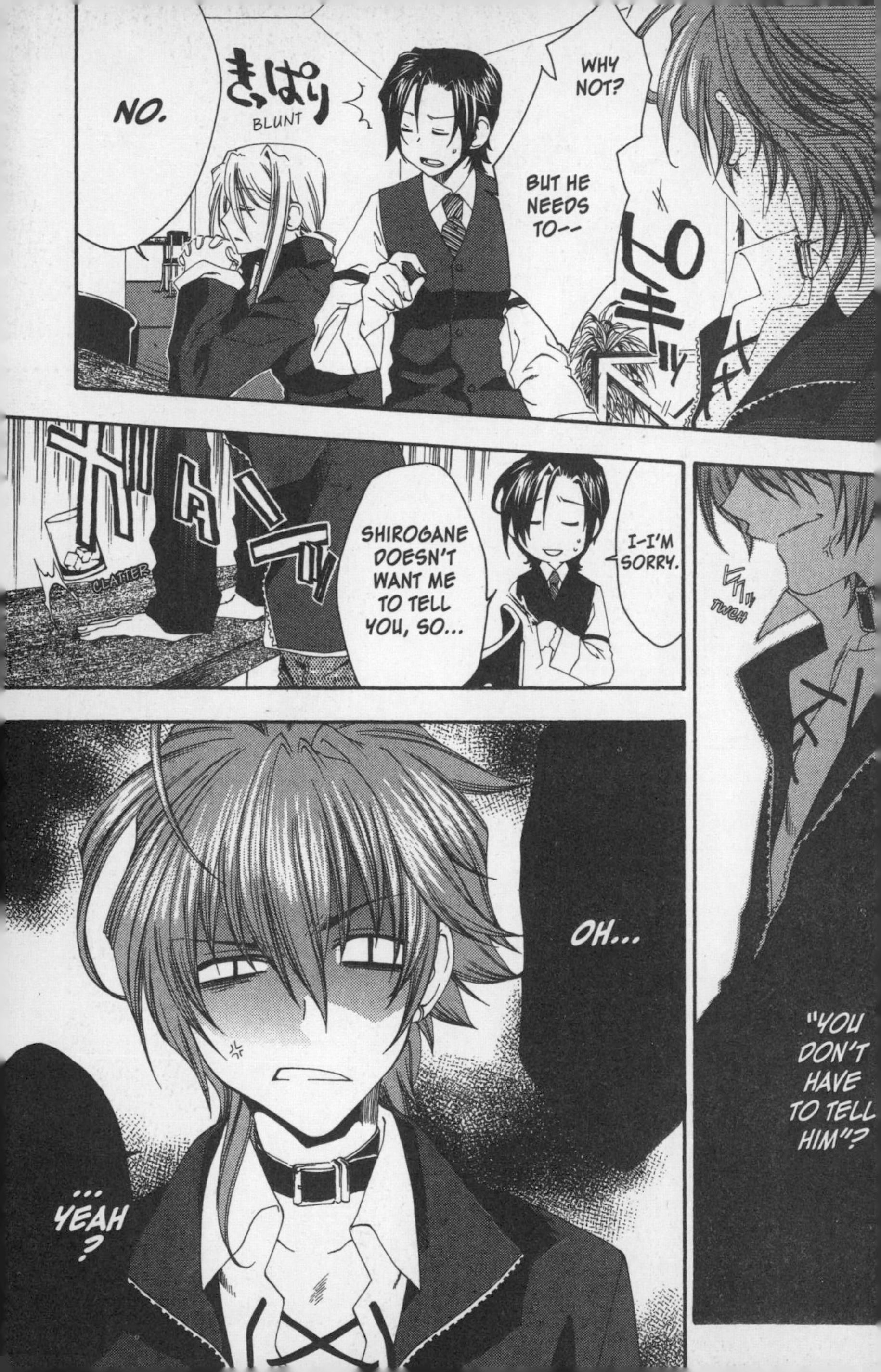

WHY NOT?
BUT HE NEEDS TO--
きっぱり
BLUNT
NO.
I-I'M SORRY.
SHIROGANE DOESN'T WANT ME TO TELL YOU, SO...
CLATTER
TWCH
"YOU DON'T HAVE TO TELL HIM"?
OH...
...YEAH?

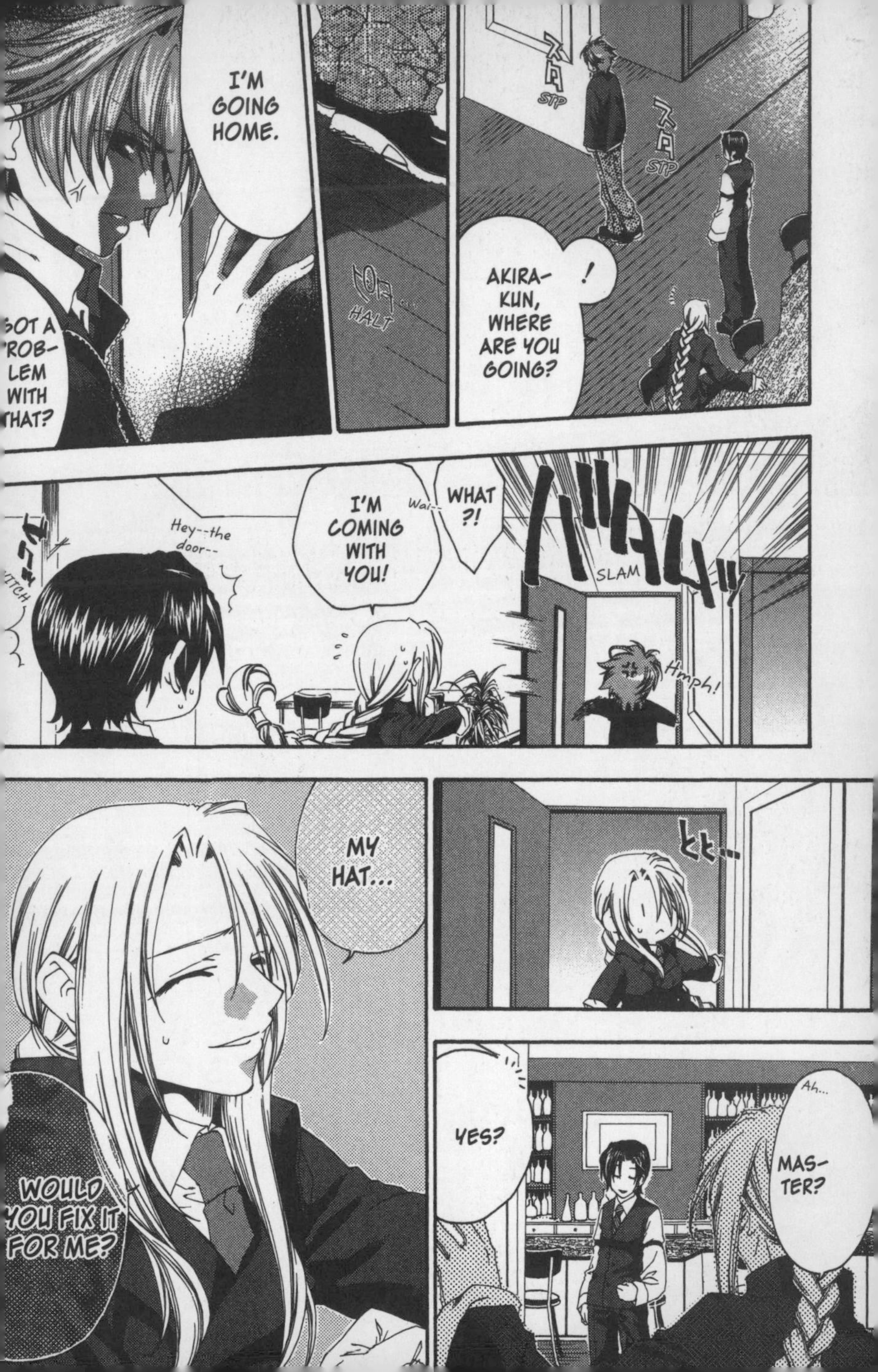
STP
STP
!
AKIRA-KUN, WHERE ARE YOU GOING?
HALT
I'M GOING HOME.
GOT A PROB-LEM WITH THAT?
SLAM
WHAT?!
Wai--
I'M COMING WITH YOU!
Hmph!
Hey--the door--
TWITCH
とと…
Ah...
MAS-TER?
YES?
MY HAT...
WOULD YOU FIX IT FOR ME?

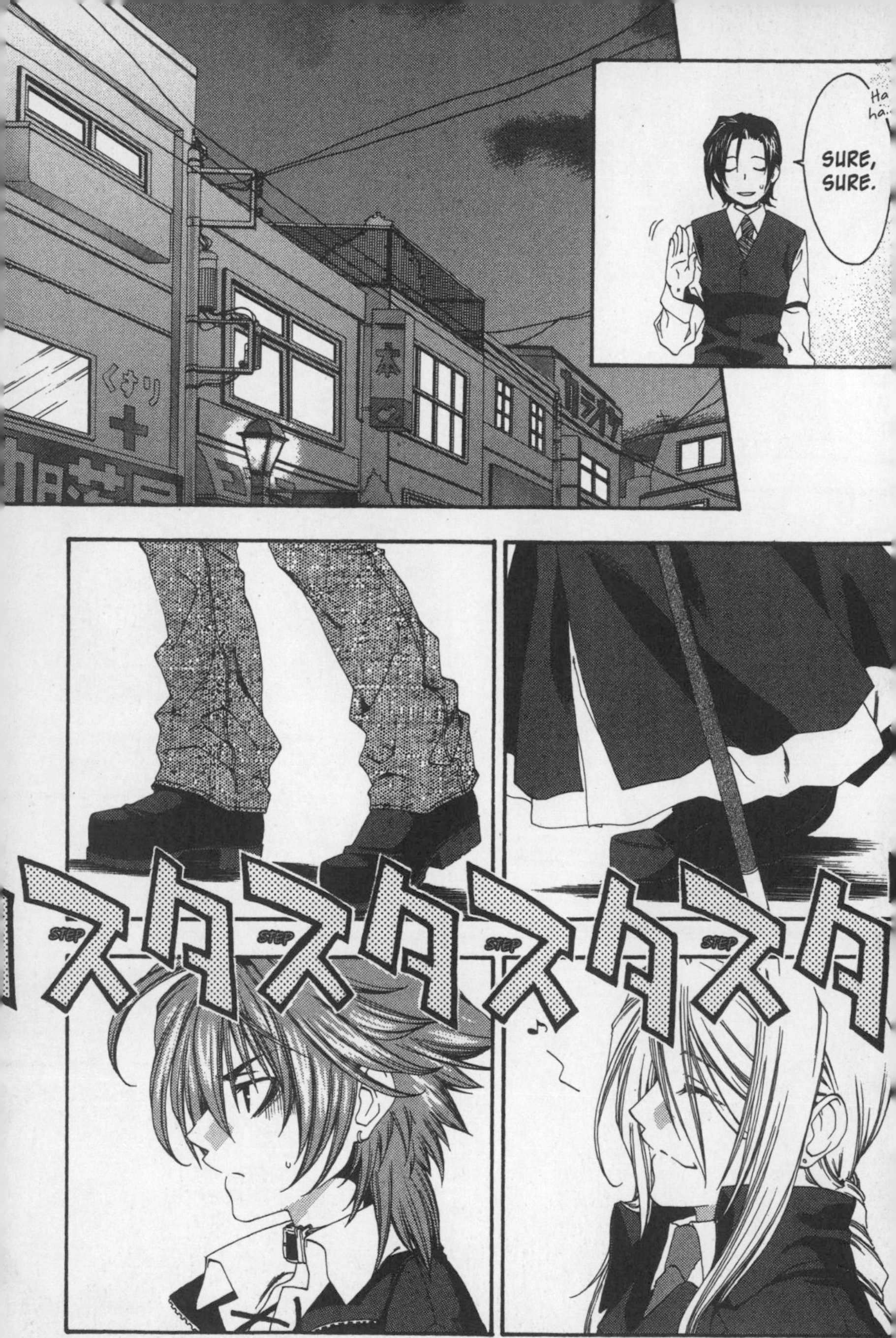
Ha ha..
SURE, SURE.
くすり
カラオケ
STEP
STEP
STEP
STEP
スタスタスタスタ

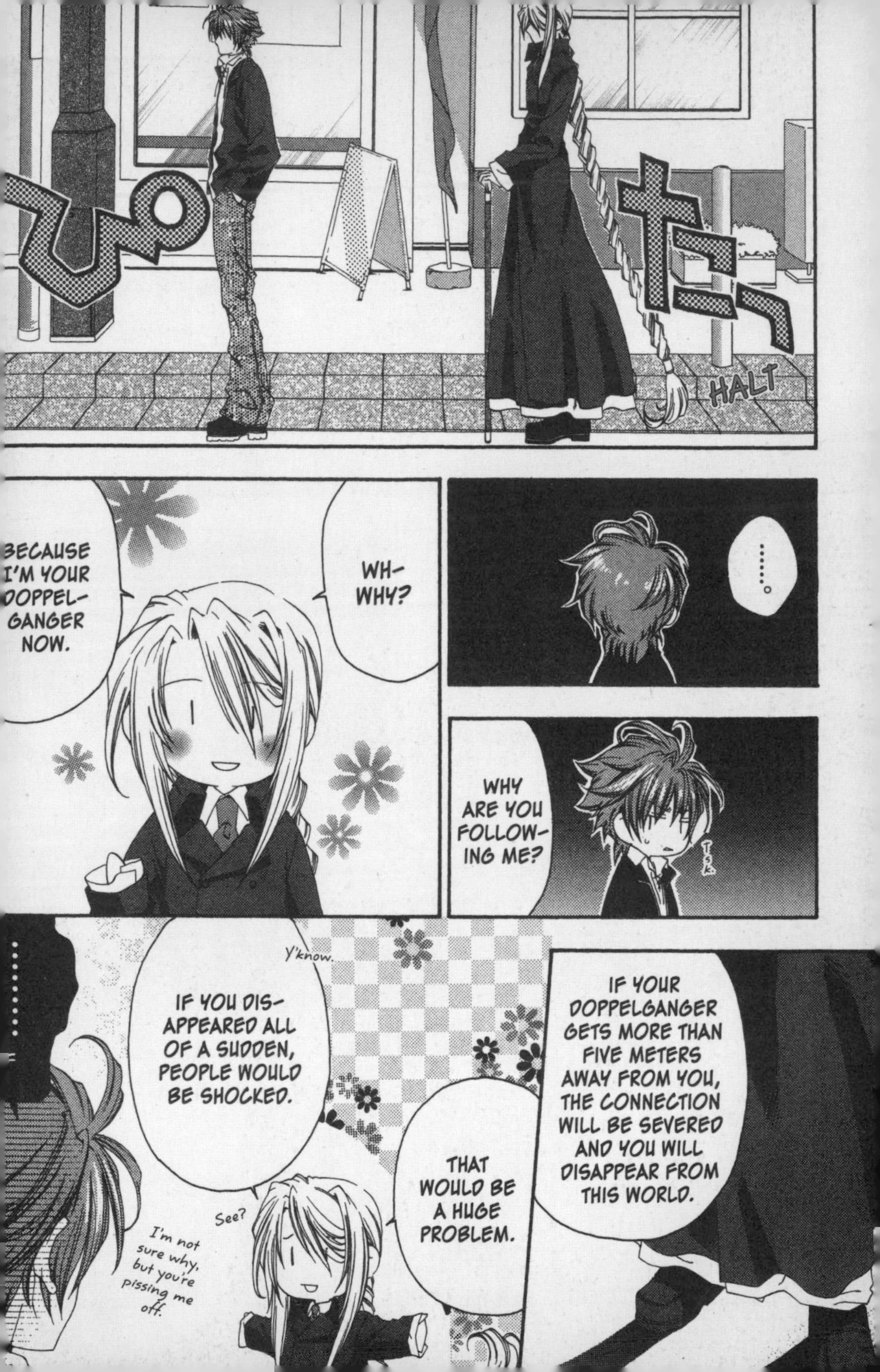

HALT
......
WHY ARE YOU FOLLOW-ING ME?
Tsk.
WH-WHY?
BECAUSE I'M YOUR DOPPEL-GANGER NOW.
IF YOUR DOPPELGANGER GETS MORE THAN FIVE METERS AWAY FROM YOU, THE CONNECTION WILL BE SEVERED AND YOU WILL DISAPPEAR FROM THIS WORLD.
THAT WOULD BE A HUGE PROBLEM.
IF YOU DIS-APPEARED ALL OF A SUDDEN, PEOPLE WOULD BE SHOCKED.
Y'know.
See?
I'm not sure why, but you're pissing me off.

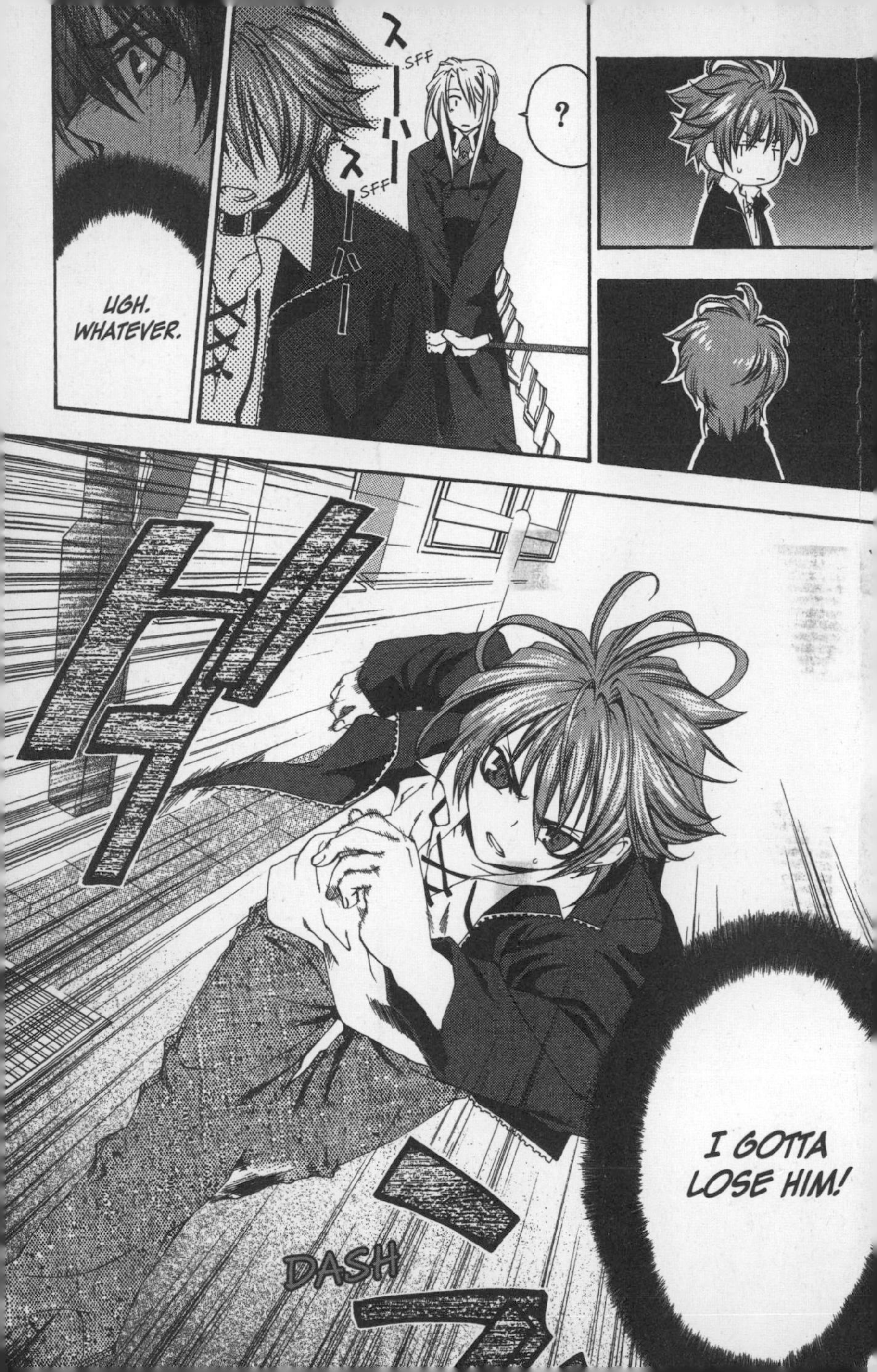

?
スーハースーハー
SFF
SFF
UGH. WHATEVER.
I GOTTA LOSE HIM!
DASH

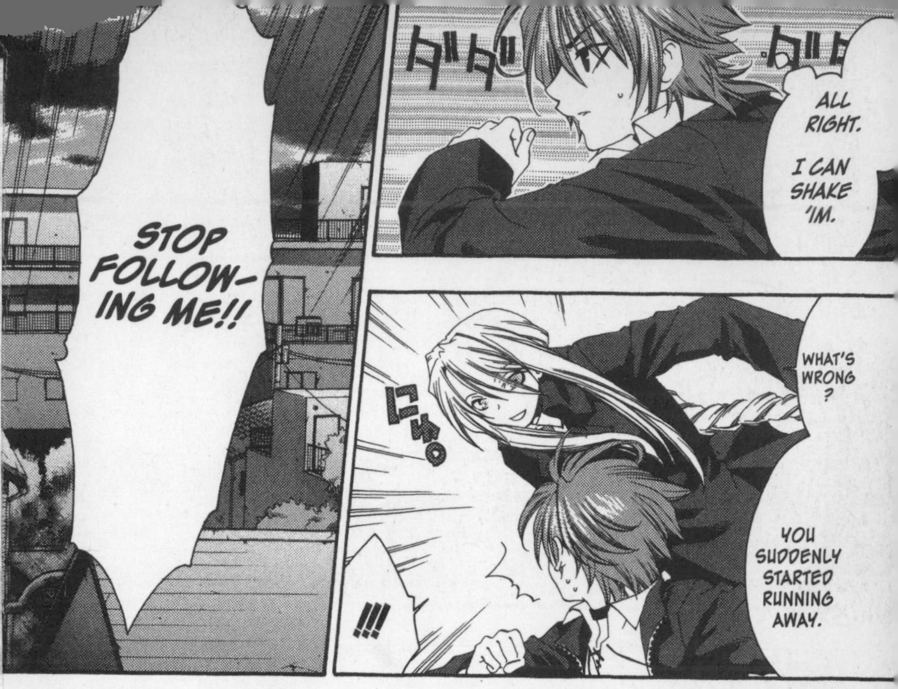
ALL RIGHT.
I CAN SHAKE 'IM.
WHAT'S WRONG?
YOU SUDDENLY STARTED RUNNING AWAY.
!!!
STOP FOLLOW-ING ME!!

—five minutes later—

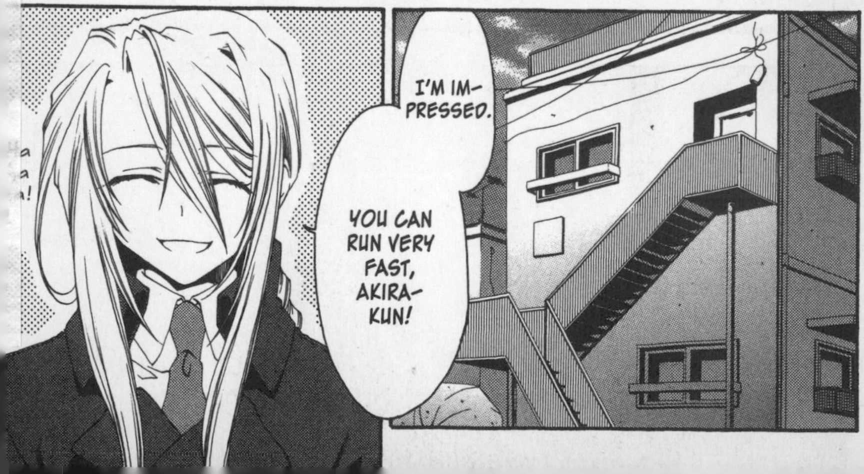
I'M IM-PRESSED.
YOU CAN RUN VERY FAST, AKIRA-KUN!

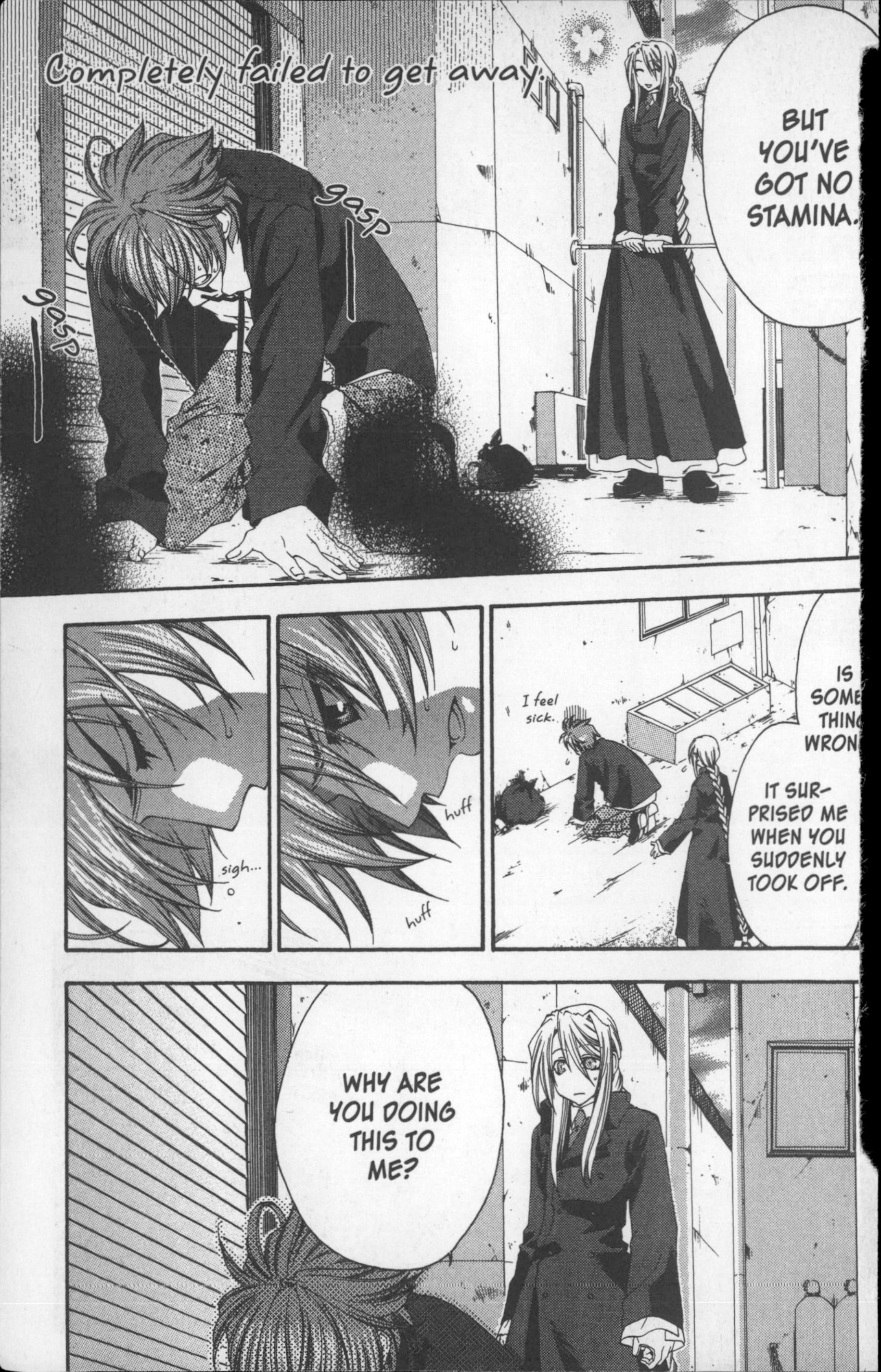
Completely failed to get away.
gasp
gasp
BUT YOU'VE GOT NO STAMINA.
IS SOME THING WRON
IT SUR- PRISED ME WHEN YOU SUDDENLY TOOK OFF.
I feel sick.
huff
huff
sigh...
WHY ARE YOU DOING THIS TO ME?

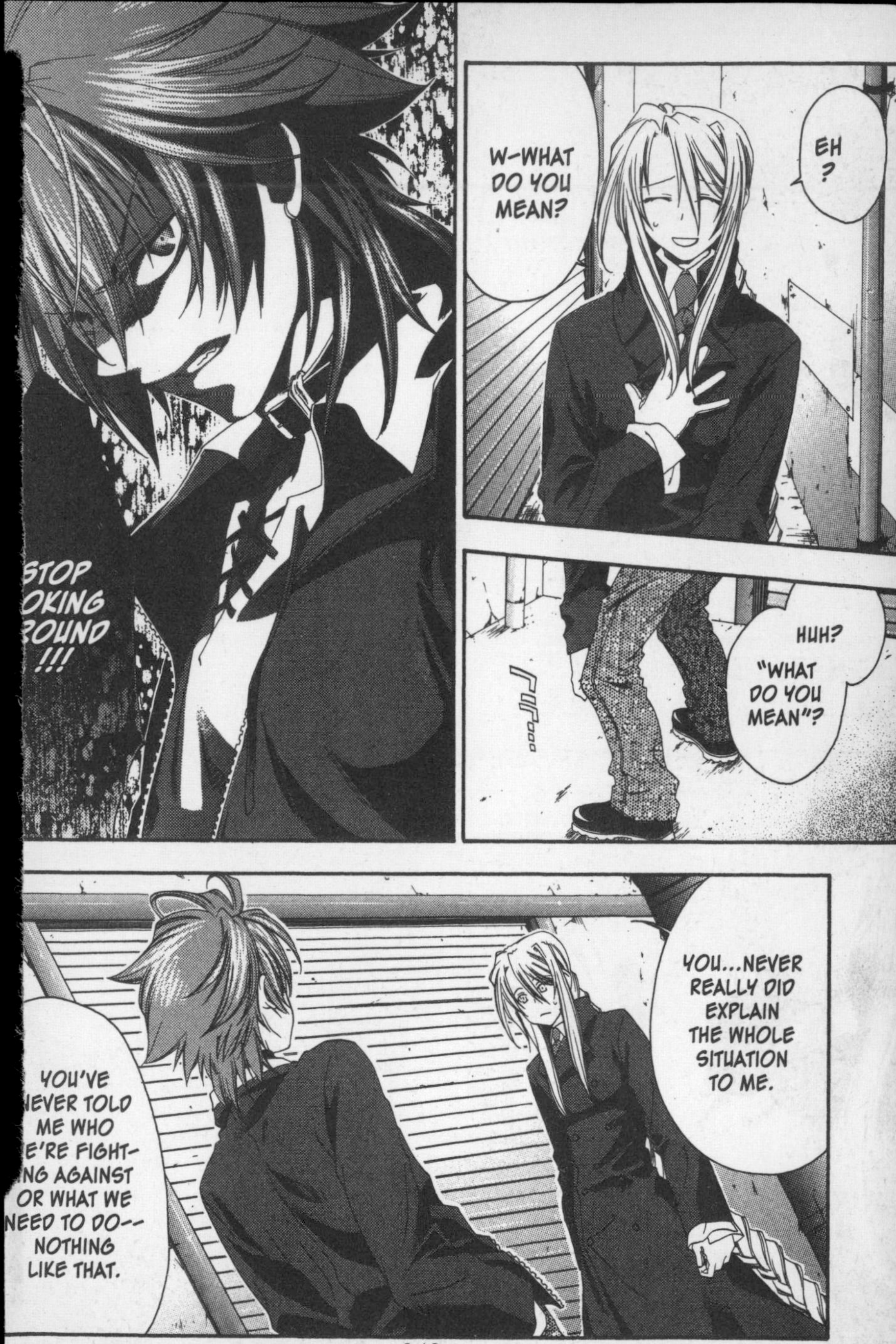
EH ?
W-WHAT DO YOU MEAN?
STOP OKING ROUND !!!
HUH? "WHAT DO YOU MEAN"?
YOU...NEVER REALLY DID EXPLAIN THE WHOLE SITUATION TO ME.
YOU'VE EVER TOLD ME WHO E'RE FIGHT-NG AGAINST OR WHAT WE EED TO DO-- NOTHING LIKE THAT.

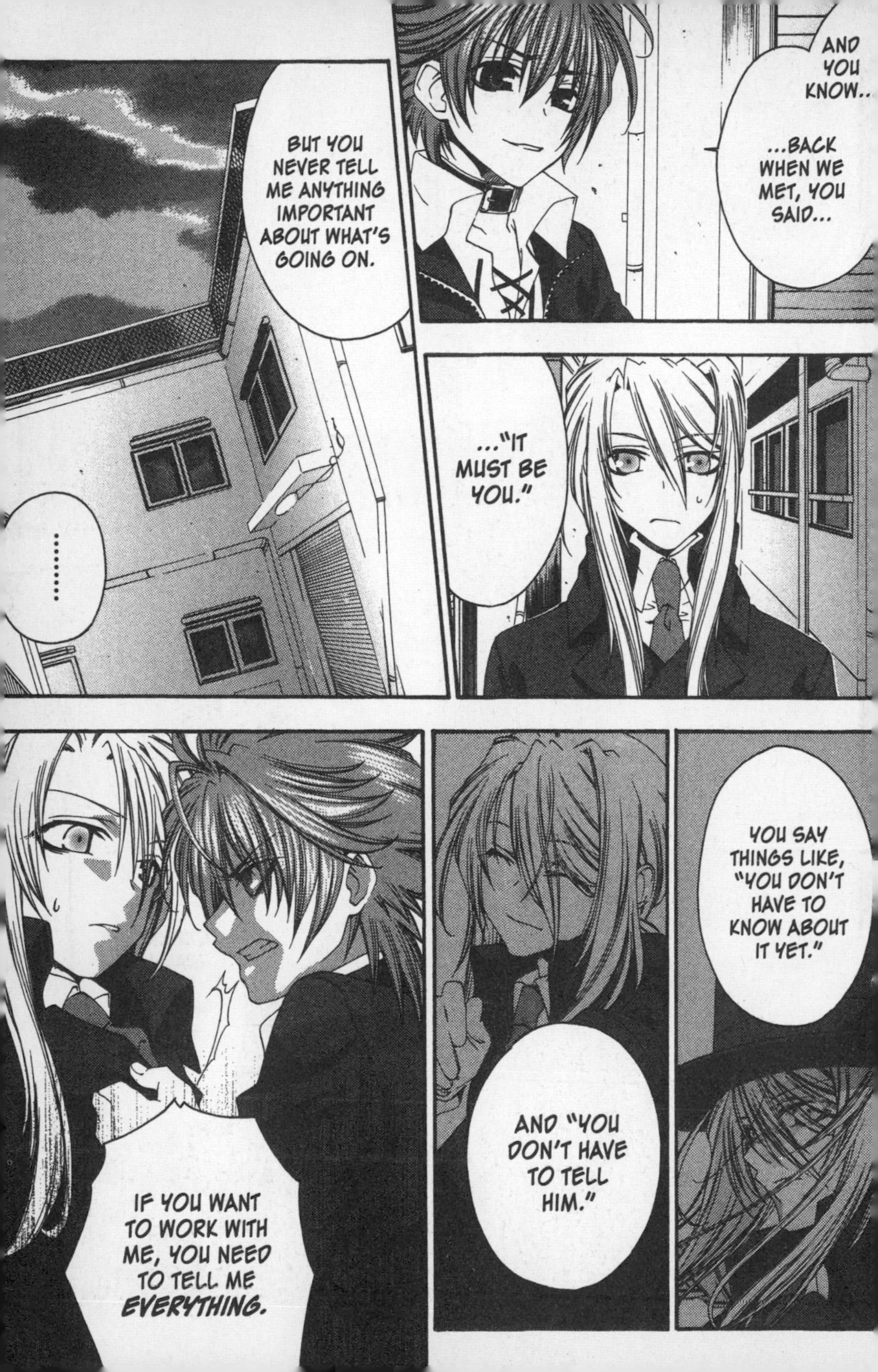
AND YOU KNOW...
...BACK WHEN WE MET, YOU SAID...
..."IT MUST BE YOU."
BUT YOU NEVER TELL ME ANYTHING IMPORTANT ABOUT WHAT'S GOING ON.
......
YOU SAY THINGS LIKE, "YOU DON'T HAVE TO KNOW ABOUT IT YET."
AND "YOU DON'T HAVE TO TELL HIM."
IF YOU WANT TO WORK WITH ME, YOU NEED TO TELL ME ***EVERYTHING***.

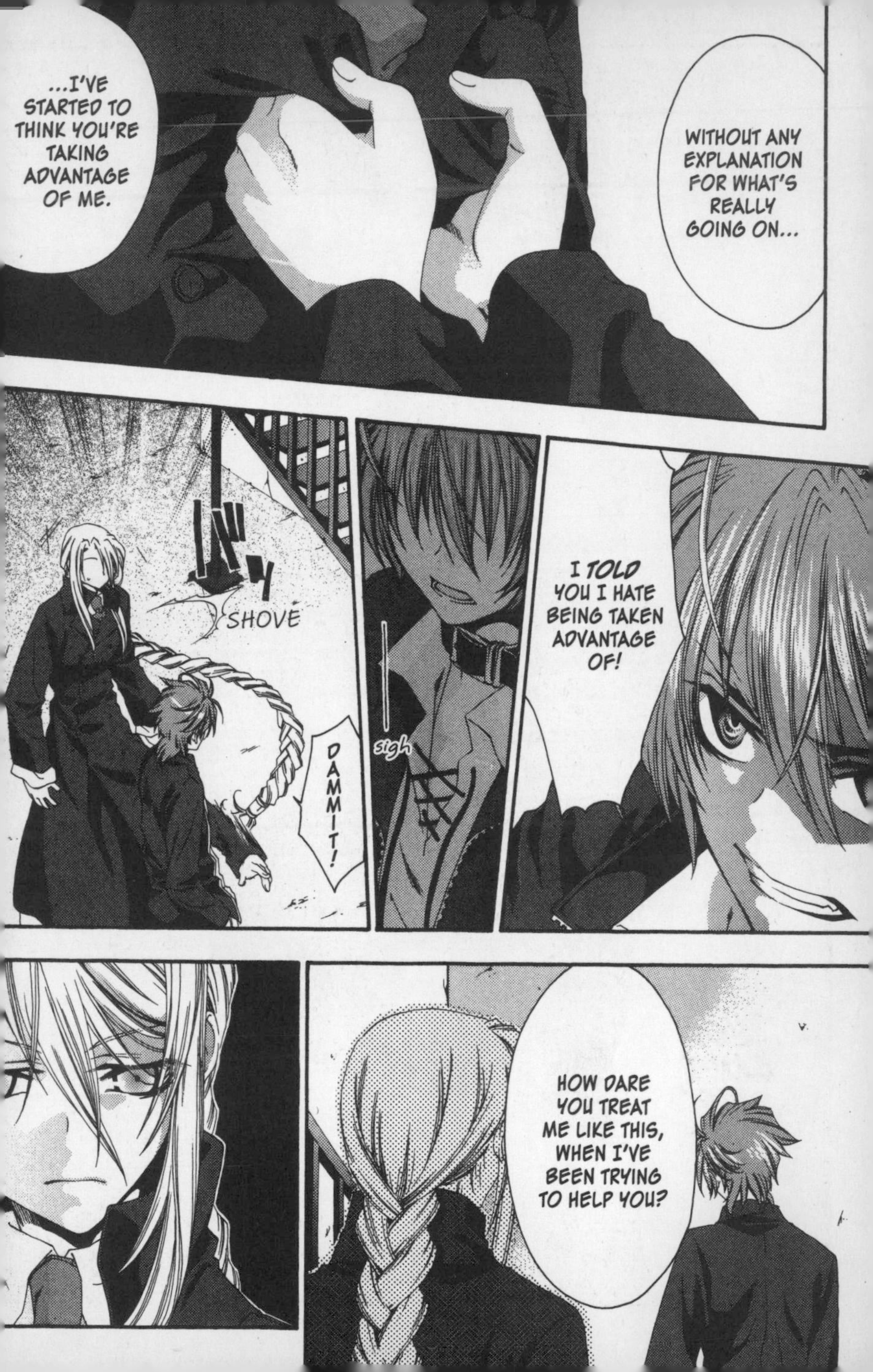
WITHOUT ANY EXPLANATION FOR WHAT'S REALLY GOING ON...
...I'VE STARTED TO THINK YOU'RE TAKING ADVANTAGE OF ME.
I TOLD YOU I HATE BEING TAKEN ADVANTAGE OF!
sigh
SHOVE
DAMMIT!
HOW DARE YOU TREAT ME LIKE THIS, WHEN I'VE BEEN TRYING TO HELP YOU?

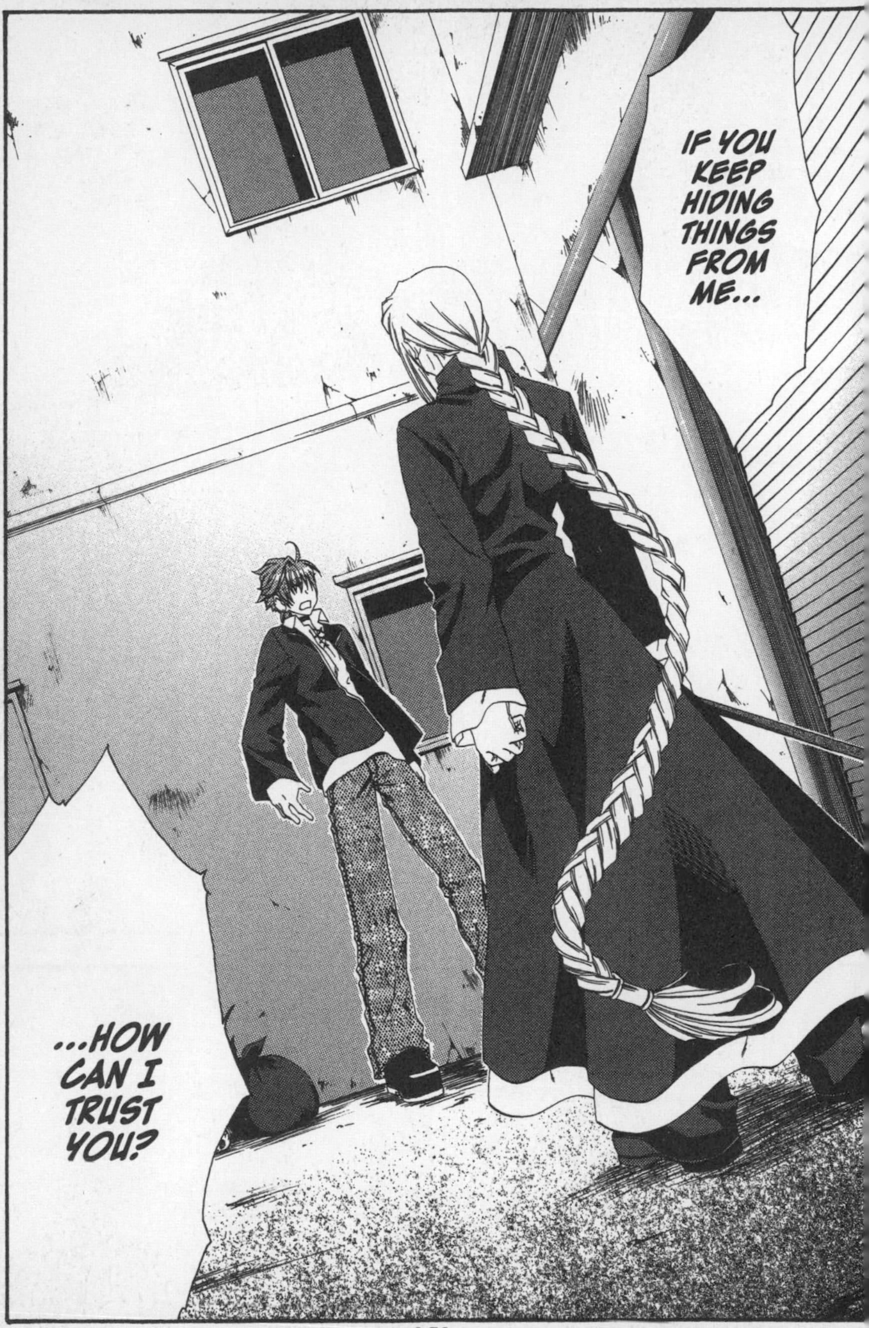
IF YOU KEEP HIDING THINGS FROM ME...
...HOW CAN I TRUST YOU?

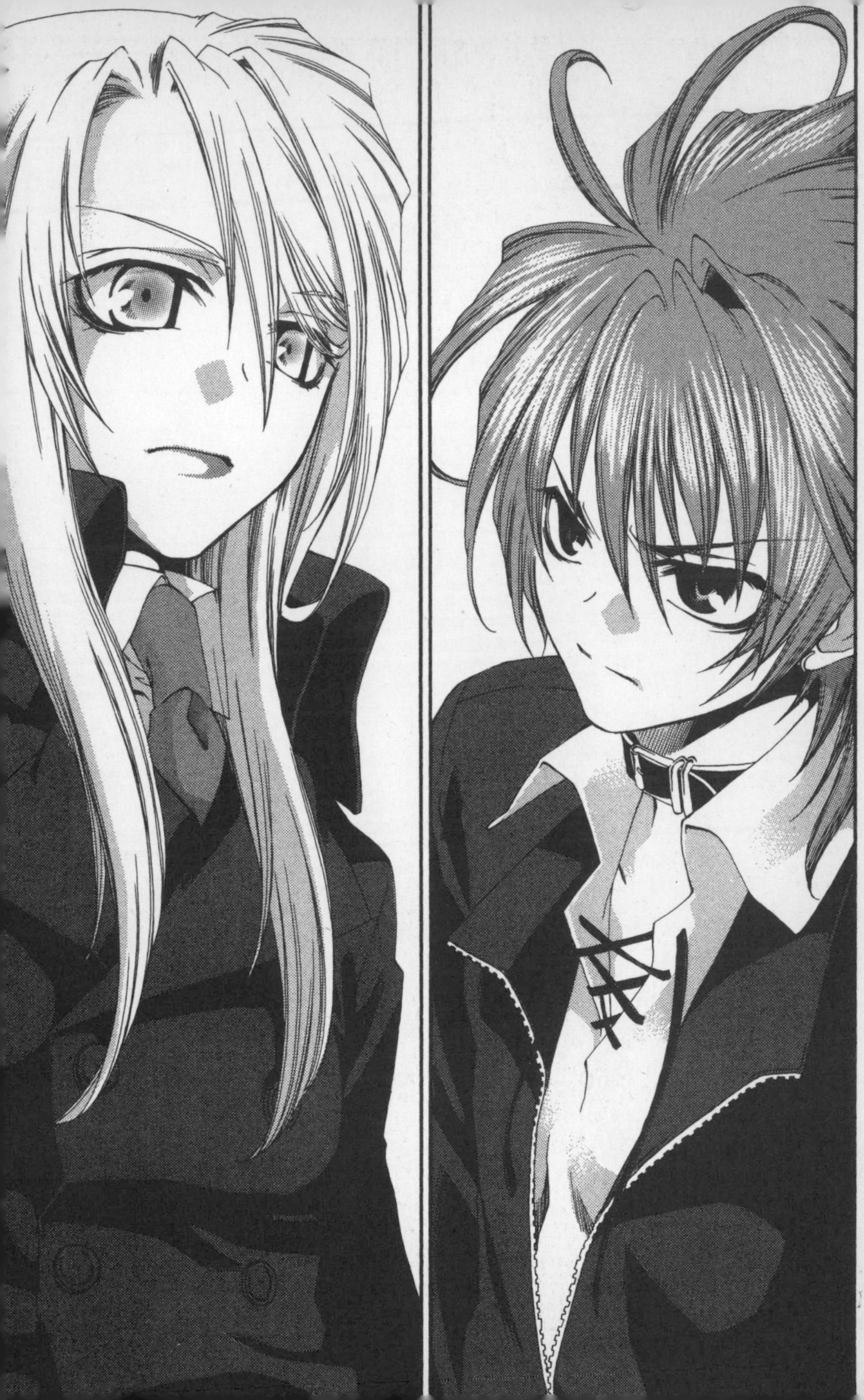

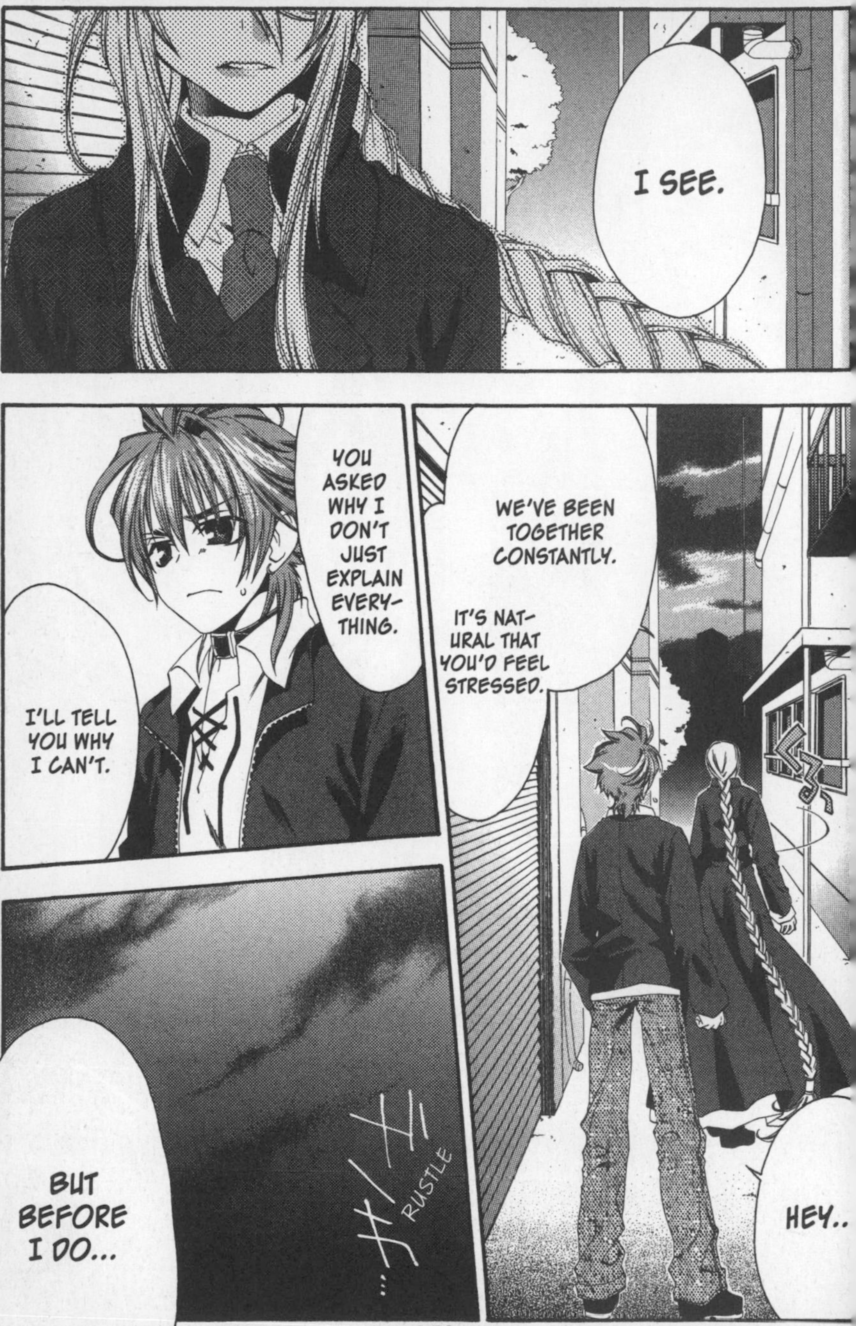
I SEE.
WE'VE BEEN TOGETHER CONSTANTLY.
IT'S NAT-URAL THAT YOU'D FEEL STRESSED.
YOU ASKED WHY I DON'T JUST EXPLAIN EVERY-THING.
I'LL TELL YOU WHY I CAN'T.
HEY...
BUT BEFORE I DO...
RUSTLE

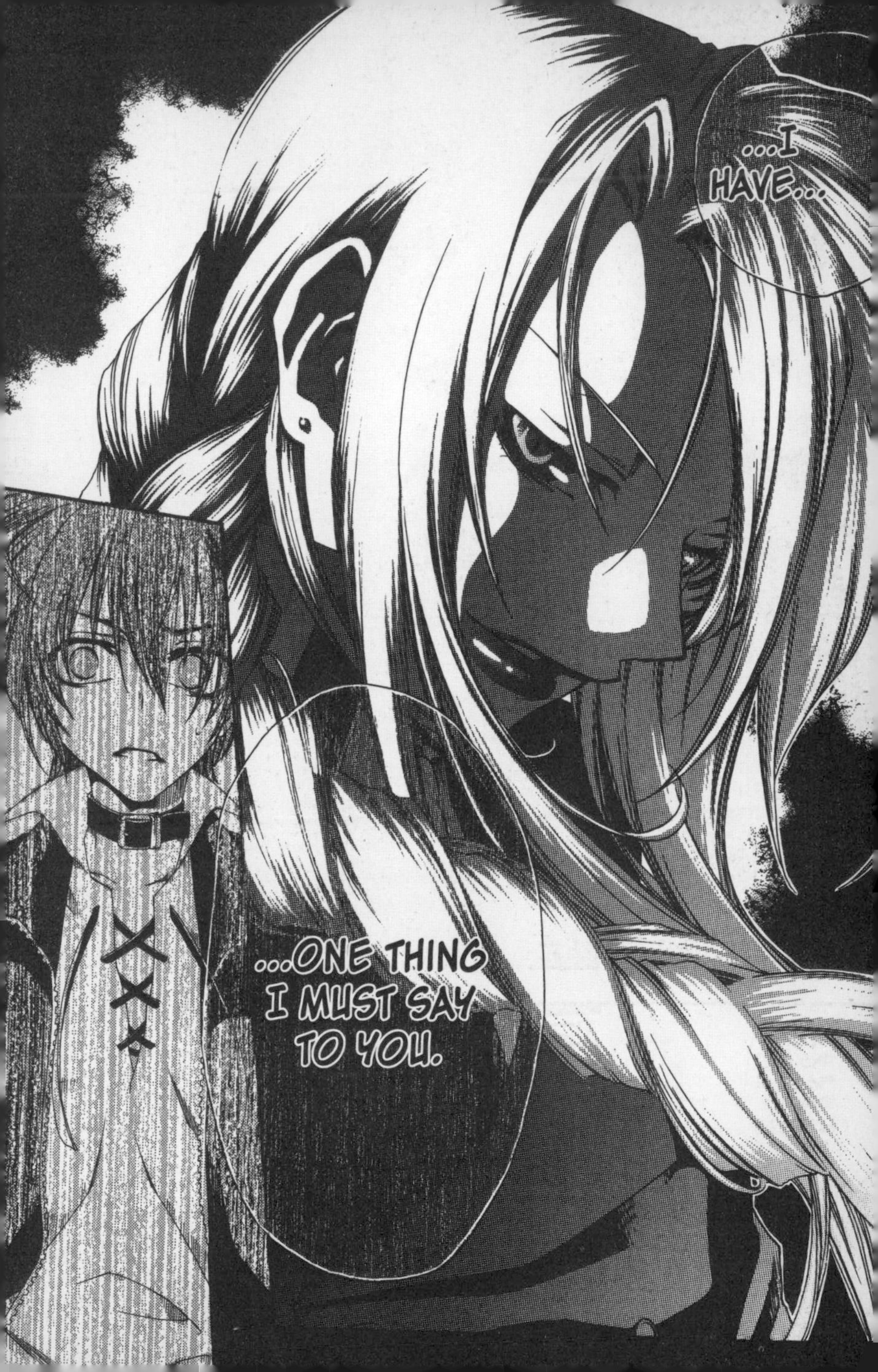
...I HAVE...
...ONE THING I MUST SAY TO YOU.

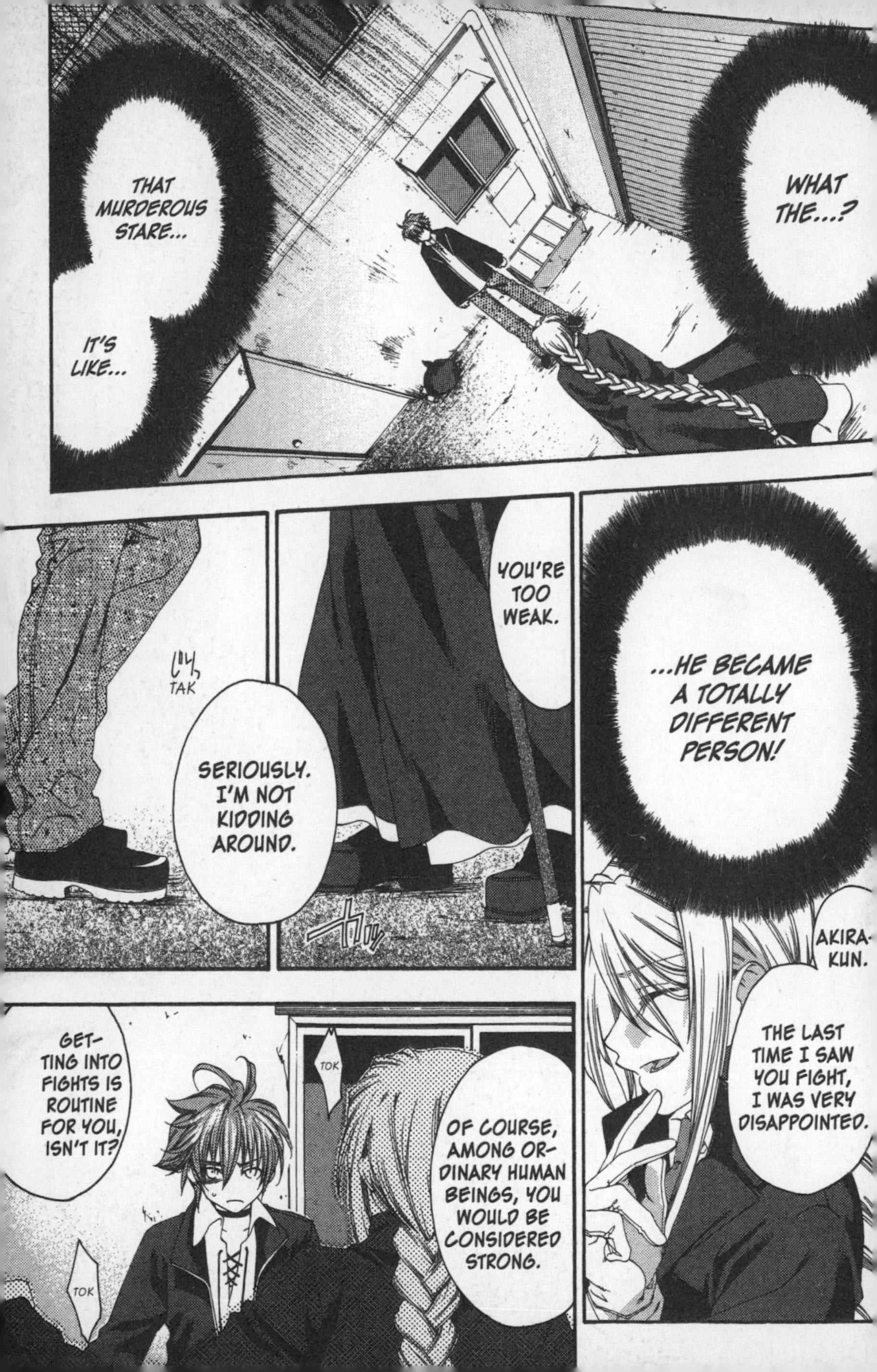
WHAT THE...?
THAT MURDEROUS STARE...
IT'S LIKE...
...HE BECAME A TOTALLY DIFFERENT PERSON!
YOU'RE TOO WEAK.
TAK
SERIOUSLY. I'M NOT KIDDING AROUND.
AKIRA-KUN.
THE LAST TIME I SAW YOU FIGHT, I WAS VERY DISAPPOINTED.
OF COURSE, AMONG OR-DINARY HUMAN BEINGS, YOU WOULD BE CONSIDERED STRONG.
TOK
GET-TING INTO FIGHTS IS ROUTINE FOR YOU, ISN'T IT?
TOK

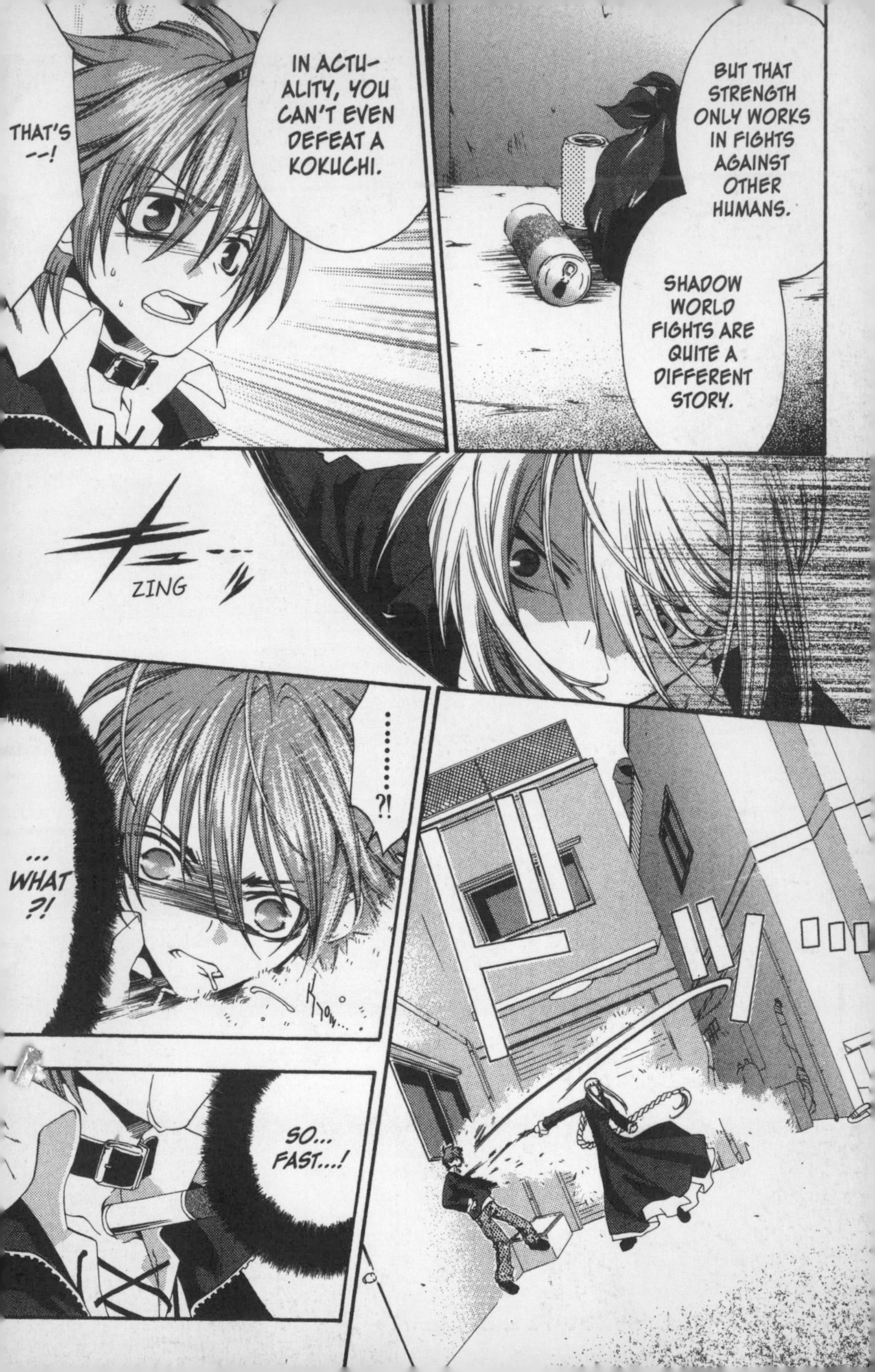
BUT THAT STRENGTH ONLY WORKS IN FIGHTS AGAINST OTHER HUMANS.
SHADOW WORLD FIGHTS ARE QUITE A DIFFERENT STORY.
IN ACTU-ALITY, YOU CAN'T EVEN DEFEAT A KOKUCHI.
THAT'S --!
ZING
......?!
...WHAT?!
SO... FAST...!

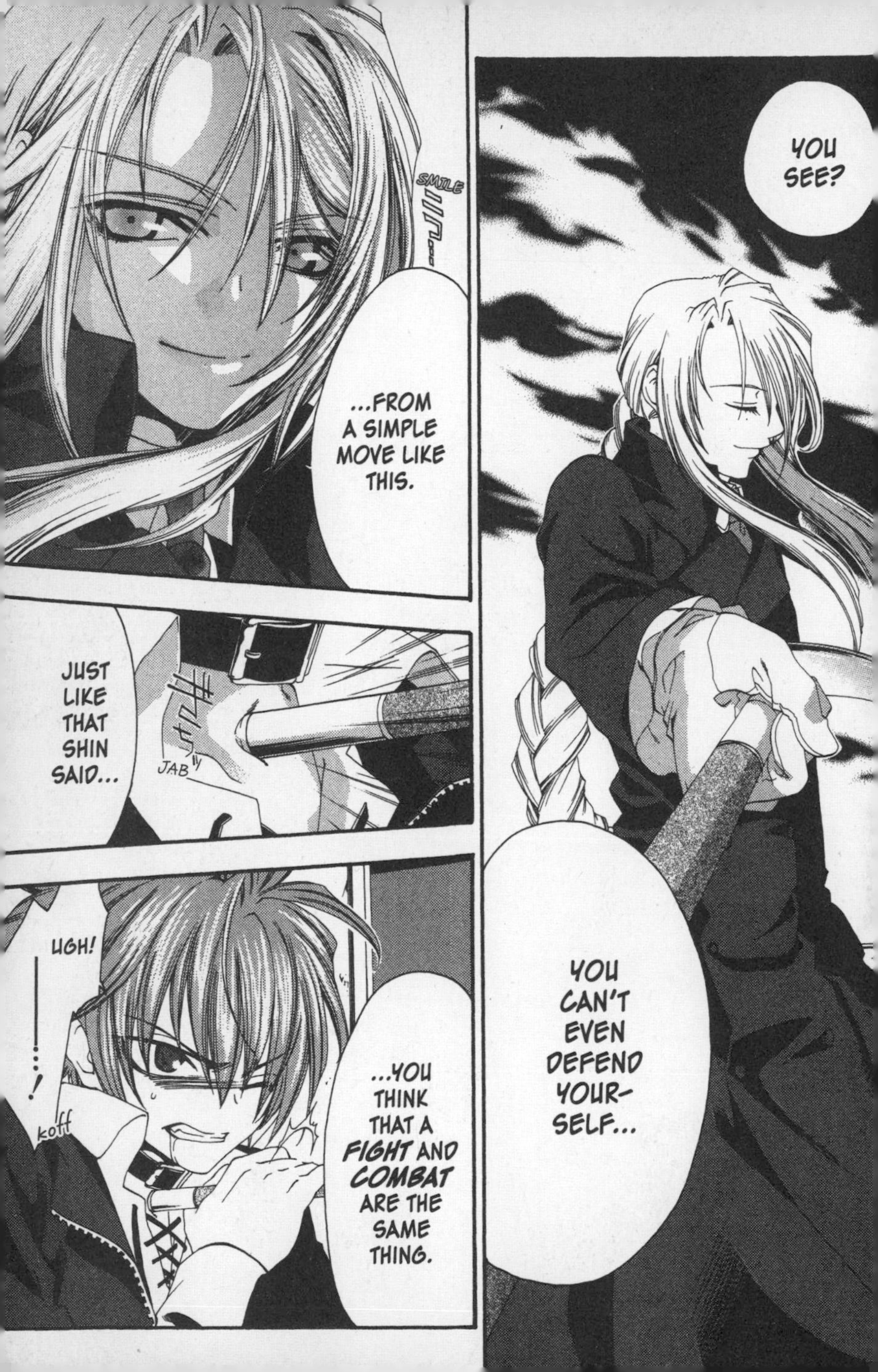
YOU SEE?
YOU CAN'T EVEN DEFEND YOURSELF...
SMILE
...FROM A SIMPLE MOVE LIKE THIS.
JUST LIKE THAT SHIN SAID...
JAB
...YOU THINK THAT A *FIGHT* AND *COMBAT* ARE THE SAME THING.
UGH!
—...!
koff

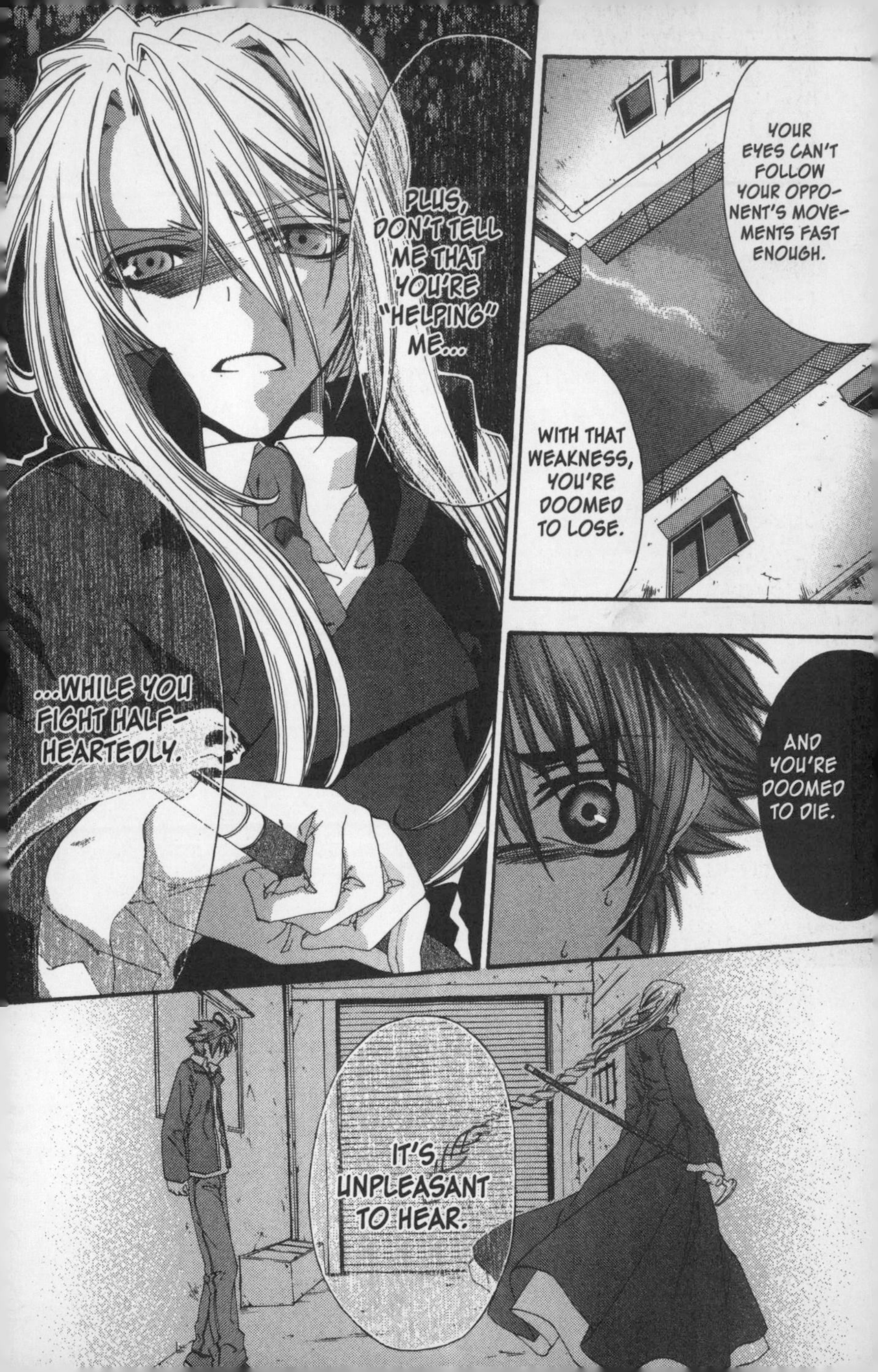
YOUR EYES CAN'T FOLLOW YOUR OPPONENT'S MOVEMENTS FAST ENOUGH.
WITH THAT WEAKNESS, YOU'RE DOOMED TO LOSE.
PLUS, DON'T TELL ME THAT YOU'RE "HELPING" ME...
AND YOU'RE DOOMED TO DIE.
...WHILE YOU FIGHT HALF-HEARTEDLY.
IT'S UNPLEASANT TO HEAR.

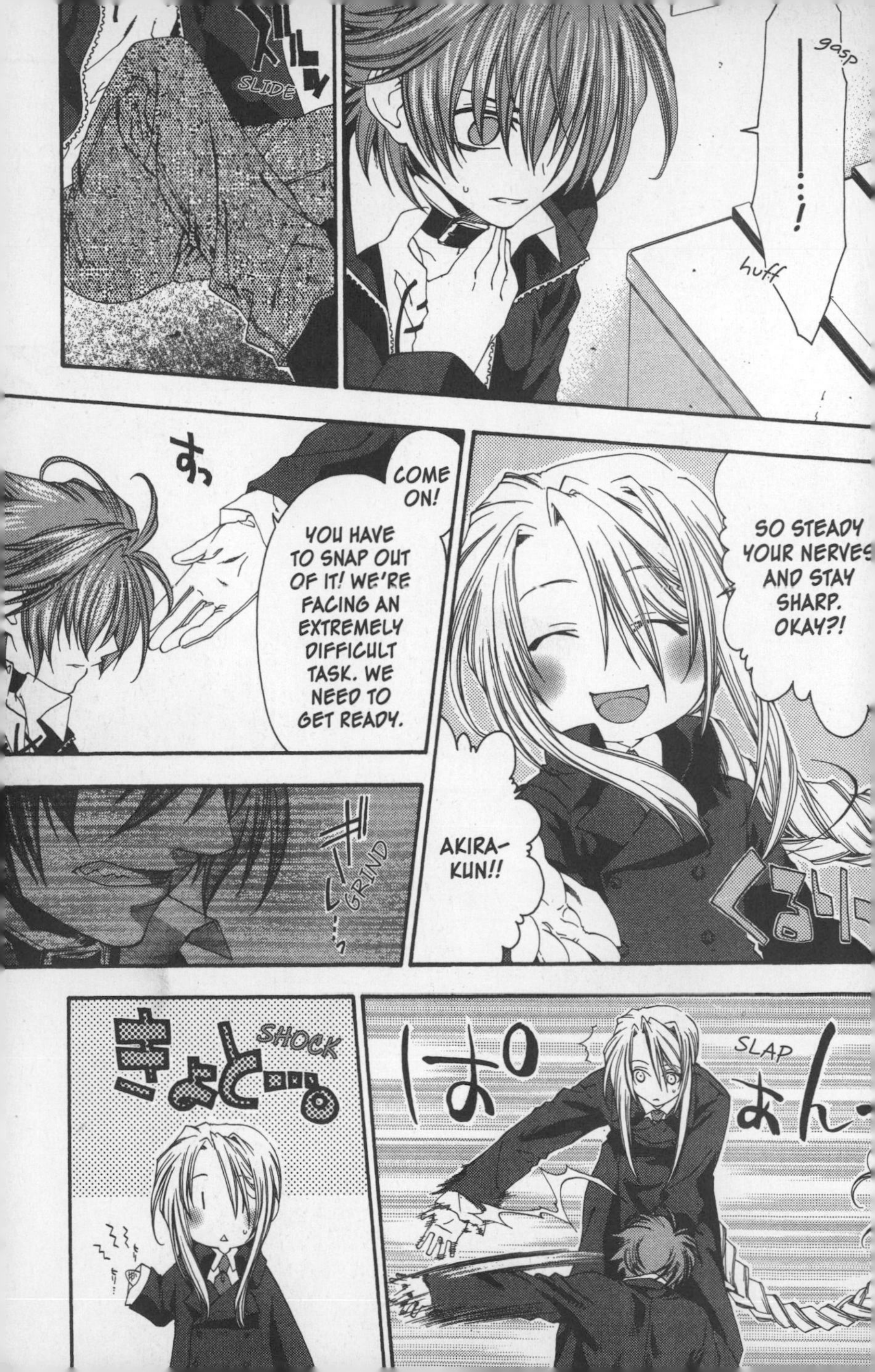
gasp
...!
huff
SLIDE
COME ON!
YOU HAVE TO SNAP OUT OF IT! WE'RE FACING AN EXTREMELY DIFFICULT TASK. WE NEED TO GET READY.
すっ
SO STEADY YOUR NERVES AND STAY SHARP. OKAY?!
AKIRA-KUN!!
GRIND
SLAP
SHOCK

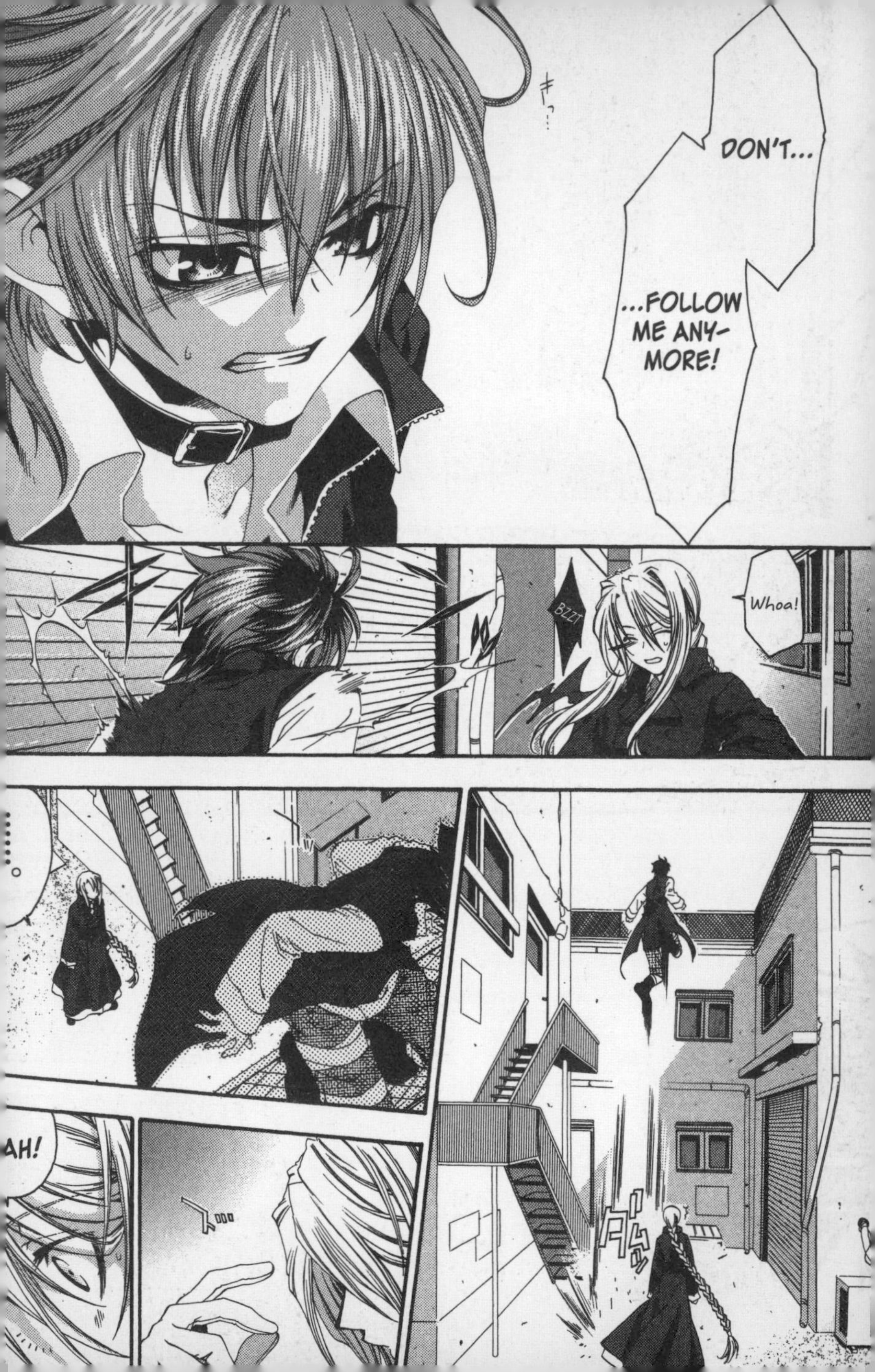

DON'T...
...FOLLOW ME ANY-MORE!
BZZT
Whoa!
AH!

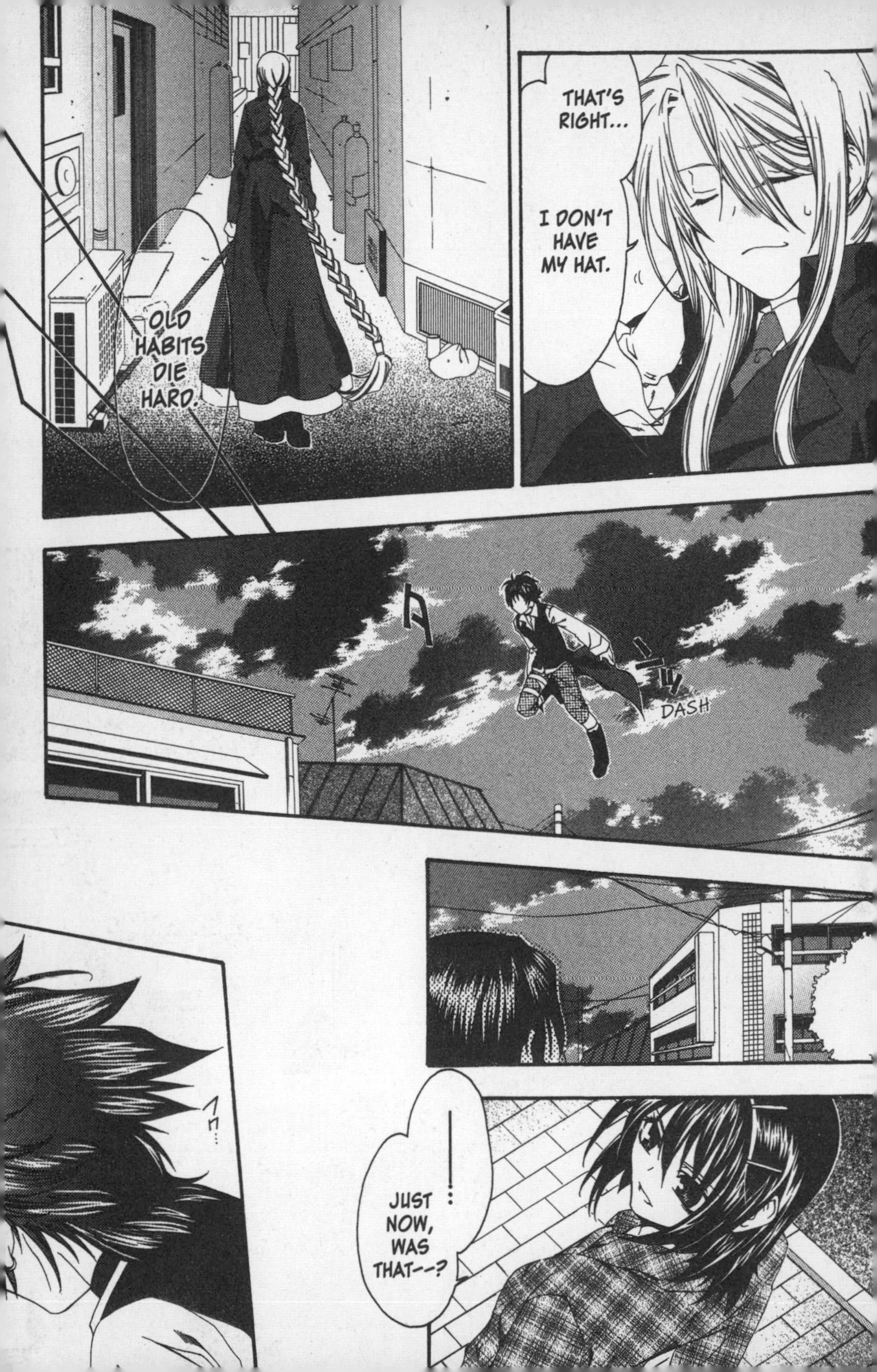
THAT'S RIGHT...
I DON'T HAVE MY HAT.
OLD HABITS DIE HARD.
DASH
JUST NOW, WAS THAT--?

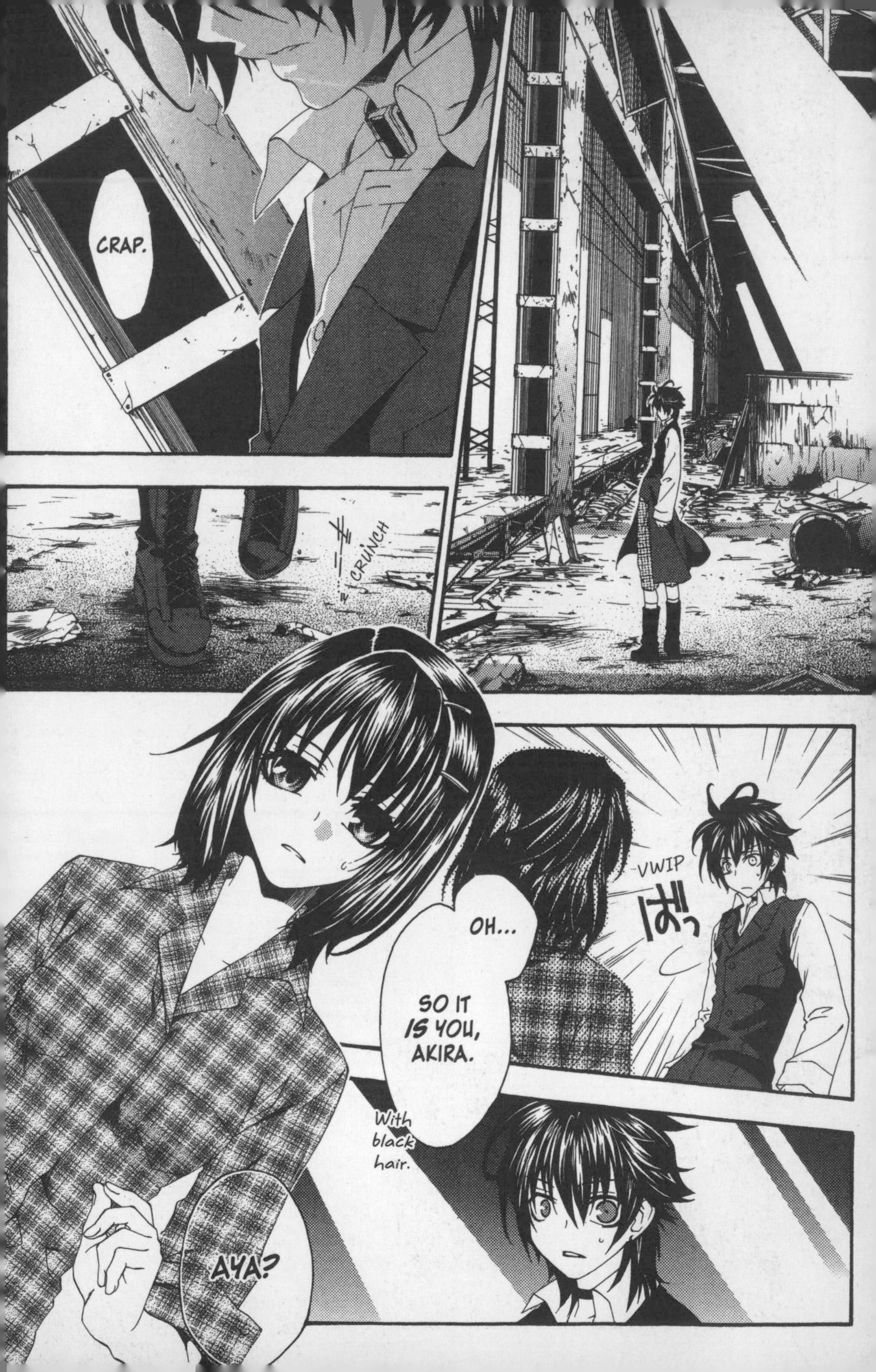
CRAP.
CRUNCH
OH...
SO IT IS YOU, AKIRA.
VWIP
ぱっ
With black hair.
AYA?

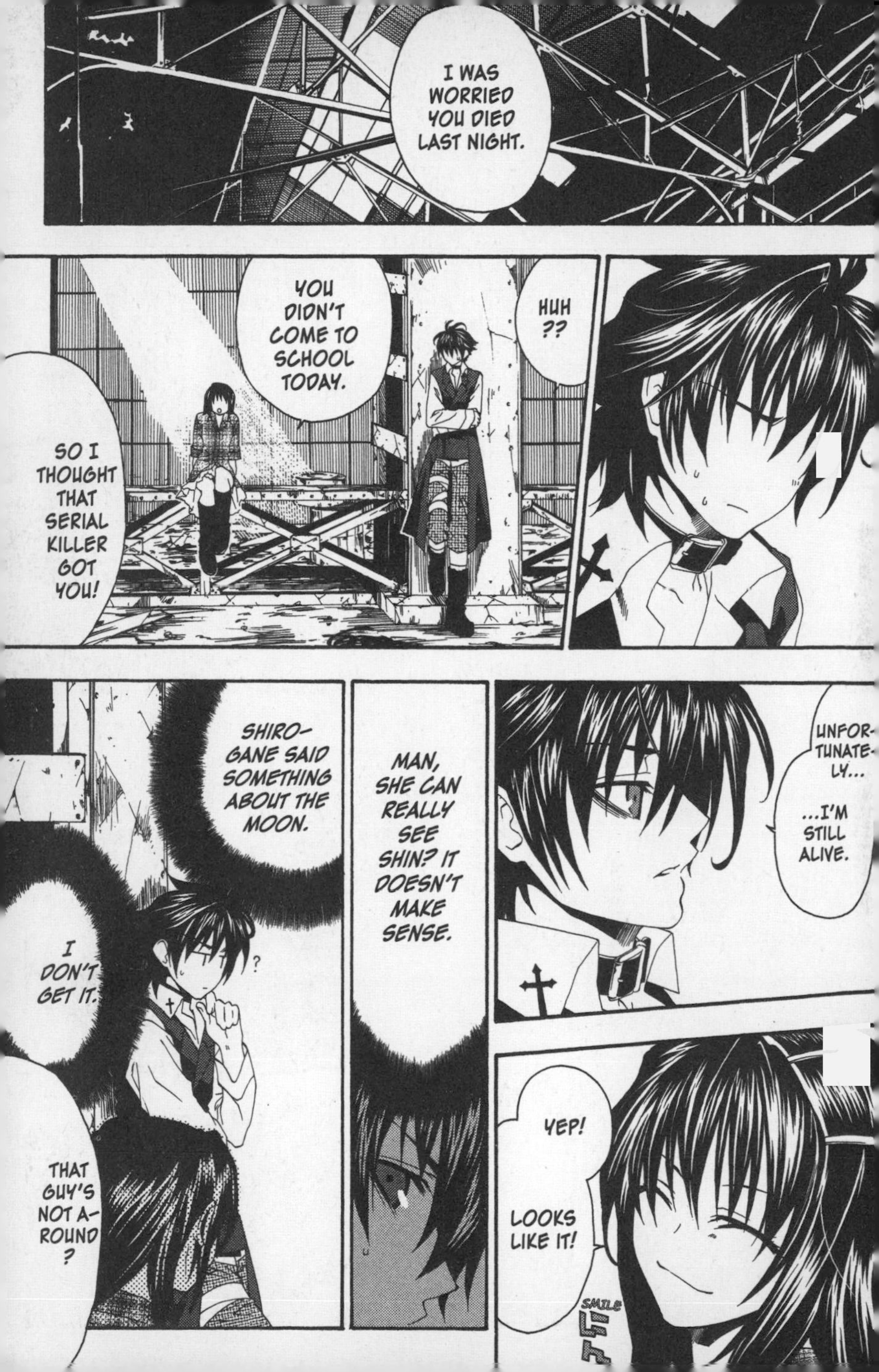
I WAS WORRIED YOU DIED LAST NIGHT.
HUH ??
YOU DIDN'T COME TO SCHOOL TODAY.
SO I THOUGHT THAT SERIAL KILLER GOT YOU!
UNFOR-TUNATE-LY...
...I'M STILL ALIVE.
MAN, SHE CAN REALLY SEE SHIN? IT DOESN'T MAKE SENSE.
SHIRO-GANE SAID SOMETHING ABOUT THE MOON.
I DON'T GET IT.
?
YEP!
LOOKS LIKE IT!
SMILE
THAT GUY'S NOT A-ROUND ?

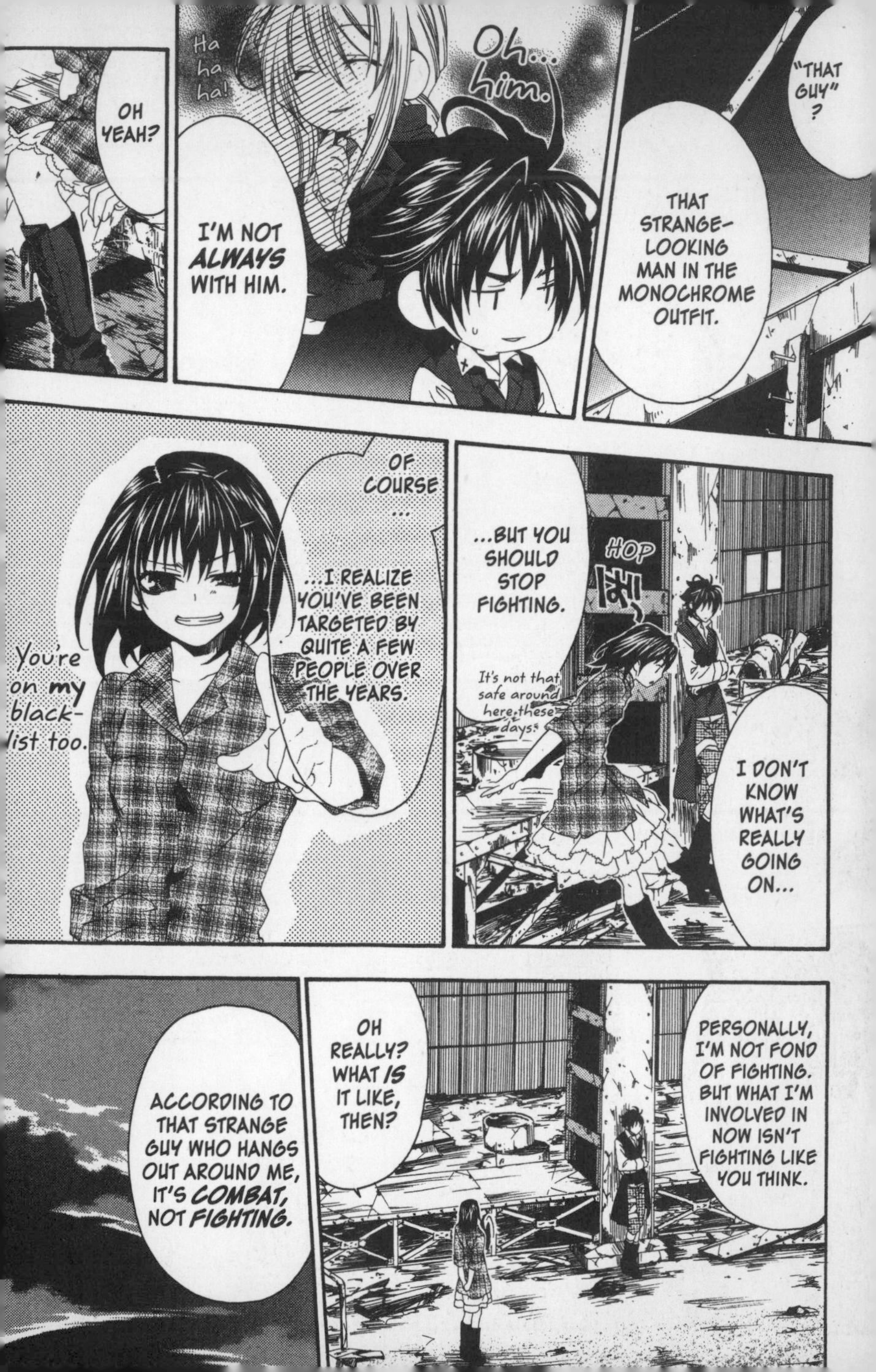
"THAT GUY"?
THAT STRANGE-LOOKING MAN IN THE MONOCHROME OUTFIT.
Oh... him.
Ha ha ha!
I'M NOT ALWAYS WITH HIM.
OH YEAH?
...BUT YOU SHOULD STOP FIGHTING.
HOP
It's not that safe around here these days.
I DON'T KNOW WHAT'S REALLY GOING ON...
OF COURSE...
...I REALIZE YOU'VE BEEN TARGETED BY QUITE A FEW PEOPLE OVER THE YEARS.
You're on my black-list too.
PERSONALLY, I'M NOT FOND OF FIGHTING. BUT WHAT I'M INVOLVED IN NOW ISN'T FIGHTING LIKE YOU THINK.
OH REALLY? WHAT IS IT LIKE, THEN?
ACCORDING TO THAT STRANGE GUY WHO HANGS OUT AROUND ME, IT'S COMBAT, NOT FIGHTING.

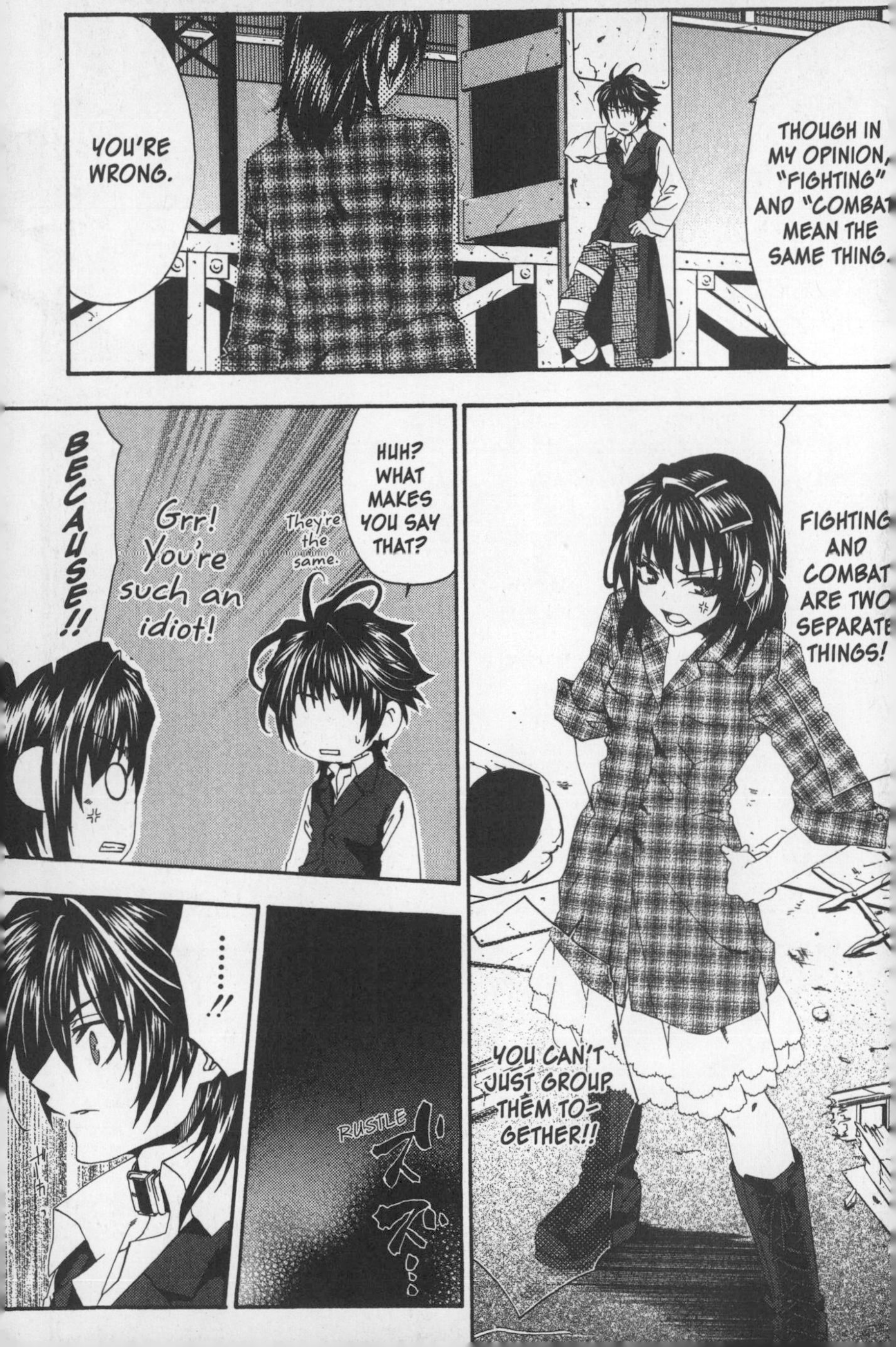
THOUGH IN MY OPINION, "FIGHTING" AND "COMBAT MEAN THE SAME THING.
YOU'RE WRONG.
FIGHTING AND COMBAT ARE TWO SEPARATE THINGS!
YOU CAN'T JUST GROUP THEM TO-GETHER!!
HUH? WHAT MAKES YOU SAY THAT?
They're the same.
Grr! You're such an idiot!
BECAUSE!!
......!!
RUSTLE

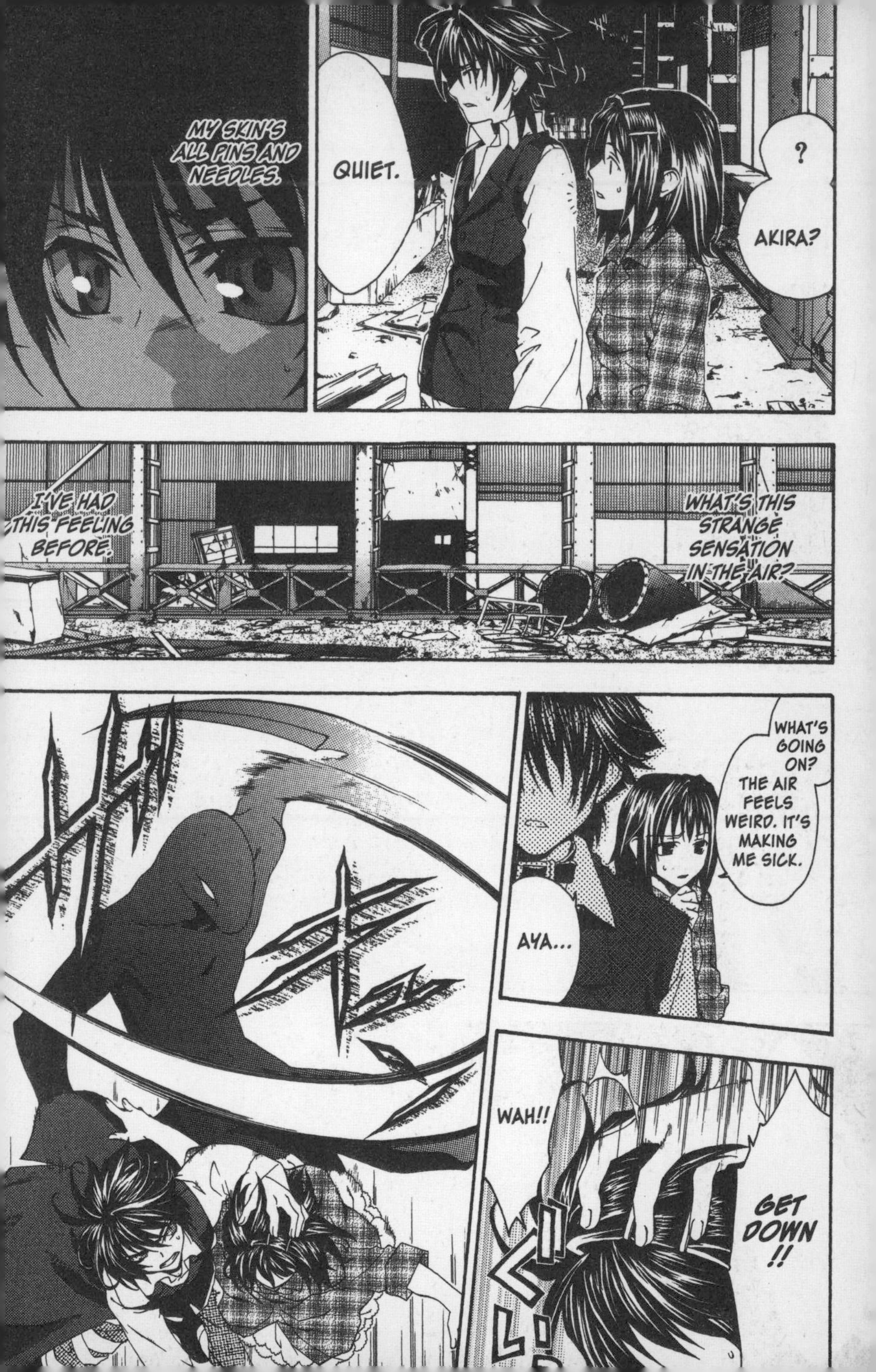
?
AKIRA?
QUIET.
MY SKIN'S ALL PINS AND NEEDLES.
WHAT'S THIS STRANGE SENSATION IN THE AIR?
I'VE HAD THIS FEELING BEFORE.
WHAT'S GOING ON? THE AIR FEELS WEIRD. IT'S MAKING ME SICK.
AYA...
GET DOWN!!
WAH!!

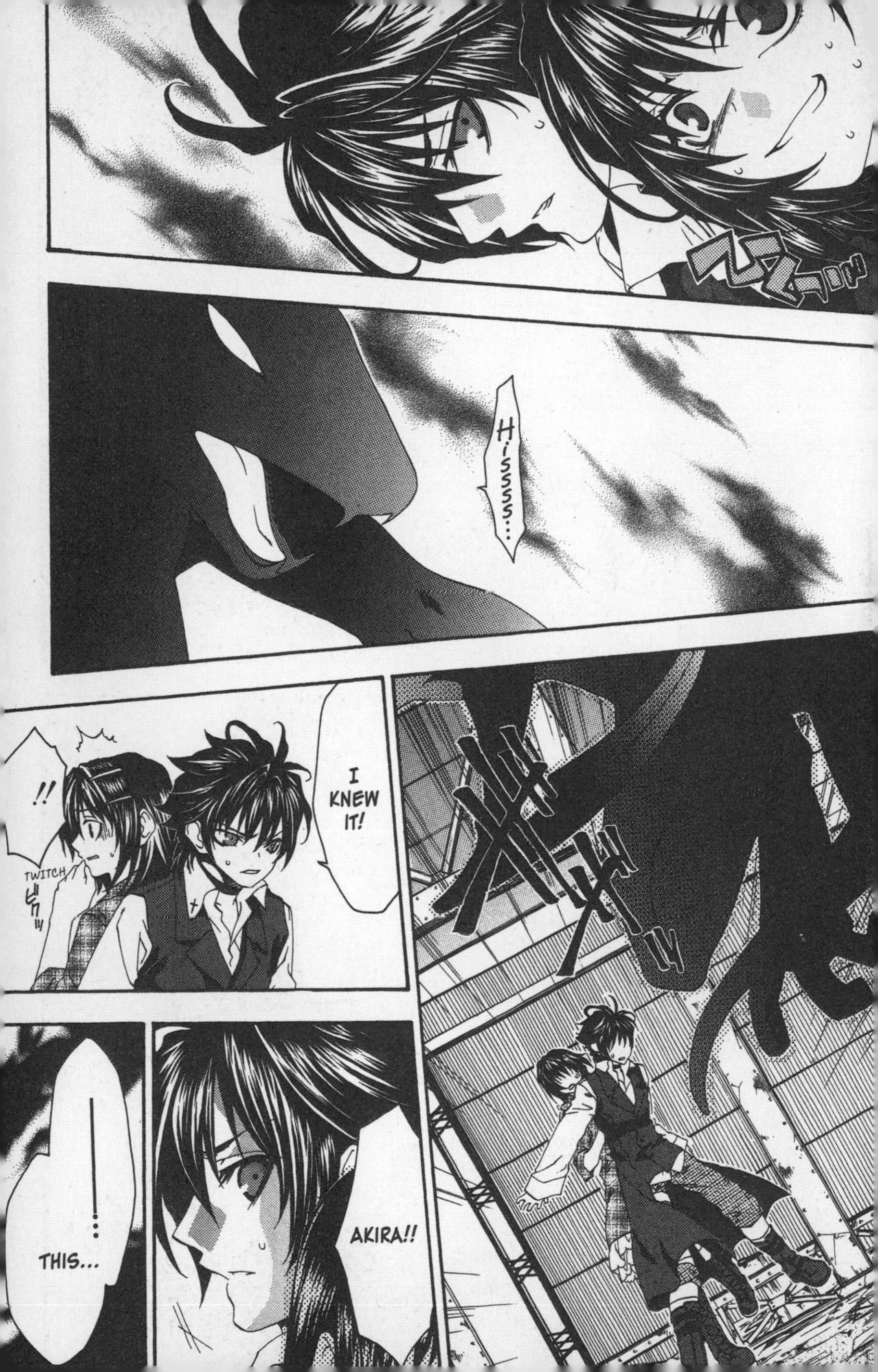

HISSSS...
I KNEW IT!
!!
TWITCH
AKIRA!!
THIS...

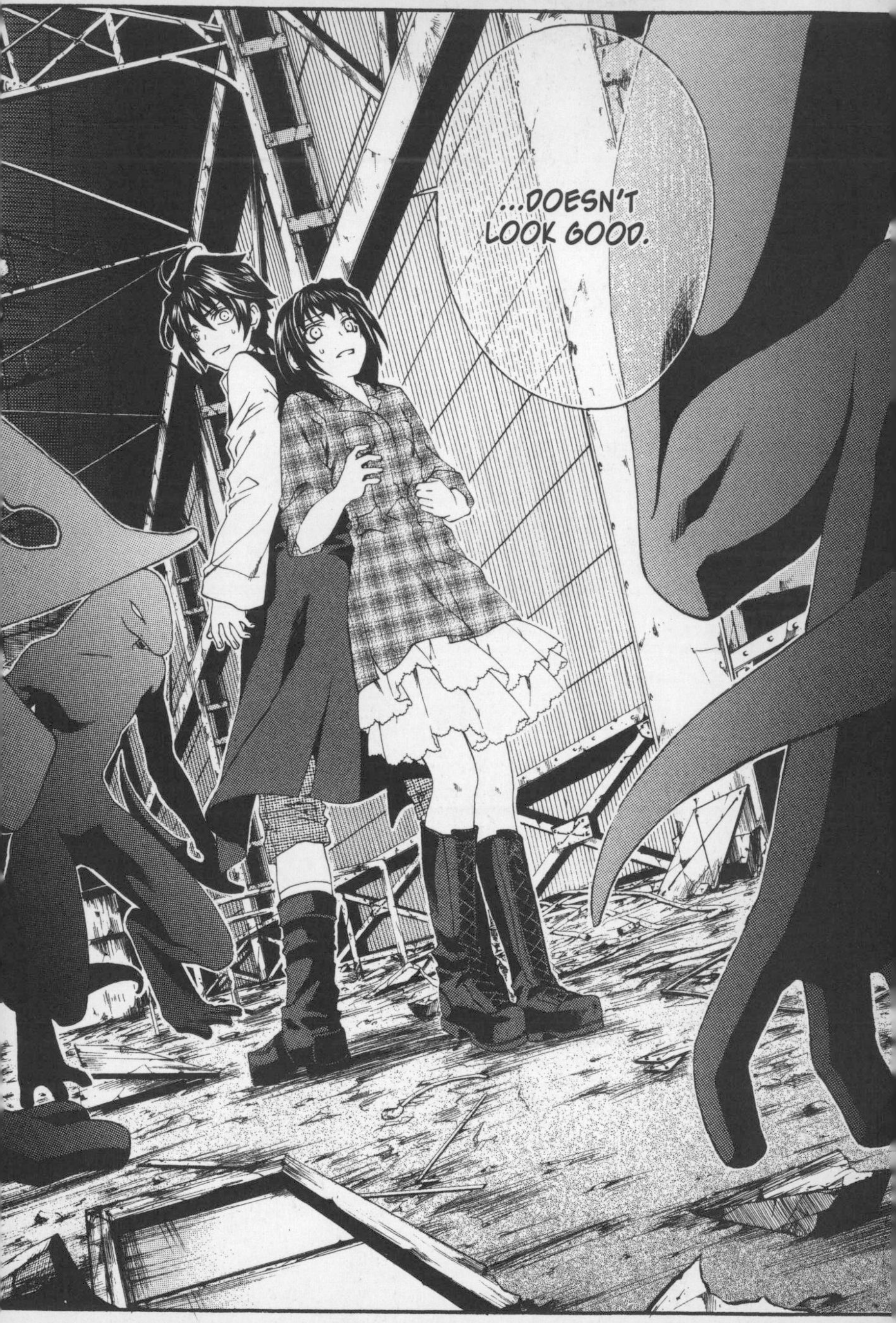
...DOESN'T
LOOK GOOD.

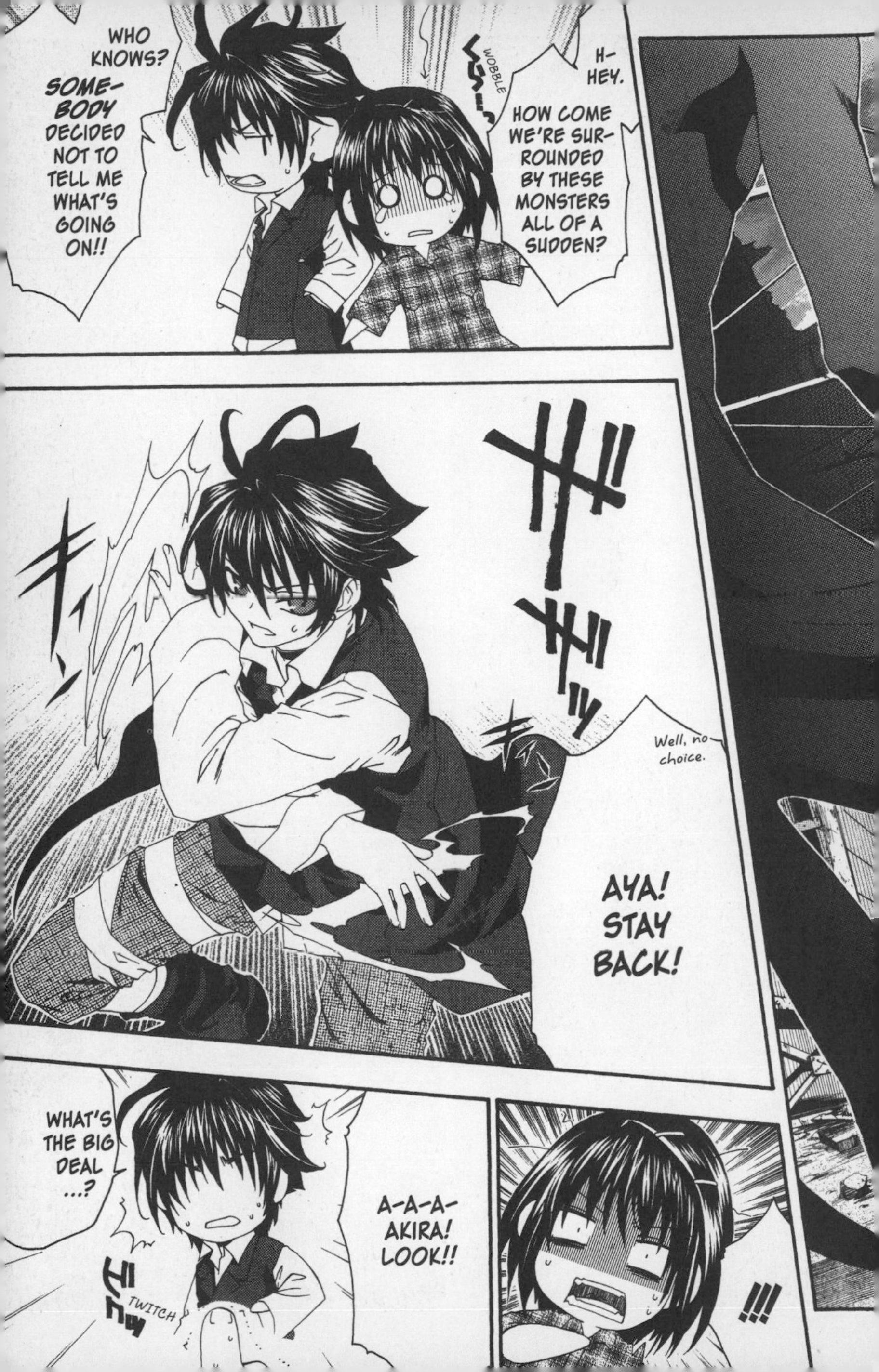
H-HEY.
HOW COME WE'RE SURROUNDED BY THESE MONSTERS ALL OF A SUDDEN?
WOBBLE
WHO KNOWS?
SOMEBODY DECIDED NOT TO TELL ME WHAT'S GOING ON!!
Well, no choice.
AYA! STAY BACK!
!!!
A-A-A-AKIRA! LOOK!!
WHAT'S THE BIG DEAL ...?
TWITCH

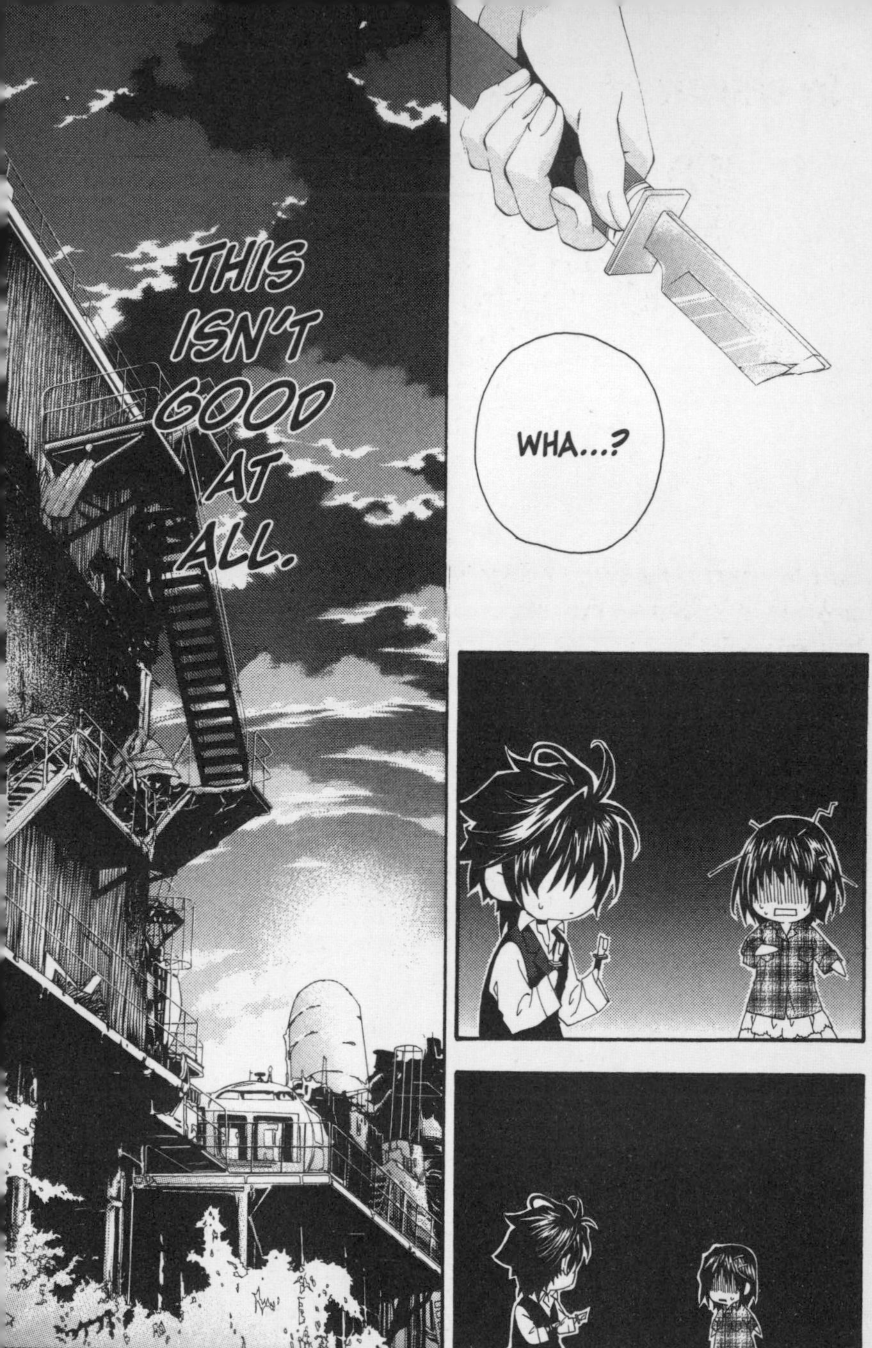
WHA...?
THIS ISN'T GOOD AT ALL.

TO BE CONTINUED IN VOLUME 3

In the next

Monochrome Factor

Surrounded by kokuchi and with Akira's shin blades broken, it's Aya to the rescue! The kokuchi's puppet master has more to say about Shirogane than he himself has been willing to reveal to Akira, so it's time to stop keeping secrets. And when Homurabi attacks Kengo, it's time for Akira to form a team to fight back!

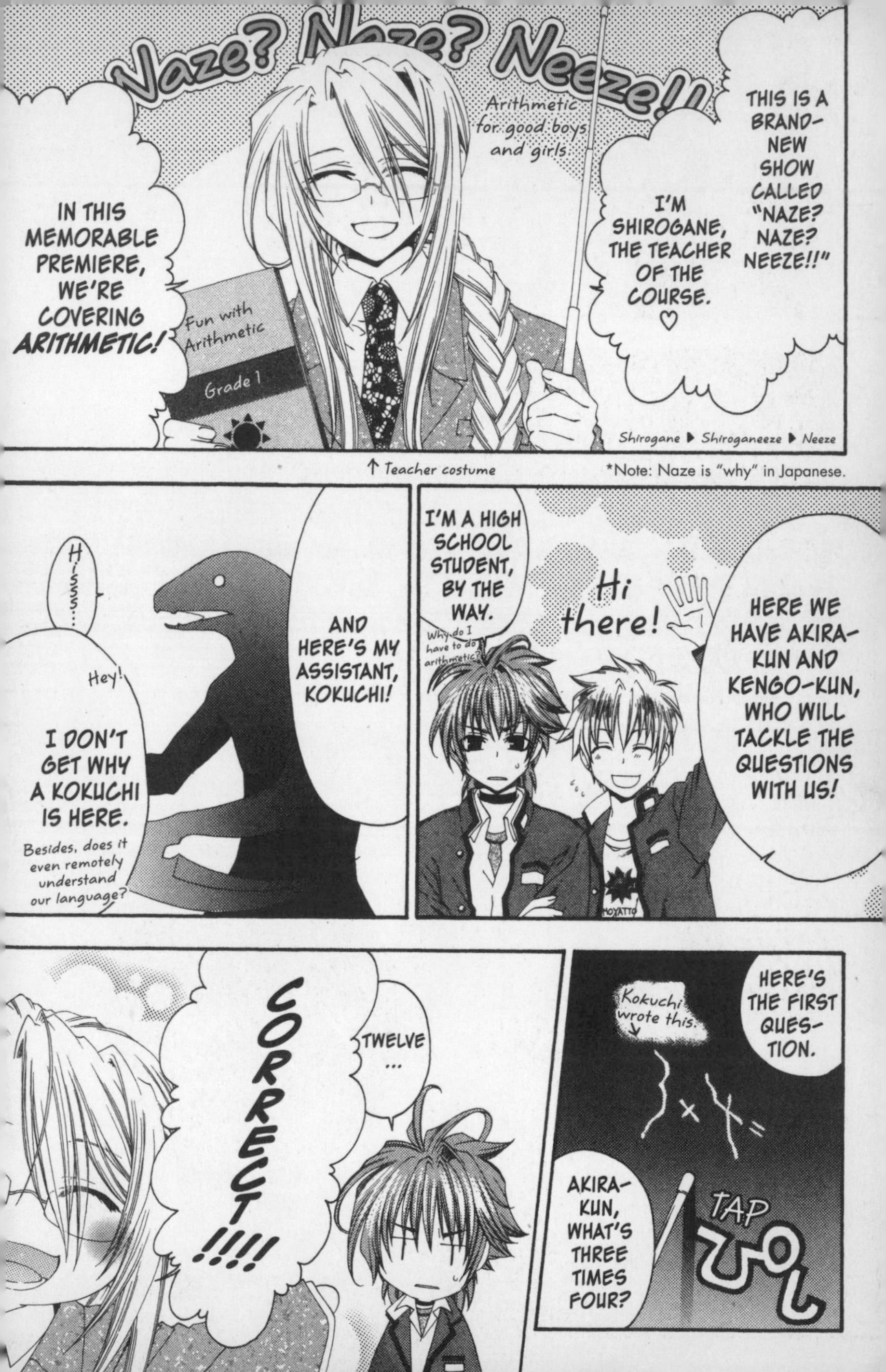
Naze? Naze? Neeze!!
THIS IS A BRAND-NEW SHOW CALLED "NAZE? NAZE? NEEZE!!"
I'M SHIROGANE, THE TEACHER OF THE COURSE. ♡
Arithmetic for good boys and girls
IN THIS MEMORABLE PREMIERE, WE'RE COVERING ARITHMETIC!
Fun with Arithmetic
Grade 1
Shirogane ▶ Shiroganeeze ▶ Neeze
HERE WE HAVE AKIRA-KUN AND KENGO-KUN, WHO WILL TACKLE THE QUESTIONS WITH US!
Hi there!
I'M A HIGH SCHOOL STUDENT, BY THE WAY.
Why do I have to do arithmetic?
HOYATTO
AND HERE'S MY ASSISTANT, KOKUCHI!
Hisss...
Hey!
I DON'T GET WHY A KOKUCHI IS HERE.
Besides, does it even remotely understand our language?
HERE'S THE FIRST QUESTION.
Kokuchi wrote this.
3 × 4 =
AKIRA-KUN, WHAT'S THREE TIMES FOUR?
TAP
TWELVE...
CORRECT!!!!

↑ Teacher costume

*Note: Naze is "why" in Japanese.

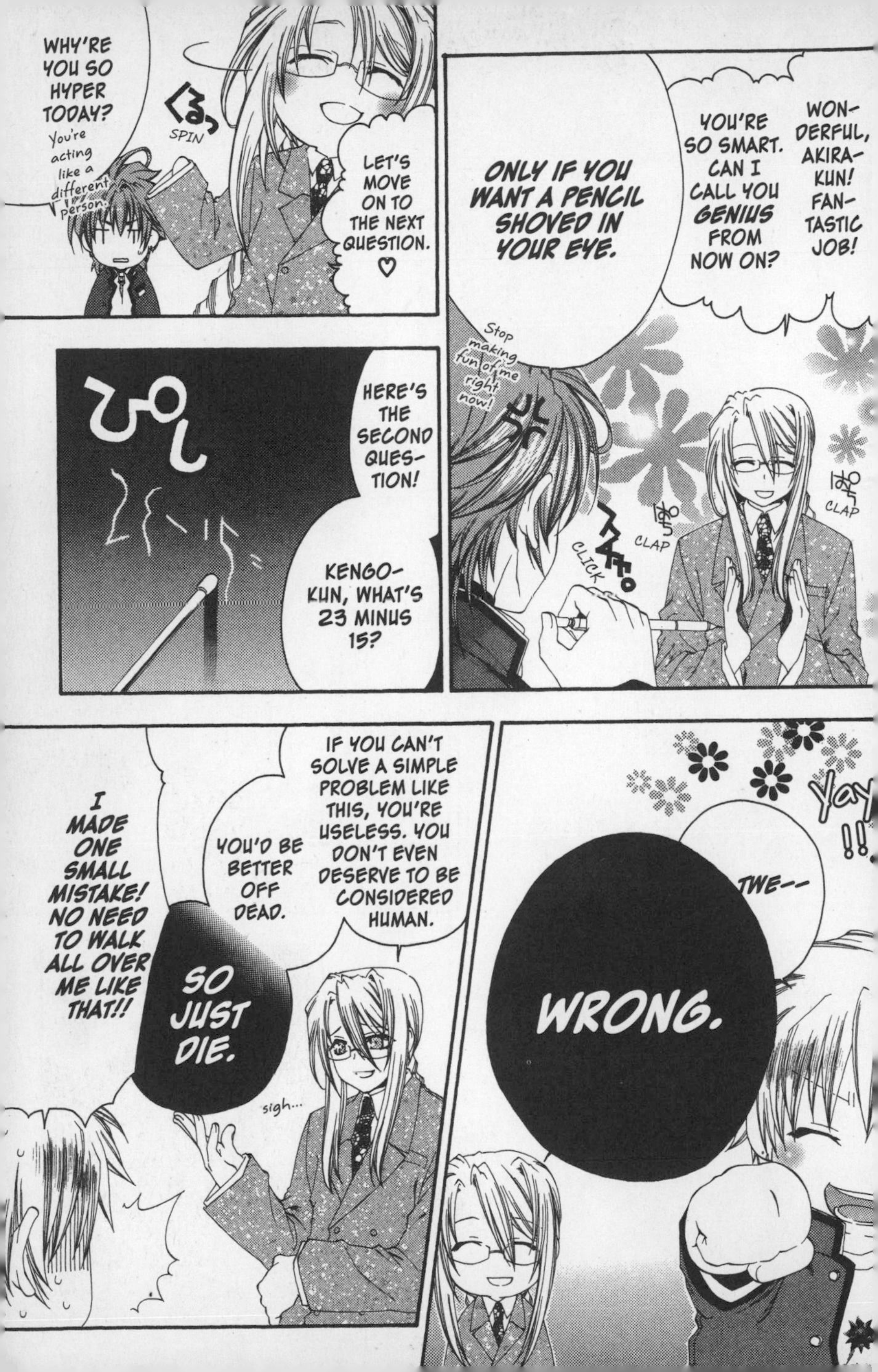
WON-DERFUL, AKIRA-KUN! FAN-TASTIC JOB!
YOU'RE SO SMART. CAN I CALL YOU GENIUS FROM NOW ON?
ONLY IF YOU WANT A PENCIL SHOVED IN YOUR EYE.
Stop making fun of me right now!
CLAP
CLAP
CLICK
WHY'RE YOU SO HYPER TODAY?
You're acting like a different person.
SPIN
LET'S MOVE ON TO THE NEXT QUESTION. ♡
HERE'S THE SECOND QUES-TION!
KENGO-KUN, WHAT'S 23 MINUS 15?
Yay!!
TWE--
WRONG.
IF YOU CAN'T SOLVE A SIMPLE PROBLEM LIKE THIS, YOU'RE USELESS. YOU DON'T EVEN DESERVE TO BE CONSIDERED HUMAN.
YOU'D BE BETTER OFF DEAD.
SO JUST DIE.
sigh...
I MADE ONE SMALL MISTAKE! NO NEED TO WALK ALL OVER ME LIKE THAT!!

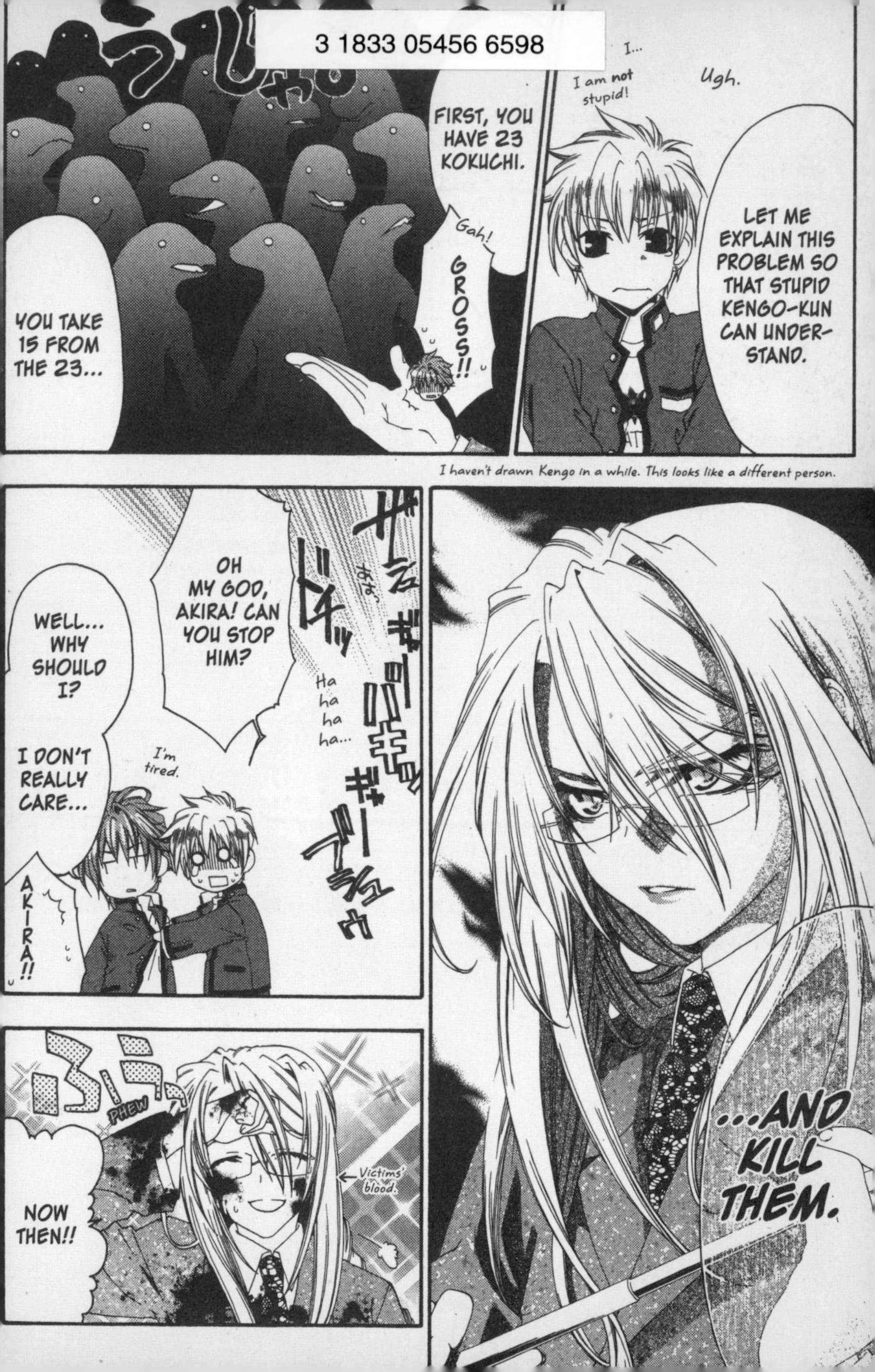
Ugh.
I...
I am not stupid!
LET ME EXPLAIN THIS PROBLEM SO THAT STUPID KENGO-KUN CAN UNDER-STAND.
FIRST, YOU HAVE 23 KOKUCHI.
Gah!
GROSS!!
YOU TAKE 15 FROM THE 23...
I haven't drawn Kengo in a while. This looks like a different person.
...AND KILL THEM.
OH MY GOD, AKIRA! CAN YOU STOP HIM?
Ha ha ha ha...
WELL... WHY SHOULD I?
I'm tired.
I DON'T REALLY CARE...
AKIRA!!
PHEW
Victims' blood.
NOW THEN!!

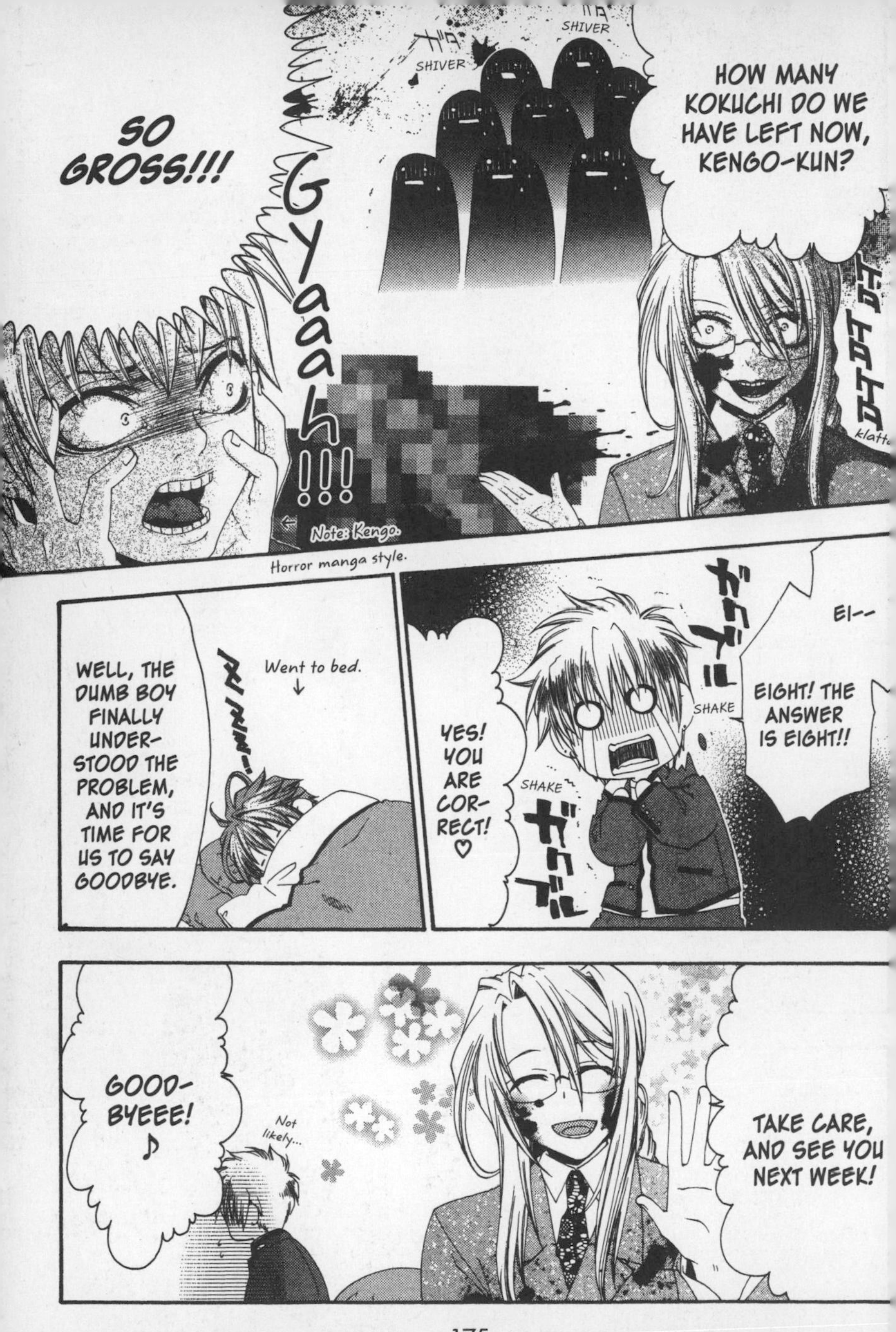
HOW MANY KOKUCHI DO WE HAVE LEFT NOW, KENGO-KUN?
klatta
SHIVER
SHIVER
Gyaaah!!!
SO GROSS!!!
Note: Kengo.
Horror manga style.
EI--
EIGHT! THE ANSWER IS EIGHT!!
SHAKE
SHAKE
YES! YOU ARE COR-RECT! ♡
WELL, THE DUMB BOY FINALLY UNDER-STOOD THE PROBLEM, AND IT'S TIME FOR US TO SAY GOODBYE.
Went to bed.
TAKE CARE, AND SEE YOU NEXT WEEK!
GOOD-BYEEE! ♪
Not likely...

Sorano Profile

Pen name	Kaili Sorano (Many people write the kanji in my name wrong.)
Birthday	October 23
Height	A "betwixt and between" height, I'm afraid.
Shoe size	25 cm (size 9)
Hobbies	Movies (I enjoy movies from the '70s, '80s and '90s, especially B movies); creating movies and games; survival horror games; bleaching and dying my hair (I try various colors such as red, blue and gray); using the computer.
Blood type	O
Vision	Left: 0.03 Right: 0.04 (I'm guessing here.)
Weight	Heavy
Hand	Big. Long, weird-looking fingers.

Art and drawing tools, etc.

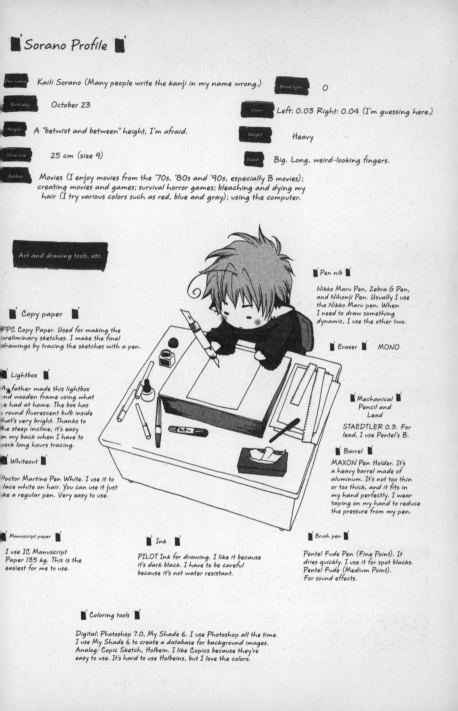

Copy paper

PPC Copy Paper. Used for making the preliminary sketches. I make the final drawings by tracing the sketches with a pen.

Lightbox

My father made this lightbox and wooden frame using what he had at home. The box has round fluorescent bulb inside that's very bright. Thanks to the steep incline, it's easy on my back when I have to work long hours tracing.

Whiteout

Doctor Martine Pen White. I use it to place white on hair. You can use it just like a regular pen. Very easy to use.

Manuscript paper

I use IC Manuscript Paper 135 kg. This is the easiest for me to use.

Ink

PILOT Ink for drawing. I like it because it's dark black. I have to be careful because it's not water resistant.

Pen nib

Nikko Maru Pen, Zebra G Pen, and Nihonji Pen. Usually I use the Nikko Maru pen. When I need to draw something dynamic, I use the other two.

Eraser MONO

Mechanical Pencil and Lead

STAEDTLER 0.3. For lead, I use Pentel's B.

Barrel

MAXON Pen Holder. It's a heavy barrel made of aluminum. It's not too thin or too thick, and it fits in my hand perfectly. I wear taping on my hand to reduce the pressure from my pen.

Brush pen

Pentel Fude Pen (Fine Point). It dries quickly. I use it for spot blacks. Pentel Fude (Medium Point). For sound effects.

Coloring tools

Digital: Photoshop 7.0, My Shade 6. I use Photoshop all the time. I use My Shade 6 to create a database for background images. Analog: Copic Sketch, Holbein. I like Copics because they're easy to use. It's hard to use Holbeins, but I love the colors.

Analysis

Antenna

Always ready to receive signals carrying good material. However, this antenna is extremely selective.

Vision

Very poor. Basically, I need glasses.

Cigarettes

About one to three per day. I used to smoke Marlboro Menthol Lights, but now I smoke Cabin Menthols.

Frame

Many people think I'm athletic and a good runner, but I'm not really either. I don't know why... Maybe people say this because I'm big-boned?

Running speed

50 meters in less than 20 seconds.

Brain

Not too bright. Especially bad at math. Can't even do two-digit addition. I grew up watching too many action movies and have a wild, unrealistic imagination going all the time.

Hearing

My hearing is extremely selective. I can hear very well when I'm willing to listen, but I'm almost deaf when I don't care.

Hands

I often put them in boiling water on purpose.

Fashion

I used to wear a lot of black outfits during my teens, but now I like jeans and military clothes.

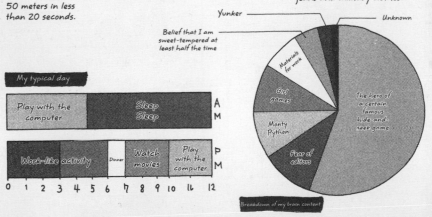

My typical day

| Play with the computer | | Sleep Sleep | A M |

| Work-like activity | | Dinner | Watch movies | Play with the computer | P M |

0 1 2 3 4 5 6 7 8 9 10 11 12

Yunker

Belief that I am sweet-tempered at least half the time

Materials for work

Girl games

Monty Python

Fear of editors

Unknown

The hero of a certain famous hide-and-seek game

Breakdown of my brain content

Optical Illusion

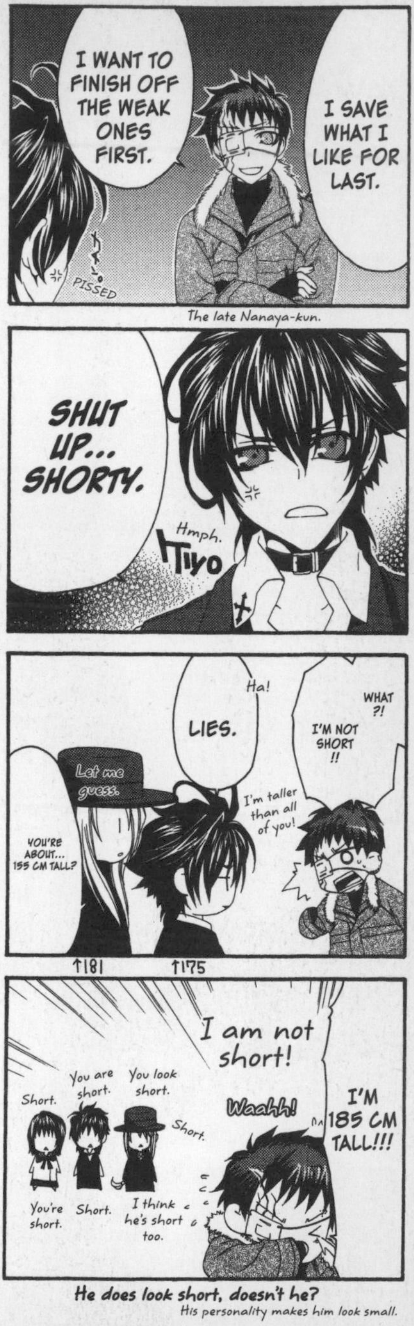
I save what I like for last.
I want to finish off the weak ones first.
PISSED
The late Nanaya-kun.
Shut up... shorty.
Hmph.
What?! I'm not short!!
Lies.
Ha!
I'm taller than all of you!
Let me guess.
You're about... 155 cm tall?
↑181
↑175
I'm 185 cm tall!!!
Waahh!
I am not short!
You look short.
You are short.
Short.
Short.
You're short.
Short.
I think he's short too.

He does look short, doesn't he?
His personality makes him look small.

Oh?

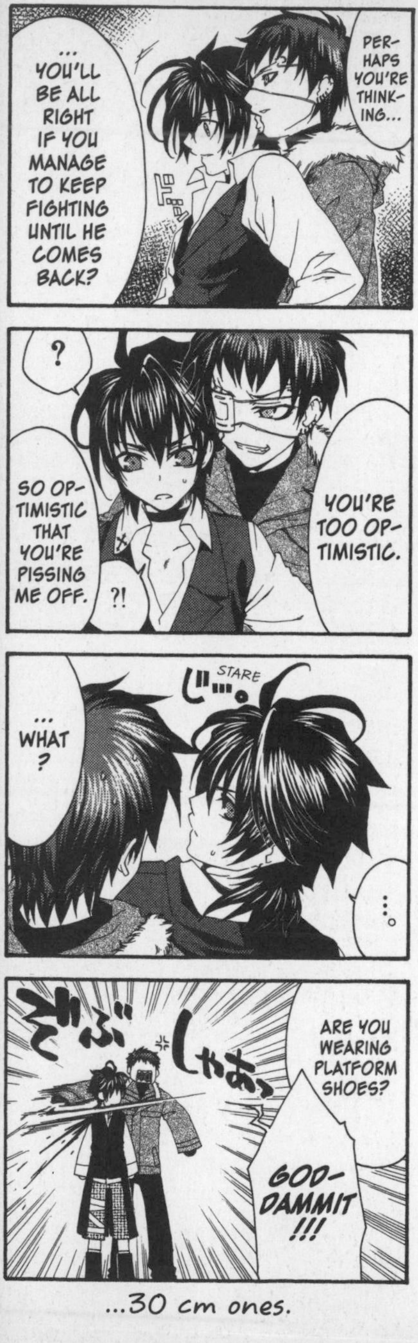
Perhaps you're thinking...
...You'll be all right if you manage to keep fighting until he comes back?
?
You're too optimistic.
So optimistic that you're pissing me off.
?!
Stare
...What?
...。
Are you wearing platform shoes?
Goddammit!!!

...30 cm ones.

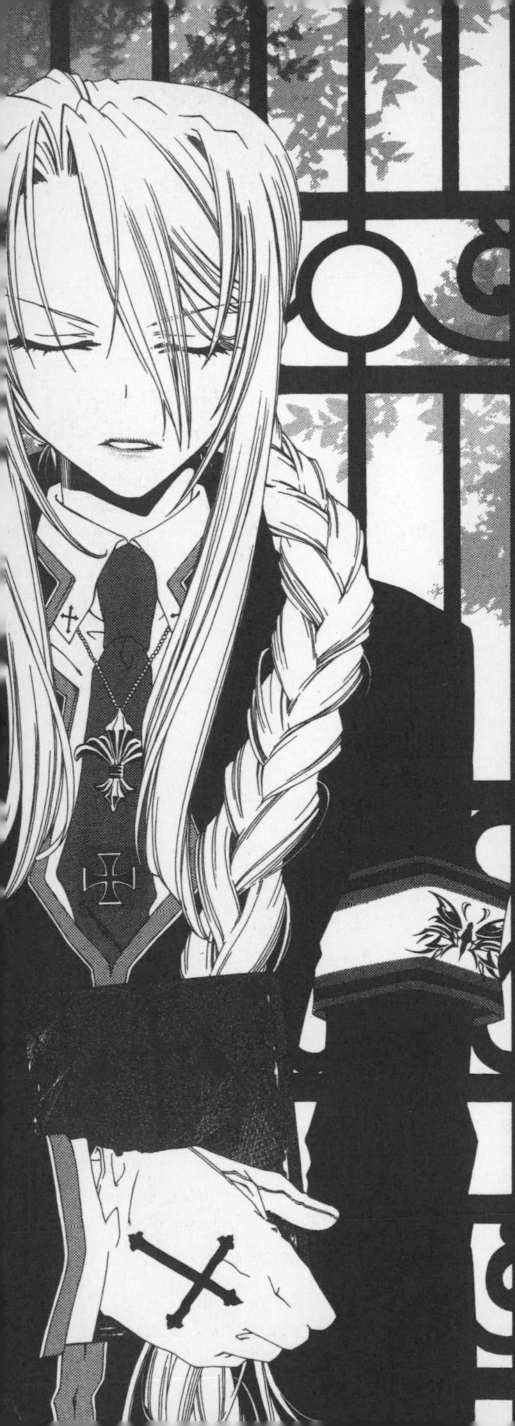

Talk

Hello to all the readers—whether you've been reading the series from volume one or are starting to read with this volume for some reason (LOL). This is Sorano. I can't believe volume two is out! We finally have some villainous characters. Good, good. Some of them are characters I've been wanting to draw for a long time, since even before I was given the chance to write Monochrome Factor, so I'm very excited.

Do you remember the "certain project" I mentioned in the last volume? It's actually "Naze? Naze? Neeze!!" Let me tell you how this special project came to life. When we were working on episode #002, my assistants and I came up with a special comedy episode of Monochrome Factor. We got really carried away (LOL) and ended up coming up with enough ideas for more than ten episodes. Some of them could be full-length episodes. It's a lot of fun because I can throw in tons of jokes and funny drawings I could never use in the main story. I hope to write a full-length episode of "Naze? Naze? Neeze!!" someday.

I appreciate the readers sending me fan mail. I receive lots of fan letters. I used to write back, but I'm afraid I'm too busy to do so these days... (Tears) But I read letters from fans over and over again. I hope I can write back someday!!

I work very slowly, but please continue to read Monochrome Factor and support the characters! (Bow) Hope to see you in volume 3...

Separation sky

Thanks

Editor ... Mr. Iida
Assistants ... Muffy, Koike, Yuuka, Yukko

...Thanks to all the people I listed above!! By the way, is it true our workshop is weird?

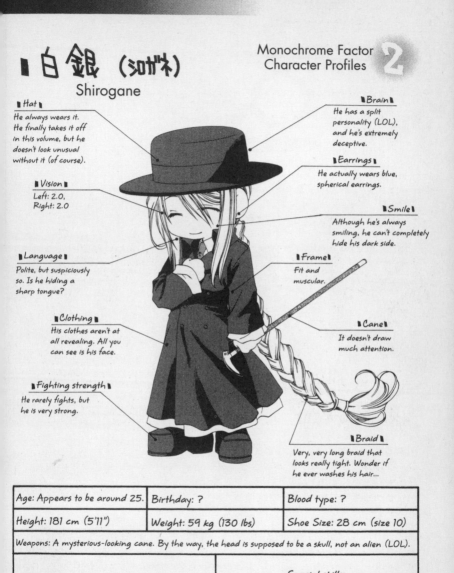

白銀（シロガネ）
Shirogane

Monochrome Factor Character Profiles 2

Hat
He always wears it. He finally takes it off in this volume, but he doesn't look unusual without it (of course).

Brain
He has a split personality (LOL), and he's extremely deceptive.

Earrings
He actually wears blue, spherical earrings.

Vision
Left: 2.0,
Right: 2.0

Smile
Although he's always smiling, he can't completely hide his dark side.

Language
Polite, but suspiciously so. Is he hiding a sharp tongue?

Frame
Fit and muscular.

Clothing
His clothes aren't at all revealing. All you can see is his face.

Cane
It doesn't draw much attention.

Fighting strength
He rarely fights, but he is very strong.

Braid
Very, very long braid that looks really tight. Wonder if he ever washes his hair...

Age: Appears to be around 25.	Birthday: ?	Blood type: ?
Height: 181 cm (5'11")	Weight: 59 kg (130 lbs)	Shoe Size: 28 cm (size 10)
Weapons: A mysterious-looking cane. By the way, the head is supposed to be a skull, not an alien (LOL).		
Hobbies: Does he have any? (Sweat)	Special skills: Keeping secrets, wearing a goofy smile, putting on an innocent face.	

His likes	His dislikes
Color: Monochromatics	Color: Pink

Food: I wonder if he ever eats. It's a mystery.

Books: I don't think he ever reads.

Music: I guess he probably listens to something like classical music. (This is just a guess.)

Games: I don't think he plays any...I'm sure he wouldn't.

TV: I think he watches what Akira watches. (This is just a guess.)

Movies: Same as above. (Hey!)

Animals: I think he just pretends to be an animal lover. I think he actually hates them.

Other: Although I wrote his profile, it just makes Shirogane even more mystifying. In fact, even the author doesn't fully understand this character... (Hey!)

I enjoy drawing Shirogane.

◄ Sorano's Babble ►

Shirogane is called "Neeze" at work. It's almost as if everyone has forgotten his real name. When I started writing the series, Shirogane was supposed to be a cool, handsome young man. Now he's nothing but a weird and funny-looking guy (sweat). To be honest, Neeze reflects my fashion tastes. His gray hair, extremely long coat (or is it a jacket?), and extremely long French braid... And he likes goth fashion (LOL). It took a long time for me to decide what his character should look like, and I remember not being able to make up my mind until the last minute. By the way, his French braid was supposed to be much shorter, but I ended up making it that long without thinking too much (sweat). To be honest, it's a pain to draw... (Punching myself).

Kaili Sorano

Caution: Working.

Photo by an Assistant.

Although it took a while, volume two has been finally published. I work very slowly, and I have to repress my innermost feelings that I might be causing people trouble. (Don't conceal such things!) But nothing really affects my speed. I always do things at my own pace and don't care what others think... A slow life is cool! (Yep, I'm a loser.)

Shirogane

slowly...

Coo Coo

WHAT'RE YOU DOING, TOUCHING MY HAT ALL OF A SUDDEN?!

HUH?!

I saw something under his hat.

Who's the?

Shock

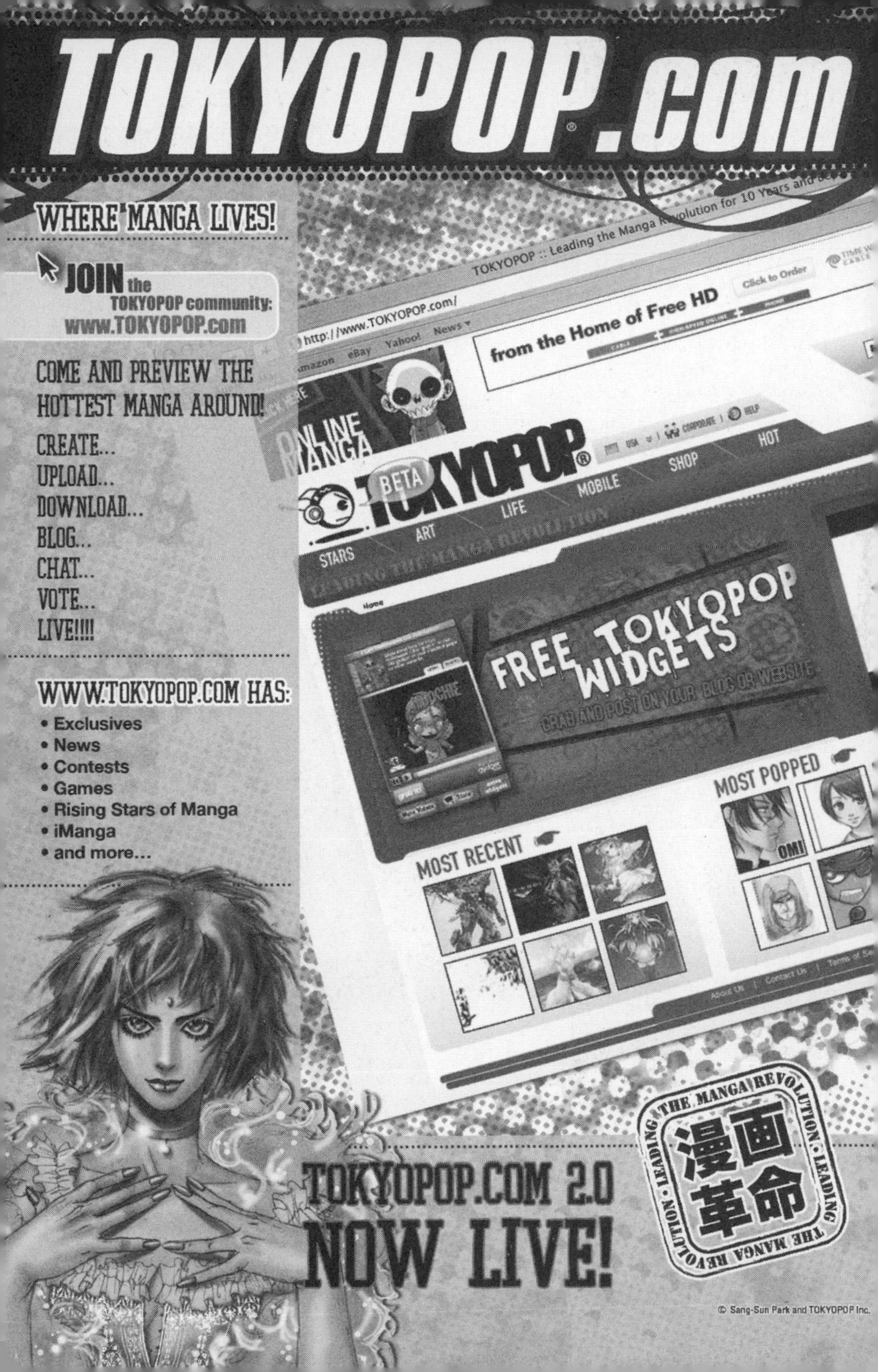
TOKYOPOP®.com
WHERE MANGA LIVES!
JOIN the TOKYOPOP community: www.TOKYOPOP.com
COME AND PREVIEW THE HOTTEST MANGA AROUND!
CREATE...
UPLOAD...
DOWNLOAD...
BLOG...
CHAT...
VOTE...
LIVE!!!!
WWW.TOKYOPOP.COM HAS:
• Exclusives
• News
• Contests
• Games
• Rising Stars of Manga
• iManga
• and more...
TOKYOPOP :: Leading the Manga Revolution for 10 Years and Beyond
http://www.TOKYOPOP.com/
from the Home of Free HD
Click to Order
ONLINE MANGA
TOKYOPOP®
BETA
STARS
ART
LIFE
MOBILE
SHOP
HOT
FREE TOKYOPOP WIDGETS
MOST RECENT
MOST POPPED
TOKYOPOP.COM 2.0
NOW LIVE!
THE MANGA REVOLUTION • LEADING
漫画革命
© Sang-Sun Park and TOKYOPOP Inc.

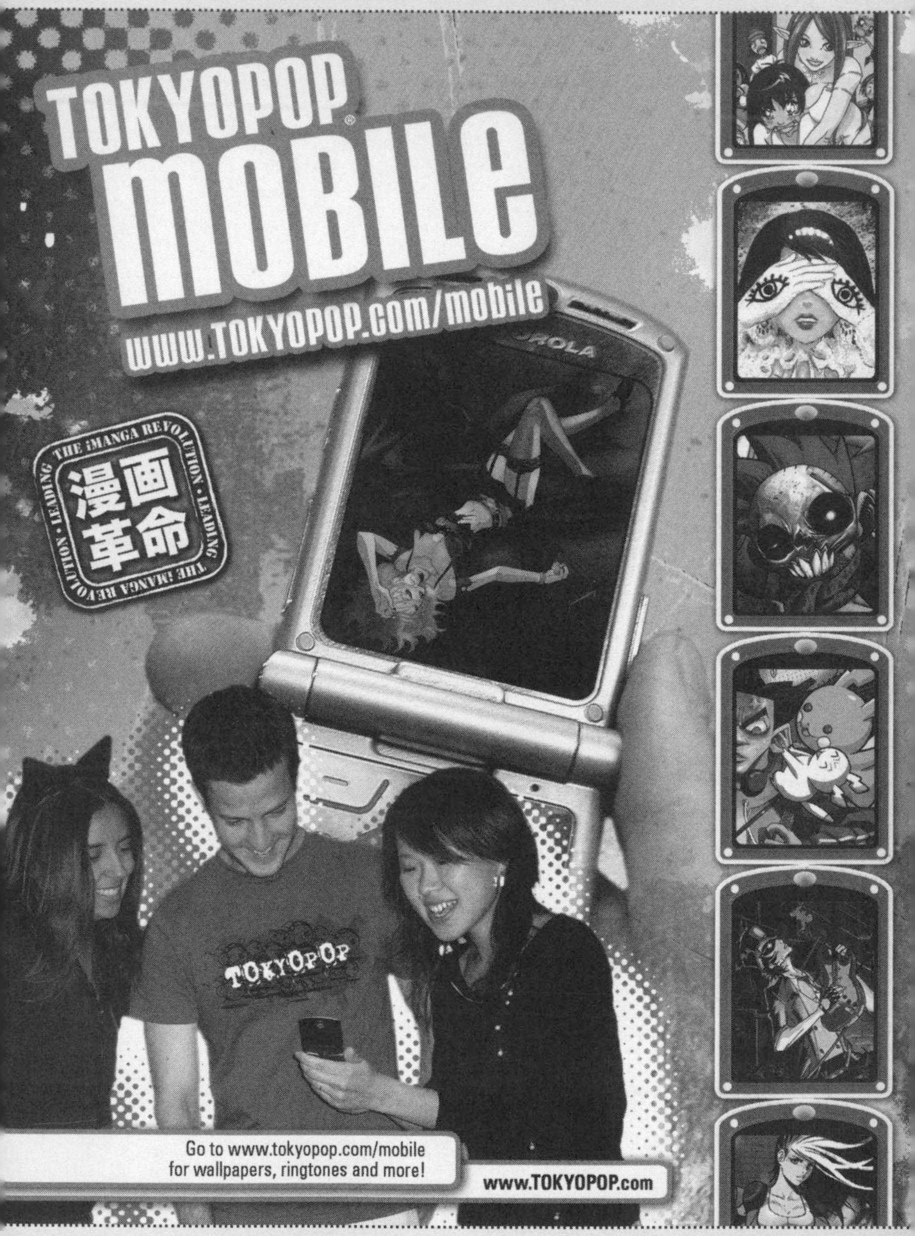
TOKYOPOP® MOBILE
www.TOKYOPOP.com/mobile
THE iMANGA REVOLUTION · LEADING THE iMANGA REVOLUTION · LEADING
漫画革命
TOKYOPOP
Go to www.tokyopop.com/mobile
for wallpapers, ringtones and more!
www.TOKYOPOP.com

FOR MORE INFORMATION VISIT: WWW.TOKYOPOP.COM

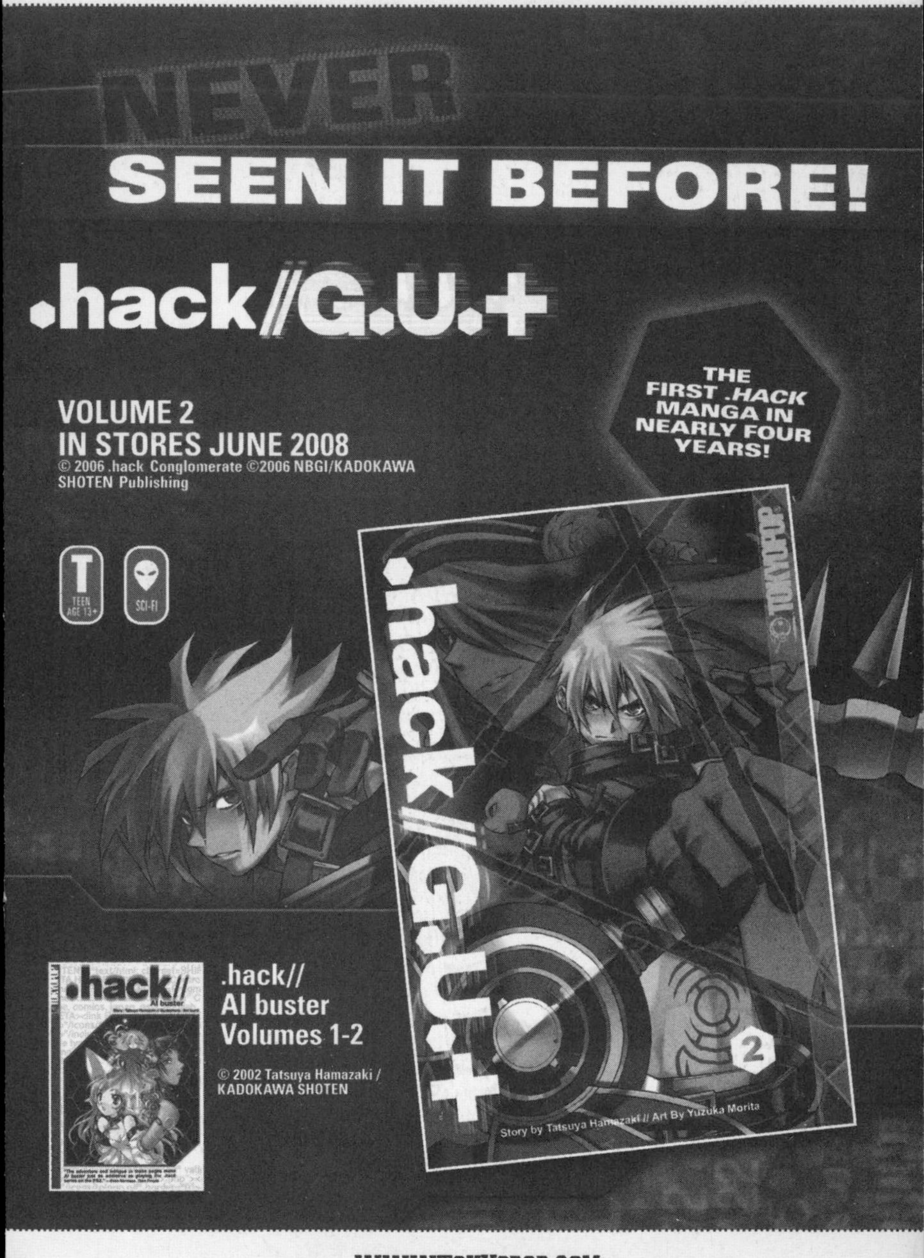
NEVER
SEEN IT BEFORE!
.hack//G.U.+
THE FIRST .HACK MANGA IN NEARLY FOUR YEARS!
VOLUME 2
IN STORES JUNE 2008
© 2006 .hack Conglomerate ©2006 NBGI/KADOKAWA SHOTEN Publishing
T TEEN AGE 13+
SCI-FI
TOKYOPOP
.hack//G.U.+
2
Story by Tatsuya Hamazaki // Art By Yuzuka Morita
.hack// AI buster
.hack//
AI buster
Volumes 1-2
© 2002 Tatsuya Hamazaki / KADOKAWA SHOTEN

.HACK UNIVERSE

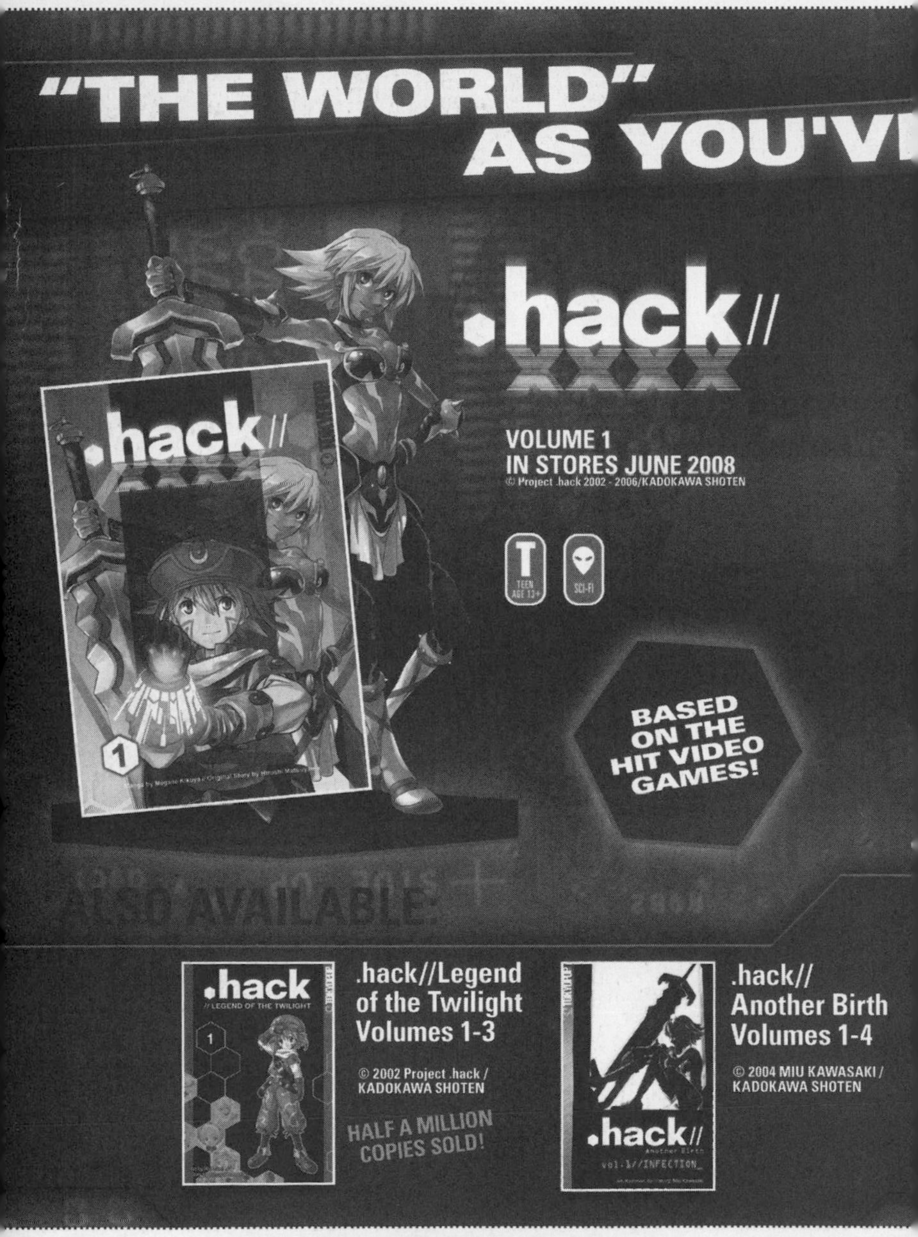
"THE WORLD" AS YOU'VE
.hack//
VOLUME 1
IN STORES JUNE 2008
© Project .hack 2002 - 2006/KADOKAWA SHOTEN
T TEEN AGE 13+
SCI-FI
BASED ON THE HIT VIDEO GAMES!
ALSO AVAILABLE:
.hack//Legend of the Twilight Volumes 1-3
© 2002 Project .hack / KADOKAWA SHOTEN
HALF A MILLION COPIES SOLD!
.hack// Another Birth Volumes 1-4
© 2004 MIU KAWASAKI / KADOKAWA SHOTEN

FOR MORE INFORMATION VISIT: